Palgrave European Film and Media Studies

Series Editors

Ib Bondebjerg
University of Copenhagen
Copenhagen, Denmark

Andrew Higson
University of York
York, United Kingdom

Caroline Pauwels
Vrije Universiteit Brussel (VUB)
Brussels, Belgium

Aim of the Series
Palgrave European Film and Media Studies is dedicated to historical and contemporary studies of film and media in a European context and to the study of the role of film and media in European societies and cultures. The series invite research done in both humanities and social sciences and invite scholars working with the role of film and other media in relation to the development of a European society, culture and identity. Books in the series can deal with both media content and media genres, with national and transnational aspects of film and media policy, with the sociology of media as institutions and with audiences and reception, and the impact of film and media on everyday life, culture and society. The series encourage books working with European integration or themes cutting across nation states in Europe and books working with Europe in a more global perspective. The series especially invite publications with a comparative, European perspective based on research outside a traditional nation state perspective. In an era of increased European integration and globalization there is a need to move away from the single nation study focus and the single discipline study of Europe.

More information about this series at
http://www.springer.com/series/14704

Paul Cooke • Rob Stone
Editors

Screening European Heritage

Creating and Consuming History on Film

Editors
Paul Cooke
University of Leeds
Leeds, United Kingdom

Rob Stone
University of Birmingham
Birmingham, United Kingdom

Palgrave European Film and Media Studies
ISBN 978-1-349-70622-8   ISBN 978-1-137-52280-1   (eBook)
DOI 10.1057/978-1-137-52280-1

Library of Congress Control Number: 2016946340

© The Editor(s) (if applicable) and The Author(s) 2016
The author(s) has/have asserted their right(s) to be identified as the author(s) of this work in accordance with the Copyright, Designs and Patents Act 1988.
This work is subject to copyright. All rights are solely and exclusively licensed by the Publisher, whether the whole or part of the material is concerned, specifically the rights of translation, reprinting, reuse of illustrations, recitation, broadcasting, reproduction on microfilms or in any other physical way, and transmission or information storage and retrieval, electronic adaptation, computer software, or by similar or dissimilar methodology now known or hereafter developed.
The use of general descriptive names, registered names, , trademarks, service marks, etc. in this publication does not imply, even in the absence of a specific statement, that such names are exempt from the relevant protective laws and regulations and therefore free for general use.
The publisher, the authors and the editors are safe to assume that the advice and information in this book are believed to be true and accurate at the date of publication. Neither the publisher nor the authors or the editors give a warranty, express or implied, with respect to the material contained herein or for any errors or omissions that may have been made.

Cover image © philipus / Alamy Stock Photo

Printed on acid-free paper

This Palgrave Macmillan imprint is published by Springer Nature
The registered company is Macmillan Publishers Ltd. London

Contents

Introduction　　xvii

Part I　Contexts of Production　　1

1　The Politics and Sociology of Screening the Past:
A National and Transnational Perspective　　3
Ib Bondebjerg

2　British Flanders: Co-produced Television Drama
and the Limits of a European Heritage　　25
Jaap Verheul

3　Whose Heritage?: *Noi credevamo* (*We Believed*)
and the National, Regional and Transnational
Dynamics of the Risorgimento Film　　45
Alex Marlow-Mann

Part II　Limits of Representation　　61

4　Towards World Heritage Cinema
(Starting from the Negative)　　63
Alan O'Leary

5 Rewriting History from the Margins:
   Diasporic Memory, Shabby Chic and
   Archival Footage   85
   Daniela Berghahn

6 Facing Dark Heritage: The Legacy of Nazi
   Perpetrators in German-Language Film   107
   Axel Bangert

7 Spectral Spanish Heritage: The Hauntology
   of *La noche de los girasoles*
   (*The Night of the Sunflowers*)   127
   Paul Mitchell

8 Adapting Balzac in Jacques Rivette's
   Ne Touchez pas la hache (*Don't Touch the Axe*):
   Violence and the Post-Heritage Aesthetic   145
   Andrew Watts

9 The Ironic Gaze: Roots Tourism and Irish
   Heritage Cinema   163
   Ruth Barton

Part III Modes of Consumption   181

10 Historical Films in Europe: The Transnational
   Production, Circulation and Reception
   of 'National' Heritage Drama   183
   Andrew Higson

11 From 'English' Heritage to Transnational
   Audiences: Fan Perspectives and Practices
   and Why They Matter   209
   Claire Monk

12 From 'Auschwitz-land' to Banglatown:
    Heritage Conflicts, Film and the Politics of Place   235
    Paul Cooke

13 Cinematic Pilgrimages: Postmodern Heritage Cinema   257
    Rob Stone

Index   279

Notes on Contributors

Axel Bangert holds a doctorate from the Faculty of Modern and Medieval Languages, University of Cambridge. He has held post-doctoral fellowships at Homerton College, Cambridge, and the University of Leeds. His main research interests are German cinema and television, in particular portrayals of the Third Reich, European heritage film, as well as transnational moving-image production. He is the author of *The Nazi Past in Contemporary German Film: Viewing Experiences of Intimacy and Immersion* (2014).

Ruth Barton is Lecturer in Film Studies at Trinity College Dublin and the author of a number of books on Irish cinema, stardom and silent cinema, including *Jim Sheridan: Framing the Nation* (2002), *Irish National Cinema* (2004), *Acting Irish in Hollywood* (2006) and *Hedy Lamarr, The Most Beautiful Woman in Film* (2010). She is also editor of *Screening Irish-America* (2009). Her most recent monograph is *Rex Ingram: Visionary Director of the Silent Screen* (2014). She is currently co-editing, with Simon Trezise, a reader on music and silent cinema.

Daniela Berghahn is Professor of Film Studies in the Media Arts Department at Royal Holloway, University of London. She has published widely on post-war German cinema, the relationship between film, history and cultural memory and transnational cinema. Her extensive work on migrant and diasporic cinema in Europe has been supported by the AHRC and is documented on the websites www.farflungfamilies.net and www.migrantcinema.net. Her publications include *Head-On* (2015), *Far-Flung Families in Film: The Diasporic Family in Contemporary European Cinema* (2013), *European Cinema in Motion: Migrant and Diasporic Film in Contemporary Europe* (co-edited with Claudia Sternberg, 2010) and *Hollywood Behind the Wall: The Cinema of East Germany* (2005).

Ib Bondebjerg is Professor Emeritus in the Department of Media, Cognition and Communication, University of Copenhagen. He has been the co-director of the

European project *Changing Media—Changing Europe* and, currently, *Mediating Cultural Encounters Through European Screens*. He is co-editor of the book series *Palgrave European Film and Media Studies*, and associate editor of the open access journal *Palgrave Communication*. His most recent English publications are: *European Cinema and Television. Cultural Policy and Everyday Life* (2015, co-editor), *Engaging With Reality. Documentary and Globalisation* (2014) and *Media, Democracy and European Culture* (co-editor, contributor).

Paul Cooke is Centenary Chair of World Cinemas at the University of Leeds. He is the author of *Representing East Germany: From Colonization to Nostalgia* (2005) and *Contemporary German Cinema* (2012). His edited volumes include *World Cinema's 'Dialogues; with Hollywood* (2007), *The Lives of Others and Contemporary German Film* (2013) and, with Marc Silberman, *Screening War: Perspectives on German Suffering* (2012). He is currently involved in an AHRC project exploring the role of film as a tool for the generation of 'Soft Power' across the BRICS group of emerging nations and a number of heritage-related community filmmaking projects in Germany, South Africa and Eastern Europe.

Andrew Higson is Greg Dyke Professor of Film and Television and Head of the Department of Theatre, Film and Television at the University of York, UK. He has written widely on heritage cinema, and on other aspects of British cinema and national and transnational cinema. He is currently leading a project on contemporary European cinema and television drama (www.mecetes.co.uk), bringing together the Universities of Copenhagen, Brussels (VUB) and York. He is the author of *English Heritage, English Cinema* (2003) and *Film England: Culturally English Filmmaking Since the 1990s* (2011), and co-editor of *European Cinema and Television: Cultural Policy and Everyday Life* (2015).

Alex Marlow-Mann is Lecturer in Italian at the University of Kent. He is a specialist on European (and particularly Italian) cinema with strong interests in regional cinemas, the politics of popular genre cinema, cognitive theory, film and emotion and film preservation. He is the author of *The New Neapolitan Cinema* (2011), the editor of *Archival Film Festivals* (StAFS, 2013) and has written numerous articles on cinema from the silent era to the present day. He is also one of the founding members of the British Association for Film, Television and Screen Studies and sits on the editorial boards of the *Journal of Italian Cinema and Media Studies* and *Cine-Excess*.

Paul Mitchell is Lecturer at the Universidad Católica de Valencia San Mártir. His research interests include both literature and cinema. He is the author of *The Poetry of Negativity* (2011) and other articles about the American writer Sylvia Plath. More recently, he has published on Spanish cinema, particularly in relation to the dynamics of rural space. His latest research projects focus on the heritage dimensions that are present in many recent Spanish comedies and horror films.

Claire Monk is Professor of Film and Film Culture at De Montfort University, UK, and a specialist in post-1970s British cinema. She is known especially for her role in the debates around British heritage cinema with reference to sexuality, gender and pleasure; and, more recently, for her work on the audiences for period screen fictions (*Heritage Film Audiences*, 2011a). Her ongoing research, initiated in 'Heritage Film Audiences 2.0: period film audiences and online fan cultures' (2011b), focuses on the place and repositioning of 'heritage' screen fictions in 21st-century, convergence-era, global internet and fan cultures. Earlier publications include *British Historical Cinema*, co-edited with Amy Sargeant (2002).

Alan O'Leary is Director of Research and Innovation in the School of Languages, Cultures and Societies, University of Leeds. He has published several books and many articles on Italian cinema and co-founded the annual Film Issue of *The Italianist*. His newest project is entitled 'Italian Cinemas/Italian Histories' (http://arts.leeds.ac.uk/italian-cinemas-italian-histories/about/) and he is currently working on a monograph on film and history in Italy and another on the 1966 film *The Battle of Algiers*.

Rob Stone is Chair of European Film at the University of Birmingham, where he co-directs B-Film: The Birmingham Centre for Film Studies, and has published widely on Spanish, Basque, Cuban, European and independent American cinema. He is the author of *Spanish Cinema* (2001), *Flamenco in the Works of Federico García Lorca and Carlos Saura* (2004), *Julio Medem* (2007), *The Cinema of Richard Linklater: Walk, Don't Run* (2013), co-author of *Basque Cinema: A Cultural and Political History* (2015) and co-editor of *The Unsilvered Screen: Surrealism on Film* (2006), *A Companion to Luis Buñuel* (2013), *Screening Songs in Hispanic and Lusophone Cinema* (2012) and the forthcoming Routledge *Companion to World Cinema*.

Jaap Verheul is a PhD Candidate in Cinema Studies at New York University, where his dissertation focuses on popular European cinema as it chronicles the dynamics of regional and national filmmaking in the European Union today. He has written on trauma and memory, fascist aesthetics, multiculturalism and violence in popular American television, and the representation of the European bourgeoisie in the work of Michael Haneke. For edited collections, he has also contributed chapters on the dual monolingualism of contemporary Flemish cinema television (*The Multilingual Screen*, 2016), and on the fluctuating stardom of James Bond and George Lazenby (*Lasting Screen Stars*, 2016).

Andrew Watts is Senior Lecturer in French Studies and co-director of B-Film: The Birmingham Centre for Film Studies at the University of Birmingham. His research focuses primarily on adaptations of nineteenth-century French literature in a variety of different media, from silent film to graphic novels and stage musicals. He is the co-author (with Kate Griffiths) of *Adapting Nineteenth-Century France: Literature in Film, Theatre, Television, Radio and Print* (2013). His current projects include a second co-authored book with Kate Griffiths, *The History of French Literature on Film*, and a monograph on adaptations of the work of Honoré de Balzac, provisionally entitled *Adapting Balzac: The Multimedia Afterlives of 'La Comédie humaine'*.

List of Figures

Graph 1.1	UK historical drama cases—Danish share % and ratings	12
Graph 1.2	Rating and share for recent Danish, historical TV drama	13
Graph 1.3	Distribution of social and cultural segments for Danish historical drama	17
Fig. 3.1	Unification as ecomonster: the use of *mise-en-scène* to prefigure the course of historical change in *We Believed* (Mario Martone 2010; Palomar/Les Films d'Ici)	54
Fig. 3.2	Puglia stands in for Cilento in the Southern scenes, shot by cinematographer Raffaele Berta according to a 'dialectical photographic style' in *We Believed* (Mario Martone 2010; Palomar/Les Films d'Ici)	55
Fig. 5.1	Gangster film iconography: Abdelkader and Faivre's meeting	92
Fig. 5.2	Archival footage of medical exams	97
Fig. 5.3	Dido looks at the portrait of herself and her cousin	101
Fig. 5.4	Belle	104
Fig. 6.1	*Wie sie es wurden: Ein junger Mann aus dem Innviertel—Adolf Hitler* (*How They Became What They Were: A Young Man from the Inn Quarter—Adolf Hitler*, Georg Stefan Troller and Axel Corti, 1973) portrays Hitler as part of a generation opposing tradition and heritage in favour of an ethnic nationalist worldview	108
Fig. 6.2	Disciplining the body: In *Aus einem deutschen Leben* (*Death Is My Trade*, Theodor Kotulla, 1977) the young Rudolf Höß absorbs the militarist ethics of obedience through physical acts	109

LIST OF FIGURES

Fig. 7.1	The representational space of Angosto in *The Night of the Sunflowers*	137
Fig. 8.1	Montriveau warns Antoinette of the punishment that awaits her	154
Fig. 8.2	Montriveau stares out to sea in the closing shot of the film	157
Fig. 9.1	'Now tell me this, Yank, what is it you're after? Is it trout or salmon?' *The Quiet Man* (John Ford, 1952)	171
Fig. 9.2	'I wonder now why a man would go to Innisfree.' *The Quiet Man* (John Ford, 1952)	172
Fig. 9.3	*Leap Year* (Anand Tucker, 2010): Anna (Amy Adams) learns to abandon materialism and embrace Irish romanticism	174
Fig. 9.4	*The Matchmaker* (Mark Joffe, 1997): reversal of the gaze as the locals look back at the tourist, Marcy (Janeane Garofalo)	176
Fig. 9.5	In *Ek Tha Tiger* (Kabir Khan, 2012), Salman Khan dances with Katrina Kaif, here dressed as a Kilkenny hurler	177
Fig. 11.1	Merchant Ivory Productions' E. M. Forster adaptations: manga- and anime-influenced styles of twenty-first-century fan art inspired by *Maurice* (James Ivory, 1987) and *Howards End* (Ivory, 1992), by ma10-mato (Japan), 2015, and endymiasyzygy (UK), 2008.	227
Fig. 11.2	RResonant sites and queer ancient heritage in *Maurice* (James Ivory, 1987). A pair of Assyrian lamassu at the British Museum, London, watch over and fascinate cross-class Edwardian lovers Alec Scudder (Rupert Graves) and Maurice Hall (James Wilby). A British Museum visitor touches one of the same lamassu in 2013.	230
Fig. 11.3	Maurice and Alec at the British Museum as visualised by one of *Maurice* (1987)'s twenty-first-century fan artists, zzigae (South Korea), drawn in 2012, posted in 2014.	231
Fig. 12.1	Chanu orchestrating his family's performance of the role of tourist	243
Fig. 12.2	A train arriving in Oświęcim	251
Fig. 13.1	Visitors to the Rovers Return public house set of *Coronation Street* pretending to pull pints. Photograph by Megan Caine.	263

Fig. 13.2	Tourists to the set of *Rome* in Cinecittà find themselves cordoned off because of a commercial shoot. Photograph by Rob Stone	265
Fig. 13.3	Tourists on the Stones and Thrones tour of Northern Ireland pose as knights on 'The King's Road'. Photograph by Rob Stone	270
Fig. 13.4	Ballintoy Harbour, renamed Pyke Harbour for the *Game of Thrones* tour of Northern Ireland. Photograph by Rob Stone	272
Fig. 13.5	Tourism Ireland campaign to lure fans of the *Game of Thrones* series to Northern Ireland	273

Introduction

Axel Bangert, Paul Cooke and Rob Stone

In *European Cinema: Face to Face with Hollywood* (2005), Thomas Elsaesser observes that 'European cinema distinguishes itself from Hollywood and Asian cinemas by dwelling so insistently on the (recent) past' (Elsaesser 2005: 23). Even if one takes the briefest of looks at the most celebrated European films internationally, he would appear to have a point. From *Das Leben der Anderen* (*The Lives of Others*, Florian Henckel von Donnersmarck, 2006) to *The King's Speech* (Tom Hooper, 2010), historical dramas seem to play a key role within national film cultures across the continent, acting as an international 'shop window' that can help support not only the domestic industry but also the wider heritage and tourist sector by attracting international visitors to the country. They can even be appropriated by governments to function (however effectively) as 'soft power' assets, in a nation's effort to gain inter-

Axel Bangert
New York University Berlin
Berlin, Germany

Paul Cooke
University of Leeds
Leeds, UK

Rob Stone
University of Birmingham
Birmingham, UK

national political or economic influence (Nye 2011: 89–102). At the same time, such films can generate major debates at home on the role of the past in contemporary national identity construction. What forms has this enduring engagement with the continent's history taken across different European film cultures? How and why do historical dramas reach big and small screens across Europe, and what is their role in the promotion of European heritage, however this might be defined, be it on screen through plots set in the past, costumes and props, or off screen through their interaction with tourist sites, the digital sphere and the heritage industries surrounding them? These are the questions that are the focus of this volume.

Screening European Heritage is the result of an AHRC Care for the Future project run by the Centre for World Cinemas and Digital Cultures at the University of Leeds and B-Film: The Birmingham Centre for Film Studies. As a starting point for the project's reflection upon the particular place that historical dramas hold in contemporary European film cultures, we returned to the 'heritage film' debates of the 1990s, which emerged in the UK in response to a wave of costume dramas that began a decade earlier, when films such as *Chariots of Fire* (Hugh Hudson, 1981) and *A Room With a View* (James Ivory, 1985) were increasingly analysed as a new style, indeed by some as a new genre, of historical film, identified by slow-moving, episodic narratives organised around props and settings as much as they were around narrative and characters. These films were often read as part of a national project of nostalgic remembrance celebrating British heritage culture just as the country was undergoing the seismic social shifts of the Thatcher years. In his defining discussion of this trend, Andrew Higson explored the manner in which heritage films present the past as a 'visually spectacular pastiche, inviting a nostalgic gaze that resists the ironies and social critiques so often suggested narratively by these films' (Higson 1993: 109). In so doing, Higson identified a key tension at the heart of this cycle of filmmaking, which, on the one hand, offered the potential for alternative, and particularly Queer, readings of history through their plots, while on the other helping to generate tourist traffic through their presentation of an essentially conservative (with both a large and small 'c') image of Englishness, readily consumable by international audiences. Claire Monk, another key voice in the early debate, underlines the political context of Higson's work, stressing how politicised the critique of the heritage film was from the beginning. 'This critique grew out of the wider, very combative, cultural-political climate that we had in Britain in the 1980s' (Monk 2013), much of which, she suggests, was predicated on an analysis of the implied spectator within the film texts themselves. In order to probe what she saw as the assumptions that flow from this, Monk focused on the empirical reception of heritage films by different audience segments. In so doing, she found 'that there is one section of the audience that was more conservative than anyone like Andrew Higson [...] ever dreamt. But there is also a left-wing or liberal, generally younger, degree-educated and quite cinephilic audience that enjoys these films but feels self-conscious guilt about it because of their awareness of the debate' (Monk 2013).

The initial discussion of the nature and status of British historical drama in the 1980s, provoked by the likes of Higson and Monk, in turn fed into a broader debate on the state of the British film industry and the nature of British 'national' film culture. Over the last two decades, Higson's original definition of the term, along with the parameters of the debates it engendered, has been repeatedly challenged, redefined and stretched almost to breaking point. Moreover, it is increasingly noted, by academics such as Rosalind Galt (2002), Lutz Koepnick (2002), Paul Cooke (2012), Ginette Vincendeau (2013), Rob Stone and María Pilar Rodríguez (2015) and others, that such films were not, and are not, unique to British cinema. Similar films can be found across Europe, suggesting that the impetus for this trend in historical filmmaking cannot all be laid at the door of Margaret Thatcher. Clearly film studies has moved on from the original debate that Higson initiated, much of which ultimately became somewhat semantic. However, its core concern, namely, what do we mean by 'heritage' and how might this be communicated, instrumentalised or challenged by cinema, remains an important concern. If we stick closely to Higson's original aesthetic definition of the concept and the debate it generated, but accept that heritage cinema is an international phenomenon, such films are produced and consumed within very different and distinct social and political contexts, all of which inflect the specific concept of heritage they seek to communicate. A country house draped in a swastika, such as we see in *Napola* (*Before the Fall*, Dennis Gansel, 2004), immediately creates a very different affective relationship with the spectator to a shot of a similar building in a British heritage drama like *Maurice* (James Ivory, 1987), two films which, on the face of it, would appear to have much in common. The disparate modes of engagement with the past we see across European heritage films (e.g. *Zemsta* [*The Revenge*, Andrzej Wajda, 2002]; *Obaba* [Montxo Armendáriz, 2005]; *En kongelig affære* [*A Royal Affair*, Nikolaj Arcel, 2012]; and *Tähtitaivas talon yllä* [*Stars Above*, Saara Cantell, 2012]) explore a very wide array of historical moments. Yet what unites them is the fact that they are always invariably inflected by the preoccupations of the present, evoking conflicting emotions among those that make and consume such films, emotions driven variously by nostalgia, mourning, or more nationalist, even jingoistic strategies. Here we should mention the more recent work of Belén Vidal, who includes in her study several productions about non-British heritages, including *The Girl With a Pearl Earring* (Peter Webber, 2003) and *Joyeux Noël* (*Merry Christmas*, Christian Carion, 2005). By drawing on a broad selection of films, with notable differences in terms of their production, representation and reception, Vidal presents the heritage film not as a rigid category but as a flexible genre: 'a hybrid genre with porous borders, a genre that is becoming less consensual and more political through its own staunch preference for emotional histories, and also more adventurous in its continuous incorporation of a popular historical iconography informed not only by literature or painting, but also by fashion, popular music and television' (Vidal 2012: 4).

This wider definition, when placed alongside the original debate, offers a particularly productive starting point for the present volume's discussion of the shape of contemporary European heritage film, its circulation and consumption across and beyond the continent. How can the concept of the heritage film, with its roots in the specific situation of 1980s Britain, be used heuristically to explore other national and transnational cinemas across Europe? What does 'heritage' mean in this context? What can 'European' heritage signify beyond the kinds of platitudinous statements of international cooperation one might expect from the European Union or Council of Europe and which might be seen to reach their cinematic nadir in the much maligned 'Europudding', a form of filmmaking that is the product of pan-European compromise, and which itself has a particular penchant for overblown historical dramas (*Enemy at the Gates* [Jean-Jacques Annaud, 2001], *Joyeux Noël*, *Henri 4* [Jo Baier, 2010])? How do the imperatives of national heritage culture interact with, enhance or resist those of the transnational? Indeed, what counts as heritage in this regard?

It is interesting to note that so much of the material that informs the European historical dramas mentioned above focuses on moments of European conflict, from the Hundred Years War to World War Two, suggesting, perhaps, that what most obviously unites Europe is its heritage of trauma and division, often termed 'dark heritage' (Biran 2011: 820–41). However, it is not only on a European level that heritage drama focuses on conflict. Here we might also mention Eric Rentschler's discussion of the political and philosophical heritage tradition in Germany, where he observes how current debates on heritage cinema tend to focus on the films that explore questions of 'dark heritage', and specifically the nation's problematic history (Rentschler 2013: 241–60). While these are, without doubt, the films that most readily circulate beyond the nation's borders, Rentschler also points to the fact that 'Millennial German cinema, in fact, has probed a decidedly wide range of pastness and recognised the contemporary resonance of a number of different heritages' (Rentschler 2013: 250). Moreover, he points to the specific philosophical and political tradition within Germany of 'heritage' as a concept, citing in particular the utility of Ernst Bloch's *Erbschaft dieser Zeit* (*Heritage of Our Times*, 1935) in this regard, and its celebration of 'nonsimultaneity'. This is the term Bloch uses to suggest the way in which it is possible to construct a heritage tradition that can protect 'thoughts out of season', thoughts which can, in turn, help protect non-hegemonic—in Bloch's case, non-bourgeois—cultural traditions and, crucially, ways of thinking. With this in mind, it is important, Rentschler suggests, to reflect upon the *heritage* of German film when discussing German heritage film. For example, reading *The Lives of Others*, which presents a present-day imagining of East Germany, alongside the contemporary East German production *Jahrgang 45* (*Born in '45*, Jürgen Böttcher, 1965), he suggests, allows us to reflect upon the elision of 'nonsimultaneity' in von Donnersmarck's film, as well as much contemporary heritage production in the country (Rentschler 2013: 252). In the later film, the past appears to be concertinaed, becoming an exotic cypher for the enlightened mores of the present. *Born in '45*, on the other hand, self-consciously challenges this view, that is of the East German population as both Other to the West—inscribed, it would seem, into the very name of the film *The Lives of Others*—and yet the same as the West, ultimately able to be incorporated straightforwardly into the unified state. *Born in '45* presents a group of young East Germans provocatively returning the gaze of a busload of West German tourists on a daytrip to the GDR. Rentschler highlights the ways in which the film presents a non-resolved, and non-resolvable, image of the GDR which returns, and thus challenges, the Western gaze he sees as informing *The Lives of Others*. While *The Lives of Others* offers an ultimately 'consensual' view of the GDR, where the traumas of the past find their resolution in the capitalist democracy of the unified German state, the youthful stare of the GDR citizens in *Born in '45* insists not upon the *otherness* of the East, but upon both its *separation* from the West and the rights of the population to be treated with equal respect to the West.

Rentschler points to a common critique of much heritage film production, films which are often seen to present a decidedly contemporary presentation of the past, inscribing present-day values as universal and atemporal, but which can, at the same time, be clearly isolated and communicated through the iconography of the past. Rentschler highlights how exploring the heritage of film can offer a counter-narrative to this view. That said, an exploration of film heritage can also point to continuities in this very same approach to the presentation of the past. Media consultant Bill Lawrence, for example, points to Gainsborough Pictures, which was well known in the 1940s, not only for its melodramas but also for its historical films, *The Wicked Lady* (Leslie Arliss, 1945) being a particularly popular example. Lawrence sees continuities with more recent films in their communication of the past via a distinct heritage iconography drenched in a very British 'nostalgia drive' that found its expression, then as now, in the British penchant for literary adaptations: 'There has always been quite a clear interest in looking back. And there is also an interest in UK cinema very early on to make films out of literature. If literature is selling well in terms of period drama, then it will transfer to cinema well' (Lawrence 2013). In Lawrence's account, producing heritage films as a strategy to achieve box-office success is by no means a discovery of the 1980s. In a similar vein, we might mention the initiative by the British Council to make its film archive available online, a collection of well over 100 short documentary films made during the 1940s that were designed 'to promote an idea of "Britain and Britishness"' (BFI 2013). Throughout these films, which range from *Cambridge* (Richard Massingham, 1945) to *Cricket* (Grahame Tharp, 1950), one finds the iconography of a Britain familiar from the 1980s heritage film cycle. But here it is presented with none of the potential critique, however implicit, seen in the ways the later films engage this iconography to tell their stories. Such films further highlight the durability of an iconographic 'shorthand' for the communication of national identities, a shorthand that is both specific to such British heritage production and yet readily understandable by international audiences.

At the same time, as Lawrence also notes and as Rentschler implies with regard to the German context, while much of the iconography might have remained constant, its meaning has changed, the aesthetics of heritage cinema now often challenging far more obviously the real or implied conservatism of the original cycle. In the process, we see filmmakers looking to widen the breadth of culture that can be constructed as part of a nation's heritage. With regard to Yorkshire, Lawrence identified this trend during his time on the board of the region's film agency in the early 2000s. The most common topic in the proposals he reviewed at the time was the Brontës. This clearly reflected the impulse to be found in the 1980s cycle. However, other common themes, most notably the history of Yorkshire's Asian community, the Yorkshire Ripper murders and the 1984–5 Miners' Strike, went beyond and ultimately challenged the cycle's ostensible founding principles. As Monk observes, one now finds an idea of heritage that is much broader than earlier understandings of the term: 'A key charge made against the heritage film in the original 1980s British critiques was that the "national" past it constructed was bourgeois and Southern, the "England" of the Home Counties and the financial City of London' (Monk 2013). This original definition expressly excluded films that were about regional heritage, or working-class heritage. More recently, agencies like Screen Yorkshire have helped extend the types of historical dramas that come to the screen. Indeed, even films that might seem ready-made to play to the sensibilities of the original cycle often take on board some of the elements of the anti-heritage-film critique of the 1980s–90s. Here one might mention the 2011 adaptation of Emily Brontë's *Wuthering Heights* (Andrea Arnold), supported by Screen Yorkshire, which presents a decidedly multicultural take on Emily Brontë's novel, the black actor James Howson's performance as Heathcliff reminding the spectator of the colonial legacy that underpins so much of British heritage culture.

This more recent trend in historical filmmaking has been defined by Monk as 'post-heritage' cinema, an approach to the representation of the past that offers a more self-conscious, postmodern take on history, one that wishes to distance itself from the drive towards 'authenticity' and, above all, the bourgeois 'restraint' she sees as at work in the 1980s cycle, particularly in its approach to sexuality and gender. She cites films such as Sally Potter's *Orlando* (1992), where Potter deliberately foregrounds the film's far more radical engagement with questions of gender and sexuality than is to be found in films of the previous decade through her casting of Quentin Crisp as Elizabeth I (Monk 1995/2001; Monk 2011: 27 n65). The more radical exploration of gender and sexuality is an impulse that one continues to see in contemporary productions, including *Wuthering Heights*, as well as *Henri 4* and *A Royal Affair*. However, countering this trend, in many recent historical dramas across Europe a post-heritage sensibility might also actually be identified in the far more radical appropriation of both the 'authenticity' and 'restraint' that many films in the 1990s seemed to reject. *Barbara* (Christian Petzold, 2012), *Lore* (Cate Shortland, 2012), *Spies & Glistrup* (*Sex, Drugs and Taxation*, Christoffer Boe, 2013)—and, indeed, one might again mention *Wuthering Heights*—all evidence restraint in their pared-down, slowly paced style. At the same time, they foreground the authentic nature of their historical narratives via the incorporation of documentary footage, or the self-conscious adoption of realist aesthetic techniques (the use of handheld camera, the lack of non-diegetic sound markers, or visual cues to carry the narrative) that attempt to present life with all its blemishes, far removed from the airbrushed version of Englishness communicated through the performance of a Helena Bonham Carter or Hugh Grant. Although these 'post-heritage' films appear very different to the types of films pointed to by Monk, they too at times challenge the sensibilities of the original cycle, their self-conscious use of restraint and authenticity foregrounding a sense of performativity that invites us to distance ourselves from, and thus to reflect upon, the world we are watching. That said, as was also noted by Monk and Higson in the original heritage debate, it is in fact perfectly possible to identify a transgressive and potentially performative reading of history in the original cycle, if one wishes to find it. Equally, the turn towards realism we see in more recent films, as well as certain recent television dramas (The UK's *Call the Midwife* [Heidi Thomas, 2012–]; *Cuéntame* [Miguel Ángel Bernadeau, 2001–]), might simply be a way to extend the durability of the heritage genre, allowing an ever-more knowing cinema and television-viewing public—a public that might be increasingly cynical towards a straightforwardly nostalgic message about the past—to continue to enjoy this same message; to have their heritage 'cake', as it were, and eat it, too.

Heritage films are powerful, even overpowering, media for negotiating a sense of history. At times one finds a heritage aesthetic employed as a tool for portraying certain locations or regions as allegorical for a larger culture or nation that is politically unrealised, such as one finds in Basque cinema of the 1980s (e.g. *Akelarre* [*Witches' Sabbath*, Pedro Olea, 1983]). It can call for the inclusion of migrant voices as part of the nation's heritage, as in, for example, the German film *Almanya—Willkommen in Deutschland* (*Almanya*, Yasemin Samdereli, Germany, 2011). Or, as one sees in recent Danish film, it can help celebrate national icons, from heroes of the resistance against the Nazi occupation to post-war figures of progress and success (*Hvidsten gruppen* [*This Life*, Anne-Grethe Bjarup Riis, 2012]). Despite the perennial accusations that such films produce comforting, consensual versions of the past, focused on visual spectacle rather than engaging the audience in critical reflection on history, in their reception, and indeed as the original heritage debate itself discussed and evidenced, these films invariably provoke heated debate, highlighting their strong potential for inciting conflicting opinions about the past and its ownership.

Among the member states of the European Union, there is no agreement on what exactly the heritage of Europe is. As Ib Bondebjerg notes, EU politics have always appealed to the rather vague formulation of 'unity in diversity'. Moreover, Europe-wide support for film production is still in its infancy, offering only a limited contribution through the MEDIA (now Creative Europe) and Eurimages funds, respectively (Bondebjerg 2013). The films that are produced frequently offer a site for continued discussion of what 'unity in diversity' might mean in practice. However, as already noted, more often than not, concerted efforts to produce European heritage films result in critical and commercial failures, so-called 'Europuddings' lacking a clear sense of identity and address. Heritage films and television series can also prompt varied and dramatic responses from governments, museums, cultural sites and the viewing public. For example, the public debate between the German producers of the Oscar-winning 'Stasi drama' *The Lives of Others* and the Hohenschönhausen Stasi memorial in Berlin led to increased footfall in the memorial and a series of government-sponsored screenings for schoolchildren, while also forcing the memorial to engage with the film in its curational strategy. As Paul Cooke describes in his chapter, the production of the film *Brick Lane* (Sarah Gavron, 2007), based on Monica Ali's book of the same name, provoked local demonstrations in the East End of London by the Bengali community who were dissatisfied with Ali's representation of their history. In the wake of the film, members of the local community began to reflect upon the competing meanings of heritage in the area, a process that ultimately led to the production of a full-length documentary film, *Our Brick Lane* (2010). In the Basque Country, a television dramatisation by the publicly funded Euskal Telebista network about the bombing of the town of Guernica by the Luftwaffe during the Spanish Civil War—*Gernika bajo las bombas* (*Guernica under the Bombs*, Luis Marías, 2012)—led to debate about the use of public funding for the dissemination of what many claimed was nationalist propaganda at a time of intense political tension relating to the definitive but tentative ceasefire of ETA. Whether despite or because of debates about political definitions, the ownership of heritage and the motives behind disparate initiatives, heritage film remains an important part of contemporary European cinema.

Of course, heritage films are prominent for economic as well as cultural reasons. They are capable of galvanising domestic audiences and, in some cases, functioning as a key export product for the international market. However, their economic impact cannot be measured only by box-office figures. This can also be judged by how they foster heritage tourism at the local and regional levels, an impact that can also have mixed repercussions for individual heritage sites. While connection with a heritage film might help increase visitor footfall, it might also force the site to rethink its curatorial strategy, compelling it to engage not only with a larger audience, but also a different one that it might not have the resources to cope with.

Heritage film in contemporary Europe offers much more than the perpetuation of a recognisable period style based on established cultural classics, as evidenced in British cinema of the 1980s. The chapters collected together in this volume reflect and extend the questions raised by the discussion of heritage film as it has developed in the last 20 years, the contributors exploring key trends in the production and consumption of these historical dramas. At times they reflect the competing tensions in the way the term itself has been understood, be it as a definable genre, an aesthetic style or a critical heuristic device. Yet, however the term is used, our discussion always focuses on how the films, and the cultures within which they are embedded, actively define what counts as heritage and to whom it belongs.

Screening European Heritage

The volume is divided into three parts, exploring three sets of interrelated questions. Part I 'Contexts of Production' examines the role that European, national and regional cultural policy plays in the production of heritage films. The authors in this part investigate how production companies in a variety of countries across Europe have negotiated the film funding landscape and endeavour to ascertain how this has impacted upon the projects chosen for development. **Ib Bondebjerg** investigates the politics and sociology of screening Europe's past. Specifically, he traces the history of EU film and media policy and the ways in which this has shaped European film culture, paying special attention to post-2000 developments. This he combines with a focus on the development of film and media policy at a national level, taking the role of the EU in Denmark as his focal point. Through case studies of transnational co-productions, Bondebjerg analyses the sociological and political dimensions of heritage cinema and television. In particular, he explores how 'national' heritage can appeal to transnational audiences, who would appear to be attracted to the ostensibly universal values such productions propagate, while at the same time noting how these same productions can generate strong, and highly particularised, ideological debates at home about the version of the past they present. Following this, **Jaap Verheul** considers the promotion of Flemish heritage in British television drama but shifts focus away from the political impetus behind the policies that drive the European film industry towards the pragmatic necessities of international co-production. Noting that, since the 1990s, the audiovisual policies of both the EU and the national and regional governments of its member states have facilitated successful collaboration in the international co-production of European broadcasting services, Verheul examines the recent cycle of heritage dramas on British television that were either co-financed or co-produced by the United Kingdom with the Belgian region of Flanders in order to argue that these miniseries demonstrate the cultural and economic benefits of pan-European cooperation at the industrial level. Indeed, Verheul demonstrates that the audiovisual policies of the British and Flemish governments promote the distinctively European heritage of both Britain and Flanders. Both Bondebjerg and Verheul investigate the ways in which filmmakers *experience* policy and their chapters are concerned with the relation between film production and the wider heritage sector. Clearly a large number of heritage films rely on tourist sites for principal photography, be they positively connoted, such as the iconic British country houses, or places of 'dark heritage', such as the former Stasi interrogation centre in Berlin Hohenschönhausen shown in *The Lives of Others*. Both Bondebjerg and Verheul consider the extent to which heritage films and heritage sites negotiate the competing demands of their approach to the communication of history. They reveal how the imperatives of the tourist industry impact upon the aesthetics of these films and describe how the film industry actively works with regional, national and transnational tourist boards to enhance what has been dubbed 'set-jetting' or 'movie-induced tourism'. In the final chapter of this part, **Alex Marlow-Mann** questions the provenance and ownership of the heritage depicted in *Noi credevamo* (*We Believed*, Mario Martone, 2010). Produced to coincide with the 150th anniversary of the Unification of Italy, against the backdrop of which the film is set, this budget literary adaptation swept the board at the 2010 Italian film awards and thus might appear to be the quintessential national heritage film. Through an analysis of the film's production history, however, Marlow-Mann challenges this perception. He points to Martone's position within the New Neapolitan Cinema, the most significant school of regional filmmaking to emerge from Italy in recent decades, as well as financial support of the project from local film commissions in Campania and Piemonte, together with funding from a French co-producer. This critique is then further developed in his close reading and contextual analysis of the film, which points to its complex utilisation of a variety of dialects and languages, along with its focus on the contradictory political agendas that underpinned the Risorgimento movement, which problematise any simplistic reading of the film as a monument to national Unification and Italian national identity. His re-evaluation of the film asks what role, in a country of continuing regional tensions and uncertain national identity, it can play within broader cultural policy and celebrations of a heritage whose ownership is unclear.

In Part II, 'Limits of Representation', contributors extend the discussion begun by Marlow-Mann to explore the ways in which heritage films can extend, or delimit, the possibilities of historical representation. They investigate how contemporary heritage films can reflect upon the heritage *of* film, and examine the various modes of emotional engagement with history via cinema and television screens their chosen case studies present. **Alan O'Leary** examines scale and address in heritage cinema. Noting that heritage cinema has typically been deplored as a mode of historical representation that implies an escapist, nostalgic and tourist gaze, O'Leary uses a variety of examples to consider how well this idea survives a consideration of the different scales—regional, national, transnational, global—of heritage cinema. He begins by examining the Italian case, where the term 'heritage cinema' has been used to refer to exportable films in which female beauty, landscape and urban heritage are part of a visual spectacle that is quintessentially national inasmuch as the films under discussion are seen at home to represent Italy abroad. Yet he also considers the notion of heritage cinema beyond Europe, examining how aspects of what has generally been considered a European mode of historical drama production have independent existence elsewhere. In relation to the cinema of India, for example, he investigates the extent to which heritage cinema has become a global cinematic trend, seeming to homogenise the way audiences around the world understand their relationship with regional, national and global heritage culture. **Daniela Berghahn**, in her chapter, proceeds to challenge the aesthetics of heritage cinema, seeking to differentiate between shabby chic, archival footage and diasporic memory. She probes the limits of heritage cinema by asking whether the imaginaries of diasporic memory can be accommodated within this particular critical paradigm. Focusing on recent films that portray the collective memory of Turkish-German and Maghrebi French communities, she examines the extent to which the narrative and visual strategies deployed in the discursive construction of diasporic heritage on screen conform to loosely defined heritage aesthetics. Furthermore, she explores how these films pluralise national heritage, still largely defined in terms of the literary canons and official historiographies of white majority culture, by articulating counter-memories that bring the blind spots of hegemonic history into focus.

This is followed by **Axel Bangert**, who looks to the prehistory of the heritage film. His chapter analyses the legacy of Nazi perpetrators in German-language cinema of the 1970s and its relationship to the present cycle of heritage film production in the country. Most specifically, Bangert examines the representation of Adolf Hitler and reveals how key films chart the ideological formation of the would-be demagogue and dictator by the ways in which he interprets and projects the notion of German heritage, while also himself having become the quintessential projection of Europe's 'dark heritage'. These films were made at the time of the so-called 'Hitler-Welle' (Hitler wave) in historiography, literature and film, which provoked a debate about the ethics and aesthetics of representing Nazi perpetrators. Linking their Nazi protagonists to cultural, social and political German traditions that helped prepare the ground for the rise of Nazism, Bangert explores how these productions achieve their unique forms of portrayal by engaging with film heritage, which is addressed for the purpose of critique both in terms of the visual legacies of Nazism and its memory in post-war film culture. This he sees as standing in stark contrast to the current wave of German heritage films and the ways in which they engage with this period of history through emotion and spectacle, rather than critical reflection. Continuing the volume's discussion of 'dark heritage', **Paul Mitchell** investigates how European heritage films and the concomitant debates they generate on the state of the nation of their production are frequently linked to complex emotional encounters with the notion of 'home'. He uses the context of the *pueblo* (village) as a prism through which to explore some of the difficult issues that underpin

Spanish heritage cinema. Traditionally, *el pueblo* has been a highly contested cultural space, a locus for fractious debates about the filmic representation of authentic national identity. Mitchell contends that such films as *La noche de los girasoles* (*The Night of the Sunflowers*, Jorge Sánchez-Cabezudo, 2006), though contemporary in their focus, are 'spectral' heritage films precisely because the past, although largely and significantly absent, is the unrepresented Other, an impossible home which haunts their ontological presents. He argues that the past as an absence—a Derridean trace—thus provides an immaterial dimension which affects how we respond to the contemporaneity of the villages we witness on screen. In a subtle analysis of the spectatorial gaze, Mitchell positions the audience as 'spectators' in a truly important sense, having a cultural/historical understanding that transcends the temporality demarcated in the films and which disrupts their apparent modernity. **Andrew Watts** further deconstructs the spectatorial gaze and its disruption in his examination of the ways in which French heritage cinema evolved between 1994 and 2007, and the key role adaptations of Balzac played in marking the emergence of a new heritage aesthetic. He provides an evocative close reading of *Ne touchez pas la hache* (*Don't Touch the Axe*, Jacques Rivette, 2007) that illustrates the extent to which heritage as a genre, if it can be termed as such, had reinvented itself since its creative and commercial zenith in the early 1990s. Although *Don't Touch the Axe* appears, superficially at least, to conform to a familiar heritage model that cultivates the 'museum aesthetic' that is a key feature of this type of filmmaking, Watts reveals that it also dramatises its struggle to break away from earlier traditions of heritage filmmaking, a struggle reflected by the director's persistent emphasis on images of cutting, slicing and violent rupture. From the title of the film—a reference to the axe used to behead Charles I during the English Civil War—to the lingering shots of actress Jeanne Balibar's sharpened fingernails, *Don't Touch the Axe* attempts to claw, cut and even hack itself free from the artistic conventions of heritage while remaining inextricably connected to them.

The tensions identified by Watts are subsequently ironised by **Ruth Barton,** who revisits her own important writing on Irish historical films from the 1990s that were defined by nostalgia for a pre-modern nation. These were often rural-based and frequently centred their narratives on children, whose state of innocence became a palimpsest for Ireland of old and, by extension, the innocent Irish people of pre-modernity. The impetus behind this wave of heritage films was a desire to make a break with the pervasive legacy of The Troubles and the image of a country defined by lawlessness and violence. Now Barton reflects upon how and why that situation has changed, with the Irish cinema of today being overwhelmingly urban-based in terms of its settings, and almost without exception favouring contemporary narratives. Her chapter considers the reasons for this shift and the implications for Irish heritage cinema. While examining the deployment of tourism as a narrative and as an aesthetic influence in this cycle of films, she also reverses the gaze of her analysis, identifying a similar sense of ironic playfulness in contemporary tourist discourse (defined in the literature as 'post-tourism').

In Part III of the volume, the attention of contributors turns to 'Modes of Consumption', beginning with a timely reconsideration of European heritage cinema by **Andrew Higson**, who presents the results of a detailed quantitative analysis of distribution and consumption patterns of European heritage dramas, broadly defined. Higson provides a series of case studies from different European production contexts and examines the extent to which they circulate in other European countries and how their audiences make sense of them. Taking as his starting point the discussion that he largely originated, Higson highlights that a great deal of what passes as national heritage cinema is actually the product of transnational circumstances and pitched at transnational, even global, markets. Yet, while he notes that historical dramas make up a large proportion of the European films that circulate, to any extent, beyond the domestic borders of the country that led their production, he suggests that this must be weighed against the fact that such films remain a very small proportion of total production. European audiences, Higson argues, are generally very poor at engaging with European culture from beyond their own national context. While historical dramas might be among the *most* visible European films internationally, they are still not *particularly* visible when compared with more mainstream (Hollywood) productions. **Claire Monk** also turns her attention to audiences by examining the importance and impact of fan perspectives and practices around the European heritage film. Noting, like many of the contributors to this volume, that heritage cinema has been persistently framed as a national 'project', she proceeds to dismantle such assumptions by a close focus upon the plural, unpredictable and surprising perspectives of transnational audiences and fans from Europe and beyond. Her analysis of transnational and transcultural fan discourses, understandings and creative/participatory practices reveals that heritage films are consumed, appreciated, understood and (at times) (re-)appropriated by audiences and fans within markedly different generic, media, fannish and transtextual contexts that depart sharply from narrowly national interpretative frameworks, and may even render them redundant. She contends that the culture of fandom itself shifts the consumption and interpretation of 'English' 'heritage' films away from the 'national' and yet reveals a passionate interest in specific 'English' tourist sites which remain uncommodified or even un-visitable in relation to the beloved film.

Many of the questions of ownership of heritage in relation to films and tourist sites come into focus in the following chapter by **Paul Cooke**, which examines the function of heritage film as a mode of 'public history'. Cooke explores how historical dramas can lead to new and unforeseen ways for individuals and groups to explore and take ownership of their heritage. His chapter investigates a number of case studies within the context of recent literature on public and community history, including an in-depth consideration of the problematic production of the aforementioned *Brick Lane* and the extraordinary community response to that film by the people it (mis)represented. Cooke duly examines how debates over the purpose of film funding, government sponsorship, engagement with curational policies and the response of those whose identity is displayed on screen can be self-consciously reflected in certain European films. To this end, he looks in detail at *Am Ende Kommen Touristen* (*And Along Come Tourists*, Robert Thalheim, 2007), a film which explores the cultural ownership of one of the world's most notorious heritage sites, the Polish town of Oświęcim, better known to the world as Auschwitz. Finally, **Rob Stone** engages in both empirical analysis and theoretical considerations of the practice of film tourism and, by applying the peculiarly relevant framework of the 'four steps to ecstasy' of Saint Teresa of Avila, works through the complications and pleasures of film tourism as pilgrimage in relation to the Cinecittà studios in Rome, the spaghetti-western film sets in Almeria, the guided tour of the locations of *Game of Thrones* in Northern Ireland and the emulative *flânerie* around Vienna of fans of the film *Before Sunrise* (Richard Linklater, 1995). Stone argues that these cinematic pilgrimages take the relation of cinema to heritage into a postmodern, even metaphysical, realm where heritage is based upon an intrahistory that fuses the memory of a favourite film with the haptic thrills of tourism. As such, his chapter explores the immediate postmodern mindset of the cinematic pilgrim by drawing in philosophical and psychological theories that explain how certain films actually create their own heritage. He argues that the 'heritage' at stake might seem to refer to nothing more historical than the incident of a film's viewing, but that cinematic pilgrimages, in reality, tap into a profound need to experience and even realise the structural myths that we see and seek in the cinema, ones that cast a light back onto heritage cinema as a mode of film production.

In sum, as the numerous examples in this volume reveal, historical dramas are a particularly visible aspect of mainstream European film production and can generate significant national debates on the role of the past in contemporary national identity construction. Defined in the 1990s as 'heritage films', the makers of such films frequently work in partnership with the wider heritage industry in order to secure funding for their productions, while the films, along with the debates they generate, often shape the subsequent marketing and curatorial strategy of the heritage sites they foreground in their stories. In addition, the consumption of these films, be that in the cinema, online or, by extension, via trips to relevant tourist sites, both official and metaphysically charged, points to an increasingly postmodernist consumption of history as something malleable, indistinct from fantasy or even visitable. Until now, however, there has been very little exploration of this relationship and how it reflects the complexity of contemporary public engagement with the past across Europe. Thus, *Screening European Heritage* provides a unique examination of the way Europe's past is represented on contemporary screens, what this says about contemporary cultural attitudes to the past, and how this reflects, and can be shaped by, the policies and practice of cultural institutions now and in the future. In the process, this volume raises questions around the role and value of the past in cultural and societal change. It investigates how history is reimagined by the contemporary film and heritage industries, and to what end, ultimately exploring the way contemporary heritage film, and its instrumentalisation of spectators' emotional engagement with history, reflects broader trends in the heritage industry. It examines the desires of the audiences for the pleasures of spectacular history and deconstructs the mechanisms of their consumption. European heritage film is certainly more diverse than it is unified, but it is also impossible to deny its persistence and impact across various European film cultures. In an interesting phrasing, Elsaesser speaks of films that 'dwell' on the past, a description which seems particularly true of films that engage with traumatic histories. As the contributors to this volume all explore, however, an examination of the entire 'life cycle' of European heritage film, from production to consumption, also highlights the many ways in which Europe builds on and develops *through* its past while continuing to dispute the place of this past in the continent's understanding of its present.

Works Cited

Biran, A. 2011. Sought experiences at (dark) heritage sites. *Annals of Tourism Research*, 38: 820–41.

Bondebjerg, I. 2013. Heritage film and cultural policy: An interview with Professor Ib Bondebjerg. *Screening European Heritage*. [Online]. Available at: http://arts.leeds.ac.uk/screeningeuropeanheritage/interview-with-professor-ib-bondebjerg/. Accessed 15 Sept 2013.

British Council Film Collection. [Online]. Available at: http://film.britishcouncil.org/british-council-film-collection/about-the-collection. Accessed 13 Dec 2013.

Cooke, P. 2012. *Contemporary German cinema*. Manchester: Manchester University Press.

Elsaesser, T. 2005. *European cinema: Face to face with Hollywood*. Amsterdam: Amsterdam University Press.

Galt, R. 2002. Italy's landscapes of loss: Historical mourning and the dialectical image in *Cinema Paradiso, Mediterraneo* and *Il postino*. *Screen*, 43(2): 158–73.

Higson, A. 1993. Re-presenting the national past: Nostalgia and pastiche in the heritage film. In: Friedman, L. ed. *Fires were started: British cinema and Thatcherism*. London: University College London Press, pp. 109–29.

Koepnick, L. 2002. Reframing the past: Heritage cinema and the Holocaust in the 1990s. *New German Critique*, 87: 47–82.

Lawrence, B. 2013. Nostalgia trips and market drives: Bill Lawrence on heritage film past and present'. *Screening European Heritage*. [Online]. Available at: http://arts.leeds.ac.uk/screeningeuropeanheritage/between-nostalgia-and-market-bill-lawrence-on-heritage-film/. Accessed 1 Sept 2013.

Monk, C. 1995/2001. Sexuality and heritage. *Sight and Sound* 5(10): 32–34. Republished in *Film/literature/heritage: A sight & sound reader*, ed. G. Vincendeau. London: British Film Institute.

Monk, C. 2011. *Heritage film audiences: Period film and contemporary audiences in the UK*. Edinburgh: Edinburgh University Press.

———. 2013. From political critique to online fandom: Claire Monk on British heritage film, its origins and afterlife. *Screening European Heritage*. [Online]. Available at: http://arts.leeds.ac.uk/screeningeuropeanheritage/from-political-critique-to-online-fandom-claire-monk-on-british-heritage-film-its-origins-and-afterlife/. Accessed 1 Sept 2013.

Nye, J. 2011. *The future of power*. New York: PublicAffairs.

Rentschler, E. 2013. *The Lives of Others*: The history of heritage and the rhetoric of consensus. In: Cooke, P. ed. *The Lives of Others and contemporary German film*. Berlin: De Gruyter, pp. 241–60.

Stone, R. and Rodríguez, M.P. 2015. *Basque cinema: A cultural and political history*. London and New York: I.B. Tauris.

Vidal, B. 2012. *Heritage film: Nation genre representation*. London: Wallflower.

Vincendeau, G. 2013. Exhibiting heritage films in the digital age: Interview with Vincent Paul-Boncour. *The Network*. [Online]. Available at: http://www.europa-cinemas.org/en/News/The-Network/Exhibiting-heritage-films-in-the-digital-age-interview-with-Vincent-Paul-Boncour. Accessed 15 Mar 2013.

PART I

Contexts of Production

CHAPTER 1

The Politics and Sociology of Screening the Past: A National and Transnational Perspective

Ib Bondebjerg

Heritage is seldom written specifically into the cultural policy documents behind national film and television production in Europe. However, historical film and television play a crucial role in European film cultures, and clearly have very high audience figures. A historical TV drama like ITV's *Downton Abbey* (2010–15) enjoyed around ten million viewers on average in the UK, and has been distributed to more than 220 territories globally. Danish historical TV drama often has a national share of between 60 per cent and 80 per cent, equal to an audience of between 1.5 and 2.5 million (of a population of 5.5 million), and the recent Danish historical drama *1864* (2014) has been sold to more than 60 countries. So, national historical productions clearly capture the national imagination and frame understandings of the past. At the same time, they often also speak to a transnational audience and are based on co-production and transnational support mechanisms. Thus, the international production of historical dramas and the success of such series tell us that the most popular national history and heritage also has a universal and transnational dimension. Within

I. Bondebjerg (✉)
University of Copenhagen, Denmark
e-mail: bonde@hum.ku.dk

© The Editor(s) (if applicable) and The Author(s) 2016
P. Cooke, R. Stone (eds.), *Screening European Heritage*,
Palgrave European Film and Media Studies,
DOI 10.1057/978-1-137-52280-1_1

the context of this present volume, it is particularly interesting to see how this transnational dimension can interact with the efforts of key European institutions to make concrete notions of a collective European heritage.

Heritage and EU Cultural Policy

The EU and the European Commission are not often thought of as major generators of cultural policy. Culture is primarily seen as a matter for the constituent nation states. However, since the 1960s we have entered an ever-more globalised film and television sector, and since the 1980s the EU has created transnational frameworks for cultural policy, broadly defined. This has included the development of policy to create a single European film and television market via European co-production and distribution structures. The recent establishing of Creative Europe represents a unification of a number of different cultural policies and agencies, but with new initiatives and an increased budget. The previous Culture Programme had a budget of €400 million and the Media Programme had a budget of €755 million. The new Creative Europe budget is €1.46 billion—an increase of nine per cent compared to the total sum dedicated to cultural initiatives from 2010 to 2014. The sub-budgets for the audiovisual sector and the sub-budgets for other cultural initiatives for other parts of European culture have only been slightly increased for the period 2014. This is clearly not a budget that can radically move things on, but it is a beginning.

The EU has increasingly looked at the creative sector as important, not just for culture itself, but also for the economy and economic growth. The creative sector has gained importance in the global economy. In the so-called communication from the European Commission *On a European Agenda for Culture in a Globalizing World* (EU Commission 2007), the Commission is almost poetic, quoting the Swiss author Denis de Rougemont: 'Culture is all the dreams and labour tending towards forging humanity. Culture requests a paradoxical pact: diversity must be the principle of unity, taking stock of differences is necessary not to divide, but to enrich culture even more. Europe is a culture or it is not' (EU Commission 2007: 2). Behind this quotation lies a new and stronger understanding of the role of narratives and culture for the creation of stronger European integration. The EU has recognised the importance of cultural narratives to develop a stronger common understanding of being European next to the feeling of belonging to a national community. Culture and media narratives are part of a cognitive and emotional battle to develop Europe as an 'imagined community'. The concept of heritage is also an important element in this same community. Heritage is a broad term, referring to history as such as well as a broad range of cultural artefacts such as archaeological sites, buildings, specific landscapes, literature, art, film, etc. In 2005, the Council of Europe adopted the *Convention on the Value of Cultural Heritage for Society* (COE 2005a) in which it defined heritage as follows: 'Cultural heritage is a group of resources inherited from the past which people identify with independently of ownership as a reflection and expression of their constantly evolving values, beliefs, knowledge and traditions. It includes all aspects of the environment resulting from the interaction between people and places through time' (Article 2). The idea of heritage is a central anchor of European cultural policy for all the key European institutions.

The stronger presence of culture and heritage in EU policies is connected with the expansion of EU policy areas after the Maastricht Treaty (1991), the Nice Treaty (2001) and the Lisbon Treaty (2004). However, we can trace the European roots of policies for cultural collaboration and cultural heritage back to 1954, three years before the founding EU treaty, the Treaty of Rome (1957). The Council of Europe (COE), an organisation independent of the EU, has often played a role as the cultural dynamo in cultural policy initiatives. COE's *European Cultural Convention* (1954) formulates a number of key issues and policy areas that later entered the EU, as can already be seen in the opening statement: 'The aim of The Council of Europe is to achieve greater unity between its members for the purpose, among others, of safeguarding and realising the ideals and principles which are their common heritage' (COE 1954: 1). The text stresses the need to further develop bilateral cooperation, among other things by encouraging the study of the languages, history and civilisation of the European nations and by promoting cultural activities of European interest. Article 4 states the aim of facilitating the movement of persons as well as objects of cultural value, whereas Article 5 stipulates: 'Objects of European cultural value in each member state must be regarded as part of the common cultural heritage' (COE 1954: 2). In the already quoted 2005 declaration (COE 2005a), the concept of heritage has an even more central position, Europe's ostensibly common heritage being placed at the heart of its democratic values and quality of life. Cultural heritage here means the common heritage of 'human rights, democracy and the rule of law' or what might be called the political democratic heritage of Europe (COE 2005a: 2, Preamble). But the preamble and the following articles also clearly point to a common European cultural heritage defined as 'the shared source of remembrance, understanding, identity, cohesion and creativity, and the ideals, principles and values derived from the experience gained through progress and past conflicts' (COE 2005a: 3, Article 2). The convention is rather forceful in its calling upon not just the diversity of national heritage traditions or 'heritage communities', but also in pointing to the fact that knowledge of, and respect for, the cultural heritage of others is the basis for a common European heritage.

In 2005, COE published *50 Years of the European Cultural Convention*, taking stock of its policy intentions and results. Between 1954 and 2005 the integration and collaboration between COE and the EU increased, and many of its initiatives were co-sponsored or simply integrated into EU policy: European Heritage Days (1985), European Heritage Prize (1991–) and the European Capitals of Culture Initiative (1985–; see Sassatelli 2009). The concept of heritage in most EU policy documents from 1957 onwards is to be understood as a broad historical, cultural and archaeological concept, often linked to cultural sites and their role in common cultural history:

> The point of the matter is that 'culture' is at the heart of all relations between people or between nations and so cannot be taken lightly or for granted. A lack of knowledge or appreciation of another's culture can result in ghastly blunders, a fact undenied by recent and on-going events and interventions around the world [...] So culture is not just one among many fields of administrative concern, it permeates, or should anyway, all aspects of life in society. (COE 2005b: 5)

The policy initiatives developed within the COE framework, which present heritage as part of a transnational European culture, were initially only indirectly represented in the EU system. The European project in the Treaty of Rome from 1957 is, from the preamble to the individual articles, clearly defined primarily as 'an ever closer union', established to 'ensure the economic and social progress of [signatories'] countries by common action to eliminate the barriers which divide Europe' (EEC 1957: 1). The Rome Treaty establishes a European citizenship and actually mentions certain goals for education and culture. Culture is, for example, mentioned in Article 3 of the treaty: 'Encouragement for the establishment and development of trans-European networks [...] contribution to education and training of quality and to the flowering of cultures of the member states' (EEC 1957: Article 3).

In Article 128, culture and heritage are addressed in more detail. This is where we find the source of the famous 'unity in diversity' concept: the union must contribute 'to the flowering of the cultures of the Member States, while respecting their national and regional diversity and at the same time bringing the common cultural heritage to the fore' (EEC 1957: Article 128.1). Further goals and policy actions are stipulated (EEC 1957: Article 128.2) by pointing to the need for improvement of the knowledge and dissemination of the culture and history of the European peoples, conservation and safeguarding of cultural heritage of European significance, non-commercial cultural exchanges, and artistic and literary creation, including in the audiovisual sector.

Until the 1980s, these principles and policy areas were not strongly implemented, but from the end of the 1980s a common European cultural policy began to take form. Milestones in this development were Television Without Frontiers (1984) and a common market for media, the subsequent development of the EU's Media programme (1987–), the Council of Europe's film support programme, Eurimages, and the Europa Cinema Initiative (both 1992), and finally the much stronger inclusion of culture and heritage after the Maastricht Treaty (1993). Behind this stronger development of a cultural dimension is a political agenda, the feeling that there is a gap between the EU and its citizens, a lack of a common communicative space and a public sphere. But there was also a genuinely cultural agenda linked to the question of national identities and how they connect with a collective European identity, and a growing understanding of the economic significance of the cultural and creative media sector. Article 128 in the original Treaty of Rome was amended and expanded in the Maastricht Treaty, most importantly by adding the cultural dimension to all other actions of the Union, thus stressing the centrality and importance of culture, heritage, media and communication. The second important amendment to the original treaty was the emphasis on the cultural dimension of transnational activities between nation states and between the EU and the rest of the world. Culture, heritage, television, film and other media thus became important in a much more direct way, not just for European integration, but also as a means of positioning Europe on the global stage.

The coming cultural turn of the EU was prefigured ideologically by a declaration of European identity by the Council of Europe. On 25 April 1985, the Council of Ministers met and issued a declaration, *On European Cultural Identity*. This stressed that 'cultural co-operation [is] an indispensable contribution to European awareness'; that unity in diversity produces the richness of the common European cultural heritage'; and that 'common traditions and European identity [are] the product of a common cultural history which is not delimited by the frontiers separating different political systems in Europe'. 'Cultural co-operation will contribute to greater mutual rapprochement of the peoples and states of Europe and thus promote lasting understanding.' It is in the common interest of all European states to maintain and develop this heritage and to expand cultural relations', as well as the necessary 'intensification of cultural co-operation among all states of Europe' (COE 1985: 1). What is striking here is a strong emphasis on a European identity along with a recognition of cultural diversity. It is not often that cultural cooperation, unity and a common culture and heritage are put on the agenda, and 1985 was particularly early for such discussions, a decade before the Maastricht and Nice treaties began to have consequences in actual cultural policy at the EU level.

National Historical Narratives and the Transnational Context

The gradual European development of a transnational European understanding of film, media and cultural heritage is not just the result of increased integration and expansion of the policy areas of the EU. It also points to a more theoretical perspective in understanding of the relation between the national and the transnational when it comes to culture, heritage and historical narratives. Benedict Anderson's widely used concept of 'imagined communities' (Anderson 1983) is sometimes interpreted as a way of conceptualising the construction of national identity through symbols, narratives, literature and communication. However, it should also be noted that Anderson finds very strong similarities between different national constructions. What Anderson argues is that within a certain historical time frame, all European nations seem to inhabit the same national imaginary and go through the same construction process.

The notion of nationality as specific and historic in concrete form and style, while at the same time having a kind of cognitive, universal commonality, is underlined by cognitive sociology. In *Social Mindscapes* (1997), Zerubavel develops a model for our social world and the cognitive basis for our perception of it. On the one hand, he refers to the notion of 'cognitive individualism'. This he uses to demarcate the subjective, personal aspects of our mentality, those parts where we differ most from each other. 'Cognitive sociology', on the other hand, refers to specific group formations and 'thought communities'. Finally, he uses 'cognitive universalism' to refer to universal, cognitive commonalities, all that makes us alike as human beings, despite our individual and collective differences. Zerubavel's main point is that we often tend to overstate the individual and collective differences and not see the universal commonalities. Social mindscapes, like imagined communities, are clearly of a much more universal nature than we tend to think. Forms of national identity will often claim a uniqueness that is false: the social, cultural and historical specificity of our history, memory and concept of heritage matters, but it is frequently based on some very universal features.

A person with citizenship in one of the member states of the EU is by definition also a European citizen. This was first established in the Treaty of Rome. By definition Europeans have both a national and European heritage and history. To what degree this actually influences our everyday social and cultural mindscape, as well as our feeling of belonging to a national and transnational community, is another issue. Drawing on the work of Zerubavel, Eder and Spohn (2005), Risse (2010) and Fligstein (2008) suggest that there is very little awareness of a specifically European dimension in our everyday engagement with the public sphere and in particular our experience of the audiovisual media environment. Despite the fact that the EU has made a deep impact on almost every aspect of our national life, we do not *feel* and *experience* it. We live in a *transnational* reality with what is still a very national, local or regional mentality. Fligstein uses the Eurobarometer data on perceived citizenship to unravel the relationship between different collective identities (2008: 141f). Over the years, he suggests, due to the efforts of European institutions, a sense of what we mean by 'Europeanness' has emerged. However, he sums up the 2004 data by saying 87.3 per cent still regard themselves mostly as nationals, only 12.7 per cent mostly as Europeans, and out of these only 56 per cent suggest that they *sometimes* feel European.

Media, both in the form of daily news and factual reporting and in the form of fiction, play a crucial role in the formation of our collective memory, our feeling of being in touch with tradition, heritage and history. Mediated cultural experiences, linked to deeper European integration, may change the relation between national and European identifications. Wilfried Spohn (2005: 2) distinguishes between three different potential outcomes of the European integration process: a strong national identity with a weak European identity as an addendum; a restructuring of national identities that incorporates a sense of Europeanness that becomes ever stronger; and finally, an enduring co-existence between a highly variable mix of national and European attachments and identifications. In the same volume Klaus Eder points to the importance of narratives: 'Europeans telling each other their past is a mechanism of identity construction [...] Collective identity [...] is a learning process in terms of narrating each other's particular past and to this extent creating a common ground in which to see each other as particular others' (Eder 2005: 213). Eder is aware that, so far, national narratives have the upper hand, despite the development of co-production mechanisms and transnational distribution. That said, nations and the rise of national narratives came about by overcoming, or integrating, regional and local dimensions within the national. All European nations are to a certain degree heterogeneous, and internal struggles continue to exist, even in aggressive ethnic forms. This kind of struggle is of course much stronger in a large EU dominated by many national and regional differences. The symbolic and communicative power to overcome this is what media and cultural policy is all about. However, stories on film and television that promote 'unity in diversity' do not develop spontaneously and Eder points to a growing gap between the national and transnational world and mentality in which we live:

> A second mechanism is triggered when widening spaces of interests no longer coincide with strong collective identities through which people recognize each other as being members of a particular group sharing a particular history. The relevant space of action becomes wider than the space covered by the stories people tell each other regarding their common past. Even being a European citizen, Europeans still live in the narrative world of the nation, as this is the world they internalized as the world of their collective belonging. (Eder 2005: 210)

AUDIENCES AND THE NATIONAL AND TRANSNATIONAL DIMENSION OF HERITAGE

In his article on European and transnational identity, Eder (2005: 214f) points to three different modes of collective learning: *the primordial mode*, which he sees as a rather superficial, atavistic and mythological construction, where ancient traditions serve to define the roots of modern Europe; *the traditional mode*, which he sees as a heroic mode underlining what fits the unified construction of a nation or modern Europe; and finally, *the reflexive mode*, which deliberately tries to grasp contradictions and differences and allow for a more dialogic approach to history and opening up of controversies. Even though these categories are not directly applicable to film and television narratives, they indicate some basic strands. The traditional mode in national, historical narratives is, for instance, very visible in national heritage drama on the formative years of a nation's life. Such narratives tend to celebrate the national and the forces that formed pre-modern times. This, however, does not necessarily mean the lack of a critical and reflexive dimension. The many British films and TV series celebrating the Tudor period, such as Tom Hooper's mini-series *Elizabeth I* (2005), *The Virgin Queen* (2005) and *Wolf Hall* (2015), all tell stories of events that constituted modern England. However, each of these narratives also illustrates how nations emerge from conflicts and the specific differences between nations and specific groups within nations, some of which continue to exist today.

The UK tradition of historical TV drama is certainly very national. The above-mentioned dramas, for example, are all about the formation of the nation, the often violent birth of modern democracy growing slowly out of strongly divided societies dominated by royalty and aristocrats. Even in UK historical drama dealing with the modern era, like *Downton Abbey*, the theme of class and the heritage of an aristocratic society lingers on. The extent to which modern audiences are fascinated by the past clearly has to do with an emotional identification with a past mode of existence and society. But seen from a broader European audience perspective, these seemingly very national UK narratives and themes are in fact just a version of something that is very universal. Furthermore, Tudor dramas are also about Europe, insofar as the formation of European nation states was also about conflicts between European nations or royal alliances. We find the same themes in heritage narratives from other parts of Europe. In addition, these UK series are also the main heritage tradition for other European audiences. British heritage dramas are the European lingua franca of historical narratives. They are as transnational as they are national.

If we look at the Danish figures for some of the UK historical series (see Graph 1.1) we see that the literary effect is quite strong. *Jane Eyre* (2006) actually scores higher than *Downton Abbey* (2010–15), even though the latter is by far the most popular series in Europe as a whole, and the adaptation of popular bestselling novelist Ken Follett's medieval story *Pillars of the Earth* (2010) is the biggest historical hit. It should be noted, however,

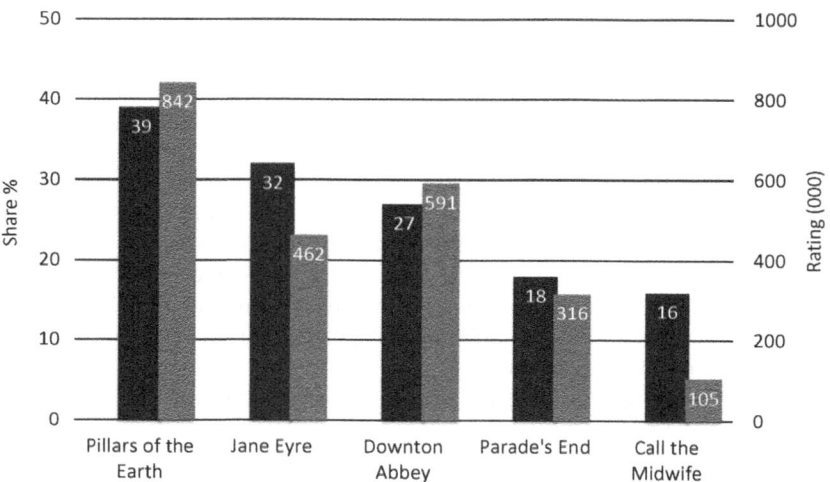

Graph 1.1 UK historical drama cases—Danish share % and ratings

that *Jane Eyre* and *Downton Abbey* are UK-US co-productions and *Pillars of the Earth* is a transnational co-production between German Tandem Productions, Canadian Muse Entertainment, The Movie Network, Canadian Broadcasting Corporation and UK-based Scott Free Productions. This underlines my previous point that drama series audiences tend to perceive as British, or indeed of any other national origin, are often transnational co-productions. The national today in film and television culture is already part of a broader European and international context.

The Danish figures indicate how strong the transnational, European dimension of historical drama is. We might expect this to have a long-term impact on the social, cultural and historical imaginaries of European audiences. When it comes to historical drama, Danes and other Europeans see many more European drama series than national, and this is to a lesser degree also the case with films. But even though UK historical drama has a strong position in broadcast hours and audience figures across Europe, the audience figures for national drama series are much stronger. This underlines the main points put forward by Eder and the data on national and European identity in Eurobarometer surveys:[1] people are first of all nationals; they strongly identify with national drama if such dramas are seen as expressing national narratives and if they manage to combine contemporary and historical memories.

In Denmark, the series *Matador* (24 parts, first broadcast 1978–81), dealing with the period between 1929 and 1947, has on average the highest rating for a national television programme ever measured, with some episodes attracting well over three million viewers (out of a population of 5.5 million). The series has been broadcast seven times since it was first aired and has entered the public imagination and memory as an almost mythological part of what Danes consider to be Danish history and culture (Bondebjerg 1993). The follow-up, *Krøniken* (*Better Times*, 22 episodes, 2004–7), dealing with Danish history between 1950 and 1972, reached the incredible share of between 85 per cent and 89 per cent in all segments of the population (see Graph 1.2). *Matador* got its amazing viewing figures in a monopoly culture with just one public service channel, whereas *Better Times* was broadcast in the modern multichannel age. Nonetheless, the Danish public service broadcaster DR managed to gather a very large and broad majority of the nation in front of the screen.

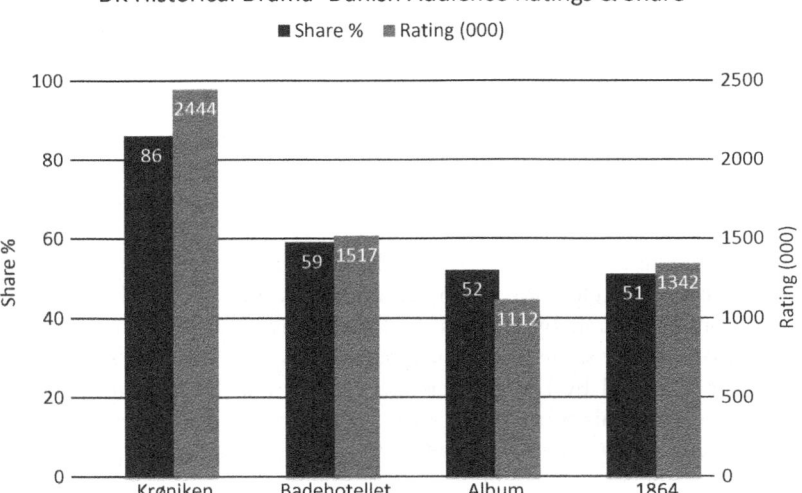

Graph 1.2 Rating and share for recent Danish, historical TV drama

Album, a more modern and reflexive series about recent history, did not do so well and, as we shall see, *1864* divided the nation. But even as it did so, the debate still suggested that national history series continue to have the ability to manifest an imagined community cutting across social and cultural differences.

We have very few large-scale empirical studies of how audiences relate to and use historical television series. One very interesting study based on viewer memories of fiction is Alexander Dhoest's study of the role of Flemish television fiction in the construction of a national identity (Dhoest 2007). This study shows the importance of 'realism' in viewers' perceptions of national fiction, the fact that television drama can create memories based on the everyday reality of a lived past. The 'authenticity' of history is important for audiences, even if they know that this is fiction. To be able to recall a memory of how it was then, or—if the past is beyond our own personal memory—to imagine and experience how it was, is a vital part of the audience fascination with heritage. Another study is Claus Ladegaard's on the Danish reception of Adrian Shergold and Dennis Potter's British series *Christabel* (four parts, 1988, broadcast on Danish DR in 1989). Ladegaard's study (1993) points to the dominance of an emotional mode of experience in the data he collected on audiences' engagement with historical drama. Identification with the characters and the personal side of the story dominate over a more cognitive approach to the historical background and factual framework of the series. Nonetheless, his interviews with viewers (ten in all) also show that the personal, emotional side of the historical everyday is often intertwined with large-scale and cognitive dimensions of history and, indeed, that the one is dependent on the other. The everyday, emotional experience of characters on screen and the conflicts they work through get their specificity from the historical context. However, emotion can become an entry point taking the audience from a personal to a collective level. The interviews underline the *universal* dimensions of television drama reception, while also highlighting that this is complemented by viewers' historical understanding of the period in question. At the same time, Ladegaard notes how the response to such dramas is nuanced by the gender and educational background of audience members. This is an aspect of research that is developed further in Claire Monk's *Heritage Film Audiences* (2011), a larger, empirical study of how audiences relate to and use period films in the UK. Monk's study of the profile of UK heritage audiences underlines the fact that we cannot speak of a homogenous audience for heritage drama. The study is based on a detailed questionnaire from two different cohorts: members of the National Trust (NT), which would indicate a special interest in national history, and *Time Out* magazine readers (TO), representing a less specific type of audience in relation to an interest in history. Based on this survey, Monk concludes that 'the period audience is not a homogenous entity' (Monk 2011: 167) and there is no such thing as a 'monolithic viewing position' (Monk 2011: 168). On the contrary we find a large variety of viewing positions and distinct subgroups, although there does seem to be a clear distinction between main attitudes in the NT and the TO cohorts.

The audience belonging to the NT group were much more focused on heritage films as their preferred film type. The fact that the NT audience had a special interest in and passion for national heritage in all its forms gave them a special perspective on heritage film. The TO audience group, on the other hand, had a broader interest in cinema and culture in general. For them, heritage films were just one genre among many others to which they were attracted. The TO audience furthermore consisted of people with a younger, more liberal or left-wing orientation, which made them look at heritage films in a slightly different way to the NT group (Monk 2011: 169). Monk's conclusion is that a common attraction to heritage films 'can co-exist with substantially different social identities, cultural-political orientations and viewing positions' (Monk 2011: 170); or in other words, our present-day attitudes and experiences influence the way we relate to and interpret films about the past.

Contested Heritage: The Past and Contemporary Politics

The audience studies of historical drama outlined here underline Robert A. Rosenstone's approach in *History on Film/Film on History* (2006). His main point is that, unlike traditional, factual historical presentations, the historical drama can visualise a past reality as lived life. By recreating, or re-establishing, a more sensuous past, combining the individual and the collective, historical drama can more easily make us connect our own memories and lives with those of the past—in terms of both the similarities and differences. The fictional distance and freedom to tell stories about the past, the various forms of dramatisation and personification of historical structures and forces, are not necessarily a diversion from cognitive historical knowledge. Just as the individual memory of the past is vital for our present identity, so the understanding of our collective history, from a national or transnational perspective, needs both emotional and cognitive inputs. Fiction can trigger the experience of a historical world in much stronger ways than factual history.

Zerubavel's concept of memory transitivity defines a 'socio-biographical memory' (Zerubavel 1997: 91) linking memories of social and cultural groups. How social memory for larger groups is transmitted from generation to generation, or from groups to individuals, is part of the ongoing battle over history and the past. This battle is often very visible in historical dramas. Historians may contest the historical accuracy of a specific drama, and different social and cultural groups may divide on the interpretation of the past. Interpreting the past can lead to cultural battles, and revisiting an aspect of history that has been forgotten, deliberately or unconsciously, can create strong public reactions:

> Not only does our social environment influence the way we mentally process the present, it also affects the way we remember the past. Like the present, the past is to some extent also part of a social reality that, while far from being absolutely objective, nonetheless transcends our own subjectivity and is shared by others around us [...]. (Zerubavel 1997: 81)

We seem to have a kind of double vision of the historical: on the one hand history is something far away, a distant and very different world, with other values and norms; and on the other, history is somehow part of our present, helping to define a collective sense of social identity. In a way, we cannot help but project our contemporary mentality onto the past, either critically or in a more nostalgic mode, as a contrast to our modern form of life. The reception of historical films and television dramas invariably highlight ideological perspectives and the ways in which the past continues to inhabit the present.

In 2014, this tension between different approaches to the past and the relationship between the past and the present was highlighted by two very different Danish historical drama series. In October 2014, the Danish public service broadcaster DR launched *1864*, a drama series in eight parts, which generated a heated public debate involving historians, politicians, media scholars and a broad variety of bloggers and ordinary viewers. Earlier that year, the other Danish public service broadcaster, TV2, launched *Badehotellet* (*The Seaside Hotel*), a series that was almost unanimously rejected by critics as popular low culture, but clearly accepted by an audience slightly bigger than the audience for *1864*. *The Seaside*

Hotel had an average audience of 1.51 million viewers, and a share of 59.3 per cent. *1864* had around 1.3 million viewers and an average share of 51 per cent.

The viewer profiles of the two series are, however, somewhat different (see Graph 1.3). Just like the immensely popular DR historical series *Better Times*, *1864* had a much higher share of viewers in 'modern segments', especially the modern social segment, whereas *The Seaside Hotel* scored much higher in 'traditional segments'.[2] Translated into social and cultural categories, this means *1864* found its core audience among the cultural elite and the better educated, those who, furthermore, lean ideologically towards centre-left political parties and attitudes. They are high consumers of all types of culture and are very much engaged in social and political matters. They also tend to be cosmopolitan in their views and less supportive of very national forms of ideology. For this group *The Seaside Hotel* seemed to be trivial entertainment. That said, *1864* also had a strong hold of the modern, individual segment. Also, the more liberal segments

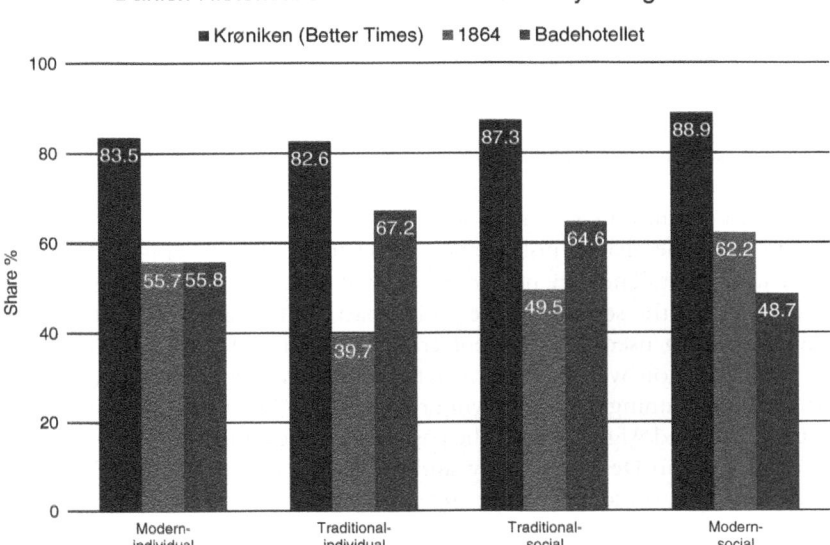

Graph 1.3 Distribution of social and cultural segments for Danish historical drama

of the audience, often employed in the private sector and in bigger cities, found *1864* much more interesting than *The Seaside Hotel*. The TV2 series also had a somewhat older audience, and an audience less educated and with a more provincial profile. *Better Times* worked across all segments and managed to attract an almost unified national audience. *1864* and *The Seaside Hotel*, on the other hand, split the population and spoke more to some parts of the audience than others.

The Seaside Hotel combines comedy and drama in a kind of upstairs-downstairs story beginning in 1928—the same period as *Matador*. It is a low-budget, very Danish version of *Downton Abbey*, where the narrative focus is clearly on the universal dimension of love, family and the local society. The series does make some vague connections between the general historical development of the period and the fictional plot, but this connection is much less integrated into the story than in *1864* and also *Better Times*. The series has elements of the mythological Danish series *Matador*, but without the same solid narrative and historical realism. There is a certain element of nostalgic looking back on life before the world crisis in 1929, a sense of nostalgia that was universally panned by the critics. Both the Danish tabloids and the Danish broadsheets saw the characters as rather flat and often caricatured. Even a provincial newspaper like *Jyske Vestkysten*, traditionally a newspaper that would support something taking place in Jutland, called the series a disaster and a 'bad version of *Midsomer Murders*' but without narrative and suspense (Eising 2014). The series was considered to be, at best, a harmlessly entertaining story about the past, and at worst a problematically nostalgic look back on early twentieth century life in the provinces.

On the other hand, nobody would accuse *1864* of being a nostalgic look at the past. The very heated debate the series generated focused massively on how the series interpreted the past, and whether this interpretation was being used to comment critically on the present. One element in the discussion was the way in which the series is constructed with a present-day framing story involving references to Denmark's role in recent wars in Iraq and Afghanistan. The past historical events it portrays seem to mirror events in Denmark today, and the debate about whether the series is historically correct was in reality a proxy for a discussion about how to interpret our national history from a long-term and short-term perspective. The Danish defeat in 1864 by a much larger German army, the probably foolish and ill-considered national political strategy that brought about the defeat and the subsequent loss of around a third of Denmark has divided nationalists ever since from more European and cosmopolitan-minded Danes. The heated public debate about the series was thus as much a discussion about the national present as about the national past.

The roots of this ideological debate can be found in aspects of the series' production history and, particularly, in the way it was funded. This, in turn, reflected the somewhat aggressive national politics of the ruling elite at the time. Some historians see the war as part of a just, national strategy; others, especially the historian Tom Buk-Swienty, on whose books the series is based, see the events as a result of national hubris. The fight over the interpretation of the past, and the relation between the past and the present, is thematised in the present-day narrative framework of the series, where the activist foreign policy of Danish governments—led by liberal-conservative parties—is seen as a continuation of national hubris. In 2010, the liberal-conservative government, with support from the nationalist Dansk Folkeparti, decided to set aside 100 million Danish kroner for the public service broadcaster DR, earmarked for a national historical drama. While this could be seen as a generous gift to the Danish people, there were also potential media policy implications arising from this 'donation'. Dansk Folkeparti in particular, but also the other liberal-conservative parties, have for the last ten years been increasingly sceptical of DR, accusing the broadcaster of not speaking to the whole of Denmark, but rather focusing more on centre-left audiences in the larger cities. This is an accusation which, it might be noted, is not borne out by the high viewing figures for the Sunday evening drama slot on DR and the broad profile of DR drama in general.

By asking DR to give the Danes a historical drama of substance, the government probably had a modern *Matador* in mind, a drama that could explicitly unite the nation. However, by choosing Ole Bornedal as both scriptwriter and director, DR gave creative power to a person known for his expressive dramatic style and controversial attitudes. Furthermore, by basing the narrative on Tom Buk-Swienty's two highly popular books on 1864, with their shocking realism and very critical interpretation of the political actions that led to the war, a divided public was to be expected. As one commentator, Gunhild Agger (2014), put it: 'The defeat in 1864 took place 150 years ago. But the fight over the interpretation has been ongoing ever since. Ole Bornedal's version [...] has created a war of attitudes. The drama demonstrates that the defeat in 1864 can still set our minds on fire.'

What started as an attack from historians on specific 'facts' in the series soon moved in the direction of a conservative, nationalist assault, not just on the series, but on DR as a whole. The climax came when the cultural spokesman for Dansk Folkeparti, Axel Ahrendsen, backed by former chairman of the party Pia Kjærsgaard, suggested that drama productions from DR should in future be fact-checked by historians, before going on to attack DR and Ole Bornedal for producing left-wing propaganda through misuse of the past (Lindberg 2014a, b). This was probably also fuelled by the fact that the outspoken critic and writer Carsten Jensen, in a strong defence of the series, called it a bold attack on the right-wing nationalists and their desire to control culture (Jensen 2014). The two Danish tabloids, the liberal *Ekstrabladet* and the more conservative *BT*, took two different positions. *BT* clearly defended the series, whereas *Ekstrabladet*'s line was that this was an incredible waste of tax payers' money. Ole Bornedal himself said that he was 'sorry for causing a civil war' (Bjørnlund 2014; Seeberg 2014), but at the same time he took strong issue with those nationalist critics who attacked his historical facts and narrative. Generally, the debate and the evaluation of the series painted a clear, ideological picture. The defence by *BT* and the very positive evaluation it offered was a surprise, but the biggest Danish broadsheet paper with a centre-left position, *Politiken*, strongly defended the series and its approach to historical reconstruction (Weiss 2014). They followed up with articles debating *1864* from historical and contemporary perspectives (Lidegaard 2014). Lidegaard saw a direct parallel between the national liberal character, Monrad, who took the nation to war in 1864, and the liberal prime minister, Anders Fogh Rasmussen, who took Denmark to war after 2001. Also, the intellectual, elite newspaper *Information* gave a positive review of the series and its message (Rasmussen 2014). The series clearly divided the audience along ideological lines. That said, it is interesting to note that, in the end, even more traditional, conservative newspapers and representatives rejected the vehement critique of the Dansk Folkeparti (Weiss 2014).

THE POLITICS OF HERITAGE AND MEMORY

1864 is as much a series about transnational, European history as it is a national historical series. German and English political characters play a crucial role in the series, which is also about the building of Germany and pan-European controversies. That said, the series set the national understanding of Denmark in Europe on fire. Earlier series such as *Matador* and *Better Times* did generate some debate on their interpretation of the past, about historical facts and the question of realism in the representation of history. However, the *1864* debate shows how intense ideological battles over the past are never just about the past, but always part of a very vital collective and individual search for cultural and social roots. (see also Hansen, K.T. (ed. 2016).

It is not only politicians, journalists, historians, TV and film critics who have invested a lot of energy in debating the value of this series. The wider public have also taken a very active part with comments on newspaper online sites and on social media such as Facebook and Twitter. On DR's own website for the series, one finds several thousand comments.[3] At the same time, the series' presentation of the historical period asks the question, 'Who would you have been in 1864?',[4] while also presenting material about the series as well as the wider historical context. This tendency to create a kind of live history class around historical drama is used frequently in the media, and special online fora such as, for example, 1864Live, where it was possible to follow the historical development in 1864 day by day. It seems our past is very much a part of the present, and that new digital media culture, with all its different platforms, can contextualise a historical drama series in ways that suggest possibilities for a broad-based re-engagement with, and ultimately a reinterpretation of, the history viewers are presented with on screen. (see also Astrupgaard, C., Lai, S. and Larsen, F. (2016).

1864 demonstrates that the fight about key past events is often, if not always, a fight about present-day politics and our national identity and self-understanding. It is still too early to judge the long-term effect of *1864* in Denmark, the UK or Germany—it has been sold to these as well as over 60 more countries. The series presents and argues for a highly cosmopolitan, European view of national history, also reflected in the fact that it was a European co-production between Swedish, German, Norwegian and Danish partners, while large parts of the series were shot in the Czech Republic. The series' narrative makes it possible for us to experience and emotionally connect with four different families in the past and to enter into the minds and actions of politicians and cultural characters in and beyond Denmark. The series creates this historical world with an eye to universal structures and the realistic recreation of the past. It is a series that illustrates that national heritage is not just national. It is part of a much broader transnational past and present.

Notes

1. See:http://ec.europa.eu/public_opinion/archives/eb/eb82/eb82_en.htm
2. The Danish TV-meter system uses a social profiling of audience groups based on a regular survey of people's work, living conditions, education, consumer patterns and certain values and attitudes. Audience segments are divided into the 'modern segments' (modern social and modern individual) and 'traditional segments' (traditional social and traditional individual). Those in the modern segment can be described as progressive in terms of the attitude to social and technological change; they have a cosmopolitan outlook, are better educated and tend to vote for centre-left parties if they belong to the social side of the segment, and for more liberal parties if they belong to the more individualist side. The modern 'individuals' most often work in the private sector whereas the modern 'socials' are generally in the public sector. The traditional segments often live in the provinces. They have a lower level of education, are often in more manual work positions, and they tend to lean towards more traditional family values and norms, just as they are more nationally oriented. Politically, they tend to belong to labour parties if they belong to the social side of this segment, or more national, right-wing parties if they belong to the individualist side.
3. See: http://www.dr.dk/Diverse/Drama/1864/index.htm
4. See: http://1864live.dk

Works Cited

Agger, G. 2014. Kampen om vores 1864. *Kommunikationsforum*, 28/10.
Anderson, B. 1983. *Imagined communities. Reflections on the origin and spread of nationalism*. London: Verso.
Astrupgaard, C., Lai, S. and Larsen, F. (2016). 1864 på DR's digitale hjemmebane. In Hansen, K. T. ed. 2016. 1864. TV-serien, historien, kritikken. Aalborg: Aalborg Universitetsforlag, p. 283-306.
BFI. 2012. *Film forever. Supporting UK film. BFI plan 2012–17*. London: British Film Institute.
Bjørnlund, F. 2014. Jeg er ked af borgerkrigen. *Ekko*, 14/10.
Bondebjerg, I. 1993. *Elektroniske fiktioner. TV som fortællende medie*. København: Borgen.
COE. 1954. *European cultural convention*. Paris: COE.
———. 1985. *On European cultural identity*. Brussels: COE.
———. 2005a. *Convention on the value of cultural heritage for society*. Brussels: COE.
———. 2005b. *50 years of the European cultural convention*. Brussels: COE.
COM. 2007. *242 final*. Brussels: COE.

de Pool, I.S. 1977. The changing flow of television. *Journal of Communication* 27(2): 139–149.
Dhoest, A. 2007. Identifying with the nation. Viewers memoirs of Flemish TV fiction. *Journal of European Cultural Studies* 10(1): 55–73.
Eder, K. 2005. Remembering national memories together: The formation of a transnational identity in Europe. In *Collective memory and European identity*, ed. K. Eder and W. Spohn, 197–220. Farnham: Asghate Publishing.
Eder, K., and W. Spohn, (eds.). 2005. *Collective memory and European identity.* Farnham: Ashgate Publishing.
EEC. 1957. *Treaty of Rome.* Brussels: EEC.
Eising, J. 2014. Anmelder sukker over *Badehotellet*: 2 stjerner. *Jyske Vestkysten* 10(2).
EU Commission. 2007. *On a European agenda for culture in a global world.* Brussels: Commission of the European Union.
Fligstein, N. 2008. *Euro-clash. The EU, European identity and the future of Europe.* Oxford: Oxford University Press.
Hansen, K. T. ed. 2016. 1864. TV-serien, historien, kritikken. Aalborg: Aalborg Universitetsforlag.
Jensen, C. 2014. 1864. *Ekko*, 12/10.
Ladegaard, Claus. 1993. Mærk historien. om receptionen af en historisk tv-serie. In *Når Medierne spinder historiens tråd*, ed. C. Ladegaard. København: Akademisk Forlag.
Lidegaard, B. 2014. 1864. sluttede i 2001. *Politiken*, 13/10.
Lindberg, K. 2014a. Politikere på kant med armslængdeprincippet. *Berlingske*, 21/10.
——— 2014b. DF kræver historiker-tjek af DRs serier. *Berlingske*, 19/10.
Monk, C. 2011. *Heritage film audiences*: Period film and contemporary audiences in the UK.
Palle, H. 2014. Tv-dramaet 1864 er forrygende flot og velfortalt. *Politiken*, 12/10.
Rasmussen, A. B. 2014. Den krigsførende nation skal stå (skole)ret. In Information, October 13.
Risse, T. 2010. *A community of Europeans. Transnational identities and public spheres.* Ithaca: Cornell University Press.
Rosenstone, R.A. 2006. *History on film/film on history.* Harlow: Pearson and Longman.
Sassatelli, M. 2009. *Becoming Europeans. Cultural identity and cultural politics.* Basingstoke: Palgrave Macmillan.
Seeberg, K. 2014. Ole Bornedal i opgør med Pia K: Jo, der var sigøjnere i 1864. *BT*, 14/10.
Spohn, W. 2005. National Identities and Collective Memory in an Enlarged Europe. In Eder, K. and Spohn, W. eds. 2005. Collective Memory and European Identity. Farnham: Ashgate Publishing. p. 1-14.

van Dijck, José. 2007. *Mediated memories in the digital age*. Stanford: Stanford University Press.
Weiss, P. 2014. Dyresex ved Dannevirke. *Jyllands-Posten*, 22/10.
Zerubavel, Eviatar. 1997. *Social mindscapes. An invitation to cognitive sociology*. Cambridge, MA: Harvard University Press.

CHAPTER 2

British Flanders: Co-produced Television Drama and the Limits of a European Heritage

Jaap Verheul

If the origins of the heritage discourse are national and political, this is most obviously the case in the United Kingdom. Stuart Hall (2005) has argued that this discourse met a British desire to preserve those sites and objects that would acquire value and meaning only in relation to a specifically English (rather than British) aristocratic and imperial past. The Conservative National Heritage Acts of the 1980s accordingly supported a heritage industry that, centred on the commercial exploitation of noble estates and the natural environment, served the economic interest and bourgeois values of the English upper class (Wright 1985; Hewison 1987). It is in this historical context of Thatcherite Conservatism, Claire Monk reminds us, that the critical debate on the British heritage film emerged in the late 1980s (2011: 14–18). The discussion addressed a collection of historical costume dramas that were said to construct a heritage of Britishness that positioned itself at the height of Britain's imperial power while refashioning its national past into romanticized representations of England's southern districts and their pastoral sceneries and aristocratic

---

J. Verheul (✉)
New York Univeristy, New York, NY, USA
e-mail: jcv239@nyu.edu

© The Editor(s) (if applicable) and The Author(s) 2016
P. Cooke, R. Stone (eds.), *Screening European Heritage*,
Palgrave European Film and Media Studies,
DOI 10.1057/978-1-137-52280-1_2

social milieus. In his 1993 essay entitled 'Representing the National Past', Andrew Higson posited that films such as *Chariots of Fire* (Hugh Hudson 1981) belonged to a cycle of heritage productions whose 'aesthetic of display' fetishized the private possessions of the English elites. In the process, these nostalgic visualizations established a 'heritage space' for 'the display of heritage properties' that, commodified into a national brand, served Thatcherism's support for England's social elite (Higson 1993: 117, 2003: 9–45). Since the publication of Higson's polemic, scholars have increasingly questioned the discursive dichotomy between those costume dramas that romanticized an elitist English past and those more socially engaged 'anti-heritage films' or 'post-heritage films' that were either set in a post-imperialist, working-class Britain or advanced alternative representations of gender and sexuality (Church Gibson 2002; Monk 1995/2001). What united these different responses, however, was their association of the heritage drama with a British national cinema.

This chapter extends the discussion by analysing the recent cycle of heritage television dramas that were co-produced by the United Kingdom with the Belgian region of Flanders. I argue that these miniseries signify the economic benefits of pan-European cooperation while simultaneously re-articulating essentialist ideas of 'Britishness'. First, I will demonstrate that the deregulation of British film and television in the 1980s and 1990s paved the way for the recent proliferation of co-produced heritage drama. I will then discuss *Parade's End* and *The White Queen*, two British heritage series that received support from the Flanders Audiovisual Fund (VAF) to promote the Belgian region and its local film industry. *Parade's End* (Susanna White 2012) is a British World War I miniseries that, although set in England and along the whole Western Front, was shot in Flanders. In like manner, *The White Queen* (James Kent 2013) transports the British Wars of the Roses to Belgium's northern region. As the VAF convinced the producers of both series to substitute a respectively war-torn or medieval Britain for Flanders, this chapter suggests that Europe's audiovisual policies are rooted in a transnational television industry that nonetheless re-establishes restricted notions of national and regional heritage at the heart of the continent's pan-European initiatives.

THE DEREGULATION OF BRITISH FILM AND TELEVISION

It was by no means a coincidence that the association of British cinema with national heritage materialized at the same time as the convergence of the UK's film and television industries. As John Caughie has demonstrated, British film and television began to merge when the public service broadcaster Channel Four went on air in 1982 (2000: 179–202). In a decade of Thatcherite deregulation, Channel Four supported the independent production of film through direct funding, co-investment and the pre-purchase of television rights while also upholding, as a decentralized and self-funded channel, a model of deregulation for a broadcasting market that had until then been rigidly regulated. The convergence and subsequent interdependence of the UK's film and television sectors was thus the result of entrepreneurship rather than stipulated audiovisual policy, and the British heritage brand encapsulated this gradual synthesis. As Belén Vidal has argued, a discourse of 'quality' had historically informed British heritage filmmaking (2012: 22–5), and British television heritage drama in the 1980s correspondingly drew, according to Charlotte Brundson, on four 'quality components': a prestigious literary source novel, an exclusive league of British theatre actors and actresses, a substantial budget and accordingly lavish production values, and a heritage brand of Englishness well-suited for export (1990: 85–6). Sarah Cardwell points out that these four facets engendered a heritage aesthetic for television that thus corresponded quite neatly to the nostalgia, fidelity and quality that had defined its cinematic doppelganger (2002: 112). At the same time, heritage television sought to differentiate itself visually and narratively in that it fetishized, as exemplified by the BBC's 1995 serial *Pride and Prejudice* (Andrew Davies), an almost obsessive attention to visual detail and literary pace.

The quality brand of British heritage television, Vidal has argued, has undergone substantial modifications since the early 2000s (2012: 35). The current, pan-European collaboration in the co-production of heritage television drama, often made possible by multiple funding bodies and converged media conglomerates, is said to have profoundly altered the culture and content of national broadcasting. Vidal's de-nationalization of the heritage debate follows from the increased scholarly opposition to the initial association of British national cinema with heritage filmmaking (Lovell 1997; Dyer 1995; Higson 2003). She suggests that, since 1989, the audiovisual policies of the European Union and its member-states have facilitated the formation of a heritage space that is now pan-European and rooted in funding bodies, private investors and creative practitioners that transcend the nation and actively promote the production and distribution of a heritage brand of filmmaking across European borders. In this 'post-national phase' of heritage filmmaking, Vidal posits, national and regional funding bodies offer supplementary financial and fiscal incentives to attract external private capital and professional expertise to the local film industry, which, in turn, creates a hybrid heritage aesthetic that does not erase popular articulations of the nation but instead rebrands them as cross-over prestige pictures to promote a certain image of the nation and to capitalize on that image in the international marketplace (2012: 63–70).

In the following analyses of *Parade's End* and *The White Queen*, I intend to challenge the presumed pan-European character of contemporary heritage drama and to re-examine it instead, in the case of these two examples, as a national enterprise that has its origins in the deregulation of the United Kingdom's film and television industries. If Conservative film policy in the 1980s had been characterized by the withdrawal of economic incentives for film production, the 1990s witnessed the gradual re-emergence of state support through the fiscal system of the tax shelter and direct public funding via the National Lottery. In 1992, Section 42 of the Finance (No. 2) Act introduced a 'large budget tax relief' that provided fiscal support through a tax shelter system designed for productions with a budget larger than £15,000,000. In addition, a 1993 Act of Parliament allocated a share of the revenues from the National Lottery to the Arts Councils of England, Wales, Scotland and Northern Ireland, whose film funds, in turn, distributed these allowances to those productions that qualified as capital expenditure (capital used to generate new projects or investments). Although the struggle to attract private investors to the British film industry would continue over the next decade, Maggie Manor and Philip Schlesinger posit that this dual strategy became the cornerstone of British film policy and subsequently shaped New Labour's legislation (2009: 304–5).

When Tony Blair's New Labour won the General Election in May 1997, the government established the Department for Culture, Media, and Sport (DCMS) to stipulate British film policy and to replace the Department of National Heritage (DNH), which had been inaugurated in 1992 to regulate art, leisure, tourism and sport. The DCMS advanced a cultural policy that promoted the commercial potential of the UK's creative industries. It emphasized, according to John Hill, the economic contribution of Britain's cultural activities to make extended government subsidy for film production socially acceptable (2012: 342–4). Gordon Brown, the new Chancellor of the Exchequer, added Section 48 to the Finance (No. 2) Act in 1997, which extended the fiscal benefits of the tax shelter system to productions with budgets smaller than £15 million.

If the Conservative 'large budget tax relief' had been designed to attract inward investment, predominantly from the United States, New Labour introduced 'low-budget tax relief' to support British domestic production (Manor and Schlesinger 2009: 305–6). Rather than privileging economic imperatives over cultural ones, however, Yet, John Hill reminds us that New Labour's creative industries agenda did not privilege economic imperatives over cultural ones, but in fact connected economic policy to cultural policy for the first time as it advanced two avenues for funding: grants and loans on the one hand, and fiscal incentives on the other (2012: 338–40).

In legislative terms, the UK Film Council (UKFC), established in 2000, was responsible for the regulation of grant-in-aid for film production (government funds that, generated from tax revenues, were allocated to a specific project and did not have to be repaid). The UKFC also introduced additional funds to co-finance productions with larger budgets and the potential to reach a wider and more inclusive audience on the domestic and international exhibition markets. Since Margaret Thatcher's time, John Hill argues, Conservative and Labour governments had ideologically framed this direct grant-in-aid as a suspicious form of state subsidy, and both accordingly favoured capital allowances (2012: 344–5). Established in 1979, these tax incentives were gradually dismantled and eventually eliminated in 1986, as Thatcher's government promoted free-market competition and consequently desired to remove all forms of public support for film production. Yet the precarious state of the British film industry at the end of the 1980s, however, obliged the Conservative Chancellor Norman Lamont to reintroduce tax breaks in 1992, which Gordon Brown then supplemented with his 'low-budget tax relief' in 1997. According to the House of Commons, the new tax regime generated a total investment of £2 billion between 1997 and 2006, with a growth from £10 million in 1997–98 to £560 million in 2005–6. Compared to the government's budget of £448 million for direct funding for the UK film industry, inward investment thus provided a substantially larger influx of capital while it also accounted for most of the overall production expenditure (House of Commons 2006).

In spite of their considerable impact, as Manor and Schlesinger point out, the tax incentives were contentious because they were seen as offering tax loopholes to the so-called 'middlemen' financiers (2009: 311–12). Consequently, Gordon Brown revised Section 48 in 2002 to limit the allocation of tax incentives to those films scheduled for a theatrical release, thereby excluding television productions from British tax benefits (HM Treasury 2005: 13). In 2004, the Inland Revenue and the Treasury closed additional loopholes that made it possible for tax partnerships either to claim 'sideways loss relief' (the deduction of a loss from other taxable income) or to exploit 'double dipping' (to claim relief on both production costs and the sale and leaseback of the final film print) (HM Treasury 2004). It soon became clear to the Treasury, however, that the dissolution of fiscal incentives seriously jeopardized the viability of the British film industry and led to a significant decrease in both inward investment and the influx of foreign capital from the United States. As a result, the DCMS introduced a 'cultural test' in 2005 to evaluate a film's 'Britishness' and to determine its subsequent eligibility for British tax allowances. The new cultural test instituted a points system that qualified a production as 'British' on the basis of its 'cultural content', its dependency on Britain as a 'cultural hub' (locations, activities and [post-]production facilities), and its employment of 'cultural practitioners' in possession of British citizenship (DCMS 2005: 3–4). The strong emphasis on the transformation of the British audiovisual sector into a 'cultural hub', particularly hospitable to inward investment from Hollywood, reflected the cultural test's focus on the training and maintenance of Britain's high-skilled production personnel and facilities.

Yet, the European Commission (EC), tasked with the promotion of fair competition between the EU's member-states, had determined that tax breaks were essentially protectionist in that they constituted a form of indirect state aid allocated after a process of selection based on national (or regional) criteria (European Commission 2006). A new directive thus stipulated that state aid, including tax benefits, should no longer focus on production expenditure and personnel only but from now on was also required to address the 'cultural content' of audiovisual works (European Commission 2001). In concrete terms, Manor and Schlesinger point out, the EC's stipulations obliged the recipients of the new Film Tax Credit (FTC), established by the Finance Act 2006, to produce 'cultural products' to qualify for national state support (2009: 313–16). The DCMS subsequently revised the cultural test and proposed a new version that more explicitly stressed the cultural content of British audiovisual works. In addition, it also added a fourth category of 'cultural contribution' for projects that promoted or enhanced British film culture, while the introduction of a 'Golden Point Rule' excluded UK-based productions, and American runaway productions in particular, whose 'British content' was limited to the English language only (DCMS 2007: 22). The EC approved the amended cultural test, which became the cornerstone of the revised tax relief system that was implemented in January 2007. The new system was designed to minimize tax fraud by allocating tax credits directly to film production companies, and by calculating tax exemption on the basis of a project's expenditure in the UK, which had to equal at least 25 per cent of the total budget (Hill 2012: 345–6).

In line with its creative industries agenda, New Labour also advanced the marketization and liberalization of Britain's broadcasting sector. This process had its origins in the Conservative Broadcasting Act of 1980, which added a fourth broadcasting service, the aforementioned Channel Four, to BBC1, BBC2 and ITV. Rather than producing its own original programming, Channel Four was designed to commission its products from independent TV producers. This new culture of commissioning stimulated the spectacular development of the UK's independent television industry in the 1980s. This was expedited by the Broadcasting Acts of 1990 and 1996, which introduced a 'statutory independent quota' mandating terrestrial broadcasters and digital networks to commission at least 25 per cent of their programming from independent producers (Goodwin 1998). In spite of these legislations, Jeanette Steemers reminds us, the independent television production sector remained a 'cottage industry' characterized by fragmentation and structural undercapitalization due to its dependency on British broadcasters for the commissioning of fully funded productions (2004: 58–9). Additionally, the British production sector was also defined by a lack of domestic competitiveness, as only 12 production houses held a total market share of 80 per cent, 40 per cent of which was attributed to the BBC (Graham 2000: 9). Finally, the formation of vertically integrated transnational media conglomerates, such as Time Warner/AOL, increasingly obstructed British distributors from competing in secondary and overseas markets, which were already dominated by affordable yet attractive American products (Graham 2000: 37–45).

The fragmentation of the British television sector, Des Freedman argues, spurred the government and the industry to support the formation of a more concentrated communications sector (2003: 33). This process of consolidation enabled Britain's two vertically integrated broadcasters, BBC Worldwide and ITV, to flourish while the corresponding drive for deregulation and integration also facilitated the emergence of a new type of 'independent' British production house: the super-indie, usually comprising several production companies merged with one distribution branch. The

Blair administration actively supported these mergers, for it presupposed that combined financial resources would reduce the risk of investment and create a level of consistency in television production, both of which would encourage the City of London to invest in the further development of Britain's audiovisual industries. To promote the concentration of television production in the UK, Jean Chalaby argues, New Labour also introduced a new intellectual property (IP) regime in 2003 that allowed independent producers to capitalize on their intellectual assets and reduce their dependency on capital injections from the broadcasting sector (2010: 683). This accumulation of capital engendered the subsequent growth of the independent production sector while the broadcasters' increased demand for content also attracted new players to the industry. According to Jeanette Steemers, the 2003 Communications Bill further expedited the formation of Britain's super-indies in that it weakened the formerly strict regulation of foreign ownership while protecting British interests in future broadcasting mergers or acquisitions (2004: 61–4).

Yet Steemers also points out that two structural concerns inhibited the sustained development of Britain's independent production sector (2004: 59–70). First, British independent producers continued to depend on major broadcasters for the distribution of their programming because they lacked the financial resources to either distribute their own productions or to establish in-house distribution arms. Furthermore, there were only a few independent distributors operating in the UK who were not reluctant to take on the risk of selling programming to smaller or less profitable international markets. A second major shortcoming of television regulation under New Labour was the aforementioned elimination of Section 48 of the tax relief system for film and television. Designed to support the realization of high-end television drama, Section 48 was eliminated in 2002, as it was predominantly used for the production of cheaper serials and reality shows, which the government regarded as a form of tax evasion in that this type of programming had traditionally been financed by the production companies themselves. According to Steemers, the elimination of the tax shelter had severe consequences. For producers, it jeopardized the financial basis for the production of high-end television drama, which, in turn, harmed those distributors that had relied on this sort of prestigious broadcasting to sell their programming packages in overseas markets. It is thus not surprising that, in the early twenty-first century, British film and television producers started the look across the Channel and the Atlantic for new funding opportunities. The recent proliferation of co-produced, high-end heritage dramas between Britain and Flanders must be situated in this context.

Co-producing Britain in Flanders

Co-productions, Barbara Selznick argues, often consolidate economic and cultural interests as each party advances its own stakes in the transnational production of television drama. If a national government, for example, signs a co-production treaty to promote an idea of national culture, producers often privilege financial benefits over cultural concerns. Selznick accordingly identifies the 'pooling of financial resources, accessing subsidies and incentives, accessing partner's markets, accessing third country markets, learning from parents, reducing risks, and accessing resources (such as stars, and other creative personnel) and locations' as the 'primary reasons for co-producing' (2008: 17–18). The pooling of international resources enables producers, and those from smaller territories in particular, to realize previously inconceivable projects with greater budgets, for a co-production treaty grants them access to additional capital while attracting potential financiers as the risk of investment is shared with multiple co-producing partners. The treaty assures the product's distribution in the territories of these partners, as well as the removal of any subsidiaries that had previously restricted the access of transnational conglomerates to their markets. Treaties often spur a wave of runaway productions that relocate one or more phases of their production process to industries with beneficial exchange rates or low-wage labour. Co-productions also allow producers to tailor their commodities to their target audience and to the regulatory conditions of the international market. Finally, they contribute to the professional and economic development of the national and regional industries involved.

The implementation of tax incentives in Britain and across Europe comprised, according to Morawetz et al., the single most important legislative measure in support of the pan-European production and distribution of audiovisual works (2007: 426–30). First, it facilitated the formation of 'competition states' that vie with each other for a limited number of high-profile, international projects. This created a climate of tax competition in which each territory was forced to establish its own tax benefits and, subsequently, to outperform its rivals' incentives in order to stay attractive for inward investment. Second, Morawetz et al. argue that in case a country should decide 'to opt out of the tax competition, it not only stands to lose incoming investment for its production service industry, but also faces a very tangible threat that its traditionally domestic production will become itself footloose and take advantage of tax incentives in a neighbouring country' (2007: 433). This is exactly what happened in the United Kingdom after the abolition of tax incentives in 2004. Britain's domestic film production declined by nearly 40 per cent, and when the tax credit system was reintroduced in 2007, television projects no longer qualified for such fiscal incentives.

Consequently, British projects became increasingly dependent on direct or indirect forms of subsidy from other nations or regions. European co-productions relied in particular on multiple tax credits to secure their funding. With producers conceiving their projects to meet the criteria of multiple, often international, funding schemes, the move towards 'creative financing' generated burgeoning private equity funds in which the amalgamation of different tax incentives created a surplus of capital that, in turn, attracted investors to medium and high-end co-productions to capitalize on the financial assets available. This had lasting consequences for European co-production. First, it provided high-end projects with new financial resources and thus made them commercially viable, which, second, led to the overall inflation of production budgets. Third, it enabled both US studios and intermediary financial advisors to divert tax money, as the former abstained from reinvesting revenues in the European market while the latter exploited the increased necessity for expert consultation. Last but not least, Morawetz et al. suggest that the 'subsidy disease', generated by the competition between different states to attract high-end projects, created a dichotomous production climate in which, on the one hand, the new tendency towards co-production restructured the formerly regional and national industries along pan-European lines while, on the other hand, it facilitated the formation of specialized clusters of regional production in which the production itself was often relocated to a lower wage industry while the post-production process usually occurred in those territories with high-skilled professionals (2007: 433–41).

The recent collaboration between the creative industries of Britain and Flanders reflects all four of these tendencies. Lured by the Flanders Audiovisual Fund's (VAF) Location Flanders and Screen Flanders initiatives, *Parade's End* and *The White Queen* moved their production to Flanders to benefit from fiscal and economic incentives and resources that were unavailable in the United Kingdom. The VAF established Location Flanders in 2008 to centralize the resources of the city film offices of

Antwerp, Bruges, Ghent, Ostend, Leuven and Mechelen, while adding, for the first time, a financial component to the support that already existed. With an annual budget of €220,000, it promoted these cities as attractive shooting destinations at international film festivals and markets, through the e-Mission project, which advertised Flanders as an ecologically responsible audiovisual industry, and via a 'location bonus', an incentive of €2,500 to fund foreign producers in their search for suitable locations in Flanders. In April 2012, Location Flanders was replaced by Screen Flanders, which currently has an annual budget of €5,000,000 and awards up to €400,000 in refundable advances to a Belgian producer or to a foreign producer who collaborates with a Belgian one. The co-production is required to contribute to the 'cultural heritage of Flanders' and to invest at least €250,000 of its own capital in the Flemish Community, while funding from Screen Flanders must be reinvested entirely in the Flemish audiovisual sector (Flanders Audiovisual Fund 2013: 81–6; Ruell 2010).

To qualify for support, Location Flanders (2008–12) and Screen Flanders (2012–) require a project to 'enrich the cultural patrimony of Flanders', which, similar to the British model, is assessed through a cultural test (Screen Flanders 2013: 4, 11). Once the test's criteria have been met, Location Flanders and Screen Flanders assist domestic and foreign producers and investors in obtaining tax shelter benefits, mostly to augment further inward investment in the Flemish audiovisual sector, while Screen Flanders also offers direct economic support through the VAF's Media Fund. Although the Belgian tax shelter is a federal incentive, each individual region must approve the allocated tax breaks. The production is also required to meet the EU's definition of a 'European audiovisual work'. The Audiovisual Media Services (AMS) Directive of 2010 demands that the project originates from an EU member-state, from a European third country that belongs to the European Convention on Transfrontier Television, or from a bilateral co-production agreement between an EU member-state and a non-EU third country, provided that the European partner supplies the majority share of the total cost of production, while foreign partners are obligated to secure a Flemish, Walloon or Bruxellois co-production partner to qualify for the tax shelter (European Parliament 2010: 12–14). Investors, on the other hand, are allowed to invest either directly through the tax shelter or via an intermediary company that matches potential investors with producers. Last but not least, some of Belgium's largest private banks, such as BNP Paribas Fortis and Belfius, have also established film funds that transfer the tax shelter's benefits to those of their investors who participate in the production of an audiovisual work in Flanders.

Location Flanders and Screen Flanders offered both logistic and financial support to the production of *Parade's End* and *The White Queen*. *Parade's End* was produced by the independent company Mammoth Screen, one of the UK's principal indies. Executive producers Damien Timmer and Michele Buck took the project, based on a series of four novels from the 1920s by English author Ford Madox Ford, to the BBC, who agreed to commission it in collaboration with the American premium network HBO. Timmer and Buck subsequently hired Tom Stoppard, one of Britain's most eminent playwrights, to adapt the saga, a World War I period piece centred on a love triangle between the English aristocrat Christopher Tietjens (Benedict Cumberbatch), his wife, Sylvia (Rebecca Hall), and the young suffragette Valentine Wallop (Adelaide Clemens), for television. It was the subsequent involvement of producer David Parfitt and his small British production house Trademark Films that brought *Parade's End* to Belgium. As the project concerned a high-end heritage drama with a total cost of £12.5 million, Parfitt felt compelled to explore those non-British territories that could serve as suitable locations and potential co-production partners. Initially, the team had considered Northern Ireland and Canada, but *Parade's End* was set in southern England and the north-western French region of Rouen, and the producers preferred the authenticity of mainland Europe and the historic battlefields of Flanders to the economic benefits of a Northern Irish or Canadian runaway production. Notwithstanding such creative considerations, Parfitt was also attracted to Belgium for the ready availability of its tax incentives for television production, which had been abolished in the United Kingdom (Mundell 2012: 20–1; Cooper 2012: 31).

The creative and financial decision to relocate the production of *Parade's End*'s non-English scenes to Flanders materialized when Parfitt met Flemish producer Martin Dewitte of Anchorage Entertainment at the Cannes Film Festival. According to Dewitte, the British producers still had a financing gap of three million euros, and a co-production with a Flemish partner such as Anchorage would enable them to submit an application, as a Flemish minority production, to the VAF's Media Fund and to the Belgian federal tax shelter. He subsequently approached the Belgian film finance company Mollywood, which, assured of the international appeal of *Parade's End* and aware of the Flemish government's initiatives for the commemoration of the First World War's centenary, agreed to close the production's financing gap (Mundell 2012: 21). The completed budget gave Mollywood a strong position in its negotiations with the Flemish public broadcaster VRT, which agreed to join the project as a co-producer in exchange for *Parade's End*'s broadcasting rights in Flanders. With the VRT on board, the production was eligible to apply to the VAF's Media Fund, which decided to fund the project for €150,000. In addition, Mammoth Screen's affiliation with Mollywood and the VRT qualified *Parade's End* as a Flemish minority production and thus entitled it to the Belgian federal tax shelter. The BNP Paribas Fortis Film Fund accordingly agreed to fund *Parade's End* via tax-shelter-raised capital, equalling an investment of €2.7 million on a total budget of €15.7 million (Media Fund 2012: 27, 39).

After the financing stage, the team hired some of Britain's most bankable celebrities for the series' major roles while the minor parts were filled by Flemish actors to qualify the project as a Flemish minority co-production and to pass the VAF's cultural test, which awarded additional points to international co-productions that employed Flemish actors. The production subsequently spent six and a half weeks in Flanders, and the post-production also occurred entirely in Belgium: Benuts qualified for Belgian tax benefits and thus managed the series' visual effects, Galaxy Studios handled its sound recording and editing, and the Brussels Philharmonic Orchestra recorded its soundtrack. With so much of *Parade's End*'s labour outsourced to Flanders, the heritage drama's Belgian co-producer, Martin Dewitte, enthusiastically proclaimed that 'a good part of the series is Belgian, or even Flemish', while Mollywood's Jan Vrints also advertised the miniseries as a Flemish success story, stating that 'the government and all the funders on the Flemish side helped close the circle and did everything in their power to make [the production] possible' (Mundell 2012: 23). Taking full advantage of Flanders' historic locations, modern facilities, skilled personnel and fiscal incentives, the producers of *Parade's End* ultimately returned nearly five million euros in investments to the region's creative industries (Mundell 2012: 22–3).

Mollywood's contribution to *Parade's End* caught the eye of Company Pictures, a British independent production company commissioned by the BBC to produce *The White Queen*, a television adaptation of Philippa Gregory's popular novel. Established in 1998, Company Pictures merged in 2003 with the media group All3Media, which has since become Britain's leading super-indie (Televisual Media UK 2013). Company Pictures initially considered Hungary and Ireland as potential destinations for *The White Queen*. During the production of *Parade's End*, however, Mollywood's Jan Vrints introduced the BBC and Company Pictures to Belgian producer Eurydice Gysel of Czar Pictures. In cooperation with Location Flanders, Gysel and Vrints began to scout for potential locations for *The White Queen* in Flanders, which set the co-production wheels in motion. A conventional British heritage drama centred on the Wars of the Roses, an often-romanticized conflict between the royal houses of Lancaster and York, *The White Queen*'s fifteenth-century backdrop necessitated such historic sites as cottages, castles, mansions and town halls. In addition to these creative considerations, the Belgian tax shelter offered Company Pictures another incentive to relocate *The White Queen* to the region under the aegis of a British-Belgian co-production, because the now Conservative-Liberal Coalition government of David Cameron had still not reinstituted the tax credit system for high-end television drama in the United Kingdom (Mundell 2013: 23).

Company Pictures and Czar TV secured historic locations in and around the medieval Flemish cities of Bruges and Ghent, and they also refurbished some of Bruges' abandoned industrial properties as studio facilities to shoot the series' interior sequences. Czar then completed *The White Queen*'s finance package by formally committing itself to the show as its Belgian co-producer. This enabled the Flemish public broadcaster VRT to join the project via its co-production fund in exchange for the series' distribution rights in Belgium. The participation of Czar and the VRT also entitled *The White Queen* to Belgian tax benefits, and the BNP Paribas Fortis Film Fund accordingly covered a tax-exempt investment of €10.5 million on an estimated total budget of €22 million. Czar's involvement also qualified the project as a Flemish majority production and enabled the VAF to support *The White Queen* through its Media Fund, which invested €150,000. Finally, Screen Flanders also came in, financing the series as one of its first projects with its maximum grant-in-aid of €400,000 (BNP Paribas Fortis Film Finance 2013: 46–7; Flanders Audiovisual Fund 2014: 72; Media Fund 2013: 22).

While *The White Queen* featured such notable British stars as Rebecca Ferguson (Queen Elizabeth), Max Irons (King Edward) and Rupert Graves (Lord Thomas Stanley), Flemish performers filled the series' minor roles to meet the requirements for European co-production and to pass the VAF's cultural test. For similar reasons as well as practical concerns, Company Pictures entrusted *The White Queen*'s costume, art, and camera departments to the Flemish sector, while it also offered assistant-director position to Flemish professionals. Although the British firm Lola handled the series' visual effects, other stages of post-production were equally outsourced to Flanders, as exemplified by the Image & Sound Factory's recording and mixing of sound. Ultimately, *The White Queen* spent 120 days in Flanders, with an average of 80 people working on set each day. The Flemish audiovisual sector had worked arduously to attract this high-end television project to the region and the Flanders Audiovisual Fund had offered substantial financial and logistical support for what was essentially a British heritage drama. In return, *The White Queen* generated significant revenues for the region as the production was accompanied by inward investments in Flanders' audiovisual industries as well as in the gastronomy and hospitality services of the medieval municipalities of Bruges and Ghent (Mundell 2013: 21–3).

The Limits of a European Heritage

The recent wave of co-produced heritage dramas for British television demonstrates the economic benefits of pan-European collaboration at the governmental and industrial level. As Andrew Higson reminds us, however, the introduction of a cultural test in Britain explicitly connected economic policy to cultural policy. In like manner, the initiatives of the Flanders Audiovisual Fund met the desire of the Flemish government to promote the region both economically and culturally (2011: 56). Herein resides the great paradox of the European heritage drama. Although *Parade's End* and *The White Queen* participated in a pan-European audiovisual industry, they nonetheless re-established essentialist ideas of national and regional heritage—and, in this case, of British and Flemish culture—at the heart of European audiovisual policy. Barbara Selznick has referred to this marketing strategy as 'the co-production of nationalism', which is, in turn, deployed by television networks to brand their own image at home and abroad. Television networks, Selznick argues, often exploit 'the reputational capital of particular products and particular product categories associated with a nation' to determine their marketing strategy for the international distribution of specific television programmes, formats and genres. In addition, a nation's reputational capital also contributes to the materialization of international co-productions, for producers will often look for partners with known expertise in a specific kind of programming. When production partners pursue the exploitation and subsequent formation of a singular and identifiable brand of national film or television, 'the process of international co-production is used not to create international appeal but to generate a very specific nationalism that is intended for an international audience' (Selznick 2008: 74–5).

Not altogether surprisingly, Selznick identifies the heritage brand as one of British television's most exportable genres. 'The heritage brand of Britishness,' she suggests, 'became associated with particular attributes, benefits, and attitudes that bolstered British producers' reputational capital in the creation of historical costume dramas' (2008: 81). It is in this context that the recent outsourcing of British heritage productions to Flanders reflects the paradox of the contemporary, co-produced heritage drama. If the reputational capital associated with the heritage brand offered the British nation a lucrative mechanism to exploit and smoothen its past, and if it established British film and television producers as the worldwide authority on period pieces, *Parade's End* and *The White Queen* transferred—or at least shared—this reputational capital with the Flemish region and promoted Flanders, its heritage and its film and television industries on an international stage. Yet there is little that is inherently 'Flemish' or 'European' about *Parade's End* or *The White Queen*. Even the shared, pan-European trauma of the First World War, which is at the heart of *Parade's End*, ultimately serves to romanticize the lives and times of England's southern elites. Indeed, *Parade's End* and *The White Queen* focus almost exclusively on English characters who operate in a specifically British historical context. Consequently, both miniseries fail to imagine the possibility of a shared heritage for Europe. As visual paeans to Flanders' historical cityscapes, *Parade's End* and *The White Queen* engaged with a pan-European audiovisual industry but nonetheless engendered the co-production of a dual nationalism. On the one hand, these productions established a distinctively Flemish brand of heritage film and television while, on the other, they deployed the heritage sites of Flanders to rearticulate an essentialist notion of Britishness.

This has profound implications for the conceptualization of British heritage drama as a mode of national cinema and television. *Parade's End* and *The White Queen* demonstrate that, while Flemish audiovisual policy may seek to attract co-productions with European partners to support the local film industry of Belgium's northern region, it still participates in the formation of the British heritage brand. In the process, British and Flemish audiovisual policies reaffirm heritage's pivotal contribution to national and regional culture. In turn, these culturalist discourses also inform European audiovisual initiatives. Contemporary European audiovisual policy represents not just the formation of tax havens and cultural hubs across Europe but also actively promotes the culture of these hubs abroad. In doing so, such legislation, and the commodities it engenders, adds a distinctively cultural element to economic incentives for film and television production. If, as Phillip Drake suggests, the creative industries agenda of the 1990s and 2000s marked a shift towards 'cultural economy policies underpinned by the belief that culture and the creative industries are key drivers of future economic prosperity' (2013: 222), the current emphasis on 'Flemishness' or 'Britishness' in audiovisual policy stresses the contribution of flourishing creative industries to national and regional culture, and it does so by explicitly connecting essentialist notions of culture to a region's or nation's illustrious heritage, thereby aligning itself, once more, with the 'culture as heritage' policies of the 1980s.

It is no surprise that the Cameron administration belatedly reintroduced tax breaks for high-end television drama in the United Kingdom in April 2013. Frustrated with the outsourcing of British products, personnel and capital to other countries or regions such as Flanders, the Treasury desired to bring the production of high-end television drama back to Britain. Aside from its traditional emphasis on the economic contribution of a tax-relief system, the Treasury also stressed the cultural significance of such a scheme, arguing that 'one of the ways in which the world sees Britain at its best is through world-class films and television made in Britain' (HM Treasury 2012: 5; Winnett 2012: 9). To determine the sorts of products that could serve this cultural function, the DCMS reintroduced a cultural test modelled on the one established for film production in 2007 (DCMS 2012: 4–8). If the latter had signified, according to Andrew Higson, 'a renationalization of British film policy, since British films did not previously have to be *about* Britain or to engage with British heritage [...] to be eligible for official support', the Treasury's introduction of a new tax regime sought to 'strike a balance between inward investment and cultural Britishness—with the two brought together in the form of investment in a UK industrial infrastructure and labour force' (2011: 63, 56–7). The explicitly cultural rhetoric that underpinned the reimplementation of a tax incentive scheme for British television marks the unmistakable renationalization of European audiovisual policy and of co-produced European heritage drama.

Works Cited

BNP Paribas Fortis Film Finance SA/NV. 2013. *Prospectus: BNP Paribas Fortis Film Finance,*. Brussels: BNP Paribas Fortis Film Finance SA/NV.
Brundson, C. 1990. Problems with quality. *Screen* 31(1): 67–90.
Cardwell, S. 2002. *Adaptation revisited: Television and the classic novel.* Manchester: Manchester University Press.
Caughie, J. 2000. *Television drama: Realism, modernism, and British culture.* Oxford: Oxford University Press.
Chalaby, J.K. 2010. The rise of Britain's super-indies: Policy-making in the age of the global media market. *International Communication Gazette* 72(8): 675–693.
Church Gibson, P. 2002. From dancing queen to plaster virgin: *Elizabeth* and the end of English heritage? *Journal of Popular British Cinema* 5: 133–142.
Cooper, S. 2012. Talent on parade. *Screen International*, March, 31.
Department for Culture, Media, and Sport (DCMS). 2005. *Cultural test for British films: Final framework.* London: DCMS.
———. 2007. *British certification Schedule 1 to the Film Act 1985: Cultural test guideline notes.* London: DCMS.
———. 2012. *Creative sectors tax reliefs. Cultural test for British high-end television: Consultation.* London: DCMS.
Drake, P. 2013. Policy or practice? Deconstructing the creative industries. In *Behind the screen. Inside European production cultures*, ed. P. Szczepanik and P. Vonderau, 221–236. London: Palgrave Macmillan.
Dyer, R. 1995. Heritage cinema in Europe. In *Encyclopedia of European cinema*, ed. G. Vincendeau, 204–205. London: British Film Institute.
European Commission (EC). 2001 *Commission adopts communication on future of cinema and audiovisual industry in Europe (Press Release). Press Release IP/01/1326 (27.9.01).* 27 September 2001. Brussels: European Commission, Press and Communication Service.
———. 2006. *State aid N 461/2005—United Kingdom: UK film tax incentive, C (2006) 3982 final.* Brussels: European Commission.
European Parliament and Council of the European Union. 2010. *Audiovisual media services directive 2010.* Brussels: European Parliament and Council of the European Union.
Flanders Audiovisual Fund vzw. 2013. *Annual report, 2012.* Brussels: Flanders Audiovisual Fund.
———. 2014. *Flanders audiovisual fund/film fund: Annual rapport 2013.* Brussels: Flanders Audiovisual Fund.
Freedman, D. 2003. Who wants to be a millionaire? The politics of television exports. *Information, Communication & Society* 6(1): 24–41.
Goodwin, P. 1998. *Television under the Tories. Broadcasting policy 1979–1997.* London: British Film Institute.

Graham, D., and Associates. 2000. *Out of the box: The programme supply market in the digital age—A report for the Department for Culture, Media and Sport.* Taunton: David Graham & Associates.

Hall, S. 2005. Whose heritage? Un-settling 'The heritage,' Re-Imagining the post-nation. In *The politics of heritage: The legacies of 'race'*, ed. J. Littler and R. Naidoo, 23–35. London: Routledge.

Hewison, R. 1987. *The heritage industry: Britain in a climate of decline.* London: Methuen.

Higson, A. 1993. Re-presenting the national past: Nostalgia and pastiche in the heritage film. In *British cinema and Thatcherism*, ed. L. Friedman, 109–129. London: University College London Press.

———. 2003. *English heritage, English cinema: Costume drama since 1980.* Oxford: Oxford University Press.

———. 2011. *Film England: Culturally English filmmaking since the 1990s.* London: I.B. Tauris.

Hill, J. 2012. 'This is for the *Batmans* as well as the *Vera Drakes*': Economics, culture, and UK government film production policy in the 2000s. *Journal of British Cinema and Television* 9(3): 333–356.

HM Treasury. 2004. *Protecting tax revenues. Pre-budget report.* 2 December 2004. [Online]. London: HSMO. Available at: http://webarchive.nationalarchives.gov.uk/20091222074811/http://www.hmrc.gov.uk/pbr2004/pn03.htm. Accessed 27 January 2014.

———. 2005. *Reform of film tax incentives: Promoting the sustainable production of culturally British films.* London: HMSO.

———. 2012. *Creative sector tax reliefs: Response to consultation.* London: HM Treasury.

House of Commons. 2006. *Written answer, 27 February 2006.* [Online]. Volume 433, Collection 328w (February 2006). Available at: http://www.publications.parliament.uk/pa/cm200506/cmhansrd/vo060227/text/60227w84.htm#60227w84.html_spnew7. Accessed 24 January 2014.

Lovell, A. 1997. The British cinema: The known cinema? In *The British cinema book*, ed. R. Murphy, 235–243. London: British Film Institute.

Manor, M., and P. Schlesinger. 2009. 'For this relief much thanks.' Taxation, film policy, and the UK government. *Screen* 50(3): 299–317.

Media Fund and the Flanders Audiovisual Fund. 2012. *VAF/media fund. Annual rapport 2011 (VAF/Mediafonds Jaarverslag 2011).* Brussels: Flanders Audiovisual Fund.

———. 2013. *Flanders audiovisual fund/media fund: Annual rapport 2012.* Brussels: Flanders Audiovisual Fund.

Monk, C. 1995/2001. Sexuality and heritage. *Sight and Sound* 5(10): 32–34. Republished in *Film/literature/heritage: A sight & sound reader,* ed. G. Vincendeau. London: British Film Institute.

———. 2011. *Heritage film audiences. Period films and contemporary audiences in the UK*. Edinburgh: Edinburgh University Press.

Morawetz, N., et al. 2007. Finance, policy, and industrial dynamics—The rise of co-productions in the film industry. *Industry and Innovation* 14(4): 421–443.

Mundell, I. 2012. The big parade. *Flandersi (Flanders Image Magazine)*. Take 24 (Autumn 2012). Brussels: Flanders Image and the Flanders Audiovisual Fund.

———. 2013. The Queen of Czar. *Flandersi (Flanders Image Magazine)*. Take 26 (Summer 2013). Brussels: Flanders Image and the Flanders Audiovisual Fund.

Rivi, L. 2007. *European cinema after 1989: Cultural identity and transnational production*. New York: Palgrave Macmillan.

Ruell, N. 2010. Cities love movies (Steden Zijn Zot van Film). *De Standaard*, October 20, D4–D5.

Screen Flanders and Flanders Audiovisual Fund ngo. 2013. *Screen flanders: Procedure manual for the 2013 calls*. Brussels: Flemish Government and Enterprise Flanders.

Selznick, B.K. 2008. *Global television: Co-producing culture*. Philadelphia: Temple University Press.

Steemers, J. 2004. *Selling television. British television in the global marketplace*. London: British Film Institute.

Televisual Media UK Limited. 2013. Production 100, 2013: Annual survey of the British independent production sector. *Televisual Magazine*. London: Televisual Media UK Limited. [Online]. Available at: http://www.televisual.com/read-reports-surveys/23/Production-100-2013.html. Accessed 22 July 2014.

Vaizey, E. 2010. *Speech: The future of the UK film industry*. 29 November 2010. London: Department for Culture, Media, and Sport. [Online]. Available at: https://www.gov.uk/government/speeches/the-future-of-the-uk-film-industry. Accessed 3 February 2014.

Vidal, B. 2012. *Heritage film: Nation, genre, and representation*. New York: Wallflower Press.

Winnett, R. 2012. Tax breaks to end exodus of Britain's best television drama. *Daily Telegraph*, March 16, 9.

Wright, P. 1985. *On living in an old country: The national past in contemporary Britain*. London: Verso.

CHAPTER 3

Whose Heritage?: *Noi credevamo* (*We Believed*) and the National, Regional and Transnational Dynamics of the Risorgimento Film

Alex Marlow-Mann

This essay will focus on *Noi credevamo* (*We Believed*, Mario Martone 2010), an ambitious and high-profile historical film about the events leading up to the Unification of Italy in the latter part of the nineteenth century. Highly acclaimed and enormously successful domestically, the film is undoubtedly one of the most accomplished and significant Italian films of recent years, although it failed to achieve a similar impact internationally. At first glance the film would appear to be a celebration of Italian culture and a commemoration of the founding of the nation, but in actual fact it constitutes a complex historiographic intervention that illuminates previously neglected or under-emphasised elements of Italian history and problematises conventional unification narratives by emphasising both the use of questionable acts of violence and the ultimate failure to achieve a true popular revolution. The tensions between the film's foregrounding of national heritage and the complexities raised by its historiographic discourse, together with

A. Marlow-Mann (✉)
University of Kent, Canterbury, UK
e-mail: A.P.Marlow-mann@kent.ac.uk

the differing receptions it achieved on the national and international stage, prompt questions about how regional and transnational dynamics impinge on national heritage narratives, which are relevant to a broader consideration of European heritage films in the new millennium.

Historical Epics, the Risorgimento and Heritage Cinema

The Italian historical epic has a long and distinguished history. Indeed, during the silent era it was with films such as *Quo Vadis?* (Enrico Guazzoni, 1913), *Gli ultimi giorni di Pompei* (*The Last Days of Pompeii*, Mario Caserini and Eleuterio Rodolfi, 1913) and, above all, *Cabiria* (Giovanni Pastrone, 1914), that Italian cinema first made an impression on international markets, while pointedly distinguishing itself from Hollywood, which was then ascending to the position of hegemony it retains until this day. Of course these films are not often described as heritage films, but they exhibit all of the characteristics that Ginette Vincendeau identifies as typifying the heritage genre (2007: 293). All of these titles were taken from 'classic' literature (*Quo Vadis?* and *The Last Days of Pompeii* from popular novels by Henryk Sienkiewicz and Sir Edward Bulwer-Lytton respectively, while *Cabiria* was an original screenplay by Pastrone, but was officially credited to the most celebrated Italian poet of the period, Gabriele D'Annunzio, who wrote the literary intertitles); they were big-budget prestige productions; they addressed a middle/upper-class audience in an attempt to legitimise cinema as a new art form; they emphasised the films' purported artistic and cultural qualities; they placed great import on *mise-en-scène* and the (supposed) authenticity of their historical reconstruction; they employed an aesthetic based around long takes and static tableaux, which by the early 1920s had already come to be seen as outmoded; they promoted a national cultural heritage to both national and international audiences through their stories of classical antiquity; and they used the past to reaffirm a fixed image of national identity. While the majority of these historical films focused on antiquity and the classical era, there were also a number of films set during the Risorgimento (literally 'Resurgence'), the turbulent period in the nineteenth century during which foreign dynasties were driven out and the Italian nation was unified. It is perhaps no coincidence that the very first fiction film to be produced in Italy, *La presa di Roma* (*The Capture of Rome*, Filoteo Alberini, 1905), dealt with the moment in 1871 when Rome was seized and made capital, the culmination of this process of Unification.

As Fulvio Orsitto notes, during the silent era 'a large number of films sought to arouse nationalistic feelings through the apotheosis of well-known Risorgimento heroes, the celebrations of the victorious battles for independence, and the heroic feats of conspirators and members of secret societies' (Orsitto 2005: 241–2). Similarly, following the advent of Fascism, films set during the period 'served the interests of a regime whose aim was to establish an affiliation between the heroic Risorgimento past and the Fascist present' (Ibid.: 242).[1] These early Risorgimento films thus used their historical setting in order to articulate a conservative message based around a celebration of national heritage in support of the political status quo. However, the publication of the Marxist theorist Antonio Gramsci's *Quaderni del carcere* (*Prison Notebooks* and *Il Risorgimento*), written from a Fascist jail in the 1930s but only published after the fall of Fascism and the end of the Second World War, offered a radically revisionist interpretation of the Risorgimento as a passive or failed revolution, and this was to influence several of the most significant cinematic depictions of the Risorgimento of the post-war period (Gramsci, 2012 [1948–51], 1996 [1949]).

It should be pointed out here that the Risorgimento was actually a complex and drawn-out process lasting over half a century and comprising a number of groups and individuals whose political positions, agendas and ultimate goals diverged significantly. For the Marxist Gramsci, the fact that the Monarchic faction ultimately prevailed over the Republican impulse meant that the Risorgimento must ultimately be considered both a failure and a betrayal of its populist origins. In failing to realise the full potential of the movement's democratic and libertarian impulse, the Risorgimento left a compromised political system dependent on national authority figures, which, for Gramsci, ultimately and inexorably gave rise to Fascism half a century later. Moreover, the fact that the first appointed King of Italy was from the Savoy dynasty in Piemonte,[2] Northern Italy, and that the national government was to be established in Rome, meant that the South—formerly the Kingdom of the Two Sicilies with its own royal dynasty based in Naples—was sidelined and the pre-existing socio-economic disparities between North and South exacerbated, creating a socio-geographic disparity that continues to blight Italy, and Italian politics, to this day.

Gramsci's reinterpretation informed the two most famous cinematic treatments of the Risorgimento of the post-war period, Luchino Visconti's *Senso* (1954) and *Il gattopardo* (*The Leopard*, 1963), whose attitude to 'the myth of the Risorgimento is […] straightforwardly critical, and at times polemical' (Nowell-Smith 2003: 71). However, as Orsitto notes, 'Visconti's neo-Marxist interpretations remained an exception in the cultural climate of the time' and, with few exceptions,[3] the Risorgimento films produced under the decades of rule by the centre-right Christian Democrat governments 'promoted a glorifying representation of national history that would appeal to a vast public ranging from the Northern industrial elite to the Southern masses and urban proletarians' (Orsitto 2005: 246). The majority of Risorgimento films produced in the post-war period thus pursued an agenda of national affirmation underpinned by a conservative, potentially reactionary historical politics that little differentiated them from those produced prior to the war.

We Believed

Undoubtedly the most significant Risorgimento film since *The Leopard*, Mario Martone's *We Believed* once again bears all the hallmarks of the heritage genre. It was a medium-budget, prestige project, directed by a cultured director of stage and screen now considered one of Italy's most respected and acclaimed filmmakers, and was based on a novel which, although a commercial failure, was well respected, particularly within academic circles.[4] The film relied heavily on historical documentation to maintain scrupulous historical accuracy and employed an elaborate and measured *mise-en-scène* to recreate the past. It also made pointed use of Italian symphonic and operatic music from the period (including Vincenzo Bellini and, especially, Giuseppe Verdi), as if to reinforce its own status as national art through reference to other Italian highbrow art forms, much as the historical epics of the 1910s and 1920s had done. Perhaps most significantly of all, the film was supported by the Comitato Italia 150 and released to coincide with the 150th anniversary of the Unification of Italy, accompanied by a large photographic exhibition in Turin and a glossy coffee-table book (Barbera 2011). As such it can be seen as a logical response to the repeated calls of Presidente della Repubblica Carlo Azeglio Ciampi for Italian filmmakers to produce a film on the Risorgimento prior to its anniversary, drawing on 'the many stories which start from different places and experiences to miraculously converge on a clearly shared objective: unity and liberty' (Ciampi 2002). The film thus bore the hallmarks of a national cultural celebration of the founding of the Italian nation on the occasion of its anniversary. Indeed its very title, with that all-important pronoun—'a sort of collective "I" with almost psychoanalytic roots' (Tabanelli 2012: 312)—apparently addresses the national populace, inviting them to participate in a reaffirmation of the shared ideals of the nation. This process is even more emphatic in the Italian trailer, which is punctuated by a series of captions ('We Dreamed'; 'We Struggled'; 'We Hoped'; 'We Never Gave Up') set to the stirring tones of Verdi, a music intimately associated with the Risorgimento and its ideals.[5]

It was perhaps to be expected, then, that the film received widespread acclaim from the Italian critical establishment and went on to sweep the national film awards, winning seven David di Donatello awards (including best film) and being nominated for five more, while simultaneously winning the Italian National Syndicate of Film Journalists Award and being nominated for the Golden Lion at the Venice Film Festival.[6] It also met with an extraordinary and, it would seem, unexpected commercial success, with its original distribution in 27 copies being increased by over 100 additional copies during the first week of release due to the unexpected audience demand (Carlo Degli Espositi, quoted in Barbera 2011: 27). All of this would seem to support its characterisation as a heritage film and to confirm that Italian audiences identified with the film and its take on national identity.

Surprisingly, however, it failed to receive a single significant award from any of the major festivals or award ceremonies outside of Italy, or to receive theatrical distribution in any of the major foreign markets, with the exception of the co-producers France. This complicates matters slightly, suggesting that while it spoke successfully to national audiences, it did not offer the kind of readily identifiable and easily exportable image of the nation typical of heritage cinema in general, which generally finds equally—if not more—appreciative audiences abroad (as Visconti's films on the Risorgimento had done). Moreover, the closer one looks at the film itself—as opposed to the promotional materials and critical reception that surround it—the less it appears to be straightforwardly nostalgic, celebratory or affirmative in its depiction of Risorgimento history and the more it appears critical, ambivalent and contradictory. As Fabio Benincasa notes, the film 'deconstructs the epic—and thus mythologizing—idea of the Risorgimento' (Benincasa 2012: 300). It is useful, then, to think of the film not only in terms of heritage cinema but also as a historical film in the sense intended by Robert Rosenstone—as an attempt to use the medium of film in order to investigate the past and construct a particular historical narrative: film as history (see Rosenstone 2006).

Problematising the Revolutionary Narrative

The first thing to note about the film's approach to Risorgimento history is that it covers a surprisingly long arc, from 1828 to 72, devoting much of its attention to a lengthy pre-history of struggle, rather than the achievement of Unification itself. The second is that it is highly elliptical, being structured in four sections, which skip over large sections of history, particularly those emphasised in earlier films on the Risorgimento. For example, it disregards the Five Days uprising in Milan in 1848, the focus of earlier films like *Le cinque giornate* (*Five Days in Milan*, Dario Argento, 1973); it sidelines the famous expedition of Garibaldi and his Red Shirts, which formed the basis of films like *1860: I mille di Garibaldi* (*Gesuzza the Garibaldian Wife*, Alessandro Blasetti, 1934); it avoids the failed attempt at the Roman republic depicted in *In nome del popolo sovrano* (*In the Name of the Sovereign People*, Luigi Magni, 1990); and it avoids the capturing of Rome in 1870 and the establishment of Rome as the new nation's capital, the event which formed the basis of *The Capture of Rome*. Instead, the film focuses on lesser events typically elided from conventional accounts of the Risorgimento, and not only those on cinema screens, but also those of the official histories taught in schools. Notably, it foregrounds the quashing of the popular uprising in Cilento in 1828 and Garibaldi's defeat at Aspromonte in 1862, choices which are extremely significant for the kind of history of the Risorgimento the film proposes. By focusing on such events, Martone articulates an account of the gradual unravelling of popular revolution which is broadly consistent with that of Gramsci. Indeed, in interview Martone has drawn attention to the tension between the Republican and Monarchist ideals underpinning the Risorgimento, which is central to an understanding of the film, describing it as 'a dualism that never healed' (Martone 2010: xi). Given this approach, the film's protagonist moves through a character arc from idealism to disillusionment, and the film acquires a markedly tragic and pessimistic tone, particularly in the latter part. Such an arc is clearly in tension with any attempt to see the film as a celebratory heritage movie.

These elements are also present in Anna Banti's novel, on which the film is based (Banti 1967). The only account of the Risorgimento written by a woman, the novel is based on factual events that befell the author's ancestor, Domenico Lopresti, a revolutionary who fought for Unification and spent periods in prison as a result of this struggle. The novel deals with the period from the 1848 uprising to the first decade of the Liberal State (Bouchard 2005: 117) and is narrated in the first person through a series of flashbacks, and in this way captures Lopresti's disillusionment with the outcomes of the Risorgimento, which mirrors that of Gramsci. The film's screenplay, by Martone and Giancarlo De Cataldo, author of the crime novel *Romanzo criminale* (subsequently adapted for the cinema by Michele Placido and for television by Stefano Sollima), jettisons both the first-person narration and flashback structure in favour of linear chronology and focalisation through three main protagonists, rather than the single focaliser of the novel. The shifts in focalisation allow the film to present clearly the contrasting agendas of the Risorgimento at the time, and thus problematise its status as a single national movement. Moreover, by focusing above all on followers of the Republican Mazzini, who remained faithful to his cause and died a clandestine revolutionary long after the process of Unification was complete, Martone emphasises their persistent and unwavering commitment to an (ultimately doomed) political ideal. The addition of the character of Salvatore, the son of a peasant, to complement the aristocratic Domenico of the novel also serves to reinforce the Gramscian historical interpretation common to both book and film. Meanwhile, the addition of the character of Angelo, who was inspired by Dostoevsky's *Devils* (1872), and who ultimately murders his comrade-in-arms, Salvatore, serves to show how dogmatic allegiance to a political cause can lead to an increasingly radical and destructive adherence to violence as a means to an end. Thus the film includes events such as the aborted attempt to assassinate the Savoia King Carlo Alberto in 1834 and the attempted assassination of Napoleon III in Paris in 1858, which are absent from the novel.[7] The emphasis on assassination attempts and public bombings also sits uncomfortably with any attempt to see the film as celebratory nation-founding myth. Instead, it teases at the blurred dividing line between political struggle and terrorism and adds an entirely new subtext, not only in relation to Italy's history of Left- and Right-wing terrorism in the *anni di piombo* ('Years of Lead') of the 1970s but also, crucially, in the post-9/11 climate and in the context of contemporary debates about the legitimacy of political violence in relation to the 'War on Terror'—a parallel explicitly acknowledged by the director himself (Martone 2010: viii, xiv).

Problematising National Unity

We have seen how the Risorgimento has been reinterpreted—by Gramsci first and then Visconti, Banti and De Cataldo/Martone—as a failed or betrayed revolution in terms of class, with the popular Republican movement embodied by Mazzini and Garibaldi substituted by an elitist Monarchic one embodied by Crispi. However, this failure/betrayal can also be understood in geographic terms, as a genuinely national movement which is usurped by a Northern agenda centred on the Piemontese Savoia dynasty. Indeed, as noted above, the exacerbation of the dramatic social and economic disparity between North and South is one of the most troubling consequences of Italian Unification, which spawned a whole new culture of historical, social and political study—Meridionalismo. This geographical tension remains the other key feature of *We Believed* and it is worth noting that while the film's protagonists cross class divides, all three of them hail from the South.

Martone signals this geographic tension in three ways. First, through a narrative progression from South to North and then abroad to France and England, as if to highlight the subsuming of local concerns to national and then international political agendas. Second, through a complex linguistic mix between archaic Italian (drawn more-or-less verbatim from historical documents), the dialects of Cilento and Sicily (in the South) and Piemonte (in the North), and the foreign languages of French and English. Martone describes these contrasts as a 'fundamental aspect of the film' and many of the actors were chosen on the basis of their origin or their linguistic capabilities. He also astutely observed that the linguistic shifts paradoxically represent both a 'conflict' between different ideals and the 'hypothesis of a [unified] populace' (Martone and Barbera 2011). This linguistic mix would not necessarily be a logical and natural choice, particularly in a country with a long history of dubbing. One need only think, for example, of *The Leopard*, which, despite the centrality of its Sicilian setting, featured a cast of American, French and Italian actors who were dubbed into standard Italian, English and French for the various international markets. Unlike Visconti, Martone is at pains to highlight the national and regional markers in speech, and consequently the geographic tensions inherent in the Risorgimento. Third, the film employs different photographic dominants to contrast the various geographic regions, creating what cinematographer Renato Berta calls a 'dialectical photographic style' (cited in Martone 2010: xliv). Thus, for example, the same green countryside illuminated by the Southern sun features both in the opening scenes and when horses pass dead bodies in a river after Garibaldi's defeat at Aspromonte, contrasting with the photography in the North and establishing the sense of a 'tragedy that takes place within an idyllic landscape' (Ibid.). Thus, these stylistic choices highlight regional fragmentation just as the choice of three protagonists and an elliptical narrative draws attention to the ultimate failures of the revolutionary impulse. In so doing the film creates an implicit parallel between the failure of the Republican movement and the failure to achieve a true and equitable geographic unity once Unification was officially completed. This is alluded to in a small but significant moment towards the end of the film after the defeat of Garibaldi's army when Domenico, now on the run and exhausted, comes to rest. Clearly visible is a large concrete and iron structure that is striking because, in a film otherwise so scrupulous about authenticity and historical accuracy, it is so obviously anachronistic. As Martone has explained, the decision to include this structure was a very deliberate one, designed to allude to the future urbanisation, abuse and decay of the South and imply that its current troubles have their roots in this historical moment (Martone 2010: xlv–xlvi). Thus, in this key moment, which provoked many questions and queries in post-screening debates, 'the Unification of Italy is represented as an ecomonster, as architecture that devastates the territory and remains unfathomable in its incompleteness' (Benincasa 2012: 310) (Fig. 3.1).

PRODUCTION: PROBLEMATISING NATIONAL CINEMA

We Believed is thus a complex piece of historiography that provides a critical account of the Risorgimento as both failed popular revolution and unresolved attempt at national unification. This problematises its construction as a prestige heritage film produced by the national film industry in response to President Ciampi's exhortations to commemorate the 150th anniversary of Unification. However, if we look at the film's genesis more closely, we can see, again, that a more complex picture of its origins and production emerges, and that these origins were significant in conditioning the direction of the film's historiography.

In actual fact, the film was not originally intended to coincide with the anniversary; rather it dates back to 2003 and it was only as a result of a particularly complex and convoluted production history that the film was eventually delayed by seven years, ultimately allowing the distributors to

Fig. 3.1. Unification as ecomonster: the use of *mise-en-scène* to prefigure the course of historical change in *We Believed* (Mario Martone 2010; Palomar/Les Films d'Ici)

capitalise on the coincidence. The initial production collapsed in 2006 when Eurimages turned down its funding application and the original producer, Feltrinelli, consequently pulled out. At this point, the producers were forced to shift attention from transnational agencies like Eurimages towards regional bodies like the Regione Piemonte and Film Commission Piemonte. Like other Film Commissions, the Film Commission Piemonte is a regionally based and regionally funded institution that promotes and facilitates film production in the region with an eye to the economic and cultural benefits that film productions bring in. The anniversary of the Risorgimento was particularly felt in Piemonte, given that it was Piemontese royalty that assumed the throne of Italy when Unification was complete, and so it is perhaps fitting that the film benefitted from funding directly from the Region of Piemonte.[8] More surprising is the fact that there was no input from the Regione Campania, despite the fact that the Southern scenes were set there and that Martone himself hails from the region and was the key figure of the celebrated 'New Neapolitan Cinema' that emerged there in the previous decade.[9] Eventually, additional support came from the Puglia Film Commission, leading to the scenes set in Cilento being shot there instead.[10] Producer Carlo Degli Espositi even observes that the production was divided into two blocks—one Northern, one Southern—just like Italy itself (quoted in Barbera 2011: 26). Another source of funding was from France—in the form of a co-production deal with Les Films d'Ici and a subsidy from Arte France Cinéma—which facilitated the shooting of a number of scenes in Paris and the recruitment of a number of French actors in secondary roles. To suggest that the input of French and Piemontese money directly determined the narrative structure of the final film might be overstating the case, but it is undoubtedly true that any screenplay must take into account the possibilities and limitations imposed by the budget and production model. It is therefore likely that these funds facilitated the inclusion of scenes set in Paris and Piemonte, and it may not be coincidental that neither the bombing in Paris nor the assassination attempt on Carlo Alberto in Piemonte feature in the source novel but were added during the screenwriting process. The irony, perhaps, is that, rather than furthering the film's status as a heritage film, these additions merely exacerbated its critique of the Risorgimento (Fig. 3.2).

An additional source of funding which was key to getting the project off the ground the second time around was Rai Fiction, the feature film arm of the State TV Network. Martone was initially contracted to deliver a longer, alternative version for screening on television in serial form; however, neither Martone nor Cataldo were ultimately able to resolve

Fig. 3.2. Puglia stands in for Cilento in the Southern scenes, shot by cinematographer Raffaele Berta according to a 'dialectical photographic style' in *We Believed* (Mario Martone 2010; Palomar/Les Films d'Ici)

the difficulties inherent in adapting such a complex series of historical events into a screenplay that could function in both these forms and the plan was abandoned. However, the version eventually broadcast on television does contain one notable difference from the theatrical release—it is dubbed into standard Italian, erasing the regional and national speech markers that play such a key role in the film.[11] It was this version that was screened on State TV in December 2011 as the 'culmination of the year-long celebration of the Unification of Italy'. By diluting the regional specificities of the language and broadcasting the film as part of a national celebration, the television version would seem to be a further attempt to homogenise the film, forcing it into the heritage cinema straitjacket against which the film's historiographic revisionism strains.

Conclusion

Martone has stated that 'Italy is a marvellous collection of geographic, linguistic and climatic contradictions. The unification of Italy becomes an extraordinary hypothesis in the moment in which it signifies the unification of this complexity, a *cultural unification*. [...] So in order to "undo" Italy the first thing is to "undo" its culture [...] and here I am talking about what is taking place in schools and universities' (Martone 2010: xxiii; emphasis in original). The central role that Martone sees culture playing in the making (or unmaking) of Italy takes us back to the notion of the heritage film and the role that, in celebrating and commemorating the past, film can play in the establishing of national identity. Yet there is a fundamental tension between the film's discourse and its cultural status. Clearly the film's convoluted production history had a determining effect on its problematic status as heritage film. On the one hand, the substitution of national and European producers with regional and French ones favoured the complication of any simplistic and celebratory narrative of national unification. On the other, the introduction of television funding and the delays that led to its release coinciding with the 150th anniversary of Unification led to a belated attempt to reconfigure and resituate a revisionist piece of historiography within the simplistic frame of a celebratory heritage film. If it is difficult to make the film-as-text cohere into a straightforward heritage film, given the complexities of its historiographic discourse, the film-as-cultural-artefact seems very much to fulfil that function, in terms of both its promotion and reception. The film can thus be considered a site of contestation between the revisionist discourse of Martone and De Cataldo, the demands of regional and foreign funding agencies, and the national audience seeking impulses from the film's distributors and State TV.

If the heritage film is, by definition, based around a celebration of cultural heritage, then this always begs the question of whose heritage it is that is being promoted—and this is precisely what originally led to political critiques that heritage cinema excludes minorities in favour of a reaffirmation of conservative, establishment values (see, for example, Higson 2003). This is even more relevant in a country with as complex a national history and as fractured a national identity as Italy. If the film's title (and trailer) appear to interpellate a national audience to participate in a celebration of 'our' heritage on the occasion of 'our' national anniversary, then the film itself begs the question who this 'we' really is and to what extent the heritage being celebrated applies to any particular individual or constituency. Moreover, the use of the past tense in the title also suggests that this belief no longer applies, and that the ideals of Risorgimento are no longer characteristic of Italian national identity. If this results in a certain pessimistic tone, it does not, itself, make the film pessimistic. As Martone says: 'The title reveals that the film is the story of a defeat, and there is no doubt that *We Believed* is a tragic film. But when I say tragic, I mean also that it is cathartic, that it is a prompt to action. The point is not that everything is over, but rather that it is just beginning' (Martone 2010: lv). And it is for this reason that special screenings of the film accompanied by a post-screening debate were organised at, for example, social centres in Naples and university halls in Rome (see Barbera 2011: 16). In this sense, the film's discourse constitutes a broader intervention into Risorgimento historiography, fulfilling for Italy the kind of film-as-history role that Rosenstone argues *JFK* (Oliver Stone, 1991) and the debates it provoked played in the US (Rosenstone 2006: 128–32). The raising of these questions thus assumes a political function at a moment when, as Martone suggests, Italian culture and State education are 'undoing' or 'erasing' Italian heritage. The film thus engages with the past not in order to repropose a static and one-dimensional image of national heritage, but rather as part of a progressive spur to action. Just as Higson and others argue that the British heritage film of the 1980s is not simple nostalgia, but rather both a product of and response to the social and political climate in which it was produced, so, too, *We Believed* is not merely the celebration of an anniversary, but a charged engagement with debates around national unity, identity, culture and politics that are as valid now as they were a century and a half ago.

Notes

1. Significant titles include *Villafranca* (1933), *Teresa Confalonieri* (*Loyalty of Love*, 1934), *Amo te sola* (*I Love You Only*, 1935), *Giuseppe Verdi* (1938), *Il cavaliere di San Marco* (*The Knight of San Marco*, 1939) and, above all, *1860: I mille di Garibaldi* (*Gesuzza the Garibaldian Wife*, 1934).
2. It is worth noting that this first king was called King Vittorio Emanuele the Second—although he was the first King of Italy, he was the second King Vittorio Emanuele in Piemonte and he saw no reason to identify himself as anything else, so fully did he see his role as an expression of continuity.
3. Significant exceptions include films made by leftist filmmakers such as Paolo and Vittorio Taviani (*Allonsonfàn*, 1974) and Florestano Vancini (*Bronte: cronaca di un massacro che i libri di storia non hanno raccontato* [*Liberty*], 1971).
4. The initial budget was dramatically reduced due to the problems in setting up and financing the project described below. Ultimately budgeted at over €6 million (Barbera 2011: 26), the film can be considered cheap for a two-and-a-half-hour historical epic, but high by the standards of Italian production of the period.
5. The trailer can be viewed online here: www.youtube.com/watch?v= OmZeKLuAVzA (accessed 19 June 2015).
6. The decision of the international jury headed by Quentin Tarantino to award the Golden Lion to Sofia Coppola's *Somewhere* (2010) generated some controversy in Italy. In retrospect, perhaps, this decision is not so surprising, since a measured historical discourse about complex national issues filtered through the restrained aesthetic of the heritage film was never likely to have been the kind of film to appeal to Tarantino's tastes. In addition to the awards mentioned above, it also won the following Italian awards: three Golden Ciak Awards, one Italian Golden Globe (plus four nominations), one Golden Grall (plus two nominations) and various other prizes.
7. These changes derive largely from the contribution of De Cataldo, who aside from his career as a crime novelist is also an investigative judge and was therefore brought on board both because of his expertise in handling historical documents and his familiarity with the clandestine and criminal world.
8. Nor did it hurt that in 2008 Martone was appointed Director of the Teatro Stabile in Turin, Piemonte, which subsequently also became involved in the production.
9. It is not clear exactly why the Campania Film Commission was not involved, although their support was sought.

10. In one scene the Sicilian coastline on the horizon was digitally added to complete the illusion that events were taking place on the western, not eastern, coastline.
11. Martone has always insisted that the model for the film was the films Roberto Rossellini made for television in the final phase of his career—didactic works based on scrupulous historical research in which great ideas are debated and which themselves constitute works of history.

WORKS CITED

Banti, A. 1967. *Noi credevamo*. Milan: Mondadori.
Barbera, A., ed. 2011. *Noi credevamo: il Risorgimento secondo Martone*. Turin/Milan: Museo nazionale del cinema, Fondazione Maria Adriana Prolo/Il castoro.
Benincasa, F. 2012. Il fantasma della politica: Il Risorgimento e l'Italia contemporanea nel cinema di Mario Martone. In *Cinema e Risorgimento: visioni e revisioni: da La presa di Roma a Noi credevamo*, ed. F. Orsitto, 296–320. Roma: Vecchiarelli.
Bouchard, N. 2005. Risorgimento as fragmented body politics: The case of Anna Banti's *Noi credevamo*. In *Risorgimento in modern Italian culture: Revisiting the nineteenth-century past in history, narrative and cinema*, ed. N. Bouchard, 117–132. Madison, NJ: Farleigh Dickinson University Press.
Bulwer Lytton, E. 1834. *The last days of Pompeii*. London: Richard Bentley.
Ciampi, C.A. 2002. *Incontro del Presidente della Repubblica Carlo Azeglio Ciampi con i candidati ai Premi David di Donatello per il 2002*. [Online]. [Accessed 19 June 2015]. Available from: http://presidenti.quirinale.it/Ciampi/dinamico/ContinuaCiampi.aspx?tipo=discorso&key=17277
De Cataldo, G. 2002. *Romanzo criminale*. Turin: Einaudi.
Dostoevsky, F.M. 1992 [1871]. *Devils*. Oxford/New York: Oxford University Press.
Gramsci, A. 1996 [1949]. *Il Risorgimento*. Rome: Editori Riuniti.
———. 2012 [1948–51]. *Quaderni dal carcere*. Rome: Editori Riuniti.
Higson, A. 2003. *English heritage, English cinema: Costume drama since 1980*. Oxford: Oxford University Press.
Mancino, A.G., et al. 2010. Speciale: *Noi credevamo* di Mario Martone. *Cineforum* 500: 56–67.
Martone, M. 2010. *Noi credevamo*. Milan: Bompiani.
Martone, M. and A. Barbera 2011. Audio commentary. *Noi credevamo*. [Blu-ray]. 01 Distribution.
Nowell-Smith, G. 2003. *Luchino Visconti*, 3rd edn. London: BFI.
Orsitto, F. 2005. Unification in postwar Italian cinema: 1954–1974. In *Risorgimento in modern Italian culture: Revisiting the nineteenth-century past*

in history, narrative and cinema, ed. N. Bouchard, 241–258. Madison, NJ: Farleigh Dickinson University Press.

———. 2012. *Cinema e Risorgimento: visioni e re-visioni: da La presa di Roma a Noi credevamo*. Roma: Vecchiarelli.

Rosenstone, R. 2006. *History on film/film on history*. Harlow: Pearson Education Limited.

Sienkiewicz, H. 1896 [1895]. '*Quo Vadis*'. *A narrative of the time of Nero*. Trans. Jeremiah Curtin. London: J.M. Dent & Co.

Sorlin, P. 1980. *The Italian Risorgimento. The film in history: Restaging the past*, 116–144. Oxford: Blackwell.

Tabanelli, R. 2012. Politica, arte e teatro: dissezione analitica di Noi credevamo. In *Cinema e Risorgimento: visioni e re-visioni: da La presa di Roma a Noi credevamo*, ed. F. Orsitto, 321–356. Roma: Vecchiarelli.

PART II

Limits of Representation

CHAPTER 4

Towards World Heritage Cinema (Starting from the Negative)

Alan O'Leary

It's a bit like taking a vacation in sixteenth-century North India, without the risk of contracting plague or being decapitated by a warlord.

(Philip Lutgendorf on *Jodhaa Akbar*)

OWNING HISTORY

To speak of 'heritage cinema' is to start from the negative. This is so because the term retains a pejorative charge from the context of its first coinage. As Claire Monk (2002) has pointed out, the critical characterisation of heritage cinema, a descriptor coined by critics rather than a genre recognised as such by industry and audiences, has to be understood as emerging from the splenetic British political atmosphere of the Margaret Thatcher premiership (1979–90). Parallel and perhaps essential to Thatcher's project of dismantling much of Britain's industrial sector in the name of defeating socialism was a narrow version of Britishness, indeed 'Englishness' (Thatcher styled herself an 'English nationalist'), which celebrated whiteness, the colonial past and the values of the upper middle classes and aristocratic elite. What came to be identified as heritage cinema was seen by scholars on the left to be a correlate of Thatcherite ideology. For these scholars, heritage cinema was a conservative and ideologically unsound form that proffered 'a highly selective vision of Englishness attached to pastoral and imperial values where the past as spectacle [became] the main attraction' (Vidal 2012: 8).

Coeval with the heritage cinema that caught the offended eye of scholars like Andrew Higson, and supplying the terminology for its dismissive characterisation, was the foundation in 1983 of a state quango, the 'Historic Buildings and Monuments Commission for England', divided in 2015 into two bodies, 'English Heritage' and 'Historic England', the joint remit of which is to manage the nation's historic built environment. To some extent, these heritage bodies do exactly what one might expect. English Heritage is responsible for maintaining monuments and historical sites like Stonehenge as well as the 'stately homes of England'—that is, the houses of the historical aristocracy considered of architectural importance. However, English Heritage also maintains more unusual sites—for example, a Cold War bunker—that point to a more ambiguous idea of heritage, while Historic England emphasises some unexpected themes in encouraging appreciation of the historic environment.[1]

Historic England devotes a section of its website to what it calls 'Inclusive Heritage', at the time of writing offering material on the legacy in the built environment of LGBT, disability and women's histories as well as of the slave trade.[2] The notion of 'inclusion' seems at once admirable and patronising in relation to the first three of these themes (suggesting a magnanimous hand extended to the previously excluded in a way that confirms their difference from an implied norm), but the idea of the heritage of the slave trade seems particularly equivocal. If 'heritage' denotes 'property which devolves by right of inheritance' or 'valued objects and qualities', then the slave trade is a heritage for whom exactly? If the answer is for the white English who profited from slavery, some of whose homes are preserved and celebrated by the English Heritage budget, then it is a negative and shameful heritage indeed. On the other hand, descendants of the enslaved may wish to ensure that the historical outrage of slavery is not forgotten, and may wish to cement an identity by 'claiming' the experience of slavery, wresting back its 'heritage' from those who profited from it and asserting a different form of ownership.

Ekhart Voigts-Virchow writes that 'heritage industries (films, novels, tourism, theme parks, etc.) re-establish the past as a property or possession, which, by "natural", or better, "naturalized" right of birth, "belongs" to the present, or, to be more precise, to certain interests or concerns active in the present' (2007: 123). The flurry of scare-quotes may imply that such 'presentist ownership' is perforce ersatz, but the 'heritage of trauma and division' (to quote this volume's introduction) exemplified by the case of the slave trade suggests that the question of the ownership of the past is a complex one indeed. 'Presentist ownership' may take a range of forms, as can be suggested by a brief consideration as heritage film of *12 Years a Slave* (Steve McQueen, 2013), the Oscar-winning adaptation of a memoir by Solomon Northup (1853). Set mostly in handsome Louisiana landscapes, the film shows the degradation and brutality of the antebellum slave economy. It is a denunciation of a historical outrage with all-too-present legacies in a country that still practises the mass incarceration of African-Americans and legalised brutality against them. Righteous anger on the part of the spectator, the desire to know and read more about historical slavery, the celebration of the resourcefulness and tenacity of forebears in impossible circumstances, the urge to fight against contemporary racism and inequality—any of these might be a response to viewing *12 Years a Slave*. Another might be the less obviously admirable one of planning a tourist visit to the American South to see the beautiful locations featured in the film. Of course this last activity need not exclude the previous four, but one of my concerns here is to take seriously (and sympathetically) a 'superficial' response that seems to privilege spectacle over contemplation and pleasure over engagement. And it is from this perspective that I find myself suspicious of the opposition accepted by Voigts-Virchow when he writes that 'heritage is not history (which seeks knowledge about the past), it is the "modern-day use of elements of the past"' (2007: 124).[3] Rather than in terms of an opposition of 'knowledge versus use', heritage culture may more effectively be thought of in terms of *establishing a relationship with the past* and in terms of *registering the persistence of the past in the present*. In heritage cinema, pleasure is the vehicle of such activity.

But I repeat: to use the term heritage cinema is to start from the negative. To describe a film as heritage cinema is to encircle it with a halo of political and aesthetic suspicion. Starting from the negative, some scholars see their task as being to list and condemn those elements in a film or group of films that illustrate and confirm the film or films' reactionary character (Higson 1993; Craven 2011). Others acknowledge but resist the negative charge by finding elements of political commentary or ambiguity that contradict the films' superficially 'touristic' vistas (Galt 2002). Still others will shift attention to the complexities of audience engagement with heritage films (Monk 2011). My approach here is to see the pejorative connotations and negative charge as *essential* to what the editors of this volume call in their introduction the 'heuristic' of heritage cinema, because heritage itself is never uncontested or uncontaminated. The 'ownership' of the past is always at issue in the heritage film, and the authority or right to interpret, employ and enjoy the traces of that past is always one of its key themes. In this chapter, I test this assertion in relation to films from different national (Italy, China, India) and transnational production contexts, moving from heritage cinema in Europe to what I dub 'world heritage cinema', and invoking UNESCO (the United Nations Educational, Scientific and Cultural Organization) as a kind of global big sister to English Heritage and Historic England. My aim is to use the heuristic of heritage cinema to treat the films in terms of their 'packaging' for different audiences of heritage 'properties': costume, architecture, the picturesque—and history as such.

Made in Italy

As evidenced by the present volume, the term heritage cinema has come to be used to characterise film production well beyond Britain, though not yet of every national (or transnational) context. With regards to Italy, it has been used to group exportable films in which landscape and female beauty are part of a visual spectacle presented for the delight of the man or male child's intra-diegetic gaze. Among these, *Cinema Paradiso* (Giuseppe Tornatore, 1988), *Mediterraneo* (Gabriele Salvatores, 1992) and *Il postino* (Michael Radford, 1995) are seen to be linked by a spectacularising representation of Mediterranean land- and seascapes (all three are set on islands) and a nostalgic register (Radstone 1995; Galt 2002). Associated with Miramax and its policy of picking up middlebrow films from Europe for the American market, such films have sometimes been seen to have been *designed* for a foreign tourist gaze and therefore to commodify the country's appeal as a kind of 'Brand Italy' for the Anglophone market.

To group these films as 'heritage cinema' is, then, to start from the negative: it is to imply that the films' construction of the past as bucolic and picturesque is consolatory, sentimental and inauthentic. Rosalind Galt

(2002: 172) starts with this negative when she speaks of the films' 'touristic spectacle', but she counters it by arguing that the beautiful landscapes in the films are infused with a sense of mourning and loss. This sense of loss is, in the films, apparently one of romantic failure, but Galt argues that it expresses disappointment with how Italy had developed since the postwar period, a period in which hope had been so strong for the renewed democracy and new republic after the disaster of fascism and the humiliations of World War II.

Galt's is a sensitive and subtle reading; the problem with it is that it requires a spectator with an ideal awareness of Italian history. Implicit in her account is something like the old value distinction between tourist and traveller, where the latter sees 'behind' appearance to the 'reality' of the place visited. And yet, as Pauline Small says, 'the political resonance of the films, emphasised in the critical appraisal by Rosalind Galt, may not be accessible to the non-Italian audience, nor perhaps to more recent generations of Italian society' (2005: 164).

Perhaps it is the case that the political and historical questions teased out by Galt are felt to earn the less recondite pleasures the films provide. Small points out that international publicity for what she dubs 'rural idyll' films suggests that 'one of the main reasons to view recent Italian heritage films is to experience again the pleasure of looking at a type of Italian beauty already familiar to the viewer of past Italian [female] stars'—stars like Sophia Loren and Gina Lollobrigida. Thus the women in the films tend to be 'markedly southern or Mediterranean in type, very much integral to the sensual beauty of the island setting' (Small 2005: 165). As Craven writes of heritage cinema in a different context: there is an 'alignment of female roles and visual spectacle'; women are 'incorporated as period features in much the same way as the set and costumes' (Craven 2011: 39, 32). Feminine beauty of a particular type is an aspect of the spectacle of the past, and by the same token this implies that the past is itself connoted by its to-be-looked-at-ness, to borrow Laura Mulvey's famous coinage. The Italian heritage film, then, offers a version of Brand Italy that acknowledges its character of display. Inasmuch as the display is earned or paid for with political commentary (on the part of the filmmakers) or background knowledge (on the part of a critic or ideal spectator) the films also fit an idea of Italy, dating at least to the international reception of Machiavelli, as at once beautiful and intensely sensual, but essentially corrupt. In *Cinema Paradiso*, *Mediterraneo* and *Il postino*, history itself becomes the element of corruption: the disappointment that coexists with the sensual experience of the beauty of the landscape and the women superimposed upon it.

Though set mostly in and around Rome, the more recent *La grande bellezza* (Paolo Sorrentino, 2013) can be seen as an elaboration of these earlier heritage films. Pauline Small talks about how the rural idyll films she discusses 'develop, with differing degrees of emphasis, narratives of courtship', and she goes on: 'The fact that the films all chart a courtship that is resolved in failure contributes directly to the sense of loss that marks closure in the individual films' (2005: 154). And so, like the protagonist of *Cinema Paradiso* in the third segment of that film, the (Neapolitan) protagonist of *La grande bellezza* lives (in a sense 'exiled') in Rome, but remembers his lost first love, pictured in a kitsch closing scene, located once again on an island.[4]

La grande bellezza very obviously proposes itself as a heritage film, with sumptuous tracking shots along the streets of Rome's old centre and 'privileged' access to the historical edifices and gardens of the city granted to us. However, the packaging is not limited to the antique or early modern, but takes in iconic elements of twentieth-century Italy. Such elements can be discussed in terms of a recognisable brand known as 'Made in Italy'; certainly, a 2013 issue of the Italian journal *Allegoria* includes *La grande bellezza* in a special section devoted to a discussion of this brand. Intriguingly, Daniele Balicco, editor of the special section, suggests that 'Made in Italy' needs to be treated as a kind of 'Italianism', by analogy with 'Orientalism' in the sense the term is used by Edward Said (1978) to refer to the manner in which the Middle and Far East have been constructed in the occidental imagination (2013a). If Orientalism necessarily implies a power relation detrimental to those pictured in the Western imagination of the East, the writers in *Allegoria* are upbeat about the implications for Italy itself of 'Made in Italy'. The brand, for Balicco, is a mark of non-standardised quality: products 'made in Italy' express a peculiarly Italian enjoyment of modernity; more precisely, they offer a vision of modernity as the immersion in and enjoyment of the present.

La grande bellezza delights in the foregrounding of this sensibility. Commodities themselves become heritage in the film. The exhilarating rooftop party sequence that opens it is punctuated with images of a billboard promoting the drink Martini, (apparently) brazen product placement that is advertising not so much the product as the sensibility that enjoys it. In fact, Martini was not one of the film's 'partners'—*La grande bellezza* had a variety of sponsors, all represented more or less prominently, but Rome itself is the product most conspicuously 'placed'. One of the paradoxes of the film is that the immersion in the present in a city like Rome is inevitably an immersion in the heritage past.

Once again, to discuss *La grande bellezza* as heritage cinema is to start from the negative. Though quintessentially a cinephile text, replete with allusions to Fellini's *La dolce vita* (1960) and Italian Golden Age cinema more broadly (part of the heritage on display), disdain for the film was loudest from the ancestral home of cinephilia, French journal *Cahiers du Cinéma*. For the *Cahiers* critics, there is 'nothing uglier than a film by Sorrentino' (Malausa 2013) and the director was accused of complicity with the spectator in the 'hypocritical condescension' of the film's representation of wealth (Chauvin and Malausa 2013). A counter-chorus of criticism put the emphasis, instead, on the political commentary that the film supposedly offers, finding a critique in it of the shallowness of Italian society in the Berlusconi era. The latter strain of criticism is, of course, of a piece with Galt's defence of the rural idyll films in terms of their lament for the disappointed promise of post-war Italy. Again, it is not that such criticism is misguided—it is rather that the insistence on the political seems to be the price to pay for the pleasures of the film.

Rather than throw in one's lot with either of the critical camps, it seems more fruitful to think of *La grande bellezza* as an ambivalent text. As Balicco writes:

> Sorrentino's film disturbs our political unconscious because while it confirms the most banal (and therefore paradoxically reassuring) reading of Italy's decline, it contradicts this reading in the form it adopts, playing explicitly with the contrary but just as powerful symbolic image of Italy as an enchanted wonderland. (2013b: 207)

Balicco's observation might usefully be generalised to heritage cinema as a whole: a defining characteristic of the form may well be its ambivalence. No heritage film is without its commentary (more or less controversial) on politics and the past, but the packaging of history as heritage implies its presentation for a tourist gaze. Packaging a national past for its to-be-looked-at-ness implies the employment of familiar conceptual schemas that make it receivable—hence Balicco's glossing of the 'Made in Italy' brand as an 'Italianism' by analogy with 'Orientalism'. We should expect to find similar branding when a heritage film is 'Made in China', 'Made in India', and so on.

Last and Later Emperors

Orientalism was one of the terms regularly employed in criticism of *The Last Emperor* (1987), Bernardo Bertolucci's multi-Oscar-winning epic that luxuriates in a Chinese heritage of architecture, costume and historical irony. *The Last Emperor* tells the story of Pu Yi (1906–67), a man who was briefly the emperor of China and grew up as prime denizen of the impressive fifteenth-century Forbidden City in Beijing; later Pu Yi became the figurehead of Japan's puppet state of Manchukuo, only to spend a third of his life under Mao Zedong. The film tells this story as a series of cross-cut episodes showing, on the one hand, Pu Yi's childhood, youth and decadence and, on the other hand, his imprisonment and 'rehabilitation' under Mao. If it was accused of Orientalism in its representation of imperial China as a place of ritual, opium and sensual delight, *The Last Emperor* was also held to be guilty, like the Italian rural idyll films discussed above, of a dubious representation of women. For Yosefa Loshitzky, the film performs a 'symbolic annihilation' of the female: 'women appear in the movie only in association with China's past. Whenever the film deals with the Maoist order, the domain of the real, women are absent' (1992: 38). Again, the more distant past in *The Last Emperor* is gendered and connoted by its to-be-looked-at-ness, characterised by rich hues of red and yellow, whereas the later, 'Maoist' sequences seem drained of colour in their blue-grey chromatic scheme: gendered male and explicitly concerned with ideology rather than sensual appeal. But once again, other, more sympathetic, critics have defended *The Last Emperor* from the accusations of cliché or exploitation by insisting on the complexity of its historical representation. Robert Burgoyne's ingenious account of the film starts from the negative by acknowledging that '*The Last Emperor* appears to be a film in which history has assumed an overtly static and emotional dimension', while its spectator seems to be encouraged 'to become a voyeur of the exotic Orient of the past' (Burgoyne 1989: 93). In reality, Burgoyne argues, the film articulates a 'highly structured argument concerning the historical process', and for him it foregrounds the importance of the image of ruler or 'model citizen' (which Pu Yi was to become under Mao) in the mass-media culture of the late twentieth century.

As with Rosalind Galt's analysis of Italian heritage films, Burgoyne's argument is subtle and persuasive but perhaps overeager to discount the franker pleasures of the film's appealing surface. David Thomson (2009) points to these when he speaks of *The Last Emperor* as 'magnificent, pioneering "tourist" cinema'. He goes on: 'The use of this term *tourist* is not meant to

TOWARDS WORLD HERITAGE CINEMA (STARTING FROM THE NEGATIVE) 71

The Last Emperor

Hero

The Curse of the Golden Flower

Big Shot's Funeral

minimise the film but rather to stress its vital historical role to bring us sights never seen.' As is well known, the filmmakers secured the necessary collaboration of the Chinese authorities and were granted unique access to the Forbidden City for the sequences of Pu Yi as a child and youth. A key role in the film was even played by the then Chinese vice-minister of culture, Ying Ruocheng (Baschiera 2014: 404). The Chinese state was therefore perfectly complicit in the packaging of Chinese history for foreign consumption: we must assume that the putative Orientalism of Bertolucci's film was a price worth paying for the export of the 'Made in China' brand, in which Chinese heritage and China itself are the products on sale or display.

The Last Emperor 'did not meet the same success in China as it did in the Western world', and Chinese critics tended to lament its factual inaccuracies (Baschiera 2014: 409), but it seems to have been successful enough in its 'will to spectacle' (Loshitzky 1992: 28) to have impacted on what I am going to describe as Chinese heritage cinema. In particular, its formal choices in the representation of the Forbidden City seem to have influenced the historical filmmaking of China's 'Fifth Generation' directors. One sees it in *The Emperor and the Assassin* (Chen Kaige, 1998) and in *Hero* (Zhang Yimou, 2002), both of which portray, even if in quite different registers, China's 'first' emperor, Qin Shihuang;[5] and it is present in later films by Zhang Yimou, such as *House of Flying Daggers* (2004) and *Curse of the Golden Flower* (2006).[6]

I will focus here especially on *Hero* because the film has generated an extraordinary amount of critical discussion such that it bears out the assertion in the introduction to the present volume that heritage films 'invariably provoke heated debate, highlighting their strong potential for inciting conflicting opinions about the past and its ownership'. As the editors of a volume devoted to *Hero* point out, 'the very appropriation and interpretation of the movie, like its subject, represents a contested narrative of history, power and national interests' (Rawnsley and Rawnsley 2010: 24).

An exquisitely made and CGI-heavy martial arts epic, *Hero* (like *The Emperor and the Assassin*) deals with the plots against the life of the man seen as the founding father of China, who unified and pacified the warring states in the third century BCE, thus establishing the beginnings of the Chinese empire (and building a first Great Wall). In Chinese culture the 'First Emperor of Qin' is a figure both admired and vilified: the standardisation of the writing, measurement and monetary systems that cemented unity was accompanied by the brutal suppression of difference and intellectual dissent. The heritage of the First Emperor is therefore a controversial and contested one, and *Hero* itself comes to be a contested text because, unlike *The Emperor and the Assassin*, which portrays him as a tragic and grotesque figure, it stages the argument about the Emperor's ambitions in ultimately sympathetic terms.

For some critics the totalitarian impulses of the emperor are celebrated in the style of the film (see Larson 2008), which seems to conform to Susan Sontag's analysis of fascist aesthetics:

> The relations of domination and enslavement take the form of a characteristic pageantry: the massing of groups of people; the turning of people into things; the multiplication or replication of things; and the grouping of people/things around an all-powerful, hypnotic leader-figure or force. The fascist dramaturgy centres on the orgiastic transactions between mighty forces and their puppets, uniformly garbed and shown in ever swelling numbers. Its choreography alternates between ceaseless motion and a congealed, static, 'virile' posing. Fascist art glorifies surrender, it exalts mindlessness, it glamorizes death. (Sontag 1975)

Sontag's words have been read as an avant-la-lettre account of the CGI-generated armies serving the Emperor in *Hero*, recalling the massed geometric gatherings arrayed before Hitler (and choreographed for the camera) in the Nazi propaganda film *Triumph of the Will* (Leni Riefenstahl, 1935). *Hero* has been characterised, as a result, as a nationalistic 'apology for the dictatorship of the Chinese Communist Party' and its imperialist policies (Larson 2008: 183).

To treat *Hero* as a heritage film allows us to understand this controversy as a more extreme version of the ideological critique of heritage cinema first made in the British context. *Hero* stands accused of expressing in the popular arena the ideology of the ruling regime, of proffering a coercive vision of Chinese-ness attached to imperial values in which the past has become pure spectacle. Critical suspicion of the film was encouraged by the fact that director Zhang Yimou had long been felt to 'reinforce the static images and warm stereotypes of Orientalism' (Lu 1997: 129). Indeed, though the term was not used, Zhang had already stood accused of creating heritage cinema for foreign consumption:

> The end result of Zhang's film art may seem to be his ability to tell the Western audience enchanting, exotic stories about the other country 'China' through stunning visual images. He has offered the western viewer a 'museum' of precious Chinese objects, costumes, and artefacts. [...] All these spectacles have been masterfully manufactured for the pleasure and gaze of the Western viewer. (Lu 1997: 126)

Inevitably, the film has also found its defenders, both in terms of its ideology and its spectacle (Larson 2008; Burgoyne 2014). But, I repeat, the challenge is not to choose between competing interpretations; it is rather to account for what generates such variant interpretations, understanding that heritage itself is never uncontested. The packaging of such heritage for consumption abroad will always be a controversial undertaking, seeming to offer a sanitised version of a painful history for a kind of tourist acquisition via the gaze. And yet, it is through the provision of a unique heritage that a film culture can declare its distinctiveness. From this perspective it is useful to note that, like the Italian rural idyll films discussed above, *Hero* became a Miramax movie, successfully distributed by the American company (by then a subsidiary of Disney) in North America, the UK and Australia two years after its Chinese release.

The heritage aspect of *Hero* was part of a project to create a specifically 'Chinese blockbuster' and to respond to the decreasing market share achieved by Chinese films at home at the turn of the century (Lau 2007).[7] The key point of reference was *Crouching Tiger, Hidden Dragon* (Ang Lee, 2000), which had been an unexpected success in the West and showed that a 'culturally Chinese' blockbuster was possible within the 'Wuxia' or martial arts genre. *Crouching Tiger* had not, however, been equally successful in Hong Kong or mainland China, and Zhang's films *Hero* and, later, *House of Flying Daggers* were an attempt to appeal simultaneously to the variety of home and foreign markets. On the one hand, *Hero* deals with ideology as heritage: it celebrates the concept of 'tian xia', literally 'all under the sun' but translated in the English subtitles as 'our land', meaning a unified China (with all its sinister implications for populations in, say, Tibet and Xinjiang). On the other hand, the film presents martial arts as one of the traditional high Chinese arts alongside music, calligraphy, Chinese chess and painting, all featured in the film. In that sense, Wuxia cinema itself becomes 'heritage' (Chan 2011), a process made clear in *Hero* and *House of Flying Daggers*, which (as in *Crouching Tiger* before them) contain specific elaborations of classic scenes from the Wuxia tradition, for example the combat in the bamboo trees in *A Touch of Zen* (Kung Hu, 1971). Viewed using the heuristic of heritage cinema, such allusions are not just the usual elaboration of genre tropes, where variation (and potential improvement) on the familiar is expected and part of the pleasure provided by the films; here the recourse is to films and motifs now perceived as cultural artefacts rather than merely as entertainment or commodities.

Hero can therefore be seen to confirm Sheldon Hsiao-peng Lu's suggestion (made almost two decades ago) that 'the greatest irony of contemporary Chinese cinema seems to be that some films achieve a transnational status precisely because they are seen as possessing an authentically "National", "Chinese", "Oriental" flavour by western audiences' (Lu 1997: 12). Of course, what seems authentic in such films is informed by the representation of China in films like *The Last Emperor*, which does not only show China's past, but shows China *as past*. *Hero* marries this 'denial of coevalness' to the most ostentatiously contemporary technical means, generating a kind of paradox of old/new, past-in-the-present, that may be held to be another defining characteristic of the heritage film.[8] And, as the author of one Chinese newspaper article remarked: '*Hero* is a symbolic film, and every frame in the movie conveys the same symbol: Made in China' (quoted in Wang 2009: 301).

World Heritage Cinema

Hero was an enormous success in China. The effective promotion of the film made it, like *Titanic*, one of its blockbuster models, an event movie that had to be seen (Wang 2009). However, if its ideological ambiguity made it uncomfortable for some, its sanitised aesthetics and solemn register also drew ironic comment. Sabrina Qiong Yu has described how the film confirmed, in mainland China, 'an emerging camp sensibility among Internet users who comprise the majority of *Hero*'s audiences' (2010: 145). She cites reports of laughter at screenings of *Hero* generated especially by the stiff or anachronistic dialogue, and quotes remarks by amateur web reviewers: 'I cannot help but suspect that *Hero* is a Model Play of the Great Cultural Revolution'; '*Hero* offers great materials for parody [...] a Chinese version of *Scary Movie* based on *Hero* would be a hit' (Yu 2010: 139, 142).

This ironic (non-)fan take on *Hero* and the epic-heritage mode had been anticipated in the 2001 'postmodern urban farce' *Big Shot's Funeral* (see Zhang 2004: 292). Directed by Feng Xiaogang, then known for Chinese New Year and social realist comedies, *Big Shot's Funeral* concerns a remake of Bertolucci's *The Last Emperor* that goes awry when its American director falls into a coma. The local cameraman he has befriended organises (prematurely) the director's funeral in the Forbidden City, attracting commercial sponsorship for every moment of the ceremony and even every inch of the would-be corpse—and thus also for the film *Big Shot's Funeral* itself, of course. The film mocks the formal vistas presented in *The Last Emperor* and bequeathed (as we have seen) to Chinese cinema in its heritage mode.[9] Arguably, *The Last Emperor* had adduced the aesthetics and artefacts of Chinese culture as chattel for a Western cinema-going public. As such, it might have been seen not only to 'colonise' the spaces of the Forbidden City and render as entertainment the painful processes of Chinese history, but also and inevitably to misrepresent the experience and aspirations of a China in the throes of accelerated urbanisation and change. Speaking on behalf of those enjoying and suffering such a vivid 'present', *Big Shot's Funeral* is social comedy ridiculing the pompous tenor of what I propose we call 'world heritage cinema'.

To start (as I have suggested we must) from the negative, let us assert that, in the reduction to spectacle it performs, and even as it celebrates uniqueness and authenticity, world heritage cinema effects an erasure of difference: it implies a transfer of ownership of a cultural heritage from a community, region or nation to a generic humanity. In the case of *The Last Emperor*, a world heritage film influences local filmmakers like Zhang Yimou, who make of their own Chinese heritage something equally exportable. In all cases, the past is that much more vivid than our own time—cleaner, brighter, more symmetrical even—enabling a voluptuous tourist gaze on the physical and temporal foreign country of the past.

The phrase 'world heritage cinema' does not seem previously to have been employed as I wish to use it here.[10] We can think of world heritage cinema in relation to certain of the activities of UNESCO just as we can consider British heritage cinema in relation to the work and ethos of English Heritage and Historic England. UNESCO recognises that 'certain places on Earth are of "outstanding universal value" and should form part of the common heritage of humankind': 'Today, 190 countries adhere to the World Heritage Convention [1972] [...] and have become part of an international community united in a common mission to identify and safeguard our world's most significant natural and cultural heritage.'[11]

The Forbidden City seen in *The Last Emperor*; the Great Wall pictured at the end of *Hero*; the Amalfi coast of which Capri, the island location of *Il postino*, is a part; the historic centre of Rome enjoyed in *La grande bellezza*: all feature on UNESCO's World Heritage List.[12] Also on the World Heritage List are several of the sites used in the Indian film I now turn to, *Jodhaa Akbar* (Ashutosh Gowariker, 2008), a Hindi epic set in the sixteenth century about a marriage of alliance that blossoms into love between Akbar, a historical Moghul (and therefore Muslim) ruler, and Jodhaa, a mythical Rajput (and therefore Hindu) princess.[13] As far as I can ascertain, heritage cinema is not a term that has been used in discussions of Indian cinema—and certainly not in relation to Bollywood—but the concept of heritage is alive and well in India itself, and prominent signs at sites of importance like the Red Fort in Agra or Akbar's palace complex in Fatehpur Sikri, both featured in *Jodhaa Akbar*, proclaim the pride felt in India's architectural legacy. *Jodhaa Akbar* restages in CGI and sets the impressiveness of Moghul building, revivifying the heritage spaces with billowing drapes and lush costumes (of which more below). As Philip Lutgendorf (no date) writes of the film:

> Anyone who has visited Akbar-period sites such as Agra's Red Fort or the ghost capital of Fatehpur Sikri will surely relish [*Jodhaa Akbar*'s] astonishing re-imaginings of what these complexes may have looked like when fully outfitted and inhabited. The dramatic hilltop palace of Amer [...] and its adjacent ravine appears starkly outlined and reforested, minus the curio shops, buses, touts, and general urban sprawl familiar to today's Jaipur tourists—a wondrous feat of digital demolition. (Lutgendorf, no date)

If the term heritage cinema has not yet been used of Bollywood, Shahnaz Khan (2011) gets very close in her critical discussion of *Jodhaa Akbar* as a film that reflects and aids the rise of Hindu nationalism in India. She draws on Andrew Higson (1993), heritage cinema's most influential theorist, to describe how the film 'situates its believability' as history not in its narrative but in its mise-en-scène and iconography: 'Each scene is presented as a tableau of opulent detail with interplay of rich colour—almost as if the actors had stepped out of miniature painting of the period. [...] Jodhaa's clothes and jewellery also appear inspired by miniatures of Moghul women' (Khan 2011: 141). For Khan, the fetishising of setting and costume serves to ratify the film's ideological project of making the Muslim empire of Akbar a preamble to the global ambitions of India in the present, and moreover of making the Muslim ruler Akbar a kind of precursor to the Hindu nationalists of today. Not only does the film's Akbar facilitate his Hindu wife's veneration of Vishnu, 'the narrative [also] domesticates him through heterosexual marital life, in the process neutralizing the excessive sexuality and violent danger the Muslim masculine normally poses in current Hindi films' (Khan 2011: 136). At the same time, Khan emphasises how Jodhaa's 'agency' in the film is illusory: 'in their cinematic form, nationalist narratives represent women's bodies, including their apparel, in ways that render them spectacles to behold and enjoy. [...] Jodhaa's "authentic" period costumes and dazzling jewellery eroticize her body even as she articulates a more transgressive insistence that she be her own woman at Akbar's court' (Khan 2011: 138).

As will be obvious by now, Khan's critique repeats several of the tropes characteristic of heritage cinema criticism. For Khan, *Jodhaa Akbar* asserts a presentist ownership of a past that is in many respects radically other; the film serves a dubious ideological agenda; and it eroticises the female body as part of the spectacle of an airbrushed (or CGI) past.[14] Certainly, the film operates in the service of a mythologised Indian identity. After all, the Moghul sites that the film delights in might well be construed as part of a specifically *Muslim* heritage. And while the mythologised romance of Akbar's marriage of alliance might be a means of offering an admirable model for Muslim-Hindu cooperation and pan-Indian identity, it reduces to a crude binary the actual ethnic and religious diversity of India and its diaspora.

In fact, Akbar already represents this kind of simplified model of cooperation in popular Indian myth. In tales for children—which have also been adapted for television—Akbar is associated in old age with his wise Hindu counsellor Birbal, a kind of homosocial marriage of minds.[15] In *Jodhaa Akbar*, Akbar is returned to his prime, given the attractive form of Hrithik Roshan, and rendered sexy as well as practical, spiritual and wise. The mythical Jodhaa is given the equally attractive form of Aishwarya Rai and a famous scene from the film shows her gazing at Akbar engaged in fencing training. The swordplay scene, characterised by throbbing crash zooms, brazen slow motion and shameless close-ups of Roshan's sculpted torso, is directly followed by another of Jodhaa in her indoor quarters. The male (Akbar) occupies in solitary action an unadorned exterior space, while the woman (Jodhaa) is first framed in the liminal space of a doorway (the editing's work of suture persuades us that the two spaces are continuous) and then shown languorous in erotic reverie in a decorated interior, accompanied by her attendants (all female apart from a eunuch). All very stereotypically gendered, no doubt; but it is notable how the eroticisation of the male body gazed upon by the woman is transferred in the next scene to female costume. The latter scene features a cut-in to a close-up on the ornate Kundan necklace sent by Akbar as a mark of his regard for his wife. This is the kind of moment in the film which, for Lutgendorf (no date), makes of *Jodhaa Akbar* 'a "consumerist" film that continues the pattern of display of conspicuous goodies established by middle-class blockbusters like *Hum Aapke Hain Koun...!* and *Dil Chahta Hai*, though here with an "ethno-historic" sensibility'. Or, as Khan less sanguinely puts it: 'Jodhaa with her stunning clothes and priceless jewels stands for a strong Hindu female presence. Upon closer inspection however, she is largely spectacle and has little agency. [...] she serves liberalism and consumerism in contemporary India' (2011: 144).

The deploring (at least in Khan) of *Jodhaa Akbar*'s 'consumerist' dimension is a version of the old 'presentist ownership' argument about heritage cinema. There is no doubting that, in the case of *Jodhaa Akbar*, the annexing of the past (the assertion of 'ownership') for contemporary purposes is supplemented by a process whereby that past is made available for purchase. In fact, the film and its publicity generated a fashion in period costume for weddings in the Hindu tradition, and designs based on Aishwarya Rai's costumes can still be bought online. Moreover, the topoi of suspicion of a feminised consumerism that we find in Khan (and consumerism has always been stigmatised as a 'feminine' dimension of modernity) can also be seen as a version of the familiar criticism of 'costume drama' as insufficiently 'historical' in its preference for spectacle over attestable fact. A less moralistic and tendentious account would suggest that *Jodhaa Akbar* catalyses a deployment of artefactual heritage that is a perfectly valid way of establishing a relationship with the past—not by reading or studying history, but by *wearing* it. Historical engagement of this sort suffers from the unexamined prejudice that discursive modes of engagement with history are superior to other forms. 'Wearing history' at a wedding conserves and employs the past to give particular form to the public declaration of gendered partnership in a social ritual. In this case, it enables the orientation of the marriage itself to the India nation inasmuch as *Jodhaa Akbar* offers a unifying vision (a myth) of India that transcends religious conflict. Indeed, this is true even for the diaspora community: over a quarter of the film's takings came from outside India and the trend for *Jodhaa Akbar* wedding jewellery remains international.[16]

The success abroad of *Jodhaa Akbar* raises a not insignificant question of terminology. If, as I am assuming, the film was watched outside India predominantly by audiences with roots in the subcontinent, then one can discuss its appeal in terms of the 'Non-resident Indian' (NRI) genre, a type of film designed to address Indian audiences in Britain and North America.[17] Ian Garwood's comments on the musical sequence in the NRI film can be generalised to the packaging of history as such in *Jodhaa Akbar*:

> The NRI romance relies on the display of 'traditional' Indian music culture to court a diasporic audience as *citizens*. But, in keeping with its project to appeal to its audience also as particular kinds of *consumers*, it subjects these traditions to a process of repackaging and reformatting. The musical number is expected to stir deep patriotic feeling in its ideal spectator, at the same time as it is pushed forward aggressively as a particular kind of commodity, as if in a shop-window display. (Garwood 2006: 356; italics in original)

The contents in *Jodhaa Akbar* of this shop-window display make up a transnational Indian heritage, and 'transnational heritage film' might seem an appropriate label not just for *Jodhaa Akbar* but for *all* of the films discussed above. Still, what the term '*world* heritage cinema' usefully connotes is an idea of the shared patrimony of human endeavour, as expressed in the philosophy and remit of the UNESCO World Heritage List. This is an ideological idea (rejected for equally ideological reasons by, for example, the Taliban and the so-called Islamic State, organisations which have deliberately destroyed World Heritage sites). As I suggest above, even as it celebrates uniqueness, the idea of world heritage posits a generic humanity, thereby erasing difference along with the history of power, oppression and struggle. Walter Benjamin's famous axiom expresses the disavowed in the UNESCO *Weltanschauung*: 'There is no document of civilization which is not also a record of barbarism' (Benjamin 1968: 256). This bleak adage is the negative from which we necessarily start in discussing world heritage cinema. In films like *Jodhaa Akbar*, conflict in the national past is aestheticised for the purposes of contemporary national pride and commoditised for international presence: 'what we are observing now, at least at the level of the high-profile, export-orientated Bombay film is the displacement of *nation as art form* by *nation as Brand*' (Vasudevan 2011: 339; italics in original).

Conclusion: Unnecessary Pasts

The organisation of the foregoing account, moving from Europe to Asia and on to the 'world', might expose me to accusations of 'unthinking Eurocentrism' (Shohat and Stam 2014). I should be clear: I am not proposing that 'European heritage film' (after all, a critical concept rather than a cinema genre) has generated some sort of global paradigm. Even the specific influence of *The Last Emperor* that I perceive on Chinese Fifth Generation filmmakers is less evidence of a migrating mode than it is an indication of how Chinese filmmakers chose to employ postcard tropes to ensure mass appeal at home and abroad. Mine is instead a *conscious* Eurocentrism. I have borrowed a term, heritage cinema, coined by critics in the British context, and used it, as the editors of this volume recommend, as a heuristic to reveal common features of a diverse group of films.

If the past is a foreign country (and if the foreign country is constructed *as past*), then heritage cinema allows a tourist visit that facilitates investments of identification and desire, and the grasping of history as a form of pleasure. Critics or constituencies with political or cultural capital to spare may scorn as 'escapist' this form of engagement with the past, but this is only to imply that the notion of escapism itself needs to be 'enlarged to a level of complexity that redeems it from the familiar charge of vacuity, frivolity and evasion of conflict' (Landy 2002: 250). Tourism, too, of course, is typically seen as a superficial form of interaction with a place or culture, but John Urry (2002) has shown the complexity and historical character of the same 'tourist gaze' I have been invoking throughout this chapter. Tourism, for Urry, is a form of 'unnecessary pleasure' (2002: 1); heritage cinema, in turn, might be understood to offer 'unnecessary pasts', pasts meant for entertainment rather than edification. But as Ginette Vincendeau has argued, 'cinematic efforts to reconstruct the past are a playful and productive experience and provide a space in which social and cultural identities can be explored' (cited in Small 2005: 172). Not in circumstances of their own choosing, perhaps, but men and women can and do use cinema to make their own heritage.[18]

Notes

1. Information about English Heritage's Cold War bunker in York can be found at: http://www.english-heritage.org.uk/daysout/properties/york-cold-war-bunker/
2. Information available at: https://historicengland.org.uk/research/inclusive-heritage/
3. Voigts-Virchow is quoting Dallen and Boyd (2003: 4).
4. The film ambiguously suggests that it may be the same island where the ferry Costa Concordia ran aground in 2012, apparently due to its captain's arrogance and incompetence, with the loss of 32 lives. Again we find the coexistence (or equation) of beauty and corruption.
5. *The Emperor and the Assassin* features a theatrical performance style and centred, frontally framed actors regularly declaiming to camera. It turns the story of the first emperor into a Macbethian drama that shows the emperor's estrangement from his wife and the cost to the man of his conquest of power. This, and the artificiality of the performance styles, tends to recall Kurosawa's version of *the Macbeth story* in *Throne of Blood* (1957). However, the film also proclaims its heritage credentials with much made of the authenticity of setting and costume in paratextual materials like the insert in the Sony Pictures Home Entertainment DVD release (2002).
6. The visual influence of *The Last Emperor* seems very clear in a recent Chinese television drama *The Legendary Last Emperor* (末代皇帝传奇), produced by Zhejiang Great Wall Television and broadcast in 59 episodes from October 2013. The story of Pu Yi had already been told in a television series of 1988, a production favourably compared by Chinese critics to Bertolucci's in terms of its fidelity to historical fact (Baschiera 2014: 409).
7. Stringer and Yu have pointed out that many of *Hero*'s creative personnel—line producer, cinematographer (the famous Christopher Doyle), costume

designer and several of those who created the film's spectacular visual effects among them—have all worked elsewhere, and often for Hollywood. Their conclusion is that 'far from being a "Chinese film", *Hero* truly is an international product' (Stringer and Yu 2007: 248).
8. 'Denial of coevalness' is anthropologist Johannes Fabian's phrase (1983) for how the study of another culture tends to imply that that culture exists in another time as well as another space: as 'primitive', perhaps, but certainly as 'unchanging', 'static', and so offering itself up to be examined and represented—or branded.
9. Ironically, the Chinese box-office records set by *Big Shot's Funeral* were overtaken by *Hero* (Zhang 2004: 292).
10. Typically, it refers to the conservation of films of international or historical importance.
11. See: http://en.unesco.org/themes/world-heritage
12. See the World Heritage List: http://whc.unesco.org/en/list/
13. Akbar certainly had a Hindu consort among his many wives, but the name Jodhaa was given to such a figure only in retrospect.
14. The temptation, as ever, is to offer or contrast a corrective, more positive interpretation of the film. For example, Philip Lutgendorf (no date) argues that director Gowariker seeks, with *Jodhaa Akbar* and his other films, 'to heal the deep wounds inflicted by religious nationalism and its most fateful consequence—Partition'.
15. The historical Akbar himself was seen to reach beyond religious bigotry with his invention of a 'syncretic' religion merging aspects of Islam, Hinduism, Christianity and others, and he was reputed to have had an otherworldly character in his sympathy for Sufism (illustrated in *Jodhaa Akbar* when he is transported by Sufi wedding music).
16. For Jodhaa Akbar's box-office takings see: http://www.boxofficemojo.com/movies/?id=jodhaaakbar.htm. For examples of a 'Jodha Akbar' jewellery range sold in Britain, see: http://www.indianjewellerystore.co.uk/Jodha-Akbar-Jewellery(1678482).htm. A television serial, *Jodha Akbar* [sic], produced by Balaji Films and inspired by the film, ran on Zee TV for 566 episodes from June 2013 and ratchets up the bling factor even further.
17. These are the two markets where *Jodhaa Akbar* earned most outside India.
18. Thanks to Alessio Baldini, Paul Cooke, Jayeeta Ghorai, Shoba Ghosh and Vidya Vencatesan for their help in the drafting of this article.

Works Cited

Balicco, D. 2013a. Guida alla lettura. *Allegoria* 68: 7–12.
———. 2013b. Paolo Sorrentino, *La grande bellezza*. *Allegoria* 68: 205–212.

Baschiera, S. 2014. From Beijing with love: The global dimension of Bertolucci's *The Last Emperor*. *Journal of Italian Cinema and Media Studies* 2(3): 399–415.
Benjamin, W. 1968. *Illuminations*. New York: Harcourt, Brace & World.
Burgoyne, R. 1989. *The Last Emperor*: The stages of history. *SubStance* 18:2(59): 93–101.
———. 2014. Colour in the epic film: *Alexander* and *Hero*. In *The return of the epic film*, ed. A. Elliot, 95–109. Edinburgh: Edinburgh University Press.
Chan, K. 2011. The contemporary *Wuxia* revival: Genre remaking and the Hollywood transnational factor. In *The Chinese cinema book*, eds. S.H. Lim and J. Ward, 150–157. London: BFI.
Chauvin, J.-S., and V. Malausa. 2013. Aristos. *Cahiers di Cinéma* 690: 27.
Craven, A. 2011. Period features, heritage cinema: Region, gender and race in *The Irishman*. *Studies in Australasian Cinema* 5(1): 31–42.
Dallen, J.T., and S.W. Boyd. 2003. *Heritage tourism*. Harlow: Pearson.
Fabian, J. 1983. *Time and the other: How anthropology makes its object*. New York: Columbia University Press.
Galt, R. 2002. Italy's landscapes of loss: Historical mourning and the dialectical image in *Cinema Paradiso*, *Mediterraneo* and *Il postino*. *Screen* 43(2): 158–173.
Garwood, I. 2006. Shifting pitch: The Bollywood song sequence in the Anglo-American market. In *Asian cinemas: A reader and guide*, eds. D. Eleftheriotis and G. Needham, 346–357. Edinburgh: Edinburgh University Press.
Higson, A. 1993. Re-presenting the national past: Nostalgia and Pastiche in the heritage film. In *British cinema and Thatcherism: Fires were started*, ed. L. Friedman, 109–129. London: University College London Press.
Khan, S. 2011. Recovering the past in *Jodhaa Akbar*: Masculinities, femininities and cultural politics in Bombay cinema. *Feminist Review* 99: 131–146.
Landy, M. 2002. Theatricality and impersonation: The politics of style in the cinema of the Italian Fascist Era. In *Re-viewing fascism: Italian cinema, 1922–1943*, eds. J. Reich and P. Garofolo, 250–275. Bloomington: Indiana University Press.
Larson, W. 2008. Zhang Yimou's *Hero*: Dismantling the myth of cultural power. *Journal of Chinese Cinemas* 2(3): 181–196.
Lau, J.K.W. 2007. *Hero*: China's response to globalization. *Jump Cut*, 49 [Online]. Available at: http://www.ejumpcut.org/archive/jc49.2007/Lau-Hero/. Accessed 18 Oct 2015.
Loshitzky, Y. 1992. Ecstasy of difference: Bertolucci's *The Last Emperor*. *Cinema Journal* 31(2): 26–44.
Lu, S.H. 1997. *Transnational Chinese cinemas: Identity, nationhood, gender*. Honolulu: University of Hawaii Press.
Lutgendorf, P. 2015. *Jodhaa Akbar* [Online]. Available at: http://www.uiowa.edu/indiancinema/jodhaa-akbar. Accessed 18 Oct 2015.
Malausa, V. 2013. Un invité envahissant. *Cahiers du Cinéma* 689: 23.

Monk, C. 2002. The British heritage-film debate revisited. In *British historical cinema: The history, heritage and costume film*, eds. C. Monk and M. Sargeant, 176–198. London: Routledge.

———. 2011. *Heritage film audiences: Period films and contemporary audiences in the UK*. Edinburgh: Edinburgh University Press.

Northup, S. 1968 [1853]. In *Twelve years a slave*, eds. Sue Eakin and Joseph Logsdon. Baton Rouge: Louisiana State University Press.

Radstone, S. 1995. Cinema/memory/history. *Screen* 36(1): 34–47.

Rawnsley, G.D., and M.Y.T. Rawnsley. 2010. *Global Chinese cinema: The culture and politics of 'Hero'*. London: Routledge.

Said, E. 1978. *Orientalism*. New York: Routledge & Kegan Paul.

Shohat, E., and R. Stam. 2014. *Unthinking Eurocentrism: Multiculturalism and the Media*, 2nd edn. London: Routledge.

Small, P. 2005. Representing the female: Rural idylls, urban nightmares. In *Italian cinemas: New directions*, ed. W. Hope, 151–173. Oxford: Peter Lang.

Sontag, S. 1975. Fascinating fascism. *The New York Review of Books* [Online]. Available at: http://www.nybooks.com/articles/archives/1975/feb/06/fascinating-fascism/. Accessed 18 Oct 2015.

Stringer, J., and Q. Yu. 2007. *Hero*: How Chinese is it? In *World cinema's 'dialogues' with Hollywood*, ed. P. Cooke, 238–254. London: Palgrave Macmillan.

Thomson, D. 2009. *The Last Emperor*, or The Manchurian candidate [Online]. Available at: https://www.criterion.com/current/posts/556-the-last-emperor-or-the-manchurian-candidate. Accessed 18 Oct 2015.

Urry, J. 2002. *The tourist gaze*, 2nd edn. London: Sage Publications.

Vasudevan, R. 2011. *The melodramatic public: Film form and spectatorship in Indian cinema*. New York: Palgrave Macmillan.

Vidal, B. 2012. *Heritage film: Nation, genre and representation*. London: Wallflower Press.

Voigts-Virchow, E. 2007. Heritage and literature on screen: *Heimat* and heritage. In *The Cambridge companion to literature on screen*, eds. D. Cartmell and I. Whelehan, 123–137. Cambridge: Cambridge University Press.

Wang, T. 2009. Understanding local reception of globalized cultural products in the context of the international cultural economy: A case study on the reception of *Hero* and *Daggers* in China. *International Journal of Cultural studies* 12(4): 299–318.

Yu, S.Q. 2010. Camp pleasure in an era of Chinese Blockbusters: Internet reception of *Hero* in mainland China. In *Global Chinese cinema: The culture and politics of 'Hero'*, eds. G.D. Rawnsley and M.-Y.T. Rawnsley, 135–151. London: Routledge.

Zhang, Y. 2004. *Chinese national cinema*. London: Routledge.

CHAPTER 5

Rewriting History from the Margins: Diasporic Memory, Shabby Chic and Archival Footage

Daniela Berghahn

Since the beginning of the heritage cinema debate in the 1980s, the concept has proven enormously popular and, in the British context, virtually all period films made subsequently have been subsumed under this proliferating critical framework (Monk and Sargeant 2002: 11). That heritage cinema has emerged as such an attractive label is all the more surprising given that it has come under attack for promoting a class-biased, conservative and consensual notion of Englishness. The excessive pictorialism, museum aesthetics, and privileging of mise-en-scène, elaborate costumes and retro fashion over narrative has even provoked some derogatory comments from critics who have dubbed heritage cinema 'the Laura Ashley school of filmmaking', the 'Merchant Ivory "Furniture Restoration" aesthetic' and the 'white flannel school' (cited in Vincendeau 2001: xviii–xix). Perhaps the lively scholarly debates that have surrounded heritage cinema ever since Andrew Higson coined the term spring from the fact that it offers a 'clear explanatory model [that] makes things look simple [...] because it confers a pleasing symmetry onto the seeming chaos of cultural

D. Berghahn (✉)
Royal Holloway, University of London, Egham, UK
e-mail: Daniela.Berghahn@rhul.ac.uk

© The Editor(s) (if applicable) and The Author(s) 2016
P. Cooke, R. Stone (eds.), *Screening European Heritage*,
Palgrave European Film and Media Studies,
DOI 10.1057/978-1-137-52280-1_5

forms' (Harper 2004: 140). The vibrant critical interest in heritage cinema coincides with the actual growth of this successful production trend. As Randall Halle notes, no other genre flourished as much during the 1990s, the decade when the European Union was founded, as the historical film. This simultaneity, he proposes, points towards a significant dialectical tension, 'because typically the historical genre has been deployed within the national ensemble precisely as a vehicle for the imagining of the *national community*' (Halle 2008: 90). It seems as if becoming part of a larger transnational community had stimulated a growing desire to be securely contained in the smaller community of the nation. The surge of heritage films since the 1990s thus reflects a certain nostalgia to be part of a specific national heritage.

To be sure, though, heritage and history are not synonymous. Heritage bestows value and kudos on the past in a way that history and memory do not. Heritage is concerned with the preservation and conservation of aspects of the past that represent those values and traditions most cherished by a particular (national) community. Heritage is inextricably bound up with 'a shared vision of the past that reinforces collective identity' (Oscherwitz 2010: 1). Yet the question of whose collective memory is valorised through its inclusion in a given 'national heritage' is a highly contested issue.

In the essay 'Whose heritage? Un-settling "The Heritage", re-imagining the post-nation', Stuart Hall defines British heritage (or 'The Heritage', as he puts it) as 'the material embodiment of the spirit of the nation, a collective representation of the British version of tradition' and a 'retrospective, nation-alised and tradition-alised conception of culture' (1999: 4). He contends that the 'selective canonisation' of the nation's 'high points and memorable achievements' (1999: 5) has a number of conspicuous blind spots and that these blind spots instantly reveal the hegemonic nature of heritage: 'It is always inflected by the power and authority of those who have colonised the past, whose versions of history matter' (1999: 6).

The emergence of 'heritage' not only as a much-debated concept but also as an industry of considerable economic value during the 1980s coincided with British and other European societies becoming increasingly multicultural. In fact, during the 1980s, diasporic filmmakers in Britain, France and Germany gained access to the means of production and self-representation—but not to heritage. Heritage continued to be imagined as ethnically homogeneous and white. The overwhelming whiteness of British and other European heritage films underscores the erasure of race from heritage. Even British Raj revival films, a popular strand of the heritage cycle including *Heat and Dust* (James Ivory, 1983) and *A Passage to India* (David Lean, 1984), by no means invalidate this argument since they are, ultimately, 'imperialist fantasies of the national past' (Higson 2006[1993]: 104). They rely on the exotic spectacle of foreign lands and fetishise the Otherness of colonial subjects, who are objects of the colonial gaze rather than the perceiving subjects whose point of view dominates the narrative. Despite 'chronicling the last days of imperial power' (Higson 2006[1993]: 104) and suggesting that imperialism is a system with no future, ultimately, these films promote neither fundamentally different hierarchies of power nor the inclusion of the subaltern in Britain's national heritage.

For Stuart Hall, any form of cultural representation, but especially national heritage, plays a powerful role in the construction of cultural identities. It is 'the material embodiment of the spirit of the nation' and of its tradition and it therefore 'follows that those who cannot see themselves reflected in its mirror cannot properly belong' (1999: 4). Given that Hall accords cinema a particularly prominent role in constituting cultural identities (2003[1990]: 245), the exclusion of diasporic subjectivities and memories from heritage cinema is highly symptomatic.

This essay seeks to probe the limits of heritage cinema in relation to films that engage with diasporic memory, a particular type of transnational memory that is inherently at odds with the overtly national project pursued by heritage cinema. Thus, one of my objectives is to examine how diasporic filmmakers pluralise national heritage by articulating counter memories that bring the lacunae of hegemonic history into focus. What strategies do they use to insert alternative accounts of the past that have hitherto been elided because, in the words of Pierre Nora, diasporic communities have no 'historical capital' (1989: 7). I shall consider three case studies that reflect the recent historical turn of diasporic European cinema. Whereas earlier phases of diasporic filmmaking had been firmly anchored in the sociopolitical realities of the present, since the early 2000s a growing number of films have engaged with historical subject matter. This shift in focus from the present to the past has gone hand in hand with a shift from social realist dramas to popular genres, reflecting diasporic filmmakers' attempts to move their films out of an ethnic niche into the mainstream.

Although the discursive construction of diasporic heritage in these films is in dialogue with the generic conventions of heritage cinema in the way the films self-consciously engage in acts of 'historical reconstruction and questions of authenticity' (Higbee 2013: 71), only a small number of films offer the kind of visual pleasure associated with heritage film. More importantly, these historical imaginaries pursue ideological trajectories diametrically opposite to hegemonic heritage cinema in as much as they challenge the Eurocentric grand narratives of colonial history and post-colonial immigration by rewriting history from the margins. The term 'counter-heritage film' (2013: 61), coined by Will Higbee, aptly describes the alternative or oppositional memorialisations of the past these films articulate. It underscores that these films are 'talking back' by appropriating certain conventions of hegemonic heritage cinema while, at the same time, seeking to subvert the genre's ideological agenda.

Drawing on recent examples from Maghrebi French cinema, Higbee distinguishes three trends, which, as I shall illustrate, are also manifest in other diasporic film cultures across Europe. First, there are films about major historical events, such as World War Two, the Algerian War of Independence or the Armenian Genocide, including the successful war film *Indigènes* (*Days of Glory*, 2006) and the controversial *Hors-la-loi* (*Outside the Law*, 2010), both directed by the Maghrebi French filmmaker Rachid Bouchareb, and *The Cut* (2014), by the Turkish German director Fatih Akın. These films dramatise painful and often traumatic memories from the vantage point of victims or colonial subjects, whose stories were hitherto untold. In a bid for mainstream and international audiences, these historical imaginaries are typically international co-productions with substantial budgets and high production values that stage history as spectacle on a grand scale and rely on the popular appeal of genre cinema. The second and most prominent trend is retro films about the ordinary lives of immigrants during the 1960s or 1970s. They include movies that narrate the immigrants' arrival in the European destination country, such as *Inch'Allah dimanche* (*Sunday God Willing*, Yamina Benguigui, 2001), *Solino* (Fatih Akın, 2002), *Almanya, Willkommen in Deutschland* (*Almanya—Welcome to Germany*, Yasemin Samdereli, 2011) and culture-clash comedies, such as the Asian-British box-office hit *East is East* (Damien O'Donnell, 1999). The narratives typically revolve around immigrant families and make the point that family life is a universal experience, notwithstanding cultural differences. Such retro films stage history from below, combining heritage cinema's penchant for period detail with the conciliatory stance of comedy in an attempt to cross over into the mainstream. The third strand marking the historical turn of diasporic cinema consists of a relatively small number of biopics whose temporal reach extends far beyond the post-war history of mass migration to Europe. They tend to portray notable figures ignored by (white) history, such as Saartjie Baartman, an African tribeswoman from the Eastern Cape of what is now South Africa, who was exhibited in freak shows in Paris and London under the pseudonym 'Venus Hottentot' and who was the object of scientific racism in the early nineteenth century (*Vénus noire* [*Black Venus*, Abdellatif Kechiche, 2010]); Solomon Northup, a free American man of African descent who was kidnapped and enslaved (*12 Years a Slave* [Steve McQueen, 2013]); and Dido Elizabeth Belle, the illegitimate mixed-race daughter of a Royal Navy Admiral and an African slave who was raised by her aristocratic uncle in eighteenth-century England (*Belle*, Amma Asante, 2014). These films, too, offer a corrective to hegemonic heritage, first, by adding 'colour' to the familiar iconography of lavish costume dramas and, second, by excavating the biographies of remarkable individuals whose lives testify to the long history of racial oppression, inequality and prejudice.

Outside the Law: Revisiting the Contested Memory of the Algerian War of Independence

Rachid Bouchareb's *Outside the* Law is the second part of 'a planned trilogy charting Algeria's long and often bloody relationship with France' (Jafaar 2011: 38). The first part, *Days of Glory*, commemorates the sacrifice of 300,000 soldiers from France's North and West African colonies, who were called upon by de Gaulle to liberate Italy and France from Fascism. While the D-Day landings in Normandy and the efforts of the French Resistance have all been commemorated, the heroism and sacrifice of the colonial soldiers has been elided in France's official accounts of World War Two. As Bouchareb commented: 'I've seen a lot of movies of the Second World War but I've never seen any Muslim soldiers' (cited in Jafaar 2011). Often described as the sequel to this successful war movie, because it stars several of the same lead actors (Jamel Debbouze, Roschdy Zem, Sami Bouajila and Bernard Blancan), *Outside the Law* begins where *Days of Glory* ends—on VE Day in 1945. Bouchareb's revisionist take on the Algerian struggle for independence and its reverberations in metropolitan France calls official French as well as Algerian historical accounts of this war into question. Until the 1990s, Algeria's armed struggle for independence was widely regarded as a taboo subject and, according to Higbee, 'legislation passed by successive French governments had actively colluded in a process of fabricating collective amnesia around' *la guerre sans nom* (2013: 63). By the time Rachid Bouchareb made *Outside the Law*, the silence had been lifted. In fact, since the late 1990s, the trauma of the Franco-Algerian war has attracted a great deal of attention in French cinema and has been depicted from the French (for example, *Mon colonel* [*The Colonel*, Laurent Herbiet, 2006] and *L'ennemi intime* [*Intimate Enemies*, Florent-Emilio Siri, 2007]) as well as Algerian vantage points (for example, *Sous les pieds des femmes* [Rachida Krim, 1997], *Vivre au paradis* [*Living in Paradise*, Bourlem Guerdjou, 1998] and *Cartouches gauloises* [*Summer of '62*, Mehdi Charef, 2007]; see Austin 2009; Durmelat 2012). Bouchareb makes a number of decisive interventions in these cinematic memory contests. Most importantly, he tries to rehabilitate the difficult position of the Algerian diaspora in France, which was excluded from the French memory of the war as well as from official commemorations in Algeria. In fact, the contributions of Algerian immigrants to the struggle for independence, financial and otherwise, were 'conveniently left out of the national genealogy rewritten by the newly founded Algerian FLN state in 1962' (Durmelat 2012: 95).

In contrast to earlier cinematic representations, Bouchareb's film expands the historical scope by situating the Algerian war in the broader context of France's long colonial history. The opening sequence, for instance, takes place in 1925 and portrays the expropriation of the land of an Algerian farmer—the father of the three protagonists, as we find out later—and the family's expulsion from their home by the Kaid (tribal chief), an Algerian working for the colonial regime. A particularly controversial event included in the film's preamble is the violent clash between demonstrators demanding Algeria's independence and the local gendarmerie in the Algerian town of Sétif that resulted in the massacre of Algerians on a grand scale. Although this event preceded the Algerian War of Independence by some nine years, for Bouchareb (2011) it represents 'the birth of the Algerian war'. The historical re-enactment of the Sétif massacres, one of the lacunae of French history, aims to shock 'spectators out of their indifference or comfortable sense of historical knowledge' (Rosello 2012: 114) into acknowledging the atrocities of France's colonial rule.

Notwithstanding Bouchareb's intention to set the historical record straight, his revisionist account is remarkably even-handed in the way it portrays the vicious cycle of carnages and revenge. For example, instead of pitting 'the French' against 'the Algerians', the film gives a nuanced account of the conflicted loyalties that transcend race and nation. The Kaid as translator and transmitter of colonial law is but one example; there are also warring factions among the Algerian freedom fighters, notably the FLN and the more moderate MNA (Mouvement National Algérien); and the film portrays French supporters of the independence struggle alongside Algerian traitors. In this respect, it articulates a corrective to 'official Algerian interpretations of the war' that have depicted Algerians as 'being naturally united against the French enemy' (Donadey 2014: 19).

The most significant departure from earlier films about the Algerian war is, however, the spectacularisation of violence and the reliance on the iconography of the gangster film. In order to render history with 'as much authenticity as possible [and] as much emotion' (Bouchareb 2011), Bouchareb looked towards Hollywood's epic gangster films such as *Once Upon a Time in America* (Sergio Leone, 1984), the *Godfather* trilogy (Francis Ford Coppola, 1972, 1974, 1990) and *Heat* (Michael Mann, 1995), while also citing *La battaglia di Algeri* (*The Battle of Algiers*, Gillo Pontecorvo, 1966) and the Algerian film *Chroniques des années de braise* (*Chronicle of the Years of Fire*, Mohammed Lakhdar-Hamina, 1975) as inspirations (Jafaar 2011; Bouchareb 2010).

Like Francis Ford Coppola's archetypal gangster film *The Godfather*, *Outside the Law* 'places the violent power struggle involving a criminal underworld, an organization that is "outside the law" [...] against the internal struggles of an immigrant family melodrama' (Higbee 2013: 90). Bouchareb also follows Coppola in the way he dramatises the fractured political allegiances of the Algerian struggle as a family saga revolving around three brothers, thereby relying on the emotive response elicited by individualised (hi)story. First, there is Abdelkader, whose revolutionary credentials are underscored by his Malcolm X-style glasses. His brother Messaoud, who has honed his rifle skills during the war in Indochina, is reluctant to be drawn into the struggle of the National Liberation Front and is haunted by moral scruples regarding how to reconcile the growing death toll with the ultimate goal of a free Algeria. The third brother, Saïd, 'represents the Algerian everyman, seeking upward mobility through cash, not dogma' (Jafaar 2011: 39). He manages an Algerian boxing champion and runs a successful nightclub in Paris's Pigalle district; nevertheless he supports the good cause financially and is eventually drawn into the vortex of violence. He is the least political of the three and the only one to survive.

Outside the Law stages the covert battle between the National Liberation Front and the Red Hand (a French intelligence and counter-terrorist unit set up to assassinate FLN leaders and other independence fighters) as a personal battle between Abdelkadar and Colonel Faivre, the mastermind behind the Red Hand. The war they wage against each other is 'more reminiscent of an underworld feud than an organised military campaign' (Jafaar 2011: 40). Their face-to-face meeting references a pivotal scene in *Heat*, in which Al Pacino, in the role of veteran LAPD detective Hanna, and Robert De Niro, as the powerful gangster boss McCauley, acknowledge their mutual respect and even something like affection for each other, while also reaffirming that neither would hesitate to kill the other if circumstances required. The conversation between Faivre and Abdelkader is suffused by the same sense of ambivalence. 'You and I are alike,' Faivre says to Abdelkader when he realises that his adversary, like himself, is prepared to sacrifice everything for his political conviction. Meanwhile, Abdelkader reminds Faivre that, not so long ago, he was on the right side of history, fighting against Nazi occupation for a free France. He then proffers an ethical argument for the inherent morality of the FLN's battle for Algeria's freedom, suggesting that it is a cause as just and fair as that of the French Resistance during World War Two (Fig. 5.1).

This provocative equation between the goals of the anti-fascist resistance and those of the FLN is reiterated by means of black-and-white archival newsreel footage (real and faux) that bookends the film: the first insert of archival footage shows the VE Day celebrations in Paris on 8 May 1945 before cutting to what an intertitle announces as 'Sétif, Algeria, on the same day'; the second, at the end, captures the Algerian independence celebrations on 6 July 1962.

Fig. 5.1 Gangster film iconography: Abdelkader and Faivre's meeting

The use of documentary footage in this and other films about the collective memory of diasporas is remarkable for three reasons. First, it is an attempt to instill a sense of historical authenticity into a film that, in other respects, is not particularly preoccupied with recreating a painstakingly accurate account of history. In interviews, Bouchareb has emphasised that *Outside the Law* is, above all, a fiction film with high production values, aiming to entertain and move audiences while also acquainting them with a part of recent French history not taught at school. However, he adds, 'if I had wanted to make a "historical" film, then I would have made a documentary' (Bouchareb 2010). This remark implicitly reinforces the common assumption that documentaries convey an objective and authentic representation of reality. *Outside the Law* proves this to be a fallacy since it blends genuine documentary footage with film stock that is made to look as if it has been retrieved from the archive (in the scene cutting from Paris to Sétif) so as to lend its political message greater authority. Second, whereas the use of archival material is not a prevalent aesthetic strategy in heritage cinema, it is very prominent indeed in what I have described elsewhere as 'diasporic postmemory films' such as *Mémoires d'immigrés—l'héritage maghrébin* (*Immigrant Memories*, Yamina Benguigui, 1997), *Mein Vater, der Gastarbeiter* (*My Father, the Guestworker*, Yüksel Yavuz, 1995) and *I for India* (Sandhya Suri, 2005), in which second-generation filmmakers excavate the memories of migration of their parents' generation, relying on oral history as well as prosthetic memory techniques (Berghahn 2013: 86–100). Third, the unexpected insertion of colour in the grainy black-and-white footage adds emphasis and immediately recalls a scene in what is arguably the most famous film about historical trauma, Steven Spielberg's *Schindler's List* (1993). The scene, which shows the liquidation of the Krakow ghetto, includes a little girl who wanders the streets in a bright-red coat. In an almost entirely monochrome film, the girl in the red coat stands out—and has attracted a gamut of critical and scholarly attention. The correspondence between this scene in *Schindler's List* and the first block of archival footage in *Outside the Law* is all the more striking, since not only the French *Tricolore* is highlighted through the use of colour, but also a little girl, whose dress is tailored out of the cloth of the blue, red and white Star-Spangled Banner. The corresponding black-and-white documentary footage at the end of the film picks out the green of the Algerian flag and, in a subsequent shot, the red star (recalling the red bloodstain on Abdelkader's white shirt when he is shot dead in a Paris metro station). The colourful French and Algerian flags, emblems of national sovereignty, commemorate the ultimate goal of the war, while at the same time suggesting that the painful and divisive memory of the war is one shared by the Algerians and the French.

The daring proposition that France's contemporary multi-ethnic society ought to embrace the separate, compartmentalised memories of this fratricidal war by sharing 'the suffering of the other' (Stora cited in Austin 2009: 125) resonates with Ernest Renan's idea that 'suffering in common unifies' nations 'more than joy does' and that, as far as 'national memories are concerned, griefs are of more value than triumphs' (Renan 1990[1882]: 19). The idea that trauma can, indeed, constitute the basis of a national heritage, in which the diametrically opposite memories of victims and perpetrators have become reconciled, underpins quite a few German heritage films such as *Aimée & Jaguar* (Max Färberböck, 1999) and *Rosenstrasse* (Margarethe von Trotta, 2003), which reimagine the relationship between Jewish and non-Jewish Germans as one of friendship, solidarity, even love (see Koepnick 2002; Cooke 2012: 147–63). Like these films, *Outside the Law* attempts to reconcile the fragmented memories of the Franco-Algerian War and to include them in France's heritage, thereby making it more inclusive and culturally diverse.

The film's unorthodox approach to a highly sensitive topic sparked considerable public debate and even protests in the streets of Cannes, where it competed for the Palme d'Or under police protection. Neither the high production values nor the stellar cast, including Jamel Debbouzze and Roschdy Zem, two of France's most bankable Maghrebi French actors, could compensate for the fact that *Outside the Law* touched a raw nerve. Even half a century later, the memory of the Franco-Algerian war is something with which the majority of French audiences are reluctant to engage (see Durmelat 2012; Stora 2014). For Bouchareb, the disappointing reception made 'clear that the Algerian war was still not over in some people's minds' (cited in Donadey 2014: 24).

ARCHIVAL FOOTAGE AND SHABBY CHIC IN *ALMANYA*: WELCOME TO GERMANY

The Turkish German comedy *Almanya—Welcome to Germany* partakes in the project of diasporic counter-heritage cinema, offering a competing version of history that pays tribute to the significant contributions Turkish labour migrants have made to West Germany's economic miracle. West Germany's official historiography identifies the Marshall Plan, which helped the defeated nation to get back on its feet, and the staunch work ethic of the Germans, who rebuilt their country from the rubble and ruins to become Europe's economic powerhouse, as the two main factors in the nation's post-war success. Until quite recently, when Chancellor Angela Merkel invited 200 immigrants to an official thanksgiving ceremony in Berlin to commemorate 50 years of immigration, the role played by labour migrants had been ignored. During the years of the economic miracle, West Germany recruited *Gastarbeiter* (literally 'guest workers', a euphemistic term used in the early days of labour migration) from Italy, Spain, Greece, Turkey, Portugal and Yugoslavia. Originally, guest workers—predominantly men— came without their families and were expected to stay only for a couple of years and then go back to their 'own country'. However, Turkish migrants, in particular, were reluctant to return to their poor and politically unstable homeland. When a law was passed in the 1970s, making it possible for family members to join a spouse who was already living and working in Germany, immigrant families were reunited and settled for good.

Taking the German word *Gastarbeiter* literally, *Almanya—Welcome to Germany* glosses over the social marginalisation and hardship immigrants actually experienced and, instead, imagines their recruitment as a cordial invitation and their arrival as a warm welcome. This kind of embellishment is made plausible through a clever framing device, which allows a child's expansive imagination to be the measure of reality and to enhance it with a magical realist touch. That child is Cenk, the seven-year-old grandson of Hüseyin Yilmaz, one of the first Turkish labour migrants to arrive in Germany during the 1960s. When Cenk is told that Germany called his grandfather and other guest workers like him, he imagines the German state as a loud, disembodied voice inviting able and willing workers from all over the world: 'Dear cosmopolitans, here speaks the Federal Republic of Germany. We are looking for a workforce. If you are young, strong and possess a good work ethic, then report immediately to the nearest recruitment office.' A sound bridge links the voice, which sounds as if it is emanating from a gigantic megaphone, to a series of snapshots in oversaturated colour, showing a group of Turkish men playing cards in Istanbul, an Italian father eating spaghetti in the family kitchen in Naples, a group of Greek men on the island of Rhodes, and three Eskimos, huddling around a fire on a vast expanse of snow at the North Pole.

The film's chief premise, that West Germany extended a warm welcome to all immigrants, is proven by the use of black-and-white archival footage. According to the fictionalised chronicle of immigration, Cenk's grandfather, Hüseyin, arrived in Germany on 10 September 1964, the same day as Armando Rodrigues de Sá from Portugal, who was the millionth guest worker to set foot on German soil and who did indeed receive a warm welcome together with a fashionable Zündapp moped, a gift donated by the Federal Republic's Association of Employers. Archival newsreel footage of this historic event is intercut with faux archival footage in washed-out colour, showing Hüseyin Yilmaz stepping off a train at the Cologne-Deutz train station at the same time. If Hüseyin had not kindly offered Rodrigues his place in the long queue of recently arrived guest workers, then he, rather than the Portuguese worker, would have made history. And so the film's humorous historical revisionism continues, juxtaposing what was and what would have been, and transforming the black and white of old documentaries and the 'faded greys of old family-album snapshots' into 'CinemaScope and glorious Technicolor'—as Salman Rushdie (1991: 10) described the retrieval of the past through memory and its magical transformation when he wrote *Midnight's Children* (1981), a book to which Samdereli's film pays homage.

There are several more inserts of archival footage from the 1960s at the beginning and end of the film. Like in the series of snapshots from a family album during the film's opening sequence, white serrated borders in the style of old-fashioned photographs also frame the archival images. However, unlike the family photographs, the black-and-white archival images are not still images, but moving ones. One particularly interesting archival insert documents the rigorous medical examinations labour migrants had to undergo at their national recruitment centres (Fig. 5.2).

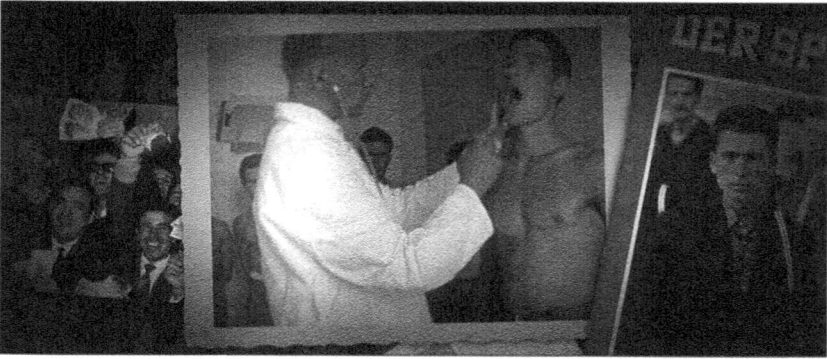

Fig. 5.2 Archival footage of medical exams

A number was written on their chests, indicating their state of health and level of fitness. As the German reporter explains, 'the selection procedure resembles that of a cattle market. Who is deemed fit may travel to Germany.' From today's vantage point, this comment is so hair-raisingly non-PC that it beggars belief while at the same time evoking surreptitious laughter. Another piece of archival footage is an excerpt from a televised interview with the manager of a crane manufacturing company, broadcast in 1963, in which he asserts: 'I would like to sum up our company's experience: if we are faced again with the choice, we will only ever choose skilled Turkish workers.' The manager's emphatic assertion of the superior quality of Turkish workers is accorded a prominent position at the very end of the film and serves as a tongue-in-cheek corrective to deeply ingrained prejudices against Turks held by majority culture Germans.

Archival footage of home movies, showing German families celebrating Christmas, lend the film a peculiar nostalgic charm, inviting audiences to remember the comparatively humble presents given in the 1970s and to take delight in the retro fashion and interior design. These home movies also fulfil important narrative and comedic functions. The Yilmaz children ask their parents to celebrate Christmas in accordance with German customs; alas, their parents do not get it quite right. The Christmas tree is tiny and bare, with hardly any decoration and no candles at all; the presents are not wrapped and more modest than expected so that, for the children at least, their first German Christmas turns out to be a rather disappointing experience. Yet in terms of the film's narrative economy, it marks the Yilmaz family's wish to integrate and to do as the Germans do.

Almanya—Welcome to Germany relies on the powerful nostalgic appeal of the past to convey a conciliatory narrative about successful Turkish integration. German retro cars, notably the iconic VW beetle and the Mercedes Benz, a status symbol for Germans and Turks alike, feature prominently. To be sure, the dull-brown apartment blocks and insalubrious living conditions with worn-out mattresses and a toilet on the half landing of the communal staircase are utterly unappealing. But the shabby chic of fixtures and fittings invites spectators to remember that, in the seventies, boldly patterned wallpaper in shades of beige and brown was all the rage. By vividly evoking the material culture of everyday life and relishing its authentic recreation, *Almanya* offers a spectacle of retro style that is redolent with nostalgia for 'the good old days'. In stark contrast to films made by diasporic filmmakers in the 1980s and early 1990s, which normally follow the gritty realism of the social problem film, this integration feel-good movie, as *Almanya* has been dubbed in the German press, does not equate shabby chic with the material culture of a particular social group, namely immigrants. Instead, it invites German audiences, whether of German or Turkish origin, to fondly remember the décor of 1970s homes, along with the cars, fashions, popular music and highlights of family life. It projects the retro look of that period as a memory shared by Germans and Turkish Germans alike and, thereby, aims to engender a collective sense of belonging.

Belle: Adding 'Colour' to English Heritage

Like the other films by diasporic directors considered in this chapter, *Belle*, by Amma Asante, a British filmmaker of Ghanaian descent, offers a revisionist account of hegemonic history. This lavish costume drama serves as a corrective to the widespread assumption that there were no black people in Britain until 1948, when the SS *Empire Windrush* arrived at Tilbury Dock, Essex, with several hundred African-Caribbean migrants on board. Although the arrival of the Windrush Generation marked the beginning of mass migration from Jamaica, Trinidad, Tobago and other Caribbean islands, 'there had been a black presence in Britain since at least the mid-sixteenth century' (Bourne 2002: 47). In fact, Lord Chief Justice Mansfield, the historical figure on whom Dido Elizabeth Belle's granduncle is based, estimated that, in 1772, there were some 15,000 people of African descent living in Britain (National Archives n/d).

Yet this historical fact is rarely shown in popular cinema. As Stephen Bourne illustrates in his concise overview of black histories and British historical films, black Africans and Caribbeans were usually portrayed as colonised 'foreign' subjects in colonial adventure films, whereas 'Britain's domestic past [was imagined] as exclusively "white"' (Bourne 2002: 50). Despite considering a few notable exceptions testifying to the black presence in Britain prior to 1948, including *Song of Freedom* (J. Elder Wills, 1936), *The Man in Grey* (Leslie Arliss, 1943) and *The Sailor's Return* (Jack Gold, 1978), Bourne concludes that 'there is ample ammunition for regarding "whiteness" as a specific generic trait of British period films' (Bourne 2002: 49).

More recent cinematic representations of black Britons, written and directed by black diasporic filmmakers such as Horace Ové, Isaac Julien,

Julien Henriques and Menelik Shabazz, are predominantly concerned with issues of black identity in contemporary British society. Meanwhile, John Akomfrah's *The Nine Muses* (2010) is an exception. It is an essayistic memory film that combines archival footage of postcolonial migrants arriving in the 'motherland' with bleak, snow-covered landscapes and a voiceover reciting Homer's *Odyssey* and other 'white' canonical literary texts. Despite engaging with Britain's black heritage, in terms of its aesthetic approach, *The Nine Muses* could hardly be subsumed under the (counter-)heritage label. Intended by Akomfrah as an epitaph to the Windrush Generation, the film unwittingly reinforces the idea that the black diaspora in Britain is a post-war phenomenon.

The biopic *Belle*, by contrast, is set during the late eighteenth century when British merchant ships transported millions of slaves across the Middle Passage to the West Indies. Dido Elizabeth Belle was born into slavery in the West Indies in 1761 as the mixed-race daughter of an African slave, Maria Belle, and Captain John Lindsay, a British naval officer, who took Maria as his concubine while stationed there. The film's narrative begins in 1765 when Lindsay takes his little daughter to London to entrust her to the care of his aunt and uncle, the Earl and Countess of Mansfield at Kenwood House.

The story of *Belle* was inspired by the copy of a painting in Kenwood House that caught the eye of Misan Sagay, who co-authored the screenplay with writer-director Amma Asante. The original painting, now hanging in Scone Place in Scotland, dates back to 1779 and is attributed to Johann Zoffany, a 'renowned portraitist of Britain's rich and royal. This unusual piece depicts two beautifully-outfitted girls, one black, one white, seemingly at leisure' (English Heritage 2014).

Sagay and Asante are less concerned with providing a historically accurate account of Dido's life, about which very little is known, than with making an impassioned plea for racial and gender equality that has 'concrete contemporary significance [and] resonates in the here and now' (Clark 2014: 32). In order to make the biography of the black Dido more pertinent to current debates about racial equality, they lend Dido a voice and a certain degree of agency in a famous court case that took place in 1783. The so-called *Zong* case refers to the massacre of some 140 African slaves, who had been thrown overboard and drowned during the Middle Passage. While under certain circumstances destroying a ship's cargo, be it livestock or slaves, was legal, the deliberate killing of the slaves aboard the *Zong* was found to be attempted fraud through which the slave owners tried to recoup insurance money. Dido's great-uncle, Lord Chief Justice Mansfield, presided over the case and passed the final verdict, deciding against the slave traders and in favour of the insurers. The *Zong* case sparked great interest and publicity at the time and paved the way for the abolitionist movement. In the film's fictional account, Dido exerts a considerable influence over Mansfield's verdict, which culminates in his public condemnation of slavery: 'It is my opinion that the state of slavery is so odious a position that nothing may support it.' His deep love of his grandniece, Dido, adds a powerful emotional motivation to his judgement. Moreover, Dido finds a strong ally in the idealistic legal clerk John Davinier, a radical abolitionist whom she supplies with important evidence relating to the *Zong* massacre retrieved from Mansfield's office.

In typical heritage style, for all her lavish period costumes and elaborate coiffure, Dido is conceived as a modern feminist heroine who defies convention on all counts in her pursuit of freedom and self-determination. She rejects the fiancé chosen for her and instead chooses the man who respects her as his equal and who fights for racial equality: the young lawyer Davinier. Hence, the film ends on a doubly triumphant note, with the promise of marriage and Dido's declaration: 'I have been blessed with freedom twice over, as a Negro and as a woman.'

Dido's path to freedom and equality is not without setbacks and humiliations. The Mansfield family, despite being portrayed as extraordinarily open-minded for their time, is by no means free from racist sentiments. When meeting his nephew's infant daughter for the first time, Mansfield is shocked to discover that she is not only illegitimate but also black and is, initially, reluctant to raise her. The large oil paintings on the walls, which Dido scrutinises with interest and bewilderment, suggest that the family is complicit with the prevailing racial inequities: they feature white ancestors who tower over diminutive black servants, squeezed to the margins or into the background. On the one hand, these heirlooms are cherished family treasures and nobody questions the blatant racism they extol; on the other hand, Mansfield is libertine enough to ignore social convention and commission a portrait of his two grandnieces depicting the two young women as equals, standing side by side. The painting created in the film differs from Zoffany's insofar as Dido does not wear a silk turban with an ostrich feather, a pictorial convention used to exoticise black people at the time. This small but significant detail signals Asante's conscious rejection of ethnic stereotyping (Fig. 5.3).

Fig. 5.3 Dido looks at the portrait of herself and her cousin

In spite of confessing to his wife that he loves Dido as if she were of his own blood, social decorum compels Mansfied to exclude her from the family dining table whenever guests are present. Paradoxically, her status is deemed too low to eat in the company of family friends and guests but too high to eat with the servants. These contradictions are hard to reconcile and reflect Amma Asante's intention to make people, especially white people, understand the subtle racism that only 'we as black people understand [...] unintentional racism, racism that runs deep, deep, deep under the surface' (Asante cited in Clark 2014: 33).

Of the three films discussed in this essay, *Belle* comes closest to the museum-aesthetic and visual opulence of heritage cinema. The pictorialist camera style that organises 'the gaze around props and settings', thereby privileging 'heritage space' (Higson 2006 [1993]: 99) over narrative space, is in evidence throughout. Consistent with the iconographic conventions of heritage cinema, the camerawork celebrates the majestic splendour of Kenwood House set amidst verdant landscaped gardens in a series of lingering long shots.

The film's production history deftly illustrates that heritage cinema, though seemingly concerned with 'the conservationist desire of period authenticity' (Higson 2006 [1993]: 101), actually does not care all that much about authenticity, as long as it succeeds in creating a credible fake. Due to major restoration work, it was not possible to film at Kenwood House, so West Wycombe House had to stand in for the stately home in Hampstead, alongside Osterley Park House and Syon House, where much of the interior filming took place. Even so, English Heritage used the theatrical release of *Belle* in June 2014 as a marketing opportunity to promote the architectural attractions of Kenwood House, notably the dairy, of which, according to historical records, Dido was in charge (although the film does not once show her working in the dairy). The June 2014 edition of *English Heritage Members' Magazine* includes an image of the film poster, which actually features Kenwood House in the background and the beautiful actress Gugu Mbatha-Raw as Dido Belle in the foreground. The article also reproduces an eighteenth-century portrait, showing the black Dido Elizabeth Belle next to her fair cousin, Lady Elizabeth Murray. Readers are invited to visit and admire the copy of the painting in the Housekeeper's Room at Kenwood House and to amble in the extensive grounds where Dido lived and worked.

The fact that neither Johann Zoffany's painting at Kenwood House nor the location where *Belle* was shot are genuine deftly illustrates heritage cinema's fascination with mere surfaces, with a certain look or style that can pass as the real thing. It is an example of postmodern pastiche that, while purporting to be concerned with the historically authentic recreation of the past, actually reflects 'our ideas or cultural stereotypes about the past' (Jameson 1985: 118).

It is thus all the more ironic that much of the public discourse surrounding heritage cinema revolves around revealing 'the true story behind the film'. Not only did English Heritage organise an English Heritage lecture held at another heritage site, Blenheim Palace, during which best-selling biographer of Jane Austen and Evelyn Waugh, Paula Byrne, revealed the 'true story of Dido Belle', but the website of *BBC History Magazine* also featured an interview about *Belle* with historian James Walvin, an expert on Britain and the slave trade. Walvin disapproved of the film's 'thunderous and didactic simplicity' and 'lachrymose sentimentality' and summed up its artistic approach as '*Downtown Abbey* meets the slave trade' (Walvin 2014). His somewhat sarcastic assessment points towards the disjuncture between the 'bucket-loads of opulent abundance [...] delivered to the screen' (Walvin 2014) and the way *Belle* mobilises the currently fashionable interest in black history and, more generally, contemporary attitudes towards race.

Conclusion

The overriding concern of this chapter has been to examine the narrative and aesthetic strategies diasporic filmmakers deploy to claim a space for the collective memory of diasporic communities in the hegemonic heritage of

France, Germany and Britain. The three case studies are apt examples of what Belén Vidal has theorised as 'politically articulate heritage cinema [, which] condenses complex historical processes into individualised narratives' (2012: 69) with a more or less overtly political agenda, be it in the guise of costume drama or the gangster film. The shared project of these diasporic counter-heritage films is to replace a biased and incomplete version of history with a more inclusive one by lending a voice to memories that have been silenced. In doing so, they aim to 'repair the symbolic injustice that such silences constitute' (Rosello 2012: 115).

The biopic *Belle* celebrates the exceptional success story of the inclusion of the racially Other, who has become immortalised in a work of art that attests to her her racial and social equality, into English heritage. In this particular context, the appropriation of the distinctive iconography of heritage cinema is entirely consistent with the protagonist's social standing as the grandniece of a wealthy aristocrat. This does not hold true, however, for the other two films whose aesthetics can hardly be accommodated under the heritage label, even though the concept has evinced remarkable elasticity over the decades since its inception. *Outside the Law* stages Algeria's political struggle for independence as a spectacle of gunfights and bomb blasts. It adopts the familiar iconography of the gangster film, with FLN fighters wearing trench coats and fedoras, the quintessential fashion accessory of the screen gangster, perhaps, because in Hollywood no other genre has been more closely associated with immigrants than that of the gangster film.

As regards the extensive use of archival footage, a staple of diasporic memory films of various kinds, Black British artist and filmmaker John Akomfrah has arguably offered the most convincing explanation. For the diasporic subject, he suggests, 'the archive acquires a special poignancy [...] because it is the space of the memorial. There are very few tangible memorials that say, "You have been here". And so, the archive is important because it is one of the spaces in which the memorial attests to your existence' (Akomfrah 2010).

The double portrait of Dido Elizabeth Belle and her cousin, which has been on public display in British stately homes for centuries, is a rare instance of such a 'tangible memorial', testifying to the long history of the black presence in Britain (Fig. 5.4). Even so, like the black-and-white footage retrieved from the archives and incorporated by Bouchareb and Samdereli in their films, this rather grand oil painting, too, forms part of the visual archive of diasporas in Europe. In this respect, all three films

Fig. 5.4 Belle

pursue the shared goal of asserting the importance of these archives of diasporic memory in relation to hegemonic cultural memory. In fact, the growing number of European films about diasporic memory and heritage resonate with cultural initiatives to generate (or respond to) increased public interest in the history of immigration and in Europe's multicultural heritage. It is certainly no coincidence that the recent emergence of diasporic counter-heritage cinema coalesced with the opening of Europe's first national museum devoted to the history of immigration in France in 2007, followed by the launch of the Migration Museum Project (a mobile precursor of a proper museum) in the UK in 2012 and concrete plans to establish a museum of migration in Germany.

Works Cited

Akomfrah, J. 2010. Chiasmus. An interview with John Akomfrah, bonus material. DVD *The Nine Muses*. New Wave Films.

Austin, G. 2009. 'Seeing and listening from the site of trauma': The Algerian War in contemporary memory. *Yale French Studies* 115: 115–125.

Berghahn, D. 2013. *Far-Flung families in film: The diasporic family in contemporary European cinema*. Edinburgh: Edinburgh University Press.

Bouchareb, Rachid. 2010. Interview de Rachid Bouchareb, cineaste de *Hors-la-loi*. Toutlaculture, 22 September.

———. 2011. Interview, bonus material of DVD release *Outside the Law*. Optimum Releasing.

Bourne, S. 2002. Secrets and lies: Black histories and black historical films. In *British historical cinema*, eds. C. Monk and A. Sargeant, 47–65. London: BFI.

Clark, A. 2014. Portrait of a Lady. *Sight & Sound* 24(7): 31–33.

Cooke, P. 2012. *Contemporary German cinema*. Manchester: Manchester University Press.

Donadey, A. 2014. Wars of memory: On Rachid Bouchareb's *Hors la loi*. *L'Esprit Créateur* 54(4): 15–26.

Durmelat, S. 2012. Re-visions of the Algerian War of independence. In *Screening integration: Recasting Maghrebi immigration in contemporary France*, eds. S. Durmelat and V. Swamy, 93–111. Lincoln and London: University of Nebraska Press.

English Heritage. 2014. Kenwood story to be told on the big screen. *English Heritage Members Magazine*, 6 June.

Hall, S. 1999. Whose heritage? Unsettling 'the heritage', re-imagining post-nation. *Third Text* 49: 3–13.

———. 2003[1990]. Cultural identity and diaspora. In *Theorizing diaspora: A reader*, eds. J. Evans and A. Mannur, 233–246. Oxford: Blackwell.

Halle, R. 2008. *German film after Germany: Towards a transnational aesthetics*. Chicago: University of Illinois Press.

Harper, S. 2004. The taxonomy of genre: Historical, costume and 'heritage' film. *Journal of British Cinema and Television* 1(1): 137–142.

Higbee, W. 2013. *Post-Beur cinema: North African Émigré and Maghrebi French filmmaking in France since 2000*. Edinburgh: Edinburgh University Press.

Higson, A. 2006 [1993]. Re-presenting the national past: Nostalgia and Pastiche in the heritage film. In *Fires were started: British cinema and Thatcherism*, ed. L. D. Friedman, 2nd Rev edn, 91–109. London: Wallflower Press.

Jafaar, A. 2011. Algeria rising. *Sight & Sound* 21(6): 38–44.

Jameson, F. 1985. Postmodernism and consumer society. In *Postmodern culture*, ed. H. Foster, 111–125. London: Pluto Press.

Koepnick, L. 2002. Reframing the past: Heritage cinema and Holocaust in the 1990s. *New German Critique* 87: 47–82.

Monk, C., and A. Sargeant. 2002. Introduction: The past in British cinema. In *British historical cinema*, eds. C. Monk and A. Sargeant, 1–14. London: BFI.

National Archives. (n/d). [Online]. Available at: http://www.nationalarchives.gov.uk/pathways/blackhistory/intro/intro.htm. Accessed 4 Dec 2015.

Nora, P. 1989. Between memory and history: Les lieux de mémoire. *Representations* 26: 7–24.

Oscherwitz, D. 2010. *French cinema and the post-colonial heritage*. Carbondale and Edwardsville: Southern Illinois University Press.

Renan, E. 1990 [1882]. What is a nation?. In *Nation and narration*, ed. Homi K. Bhabha, 8–22. London and New York: Routledge.

Rosello, M. 2012. Rachid Bouchareb's *Indigènes*: Political or ethical event memory. In *Screening integration: Recasting Maghrebi immigration in contemporary France*, eds. S. Durmelat and V. Swamy, 112–126. Lincoln and London: University of Nebraska Press.

Rushdie, S. 1991. *Imaginary homelands: Essays and criticism*. London: Granta.

Stora, B. 2014. Close-up: Postcolonial filmmaking in French-speaking countries. The Algerian War: Memory through cinema. *Black Camera: An International Film Journal* 1: 96–107.

Vidal, B. 2012. *Heritage film: Nation, genre, representation*. London: Wallflower Press.

Vincendeau, G. 2001. Introduction. In *Film/literature/heritage*, ed. Ginette Vincendeau, xi–xxiv. London: BFI.

Walvin, J. 2014. Historian at the movies: *Belle* reviewed. *History Extra* [Online]. Available at: http://www.historyextra.com/feature/international-history/historian-movies-belle-reviewed. Accessed 2 July 2015.

CHAPTER 6

Facing Dark Heritage: The Legacy of Nazi Perpetrators in German-Language Film

Axel Bangert

On 30 November 1973, the docudrama *Wie sie es wurden: Ein junger Mann aus dem Innviertel—Adolf Hitler* (*How They Became What They Were: A Young Man from the Inn Quarter—Adolf Hitler*, 1973) was broadcast simultaneously by Austrian and German public television. Written by Georg Stefan Troller and directed by Axel Corti, it was the first German-language film to offer an in-depth portrayal of Adolf Hitler (Kansteiner 2006: 376), focusing on his coming-of-age, from his schooldays to the outbreak of the First World War. In several scenes, the production shows the young Hitler contemplating the architectonic landmarks of Linz, Vienna and Munich. Hitler is set against imposing facades, first in straight-on wide shots that dwarf his figure, later in low-angle medium close-ups monumentalising his torso, with towers and statues in the background. It is not for the sake of visual pleasure that Hitler contemplates the buildings—in his imagination, he enlarges them to express his will to power. And, particularly in Munich, which he enthusiastically calls 'eine deutsche Kunststadt' (a German city of art), he moreover derives his understanding of nation and people from them. In other words, Troller and Corti chart the ideological formation of the would-be demagogue and dictator by

A. Bangert (✉)
New York University, Berlin, Berlin, Germany
e-mail: axel.bangert@nyu.edu

© The Editor(s) (if applicable) and The Author(s) 2016
P. Cooke, R. Stone (eds.), *Screening European Heritage*,
Palgrave European Film and Media Studies,
DOI 10.1057/978-1-137-52280-1_6

how he interprets and projects heritage sites. *How They Became What They Were*—a heritage film about Adolf Hitler (Fig. 6.1)?

In this chapter, I examine two German-language films from the 1970s that portray Nazi perpetrators, illustrating how their understanding of heritage contrasts with contemporary films about the Third Reich made in Germany. In addition to *How They Became What They Were*, a co-production between public broadcasters Österreichischer Rundfunk (Austrian Broadcasting Corporation) and Zweites Deutsches Fernsehen (Second German Television), I also discuss *Aus einem deutschen Leben* (*Death Is My Trade*, 1977) by writer/director Theodor Kotulla, a German feature film co-produced by Westdeutscher Rundfunk (West German Broadcasting) and Iduna-Film about Rudolf Höß, the first and longest-serving commandant of the Auschwitz concentration camp. The two films were made at the time of the so-called 'Hitler-Welle' (Hitler wave) in historiography, literature and film which provoked a debate about the ethics and aesthetics of representing Nazi perpetrators. Heterogeneous and

Fig. 6.1 *Wie sie es wurden: Ein junger Mann aus dem Innviertel—Adolf Hitler* (*How They Became What They Were: A Young Man from the Inn Quarter—Adolf Hitler*, Georg Stefan Troller and Axel Corti, 1973) portrays Hitler as part of a generation opposing tradition and heritage in favour of an ethnic nationalist worldview

short-lived, the 'Hitler-Welle' consisted for the most part of eyewitness accounts as well as biographies by amateur historians published in Germany between 1973 and 1975. While these works were often criticised by professional historians, there was a parallel debate in historiography about psychological interpretations of Hitler which showed a similar fixation on his persona. With regard to film, an example for the 'Hitler-Welle' would be *Hitler: The Last Ten Days* (1973), directed by Ennio de Concini with Alec Guinness in the lead role. The bunker drama was based on Gerhard Boldt's eyewitness account, *Hitler: Die letzten Tage in der Reichskanzlei* (*Hitler: The Last Days in the Reich Chancellery*, 1947) republished in extended form in 1973 (Fischer and Lorenz 2007: 220–1) (Fig. 6.2).

How They Became What They Were and *Death Is My Trade* can be seen as exceptions to this trend in that they portray Hitler and Höß, respectively, not as anomalies but as products of society. In contemporary reviews, some critics applauded Troller and Corti as well as Kotulla for examining the genesis of a Nazi perpetrator on the collective level (e.g. Löbl 1973 for *How They Became What They Were* and Knapp 1978 for *Death Is My*

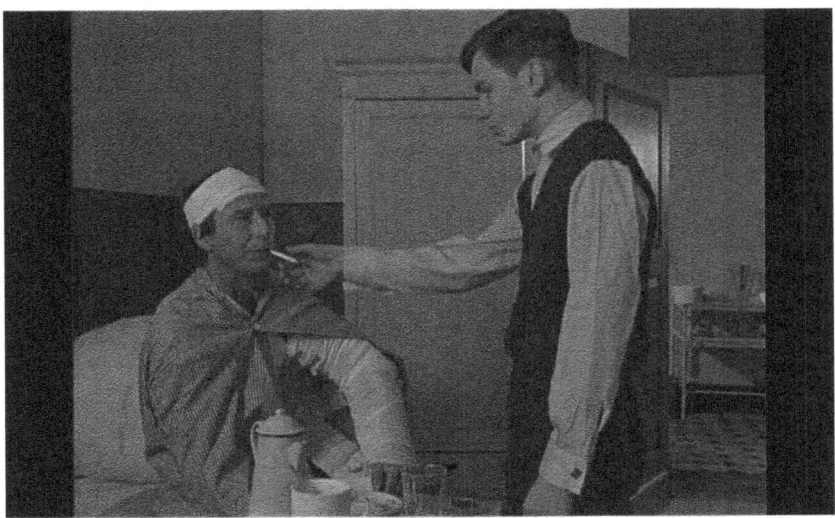

Fig. 6.2 Disciplining the body: In *Aus einem deutschen Leben* (*Death Is My Trade*, Theodor Kotulla, 1977) the young Rudolf Höß absorbs the militarist ethics of obedience through physical acts

Trade). As I intend to show, ideas of heritage, as they are discussed across this volume, play an important role in this approach, as the two films link their protagonists to traditions—understood not only in cultural, but also in social and political terms—that helped to prepare the ground for the rise of Nazism. Moreover, I examine how both productions achieve their unique forms of portrayal by engaging with film heritage. Also in this regard, heritage is addressed for the purpose of critique, both in terms of the visual legacies of Nazism and its memory in post-war film culture, a historical tradition that continues to be mined by the country's filmmakers today.

Indeed, not only by German filmmakers. While one would struggle to offer a clear definition of 'European heritage', the Second World War and more recently the Holocaust are often referred to as the continent's shared legacy (Boswell 2013). And while, in the words of Thomas Elsaesser, 'European countries are notoriously bad at watching each other's films' (Elsaesser 2005: 120), the Nazi past is one of the few subject matters that may allow a film to cross national borders and speak to audiences Europe-wide. Of course, dictatorship and war, occupation and resistance, as well as persecution and genocide, are a far cry from the subject matter of the heritage film as it is commonly understood. The world of the heritage film, as it has come to be defined, derives from the literary imagination, for which history provides the idealised setting. And the stories with which it is frequently associated usually occur before the Second World War, in the elite sphere and rural seclusion of the British homelands (Higson 1993, 2003), remote from the political violence that would soon arise in mainland Europe.

Yet, in view of the abundance of audio-visual dramatisations of the Third Reich produced in Europe, some scholars have begun to speak of a filmic engagement with 'dark heritage'. In his interview with Screening European Heritage, Matthew Boswell argues that dark heritage performs a social function similar to that of heritage in the original sense: 'Although dark heritage is difficult and traumatic, it's still connected to exactly the same ideas and processes, often in a positive way: things like community-building and the construction of group identities' (Boswell 2013). As an example, Boswell cites the German production *Der Untergang* (*Downfall*, Oliver Hirschbiegel, 2004), a national as well as international success about Hitler and the Nazi leadership's final days in the Berlin bunker. He sees the film's positive representation of national identity as being based on a shared experience of suffering. 'It's a film that represents Germans as victims. It doesn't really attempt to deal with them as perpetrators of terrible crimes—apart from Hitler who is virtually the sole perpetrator, the sole source of evil. *Downfall* is about communities being restored and positive, harmonious group identities arising out of a dark chapter of the past' (Boswell 2013).

Reading *Downfall* through the lens of dark heritage places the emphasis on the experience of Germans as a collective and their victimisation through Hitler. But what about the figure of the Nazi perpetrator as such? Owing to Bruno Ganz's spectacular performance, Hitler clearly stood at the centre of the film's grim vision of defeat and collapse. Can a perpetrator be regarded as a kind of heritage? Undoubtedly, figures such as Hitler have a special—or especially problematic—place even within the broader category of dark heritage. The conservative or nostalgic idea of heritage as something passed on to us that requires preservation or recuperation is not applicable to them. At most, such figures may be presented as a warning from history, as a difficult and dangerous legacy calling for a critique of heritage in the cultural, social and political sense.

The portrayal of Nazi perpetrators was and remains particularly contentious in German-language film, where these figures are fraught with inner controversy about the Nazi past. Were the perpetrators of the regime the exception? Or were they ordinary Germans, and if so, how did they become agents of mass murder? In post-war Austria and West Germany, representing a Nazi perpetrator meant raising a neglected but crucial issue about the Third Reich, namely, the perpetrator's position within society. Focusing on prominent figures, neither *How They Became What They Were* nor *Death Is My Trade* directly investigate the broad spectrum of low- and mid-level functionaries within the Nazi state. The two films also do not lay open personal continuities between the Third Reich, on the one hand, and post-war Austria and West Germany on the other. At the same time, as Alexandra Hissen points out with regard to *How They Became What They Were*, the film aims at 'broadening the basis of responsibility' (Hissen 2010: 67). This intention can also be seen in Kotulla's *Death Is My Trade*, a film which, similarly to Troller and Corti's, portrays Höß as absorbing and executing ideas that already exist around him. In this way, the two films extend our understanding of historical responsibility towards a complicity with the heritage that led to and, potentially, endured after the Third Reich.

Discussing the portrayal of the GDR past in Florian Henckel von Donnersmarck's *Das Leben der Anderen* (*The Lives of Others*, 2006), Erich

Rentschler argues that, in order to understand the role of heritage films in today's Germany, one needs to consider their interaction with German film heritage (Rentschler 2013: 252–60). Taking inspiration from Rentschler's approach, this chapter reviews 1970s German-language films about Nazi perpetrators in their own right as well as to shed light on contemporary German 'dark heritage' films about the Third Reich such as *Downfall*. What emerges from this comparison is that the earlier films are much more concerned with heritage in the sense of what is socially inherited, both with regard to the Nazi perpetrators' biographies and the insufficiencies of 'Vergangenheitsbewältigung' (coming to terms with the Nazi past) at the time of the films' production. By contrast, in *Downfall* the figure of the 'Führer' stands at the centre of a spectacular re-enactment of a dark past. In addition to the community-building aspect mentioned by Boswell, the bunker drama corresponds to the heritage film in terms of a style that presents diegetic space as both historically authentic and an attraction for the eye. Finally, in accordance with the broader definition of the 'genre' by Belén Vidal, *Downfall* tells the story of Hitler's last days as an emotional history by creating a sense of intimacy with his persona (Vidal 2012: 4).

How They Became What They Were: Tracing Ideological Formation Through Heritage Discourse

How They Became What They Were narrates Hitler's development from a boy without a sense of direction or purpose to a young man who frequents the ethnic nationalist and anti-Semitic circles of Vienna and Munich. Interestingly, Corti decided to give the dramatised parts of the film a sepia-tinted look. In Hissen's reading, this conveys a sense of historical distance, likening the fictional episodes to footage from the Nazi past (Hissen 2010: 58). Given that tinting was particularly popular up to the 1920s, one could also read this stylistic choice in a different way: as an attempt to let the dramatised parts seem like footage from the time in which the film is set, predating the well-known images of Hitler from the Third Reich. One could even go as far as to say that by means of this old-fashioned look, Corti presents *How They Became What They Were* like a non-existent, invented piece of film heritage that allows us to gain insight into Hitler's early development. The film's fictional episodes are intercut with a number of interviews with people who had a private connection to

Hitler, interviews which Corti conducted during the production's research phase. For instance, we get to know some of Hitler's former classmates, the widow of his friend during his Viennese days, when he tried in vain to be admitted to the Academy of Fine Arts, as well as the daughter of his landlord in Munich. While these interviews have a personal character, the aim is not to give an intimate portrait of the young Hitler. On the contrary, the interviews serve to clarify the conditions under which Hitler grew up and came of age. *How They Became What They Were* presents Hitler's early development in a mixture of historicised re-enactment and present-day enquiry, both of which aim to reshape our collective image of the future 'Führer'.

The beginning of the docudrama serves to illustrate the collective thrust of this portrayal. The first fictional episode begins in a train carriage where a group of mainly middle-aged men start a discussion about society and politics. We can identify an ethnic nationalist, a philosopher, a student and a priest. Their views diverge: while the ethnic nationalist, for instance, wants to strengthen German consciousness by defending the purity of the German language, the philosopher sees the destruction of interiority through the intellect as the real threat of the time. The only attitude that the men have in common is their anti-Semitism. Eventually, the camera moves towards a young man sitting at the back of the carriage, gazing out of the window in silence. This, as we easily guess, is Hitler. A freeze frame allows us to contemplate his profile. Yet, before the full title of the film is superimposed and our suspicion confirmed, we merely read the words 'Wie sie es wurden' (How they became what they were). From the start, Hitler is presented not as an individual, as singular, but by means of the plural 'they'. His development as politician and perpetrator is viewed as a collective phenomenon. In this context, the second part of the film's title, *A Young Man from the Inn Quarter*, takes on a new meaning: Hitler was a young man like many others.

Much of the literature on *How They Became What They Were* argues that Troller and Corti approach Hitler from a psychological point of view. In fact, particularly in the early stages, Troller's screenplay was strongly shaped by a psychoanalytic interpretation of Hitler's persona. In his autobiography, Troller calls Hitler a 'typically Austrian backwoodsman' and remarks that, to his astonishment, he had no problem trying to understand him (Troller 1988: 364). However, an article in the German weekly news magazine *Der Spiegel* published a few days before the film's broadcast suggests that Troller's psychologisation of Hitler was eventually revised

(*Der Spiegel* 1973). The article states that, initially, Troller took inspiration from American psychoanalyst Walter C. Langer's secret report on Hitler. Written in 1943 for the Office of Strategic Services, the report was published in revised form under the title *The Mind of Adolf Hitler* in 1972 when the 'Hitler-Welle' was in full swing. Based on Langer's analysis, which was praised for predicting Hitler's suicide, Troller devised a few scenes narrating formative experiences of the young Hitler. In one scene, Hitler witnesses his father raping his mother, but is unable to intervene; in another, Hitler stands at his mother's grave and starts touching his genitals.

According to *Der Spiegel*, ZDF commissioning editor Dr Franz Neubauer and historian Dr Werner Maser, as well as ORF commissioning editor and historian Dr Werner Swossil, urged Troller to omit this kind of speculative and crude psychologisation. Moreover, in contrast to Troller, Corti placed a strong emphasis on authenticity in researching the docudrama (Neumüller et al. 2003: 89–90). In addition to interviewing friends and acquaintances of Hitler, he insisted on shooting in real locations wherever possible, for instance, in the former house of Hitler's parents in Leonding near Linz (*Der Spiegel* 1973). What had begun as a bold attempt to explore the depth of Hitler's psyche thus came to be accommodated within the boundaries of public broadcasting, and its insistence on cautious, fact-based dramatisation.

That said, psychology still plays a significant role in the finished film, on both the individual and collective level, as Hitler is characterised as a child of his time. Hiller has analysed in detail how *How They Became What They Were* charts Hitler's development in three roughly divided stages. The first stage focuses on the conflict between Hitler and his father, a patriarch and representative of the Habsburg monarchy. Hitler's 'Ohnmachtserfahrungen' (experiences of powerlessness) in confronting his father turn him into a vilified egomaniac searching for compensation (Hissen 2010: 63). In the second stage, Hitler transforms his bitterness into a worldview that allows him to gain a sense of superiority and find an object for his hatred. Finally, the third stage shows Hitler learning to manipulate the people around him so they will accept his ideas and put them into practice (Hissen 2010: 64–7). The collective aspect of this psychologisation particularly, I argue, is better understood in conjunction with the film's heritage discourse, as it helps situate the figure of Hitler within contemporary politics, society and culture.

In fact, the conflict between father and son finds expression as a conflict about heritage. Hitler's wish to become a 'Kunstmaler' (artist)—the only word that he ever directs at the patriarch—is a protest against the Habsburg tradition that his father proudly personifies and that he demands Hitler continue. Hitler is shown to form his political identity by rejecting the heritage that surrounds him, and against which he pits his emerging ethnic nationalist convictions. At the local celebration of Franz Joseph I's diamond jubilee, for instance, Hitler is among the young men who try to drown the 'Kaiserhymne' (Emperor's Hymn) by chanting the 'Deutschlandlied' (Song of Germany). An important site for this political formation through heritage critique is the school, where we see Hitler and his classmates ridiculing a priest teaching religion, the priest functioning, for the young men, as a synecdoche for the entire Catholic Church. If Jesus was a Jew and not 'a Germanic luminary', how is the Germanic race supposed to believe in him, Hitler challenges the priest. Hitler, it becomes clear, is part of a generation intent on overthrowing tradition and revolutionising culture. Their disrespect for Habsburg and Catholic heritage is a reflection of their growing ethnic national zeal, which at this point still lacks a figure of identification.

It is worth looking beyond the nuclear family in *How They Became What They Were* because the school is where Hitler is first exposed to contemporary ideas about race and learns to embrace them. And, again, heritage is the medium through which he is shown to forge his political views. One of his teachers captivates him by interpreting the 'Nibelungenlied' (Song of the Nibelungs) not only as a German-Austrian national epic, but also as having the deeper meaning of an ongoing struggle against the dark enemy of the Slavic race. Hitler's early thoughts on race are thus equipped with cultural legitimacy and historical necessity. And they are shown to be conditioned by his surroundings: as the interviews with his former classmates illustrate, nationalist sentiments prevailed at his school, among both pupils and teachers. Troller even goes so far as to speculate that the school was also the place where Hitler began to apply his new convictions. In one scene, Hitler turns a game of dodge ball, literally called 'Völkerball' (ball of peoples) in German, into an ethnic nationalist competition, as he insists on only accepting Germanic pupils into his team. Already, even before the outbreak of the First World War, *How They Became What They Were* suggests, racial selection is prevalent, secretly approved of by Hitler's teacher and enthusiastically embraced by his Germanic comrades.

Uninterested in the art of his time—at the Academy of Fine Arts in Vienna, a professor criticises his lack of engagement with Impressionism or the Vienna Secession—Hitler explores the arsenal of cultural heritage to construct a counter-tradition to Habsburg Catholicism. In *How They Became What They Were*, heritage is what Hitler uses to give credibility and continuity to his understanding of nation and people, as well as to define his place in history and society. The importance which Troller and Corti give to this identity-building aspect of heritage is illustrated by the film's broad range of cultural references. Apart from architecture as a mirror for Hitler's ambition, and the 'Nibelungenlied' as a foil for his racial ideology, heritage in *How They Became What They Were* moreover includes music and philosophy. Wagner and Nietzsche are figures of identification for Hitler because of their striving for pre- and post-Christian values, respectively. Hitler chooses these figures to build an intellectual genealogy for himself, to place himself into a line of untimely yet prophetic national heroes. When he attends speeches by Dr Karl Lueger and Georg Heinrich Ritter von Schönerer in Vienna, Hitler's heritage-based self-image meets nationalist, anti-Semitic populism. There is an instant, strong affinity—if not continuity—between the two: although highly idiosyncratic in his coming-of-age and political formation, Hitler mirrors the ideological tendencies of his time.

As Hitler constructs his heritage and absorbs the ideologies surrounding him, he bit by bit acquires the words, expressions and gestures that we are familiar with, that we recognise him by. This change in performance reaches its culmination in the film's final scene, when Hitler welcomes the outbreak of the First World War. Observing himself in the mirror, he gives an impromptu speech about war as sacrifice and renewal, in actual fact an extract from his autobiographical manifesto *Mein Kampf* (*My Struggle*, 1925), still unpublished at the time the scene is set. There is a transformation in this scene which we can observe throughout *How They Became What They Were*: everyday situations turn into performances in which Hitler rehearses and consolidates his political persona. The fact that the entire speech is shot through a mirror of course underscores the narcissistic quality of this performance. However, more interesting in terms of the film's heritage discourse is Corti's second use of a freeze frame, following which Hitler's speech continues as a voiceover. It is an image clearly imitating the iconic photographs of the young Hitler taken by Heinrich Hoffmann in the 1920s. According to Hissen, this reference disrupts the film's focus on Hitler's development by citing the future 'Führer' and his 'negative myth' (Hissen 2010: 67). But perhaps one could also argue that the aim of *How They Became What They Were* is to change our perception of this imagery. Corti concludes the film with a kind of image that is well known to us but which, given the insight that we have gained into Hitler's personal and political development, we now see with different eyes. The Hitler myth such images helped to create has been debunked; the exceptional figure of the charismatic 'Führer' revealed to be a product of his time. *How They Became What They Were* thus also seeks to deconstruct the visual legacy of Nazism, the dark heritage of propagandistic iconography.

Similarly, in *Downfall* reference is also made to a historical photograph – to one of a rather different kind, however. In line with the film's aim of understanding the Third Reich from its end, *Downfall* does not cite a photograph of the young Hitler but one of the last photographs ever taken of him. Dated 20 April 1945, his birthday, it shows Hitler in front of his Berlin bunker, honouring a group of very young 'Volkssturm' (home guard) soldiers. In contrast to *How They Became What They Were*, the intention is not to deconstruct the iconography of the 'Führer' by revealing the disparity between reality and propaganda. Instead, *Downfall* re-enacts the photograph, emphasising how accurate the film's reconstruction of history is, while at the same time integrating the image into its period style. If *How They Became What They Were* is a heritage film in the sense of working through a political, social and cultural legacy, then *Downfall* is one in the sense of suggesting a coherent and complete audiovisual experience of history to the viewer.

Death Is My Trade: Criticising German Memory Through Film Heritage

In terms of its interest in the individual as a prism of social conditions and tendencies, Kotulla's *Death Is My Trade*, about Höß, is somewhat similar to Troller and Corti's *How They Became What They Were*. An adaptation of Robert Merle's novel *La mort est mon métier* (*Death Is My Trade*, 1952), the film also draws on Höß's statements during the Nuremberg trials as well as his autobiographical text *Kommandant in Auschwitz* (*Commandant in Auschwitz*), written while imprisoned in Poland and posthumously published by Martin Broszat in 1958. Interestingly, the German release title literally translates as 'from a German life', again situating the perpetrator figure within society and history more broadly. And, again in analogy to Troller and Corti, Kotulla also uses an episodic structure to narrate the genesis of a Nazi perpetrator. These episodes range from 1916, when Höß, being too young to join the German army, volunteers in a military hospital, to 1946 when he is arrested by the Americans and handed over to the Poles. Finally, the film uses the name 'Franz Lang' for its protagonist, the name which Höß himself took on when trying to hide from the Allies. In *Death Is My Trade*, 'Franz Lang' becomes a cipher for the ordinary German: just as many did after the Third Reich, Höß tries to pass as a normal person. In the process he becomes a symbolic everyman, both symptom and cause of the dictatorship and war.

Kotulla's film has a special place in German cinema for the analytical clarity and sociological sobriety with which it portrays one of the most notorious Nazi perpetrators. This achievement needs to be seen against his background in film criticism, most importantly his role as co-founder of the influential magazine *Filmkritik*, to which he contributed until 1969. For the founding generation of *Filmkritik*—apart from Kotulla, Wilfried Berghahn, Ulrich Gregor and Enno Patalas—the heritage of Weimar cinema, its socio-psychological interpretation by Siegfried Kracauer, as well as the 'Ideologiekritik' (ideological criticism) of the Frankfurt School, were major points of reference. Moreover, the magazine closely followed foreign developments such as Italian Neorealism, which it applauded for showing the social and political awareness that German cinema at the time severely lacked (Nechleba 2007: 24–5). As Kotulla moved from being a film critic to also being a filmmaker, his concern with film culture remained strong. This is illustrated by the fact that his first film was a television documentary about Robert Bresson, entitled *Zum Beispiel Bresson* (*Au hazard Bresson*, 1967), in which Kotulla accompanies and interviews the French *auteur* during the shooting of *Mouchette* (1967).

In *Death Is My Trade*, Kotulla not only examines the genesis of a Nazi perpetrator, but also, based on his understanding of film heritage, criticises the engagement with the Third Reich in post-war West German cinema. Kotulla expresses strong discontent with the image of the Nazi past in post-war film in a radio essay for Südwestfunk (Southwest Broadcasting) from 1962. In his view, the cinema of the Federal Republic lacks both art and conscience; it is a medium 'without sufficient self-awareness' (Kotulla 1962: 140). His scathing criticism is directed above all at what he recognises as the 'apologetic nature' of West German films about the Third Reich (Kotulla 1962: 146). Productions such as Bernhard Wicki's *Die Brücke* (*The Bridge*, 1959) or Frank Wisbar's *Nacht fiel über Gotenhafen* (*Darkness Fell on Gotenhafen*, 1959) are accused of systematically avoiding questions of guilt and responsibility. Dictatorship and war, Kotulla argues, are presented as 'inevitable natural disaster[s]' engulfing 'the innocent German people' (Kotulla 1962: 147). Dutiful soldiers are neatly separated from criminal Nazis, and the heroes of the resistance celebrated (Kotulla 1962: 147–8). This critique, which is canonical today, illustrates Kotulla's sustained occupation with the ethics of historical representation, and the importance which he gave to film as a medium for remembering and reflecting the dark heritage of the Nazi past.

A partial exception in Kotulla's account of post-war film is Wolfgang Staudte's *Die Mörder sind unter uns* (*The Murderers Are Among Us*, 1946). This has a lot to do with how Staudte dramatises issues of guilt and responsibility, in the ethical not juridical sense. In an article for *Filmkritik* from 1960, Kotulla emphasises how the character of Brückner, who as Wehrmacht captain gave the order to shoot 121 civilians, is unable to grasp his guilt. It is moreover significant for Kotulla that the protagonist Dr Mertens, a military surgeon and bystander to the crime, reveals through his compulsive behaviour how conscience-stricken he actually is. Yet, while Kotulla is sympathetic to some of the messages that Staudte intends to convey, he deems his aesthetic strategies anachronistic and problematic. He identifies 'questionable clichés of the German film tradition' in *The Murderers Are Among Us*, 'that of the passive hero first of all, who only has the powers of the mind to stake against the blows of fate' (Kotulla 1960a: 101). Kotulla judges Staudte's 'Trümmerfilm' (Rubble film) as both a beginning and an end: a beginning for its attempt to work through the Nazi past, and an end for yielding the insight that 'the new reality demanded a new style' (Kotulla 1960a: 101). A productive engagement with the legacy of the Third Reich, Kotulla insists, requires a renewal of German film, and a rupture with a part of its heritage.

While Kotulla did not belong to the generation of the New German Cinema, like many of the younger filmmakers he also looked abroad to find models for his film language. Already as critic, and later as writer/director, he was intrigued by a kind of cinema in which style is not used for effect but as a way of viewing the world. What fellow critic and long-time commissioning editor Heinz Ungereit says about Kotulla's reviews of films by Bresson and Buñuel, for instance, can be taken as an implicit agenda for Kotulla's own practice: 'aesthetic structures and details' are understood as being one and the same as the 'ideological substance' of a film (Ungereit 2005: 13). In contrast to Christine Haase, who stresses the influence of Brechtian 'Verfremdung' (defamiliarisation) on *Death Is My Trade* (Haase 2002: 50–2), I would therefore highlight Kotulla's engagement with the European art-house cinema of his time. Apart from Bresson—particularly his *Mouchette*—Kotulla moreover appreciated the work of Michelangelo Antonioni, whose *Il Grido* (*The Cry*, 1957) he closely analysed in terms of style and perspective. As Kotulla concludes his review of the film in *Filmkritik*: 'Antonioni's point of view is "phenomenological". [...] He keeps an agonising, cool distance from what he shows' (Kotulla 1960b: 104). What interests Kotulla is not character psychology or viewer identification, but the acts of showing and seeing, and the space of reflection that opens up between the two.

For Kotulla's exploration of how Höß turns into a Nazi perpetrator in *Death Is My Trade*, this means that he proposes neither individual psychology nor social determinism as explanations. Instead of trying to demonstrate the causes of Höß's development, he describes its circumstances, what prepared the ground for his career as camp commandant, without this being an inevitable outcome of his life. Kotulla does not at all present Höß as an incarnation of evil, or as someone who, filled with hatred, relishes in his crimes. Rather, his figure—as well as our understanding of it—is always situated in the specific cultural, social and political context of the time. Following Haase, three traditions can be said to form the conditions for the possibility of Höß: 'religion, absolutism, and patriarchy', 'higher powers that "know best"' and demand submission (Haase 2002: 52). I would add to this militarism, which seems particularly important for training Höß to obey. Throughout his career, Höß defines himself as a soldier, and he states, while in American captivity, that he would repeat the extermination of Jews if he was ordered to do so. Yet Kotulla's film refrains from drawing a direct connection between any of these traditions and Höß's crimes. In fact, one could argue that the three traditions that Haase mentions are in a state of crisis: there is no reference to the influence of the church—instead, as a young man, Höß learns the mantra 'my church is Germany'. He turns not towards absolutism, but Nazism, and, due to his father's early death, the Höß family lacks its patriarch. We may see Hitler as replacing and uniting these three traditions, as Haase does. However, the figure of Hitler is curiously absent from the entire film, appearing only sporadically in iconic portraits, without Höß reacting to them. This openness in representation is precisely what makes Kotulla's film so unsettling: it situates the character of Höß in such a way that we are prevented from gaining a clear-cut explanation for his later development. In *Death Is My Trade*, we do not discover an essence but observe a process of becoming, a process that also implicates the spectator, forcing us to reflect upon its workings.

This approach is particularly challenging when Kotulla shows how Höß learns to obey unconditionally and ceases to act with empathy. *Death Is My Trade* narrates Höß's development in small steps, with a focus not on inner but outer transformation. The first episode, for instance, shows Höß as a young man, volunteering in a military hospital as he is too young to join the army. Here, a wounded captain introduces him to the spirit and ethics of militarism, namely, to give absolute value to obedience in the name of the fatherland. What I would like to highlight in Haase's detailed interpretation of this scene is the fact that Höß acquires obedience through action (Haase 2002: 53). The captain, whose wounded arms are in a cast, orders Höß to help him smoke a cigarette. In a grotesque shot, Höß follows the captain's commands, putting the cigarette into his mouth and taking it out again in a mechanical fashion. Coupled with this literal obedience is an increasingly bewildering lack of empathy. The extent of this lack is revealed in stages: during the First World War, Höß turns against a comrade to enforce an order from his superior, and after the war, as a factory worker, he refuses to show solidarity with his co-workers to meet the quota set by his foreman. Again, Kotulla operates not on the psychological level but views Höß from an ethnographic perspective. There is a stark difference here from how *How They Became What They Were*—although also concerned with the becoming of a perpetrator figure—engages with the dark heritage of the Nazi past: *Death Is My Trade* does not trace Höß's ideological formation but analyses how he conditions his body into a tool for authority (see Jansen 1977).

A crucial moment occurs when Höß's obedience begins to have deadly consequences. In 1920, having joined the Freikorps Roßbach, Höß guards a group of Communists who are destined for execution, among them a comrade from the First World War. Höß tells his lieutenant about the comrade, but to no avail: he has to accept that orders are to be followed at all costs. Mise-en-scène is vital for conveying how Höß learns this lesson, illustrating the unity of style and ideology throughout the film which Kotulla valued about the works of Bresson and Antonioni. Sound design, and its selective use, is also an important feature of *Death Is My Trade*. Except for the opening credits, there is no music, the dialogue is for the most part minimalistic, and atmospheric sounds feel muted, making the surrounding world seem remote and uninvolved. The cinematography is likewise restrained and characterised by a sense of distance. Close-ups of Höß and the lieutenant at the beginning of the scene serve to convey not intimacy but the giving and receiving of a command. Static frames and slow pans, combined with the subdued performances of leads and extras, create a scene which, despite steering towards the inevitable—Höß's killing of the comrade—is devoid of suspense. A silent exchange of gazes between Höß and the comrade reminds us that following orders requires the suppression of empathy: the comrade smiles at Höß who adjusts his collar and looks away, implicitly acknowledging how unsettling the comrade's look is for him. By trying to flee, the comrade turns into a moving target—a rare, effective tracking shot focuses on the back of his head—and Höß chases and shoots him as we expect him to. Both sound and image concentrate on the basic actions that Höß, following orders, learns to perform and that, step by step, make him the perpetrator that history knows him to be. Taking inspiration from the art-house cinema of the time to break free from the (West) German film tradition, Kotulla offers a perspective that is immanent, dissecting Höß's career in order to treat it didactically.

As camp commandant, Höß has not only perfected control over his body but also disciplined his vision. The act of killing has been depersonalised, from pulling the trigger to lifting the receiver to demand a higher number of people to be gassed. When asked by his wife if he would kill his own children if ordered to do so, Höß replies that it is 'physically impossible' for him not to obey a command. Action by action, deed after deed, the ethics of militarism has penetrated his body and mind. As Höß explains, first to his wife and later to an American investigator, he believes that his convictions are irrelevant, and that responsibility lies with those in command. He is unable to grasp that he has an innate responsibility for his own actions, and that he reaffirms Nazi ideology by enacting it. Höß's perspective is a radically internal one, and this is reflected in the film's visual regime. For instance, throughout the scenes set in the camp, we hardly see a dead body, and all of the killing happens off screen. Mise-en-scène in *Death Is My Trade* is shaped by Höß's view of the world.

In a critical review published at the time of the film's release, Gertrud Koch argues that *Death Is My Trade* forces us to assume the perpetrator's gaze on his victims. In such moments, Koch explains, the film meets 'the limits of reconstruction', presupposing that the viewer has sufficient knowledge about Auschwitz to fill the gaps in what is shown. In contrast to Koch, I would not speak of identification, but rather of a style which allows us to see the limitations of Höß's vision. As Peter W. Jansen has said about Kotulla's films in general, looks do not only tell a story but also configure how a story is told (Jansen 2005: 27). A case in point is the scene in which an inmate is shot and the camera stays on Höß, walking away from the scene without turning around, and ordering his assistant to do the same and wait for the report. While there is visual reference to the Holocaust, it is mediated through the perspective of the Kulmhof commandant who describes the sight of the murdered in drastic images that betray his racist perception. When Lang stops him to keep knowledge of the murder of Jews from his wife, it becomes clear that his work relies on the censorship of vision, for others as well as for himself. In *Death Is My Trade*, Nazi ideology is visualised through a selective and distorted point of view. In response to the pseudo-realist, effect-heavy cinema of Wisbar, for instance, and post-war West German film more broadly, Kotulla develops a style that works with omissions, aiming to, as he puts it, mobilise 'the critical phantasy' of the viewer (Stempel 1977).

In *Downfall*, we find neither a comparable phenomenological distance from the events and the 'Führer', nor a comparable style that seeks to highlight the distortions and omissions of his worldview. By contrast, our perspective is closely aligned with that of Traudl Junge, Hitler's private secretary, bringing us close to and sometimes even encouraging us to empathise with him. As I have argued elsewhere, *Downfall* thus sets up a play of attraction and repulsion in the face of the seductive powers of the charismatic 'Führer', a dialectic which in fact can be found in a range of German films about Nazi perpetrators since the 1990s (Bangert 2014: 4–6, 55ff.). When *Downfall* works with omissions, in most cases these have to do with the limitations of Junge's point of view, what she fails to recognise or put into context. Junge's character serves to convey dark heritage as emotional history, to the point of inciting highly ambivalent feelings of intimacy with Hitler.

Untimely Enquiries into Dark Heritage

The two films prompt us to face the dark heritage of Nazi perpetrators in rather different ways. While in *How They Became What They Were*, we follow the genesis of Hitler's political ideology, and how it becomes a tool for social manipulation, in *Death Is My Trade*, the focus is on obedience and the disciplining of Höß's body and vision. And while Troller and Corti mostly remain within the conventions of post-war West German/Austrian television docudrama, Kotulla uses foreign influences to formulate a critique of the West German coming to terms with the Nazi past that is both aesthetic and political. Yet, by tracing the collective roots of how Hitler and Höß became what they were, both films engage with the legacy of Nazi perpetration in a way that was untypical of its time.

How untimely *How They Became What They Were* and *Death Is My Trade* were is illustrated by the fact that the most successful portrayal of a Nazi perpetrator in 1970s German-language film was *Hitler—eine Karriere* (*Hitler, a Career*, Joachim Fest and Christian Herrendoerfer, 1977), a compilation film consisting almost entirely of propaganda footage. Its portrayal of Hitler as charismatic leader and seducer of the German people had a much stronger impact on historical consciousness than the engagement with the social and political circumstances of perpetrator biographies in the films by Troller and Corti, as well as Kotulla. Moreover, while the Landesbildstelle Bayern, a public institution providing access to audiovisual materials for education in Bavaria, recommended *Hitler, a Career*, it excluded *Death Is My Trade* from use in schools. Given the critical success of Kotulla's film, as well as the fact that it had been rated 'particularly valuable' by Filmbewertungsstelle (National Board of Film Classification) Wiesbaden, this led to critical articles in the German press as well as a polemic response by the director himself (see Frank 1978; Kotulla 1978). The rejection of Kotulla's and embracing of Fest and Herrendoerfer's film in Bavaria reinforces a point that *How They Became What They Were* makes about the challenge implicit in portraying Hitler: that to engage with the dark heritage of Nazi perpetrators requires one to reflect the influence of propagandistic images instead of reproducing them, as in *Hitler, a Career*. If, from today's point of view, *How They Became What They Were* and *Death Is My Trade* appear as important works of German-language film heritage, it should be kept in mind that their collective enquiry into the legacy of Nazi perpetration was an exception.

Finally, the films by Troller and Corti as well as Kotulla illustrate what by comparison is unique about a contemporary German dark heritage film such as *Downfall*. Instead of allowing for a critical distance between viewer, perpetrator figure and strategy of portrayal, the heritage style of Hirschbiegel's film plunges us into history as happening in the 'here and now'. And, through the figure of Junge, *Downfall* brings us seductively close to Hitler as the Third Reich's main perpetrator. Without wanting to ignore the problems of this approach, one could argue that the film thus adds a new layer to the discourse about dark heritage and Nazi perpetrators, namely, by shifting the focus from the social conditions of how they became what they were to their relationship with ordinary Germans who, like Junge, for instance, believed and trusted in Hitler. This interpretation would again understand the heritage film as a vessel for emotional histories, in this case feelings of identification with, and attachment to,

Nazi perpetrators—an extremely difficult and rarely addressed legacy of the Nazi past.

WORKS CITED

Aurich, R., and W. Jacobsen, eds. 2005. *Theodor Kotulla: Regisseur und Kritiker.* Munich: Edition Text + Kritik.
Bangert, A. 2014. *The Nazi past in contemporary German film: Viewing experiences of intimacy and immersion.* Rochester: Camden House.
Boldt, Gerhard. 1947. *Hitler: Die letzten Tage in der Reichskanzlei.* Hamburg: Rowohlt.
Boswell, M. 2013. Dark heritage, identity and community: In conversation with Matthew Boswell. [Online]. Available at: http://arts.leeds.ac.uk/screeningeuropeanheritage/dark-heritage-identity-and-community-in-conversation-with-matthew-boswell/. Accessed 14 June 2013.
Elsaesser, T. 2005. *European cinema: Face to face with Hollywood.* Amsterdam: Amsterdam University Press.
Fischer, T., and M.N. Lorenz, eds. 2007. *Lexikon der 'Vergangenheitsbewältigung' in Deutschland: Debatten- und Diskursgeschichte des Nationalsozialismus nach 1945.* Bielefield: Transcript.
Frank, M. 1978. Eine bayerische Behörde und ein deutsches Leben. *Süddeutsche Zeitung*, 16 October.
Haase, C. 2002. Theodor Kotulla's excerpts from a German life (*Aus einem deutschen Leben*, 1977) or The inability to speak: Cinematic holocaust representation in Germany. *Film & History: An Interdisciplinary Journal of Film and Television Studies* 32(2): 48–61.
Higson, A. 1993. Re-presenting the national Past: Nostalgia and pastiche in the heritage film. In *British Cinema and Thatcherism*, ed. L. Friedman, 109–129. London: University College London Press.
———. 2003. *English heritage, English cinema: Costume drama since 1980.* Oxford: Oxford University Press.
Hissen, A. 2010. *Hitler im deutschsprachigen Spielfilm nach 1945: Ein filmgeschichtlicher Überblick.* Trier: Wissenschaftlicher Verlag Trier.
Hitler, Adolf. 1925. *Mein Kampf.* Munich: Eher Verlag.
Höß, R. 1958. In *Kommandant in Auschwitz*, ed. M. Broszat, Munich: Deutsche Verlags-Anstalt.
Jansen, P.W. 1977. Der vermeidbare Aufstieg des Rudolf Höß. *Vorwärts*, 15 December.
———. 2005. Sehen, Schreiben, Zeigen. In *Theodor Kotulla*, eds. R. Aurich and W. Jacobsen, 20–34.
Kansteiner, W. 2006. *In pursuit of German memory: History, television, and politics after Auschwitz.* Athens: Ohio University Press.

Knapp, G. 1978. Aus einem deutschen Leben. *Süddeutsche Zeitung*, 17 February.
Koch, G. 1977. Aus einem deutschen (Faschisten-)Leben. *Frankfurter Rundschau*, 19 November.
Kotulla, T. 1960a. Die Mörder sind unter uns. In *Theodor Kotulla*, eds. R. Aurich and W. Jacobsen, 100–102. 2005.
———. 1960b. Der Schrei. In *Theodor Kotulla*, eds. R. Aurich and W. Jacobsen, 102–105. 2005.
———. 1962. Das Gesellschaftsbild des modernen Films. Die Filme der Bundesrepublik. In *Theodor Kotulla*, eds. R. Aurich and W. Jacobsen, 139–149. 2005.
———. 1978. *Aus einem deutschen Leben* – ein mißverstandener Film? Erfahrungen mit Zuschauern und einer Behörde. In *Theodor Kotulla*, eds. R. Aurich and W. Jacobsen, 2005, 215–224.
Löbl, K. 1973. Kunst für Wahrheit. *Kurier*, 1 December.
Merle, R. 1952. *La mort est mon métier*. Paris: Gallimard.
N.N. 1973. Wie wurde der das? *Der Spiegel* 48: 169–170.
Nechleba, M. 2007. 50 Jahre Filmkritik. In *Programmheft*, vol 13, ed. Filmmuseum München, 24–27.
Neumüller, R., I. Schramm, and W. Stickler, eds. 2003. *Axel Corti: Filme, Texte und Wegbegleiter*. Weitra: Bibliothek der Provinz.
Rentschler, E. 2013. The lives of others: The history of heritage and the rhetoric of consensus. In *The lives of others and contemporary German film*, ed. P. Cooke, 241–260. Berlin: De Gruyter.
Stempel, H. 1977. Weder Unmensch noch Psychopath. *Frankfurter Rundschau*, 4 March.
Troller, G.S. 1988. *Selbstbeschreibung*. Hamburg: Rasch und Röhring.
Ungereit, H. 2005. Das Widerständige der Hagemann-Clique. In *Theodor Kotulla*, eds. R. Aurich and W. Jacobsen, 7–19.
Vidal, B. 2012. *Heritage film: Nation genre representation*. London: Wallflower.

CHAPTER 7

Spectral Spanish Heritage: The Hauntology of *La noche de los girasoles* (*The Night of the Sunflowers*)

Paul Mitchell

Notions of heritage and, in particular, its association with nostalgia are without doubt highly problematic when applied to the context of Spain, not least because of the brutal Civil War that ravaged the nation in the 1930s and which led to 36 years of nationalist autocratic rule under Franco, the self-proclaimed *el Caudillo de la Última Cruzada y de la Hispanidad* (Leader of the Last Crusade and of Spanish Heritage). Barry Jordan and Mark Allinson have described how 'Spain's natural geography works against a strong sense of national identity' (2005: 137). Nonetheless, this was the central aim of Franco's project, his desire to achieve linguistic homogeneity by outlawing the Basque, Galician and Catalan languages, the clearest example of how Spain's cultural diversity was suppressed. In addition, Franco's promotion of bullfighting and flamenco as typical Spanish customs reveal his attempt to impose nationally what Benedict Anderson refers to as an 'imagined community' (1991: 6). The problematic nature of such a strategy, a reflection of a fundamentally reductive understanding of Spanish heritage upon which Francoism was

P. Mitchell (✉)
Universidad Católica de Valencia San Mártir, Valencia, Spain
e-mail: paul.mitchell@ucv.es

© The Editor(s) (if applicable) and The Author(s) 2016
P. Cooke, R. Stone (eds.), *Screening European Heritage*,
Palgrave European Film and Media Studies,
DOI 10.1057/978-1-137-52280-1_7

based, is conveyed by Ernest Gellner's belief that nationalism 'is not the awakening of nations to self-consciousness: it invents nations that do not exist' (1964: 169). Rather than solely conquering the land to unify the diverse provinces and populations of Spain under one ruler, therefore, the legacy of the Civil War meant that the landscape itself remained an ideological battlefield, a palimpsest upon which Spanish heritage could be reinscribed with the image of Francoist nationalism and erased by those who opposed it. As Nathan Richardson suggests, 'Franco's government overtly attempted to employ space as a key weapon in their blitzkrieg of Spanish identity' (2011: 33).

Spanish cinema, like other European cinemas, has a long tradition of figuring the rural milieu in terms of 'homeland'. Indeed, during the early years of the dictatorship, rural existence became glorified in much government-endorsed cinema as a locus of authentic *Spanish* identity.[1] As Juan Andrés Blanco Rodríguez explains, 'Francoist values, at least those in the early years, were fundamentally rural' (1998: 368). Hence, in *Raza* (*Race*, Sáenz de Heredía, 1942), a story drafted by Franco himself (although under the pseudonym of Jaime de Andrade), the timeless stability of the Spanish homeland is figured metonymically through repeated landscape shots of Galicia—'an attempt to establish national unity through an imaginary common patrimony and past' (Pavlović 2009: 64); whereas, in *Surcos* (*Furrows*, José Antonio Nieves Conde, 1951), a family migrate from their village to the city in search of prosperity but find only corruption and degradation. Although the film emphasises the hardship of agrarian existence, the rural environment is clearly posited by Nieves Conde in ideological terms, its Manichean difference from the urban suggesting it as the crucible of traditional family values. To this extent, *Surcos* is complicit with the moral conservatism that underpinned Francosim. Thus, the opening intertitle informs us that, in their removal from the countryside, the family become 'rootless trees, suburban splinters that life destroys and corrupts'.

The traditionalist outlook of a regime that chose to adopt a nostalgic attitude to the pre-industrial world is clearly indicated by Franco's fanciful envisioning of Spain as 'a peaceful forest' (Kinder 1993: 348). Central to this mythopoeia was the figure of the noble *campesino* (agrarian peasant), whose 'robustness, authenticity and austerity [...] represented, from the Francoist perspective, Spanish racial values in their purest form' (Blanco Rodríguez 1998: 368–9). Such propaganda, an imagining of the populace in keeping with the rural priorities of Francoism in the immediate postwar years, has had a significant impact on the Spanish social and cinematic landscape; and yet, as much as it initially encouraged a laudatory (quasi-paradisiacal) representation of the nation's countryside—one which, as Ann Davies suggests, is ironically mirrored by several more recent Basque films (2012: 69–77)—it has ultimately provoked a significant and sustained backlash, with a number of dissident directors from the 1950s onwards, including Carlos Saura (*La caza* [*The Hunt*], 1966), José Luis Borau (*Furtivos* [*Poachers*], 1975) and Ricardo Franco (*Pascual Duarte*, 1976) among others, choosing to express their opposition to the dictatorship in terms of landscape and, in particular, via the depiction of a rural space that is both hostile and destructive (Faulkner 2006: 35). From this, it is clear that the Spanish countryside has become a highly contested filmic terrain, a culturally imagined (and imaginary) site upon which complex ideological conflicts about Francoism and its (mis)representation of national identity have been often acrimoniously inscribed.

This chapter will evaluate the representation of the village in the Spanish film *La noche de los girasoles* (*The Night of the Sunflowers*, Jorge Sánchez-Cabezudo, 2006) from the perspective of heritage cinema and, thereby, intends to explore the manner in which Sánchez-Cabezudo uses a rural location to interrogate persistent elements of the nation's cultural (and Francoist) legacy. Throughout my analysis, I will make reference to several other rural-based films as *The Night of the Sunflowers* achieves much of its impact when it is considered dialogically, that is as an intertext in conversation with the historical imagining of location in Spanish cinema. The term 'location' is used here to refer to a confluence of place, space and landscape and, in doing so, I acknowledge Davies's key observation that location must be understood as something which is invested with the unstable dynamism of subjective meaning. It is not my intention to explore the village as a cinematic location in order to uncover any essentialist notions of 'true Spain'—to do so is 'an impossible possibility' (Davies 2012: 5)—but rather to observe the manner in which films 'do not simply represent or express the stable features of a national culture, but are themselves one of the loci of debates about a nation's governing principles, goals, heritage and history' (Hjort and Mackenzie 2000: 4).

Heritage as Hauntology

The Night of the Sunflowers is not a heritage product in any conventional sense. Most significantly, it flouts the usual stipulation that a heritage film should convey 'the *material world* of the past' (Monk 2011: 17; emphasis in original)—whether that be distant or more recent—because the village in which it is set is of the contemporary world. As a consequence, nor does it bear witness to heritage cinema's 'discourse of authenticity' (Higson 1995: 26) and its attempt, through the use of costume and artefacts, for example, to convince the spectator that the world it embodies is a faithful reproduction of the historical reality on which it is based. Furthermore, the function of nostalgia, frequently a key element in conventional heritage cinema, is also problematic in the context of *The Night of the Sunflowers* when we take into account the cultural ramifications of *el pacto de olvido* (the pact of forgetting) which was enshrined by the 1977 Amnesty Law as an attempt to deal with the legacy of Francoism during the period of transition after the dictator's death.[2] The direct cultural impact of this has been that many Spaniards wilfully refuse to remember the past, a resonant silence about their heritage more typical than any sense of nostalgia. In the words of Jo Labanyi, 'contemporary Spanish culture [...] is based on a rejection of the past' (2000: 65). Indeed, the recent post-heritage film *La isla minima* (*Marshland*, Alberto Rodriguez, 2014) symbolically enacts this cultural amnesia when, in the final shot, Pedro (Raúl Arévalo) tears up the photographic evidence of his police colleague's crimes during the dictatorship.[3]

Owing to the contemporaneity of its setting, *The Night of the Sunflowers* is most often identified as a thriller or *noir* (Herrero 2010; Whittaker 2013) and yet it still contains significant heritage elements that reflect the manner in which Sánchez-Cabezudo implicitly explores Spain's ambivalent relationship with its past. In this sense, heritage cinema is an intertextual prism through which the director can refract the present as conterminous with what it is not, a filmic history that is figured not as an absence but as what Derrida terms a 'hauntology': '[it] is neither [...] present nor absent [...] [it is] an interpretation that transforms the very thing it interprets' (Derrida 1994: 63). This absence is rendered perceptible in the film by the spectators' awareness that something is lacking and, in this way, we sense how the contemporary moment is necessarily determined by a no longer materially existent past. These vestiges of history, which become embodied through the film's use of landscape, are spectres that dislocate the homogeneity of the present by disrupting 'the border between the present, the actual or present reality of the present, and everything that can be opposed to it: absence, non-presence, non-effectivity, inactuality, virtuality, or even the simulacrum in general' (Derrida 1994: 48). Thus, if heritage cinema can be understood as the mode in which contemporary concerns are filtered through the past—or, as Belén Vidal suggests, 'a disturbing symptom of our inability to think historically about the present' (2012: 17)—what I will refer to as 'spectral heritage' reverses this process, reifying the present in order to indicate how it is haunted by a 'non-object, [a] non-present present' (Derrida 1994: 5), the ghost of history that is sensed within the cinematic text as the presence of an absence.

In recent years, the concept of haunting has become increasingly important to the analysis of post-Franco film (Labanyi 2000, 2001a; Davies 2012; Whittaker 2013, 2014; Marsh 2014)—although not until now in relation to heritage cinema as a mechanism which self-reflexively reveals such spectrality. In this chapter, I will argue that *The Night of the Sunflowers* exemplifies spectral heritage cinema because the past, although temporally absent, is a ghostly presence that haunts and informs its ontological present. In particular, this chapter will focus on how the historical reality of Spanish rural-urban migration is spectrally evoked through the film's exploration of contemporary rural tourism. This ghost of the past in inscribed upon the film's diegetic landscape and yet, in contrast to conventional heritage cinema, *The Night of the Sunflowers* fails to sustain the usual ideological association between land and cultural nostalgia, indicating instead how the Spanish countryside is a locus from which the negative imprint of historical suffering cannot be exorcised or erased. Heritage, as a Derridean hauntology, thus provides a (material and immaterial) dimension that inscribes itself on the representation of the modern Spanish village in which the film is set and which renders the landscape as a site of (dis)location. My analysis is indebted to Henri Lefebvre's understanding of how physical landscape (or 'perceived space') interacts with the manner in which it is experienced (as either 'mental space' or 'social space'), so as to explore how cinema subjectively produces (rather than objectively reflects) location. Lefebvre differentiates spatial practice (*espace perçu*), or 'the deciphering of [society's] space' (1991: 38), from representations of space (*espace conçu*), which, through the work of 'scientists, planners, urbanists [and] social engineers' (1991: 28), take on specific cultural meanings. As the latter involves the organisation or cultural production of space, it is intrinsically linked to the socio-political hegemony. Thus, 'in addition to being a means of production it is also a means of control, and hence domination, of power' (Lefebvre 1991: 26). For Lefebvre, however, perceived and mental spaces are fundamentally symbiotic because they 'embody and nourish each other' (1991: 30). In contrast to these, Lefebvre identifies representational (or social) space (*espace veću*) as that which 'the imagination seeks to change and appropriate. It overlays physical space, making symbolic use of its objects' (1991: 39). Taking these three concepts, I will argue that *The Night of the Sunflowers* self-reflexively interrogates the political structuring of the film's Spanish village as a heritage site and, in so doing, demonstrates how representational space, 'a tool of thought and action' (Lefebvre 1991: 26), functions as a counterpoint to representations of rural space in the historical/cinematic past. In this way, the rural landscape of Spain becomes a palimpsest upon which the nation's cultural memory is both marked and, through the process of Sánchez-Cabezudo's filmic reinscription, overwritten with new historical traces. For Whittaker, this is manifested by the centrality of violence in the film which, as mentioned above, is a key constituent of post-heritage cinema. Here it functions as an historical echo, 'the immaterial traces of a violent past that resounds in the present' (Whittaker 2013: 166). However, my own analysis will explore *The Night of the Sunflowers* in terms of three further symbolic elements that constitute its representational space and which contribute to its cinematic hauntology: the film's exploration of modern tourism, the theme of historical rural depopulation, and, as a segue between the two, the importance of Castile as a cinematic location.

Heritage, Landscape and Tourism

The Night of the Sunflowers is a film about contemporary Spain in which heritage, as it is manifested by the Spanish landscape, is a primary concern. Indeed, the reason for Esteban's (Carmelo Gómez) arrival in the Castilian village of the film's diegesis is precisely because, as a speleologist, he has been brought from Madrid to inspect the cave that the residents hope to exploit for its touristic potential. In Lefebvrean terms, they seek to transform the spatial practice of the cave into a representation of space, a rural heritage site with economic advantages for the local community. As local mayor, Julián (Enrique Martínez) explains, '"Rural tourism", that's what they call it. It's all the rage. This area has possibilities, but first we need to be on the map.' Whittaker has rightly suggested that *The Night of the Sunflowers* provides an archaeology of Spain's rural memory, where the rural emerges as traces of a violent and monstrous nightmare' (2013: 159), but the film is also significant for the manner in which it self-reflexively explores the rural as a problematic Spanish heritage location, a place 'for both the articulation and interrogation of nostalgia' (Faulkner 2006: 35). The commodification of cultural authenticity is a key element of the film, a notion that is reinforced by the weight given to Esteban's expert evaluation of the cave's potential marketability. Yet, as Sánchez-Cabezudo chooses to locate his narrative in the fictional Castilian village of Angosto, *The Night of the Sunflowers* also foregrounds the important function of artifice within the economy of (cinematic) heritage. In this way, the timeless materiality of the Spanish landscape, which the camera's tracking and establishing shots try to 'capture [...] in its totality' (Whittaker 2013: 162), is rendered as a representational space, an intertextual absence/presence—in this case literally, via the film's central symbol of the cave—which is reinscribed with the ghostly presence of historical socio-cultural and cinematic references. In fact, the resonant motif of the cave in *The Night of the Sunflowers* is intertextually reminiscent of the hollow tree stump that lies at the heart of the forest in Julio Medem's *Vacas* (*Cows*, 1992), both of them encapsulating the interface between material existence and its erasure, or how physical landscape becomes transformed through its cinematic representation into a culturally encoded space. As Derrida suggests: 'Representation *in the abyss* of presence is not an accident of presence; the desire of presence is, on the contrary, born from the abyss (the infinite multiplication) of representation' (1998: 163; emphasis in original).

In attempting to reconstruct Angosto (in English, the name means 'narrow') from the perspective of the 'tourist gaze' (Urry and Larsen 2011:5), the Castilian locals wish to invest this space with cultural meaning, a hegemonic reimagining of the village as a heritage location fit for the consumption of a modern, urban Spain that is embodied by Esteban and his companions.[4] In this sense, the presence of Carmelo Gómez in *The Night of the Sunflowers* is particularly interesting, given that his screen persona is often intimately associated with a sense of rootedness to the landscape whereby he embodies an 'allegiance to what Anderson has famously called "imagined community"—to "being Spanish" at a number of different levels' (Perriam 2003: 72). Indeed, Whittaker suggests that 'rural space is refracted through the urban gaze of Pedro, Esteban and Gabi—an effect which is created through a conspicuous use of eye-line matches and point-of-view shots' (2013: 163). Yet, the impulse to envision (and demarcate) the landscape as a tourist spectacle seems decidedly at odds with the reaction of 'los chicos de la ciudad' (the city folk) themselves. Although Whittaker argues that Pedro's (Mariano Alameda) camera fixes the rural as 'an exotic Other' (2013: 163), his character actually undermines such a viewpoint, perceiving instead the hollow performativity that the representation of (tourist) space in Angosto entails. Pedro's dismissive reference to the cave as 'una mierda' (a piece of shit), an echo of Esteban's equally cynical statement, 'I know the story, I've seen hundreds of pueblos like this', thereby draws attention to Urry and Larsen's observation that 'the [tourist] gaze in any historical period is constructed in relationship to its opposite, to non-tourist forms of social experience and consciousness' (2011: 3). This ironic opposition—between the locals who see their village as a representation of space (for the imagined/imaginary tourist) and Pedro/Esteban (themselves 'tourists') whose resistance to such commodification symbolises the film's representational space—reveals how the dual perspective of the insider/outsider is crucial to the impact of *The Night of the Sunflowers*. In short, it is through this mechanism that we are better able to appreciate the film's inscription of the heritage it represents as a hauntology.

This is particularly well illustrated by the manner in which Cecilio's (Cesáreo Estébanez) movement within his local landscape is parallelled and contrasted with that of the outsider, Miguel (Manuel Morón). The two characters demand to be understood in tandem given that Cecilio is introduced into the film via the intertitle 'The Man on the Road', a reference that implicitly connects him with Miguel, the travelling vacuum cleaner salesman whose rape of Gabi (Judith Diakhate) ironically precipitates Cecilio's later murder. Whittaker sees this death metaphorically as a comment on the plight of Spanish agrarian culture in the contemporary world, arguing that, 'killed in part by his own tool, [it] more widely suggests the greater implosion of rural Spain' (2013: 161). While this might be true, it is of course also significant that Cecilio is killed by another outsider, Esteban, and, in this sense, *The Night of the Sunflowers* recalls Nieve Conde's suggestion in *Surcos* that violence is a destructive force of external origin. (At one point in the film, a mid-shot of Miguel's car tellingly reveals that it has been registered in the Valencian region.) The film begins with a static long shot of Miguel emerging from a field of sunflowers before he gets into his car and drives away, the fecundity of the darkened landscape in significant opposition to the brightly lit shot that first introduces Cecilio standing on the arid soil of his field. The subsequent montage of newsreel footage indicates that Miguel is in fact the murderer of Elena Marcos, a young woman from the local village of Cerredo, and that we have just witnessed the disposal of her corpse. As a travelling salesman, Miguel has a peripatetic lifestyle that facilitates his crimes, allowing him to target isolated victims before absconding from the murder scene and, as the end of the film makes clear, from ultimate detection by the police—a fate which parallels that of Cecilio, whose corpse remains undetected in the cave into which it was thrown by Esteban.

Structurally, *The Night of the Sunflowers* both begins and ends with Miguel and, in an intertextual echo of both the Castile-based *El espíritu de la colmena* (*The Spirit of the Beehive*, Víctor Erice, 1973) and *Tierra sin pan* aka *Las Hurdes* (*Land Without Bread*, Luis Buñuel, 1933), the film closes with an over-the-shoulder shot of Miguel watching a documentary about beekeeping in the village of Las Hurdes, the voiceover of which emphasises that what we have just witnessed is a manifestation of specifically human brutality: 'Bees don't attack people as much as you might think. If you don't bother them, they won't bother you.' Whittaker wonders if this 'homage' to Buñuel is 'accidental' (2013: 166). However, the fact that such cinematic ghosts can be sensed within (or beyond) the film's material diegesis is more significant than whether Sánchez-Cabezudo intends them to be there or not. Indeed, it is this absence/presence that constitutes the film's hauntology, its self-reflexive and spectral exploration of the national cinema. Faulkner has commented on the beehive metaphor as a reflection of 'a fractured society of atomized lives' (2006: 174), a notion that seems to be particularly appropriate to describe the nature of Miguel's enigmatic character in *The Night of the Sunflowers*. He himself functions almost spectrally, a ghostly predator whose misogynistic violence haunts and fleetingly disrupts the superficial tranquillity of rural Castile. In fact, it is interesting to note that many of the film's conventional heritage landscape shots are used in relation to Miguel, such as when he stops on the road to observe from afar the picturesque white houses of Angosto set among the verdant splendour of the surrounding countryside, the over-the-shoulder shot positioning his viewpoint as typically touristic. Yet, Miguel resists (or deliberately misinterprets) such a perspective, seeing the remoteness of the Castilian landscape instead as an environment in which he can prey upon and brutalise vulnerable women. In essence, therefore, Miguel's rape of Gabi symbolically reveals the function of Lefebvre's spatial hierarchy: whereas the hegemonic cultural production of heritage cinema encodes the rural as a locus of natural/national beauty, as a representation of space which is nourished by the physical landscape (or spatial practice) on which it is based, Miguel's appropriation of this site for his own sadistic purposes is transformative, rendering it a subversive, representational space.

Castile as Cinematic Location

By self-reflexively emphasising rural space as both representation and representational, *The Night of the Sunflowers* foregrounds how landscape is cinematically produced in the construction of spatial (and spectral) heritage. Marvin D'Lugo has argued that, in the context of Spanish cinema, 'the depiction of landscape is seldom a matter of neutral cinematic-narrative setting' (2010: 119). In *The Night of the Sunflowers*, the specific choice of Castile is crucial to the film's meta-heritage dimension, its self-conscious exploration of heritage cinema, as it is a region that has been important to Spanish film production for many decades—not least because, in the historiography of the Franco regime, it became reimagined as 'the spiritual centre of the nation, a marker of authentic Spanishness' (Whittaker 2011: 47).[5] As an intertext, *The Night of the Sunflowers* deliberately draws on and subverts this cinematic tradition, with its use of long shots that dwell upon the barren, sun-beaten landscape. As Cecilio heads to buy provisions from the local store, cinematographer Ángel Guácel captures the inhospitality of the place in an arresting *mise-en-scène*: Cecilio and his donkey are in the centre but the frame is dominated by the dusty brown, weed-strewn field across which they trek and the hazy blue sky in the upper part of the screen. In the background, the ramshackle remains of previous dwellings and outhouses can be seen, testimony to their years of abandonment and neglect. Such is the composition of the frame that this could be an historical painting of traditional agricultural existence were it not for the presence of a dilapidated car, prominently positioned in the bottom right of the frame. This token of modernity strikes the spectator as incongruous but it serves to underscore Sánchez-Cabezudo's awareness of the difficulties of finding in the Spanish countryside a repository for nostalgic (cinematic) heritage. Therefore, rather than the rural idyll of *Nobleza baturra* (*Rustic Chivalry*, Juan de Orduña, 1965) or other dictatorship-era films which laud Castile as the national heartland, Sánchez-Cabezudo chooses to reinscribe the landscape of *The Night of the Sunflowers* in terms of what Maria Tumarkin refers to as a 'traumascape', a site that is 'transformed physically and psychically by suffering' (2005: 13) (Fig. 7.1).

At this moment in the film, the *mise-en-scène* bears witness to an interface between Lefebvrean spatial practice—Cecilio's movement through and within the arid landscape—and the representation of space, the manner in which it is voyeuristically observed/invested with meaning by the static cinematic spectator. Indeed, one of the first shots of Cecilio is of him erecting a scarecrow in his field. Cecilio looks down as he digs, his focus on the dusty earth that sustains his existence, while the spectator's eye is drawn to the background of the frame and to the verdant hillside that surrounds him but which he does not observe. The use of deep focus here efficiently contrasts Cecilio's physical engagement with the land and our more aesthetic response to it. In doing so, *The Night of the Sunflowers* draws attention to what both John Hopewell and Sally

Fig. 7.1 The representational space of Angosto in *The Night of the Sunflowers*

Faulkner have referred to as the contradictory nature of the Spanish rural, whereby the artful construction of the film's landscape shots creates 'an effect of picturesque poverty' (Hopewell 1986: 227). For Faulkner, this creates a 'problematic viewing experience' (2006: 40) as we are encouraged to find aesthetic pleasure in the portrayal of suffering, an observation that seems particularly apposite in relation to *The Night of the Sunflowers* for the manner in which it shows a profound concern for how location is cinematically imagined.

Whereas Sánchez-Cabezudo depicts the harsh reality of traditional Castilian existence from the perspective of Cecilio—and, in so doing, may be said to rewrite the historic(ised) depiction of the agrarian peasantry promoted under Franco—the film also seems to offer, through its repeated use of static long shots, a visual fetishisation of the landscape that is a hallmark of much heritage cinema. As such, it deliberately brings into focus the intersection between Lefebvrean spatial practice and the representation of space and, in so doing, structurally replicates the manner in which the rural imaginary (whether that be touristic or Francoist) is embodied by the materiality of Castile as land. *The Night of the Sunflowers* promotes a profound ambivalence about this location that reveals its self-reflexive concern with how cinematic landscapes function as palimpsests inscribed with shifting cultural meaning. At one point, a long shot of Cecilio's ramshackle house is seen from Esteban and Julián's shared perspective as they observe it from the opposite hillside, the muted brown hue of the house suggesting that it and its occupant are decomposing into the bleak surrounding landscape. As Julián observes, 'The thing is that, when the last neighbour dies, it will be over. This hamlet will be dead. In fact, it already is.' Thus, as much as *The Night of the Sunflowers* may seem to fetishise Castile through its occasional adoption of the audience's (or tourist's) hegemonic viewpoint—a representation of space that the local villagers themselves hope to exploit—it also expresses unease at what such a mythopoeia seeks to erase by characterising rural space in terms of its emptiness and isolation, its inertia and stagnation, rather than its vitality. In doing so, the film retraces and reinscribes the cinema of those dissident directors mentioned earlier who sought to offer a more authentic vision of Spain's geographical and cultural landscape than was available in much dictatorship-era cinema (Triana-Toribio 2003: 124). However, as much as *The Night of the Sunflowers* reclaims Castile cinematically (by transforming it into a representational space) from its Francoist ghosts, Sánchez-Cabezudo also exposes the performative artifice of modern Spanish heritage tourism, whose hegemonic representation of cultural space erases the traumascape on which it is founded. In the process, the film subverts the cultural amnesia occasioned by *el pacto de olvido* by spectrally reinscribing historical suffering (and its filmic representation) as ghostly traces—a hauntology—within the rural environment. The important symbol of the cave visually manifests how landscape embodies the tension between cultural remembering and forgetting in *The Night of the Sunflowers*. Whereas the local residents see it in terms of its materiality, its spatial practice a tabula rasa on which they can inscribe their hegemonic narrative of rural heritage, the cave is equally constituted by its physical absence—the hollow promise of its touristic viability as well as the nothingness (of disremembering) into which Cecilio's corpse is cast. In this sense, *The Night of the Sunflowers* deliberately unravels the association between Castile and cultural forgetfulness through its spectral reinscription of the trauma that is a fundamental constituent of its ontology. Despite Amós's (Walter Vidarte) confession that 'I don't remember', the voices of 'los muertos' (the dead) who speak to him in the mountains are ghosts that haunt the film's rural space, historical remnants echoing and disrupting its cinematic diegesis as a hauntology.

Conclusion

In *The Night of the Sunflowers*, the historical reality of rural depopulation is figured as a hauntology, a ghostly absence/presence that adds to the spectral nature of the Spanish heritage it explores. The film makes several oblique allusions to the phenomenon of rural-urban migration that devastated the Spanish agrarian population during the years of the dictatorship. Beni (Fernando Sánchez-Cabezudo) and Tomás (Vicente Romero) seek to leave the village in the hope of finding a more fulfilling existence elsewhere, while the house in which Esteban lodges is empty because the previous residents 'left the village 15 years ago'. Furthermore, after Cecilio has been murdered and the plot devised to dispose of his corpse, Tomás suggests that 'it's normal that people leave these hamlets and are never heard of again'. Indeed, it is implied that the primary motive for the locals inviting Esteban to Angosto in the first place is to use tourism to reinvigorate a local economy, which has become stagnant in the years following the rural exodus. The countryside of Angosto is haunted by the spectres of previous historical and cinematic migrants and, as such, the film's long shots of the landscape, which transform the spatial practice and representation of Castile into a subversive representational space, thus function symbolically, the barren terrain of Cecilio's field a poignant visual metaphor for how, after so many years of depopulation, no sense of cultural nostalgia can be cultivated from such aridity. This notion is further visually underscored by the contrast between the modern village of Angosto and its now moribund adjunct, where Cecilio lives. *The Night of the Sunflowers*'s shots of the remnants of now dilapidated dwellings on the Castilian hillside point to a rural existence under erasure but still physically existent, a spectral trace that is embodied in the figures of Amós, Cecilio's senile neighbour and antagonist, and Cecilio himself, who spends his evenings in lonely, nostalgic contemplation of old family photos. Both are profoundly anachronistic, living on the periphery of modern society and beyond its concerns, a notion that is suitably illustrated when, after Cecilio's murder, Tomás suggests that 'this gentleman lived alone in an abandoned village. Nobody will report him missing.'

From the above, it is clear that *The Night of the Sunflowers* offers a new perspective on how heritage cinema can be used as an analytical tool to explore the thematic and stylistic facets of contemporary European films. Although not a heritage film in any standard sense, *The Night of the Sunflowers* self-reflexively posits Spanish heritage as a cinematic hauntology, tracing the Castilian landscape and its filmic representations as intertextual spectres which are reinscribed within the contemporary moment. The rural milieu, a Lefebvrean representation of (hegemonic) space that has served as a controversial repository of Spanish cultural memory throughout the nation's cinematic history, is thus interrogated by Sánchez-Cabezudo's exploration of modern heritage tourism and its artifice in the fictional village of Angosto. In doing so, the landscape is transformed into a representational space which overlays the spatial practice (or materiality) of the land. Rather than evoking nostalgia for the past, the spectral heritage of *The Night of the Sunflowers* emphasises the devastating consequences of a historical rural depopulation whose ghostly traces are etched upon the contemporary 'traumascape' of Castile itself. In this way, the film represents an interesting example of how contemporary European cinema can engage with issues of historical and cultural legacy. Through its awareness of how the past is coterminous with the present, a ghostly non-presence that inscribes itself upon the filmic text, *The Night of the Sunflowers* inverts the temporal priorities of traditional heritage cinema. In the process, it opens up our understanding of what constitutes a heritage film to new possibilities because it sees the contemporary landscape of Spain as a palimpsest upon which are etched the phantasmic traces of the nation's historical and cultural past as a hauntology.

Notes

1. Jesús Gonzalez Requena's 'Apuntes para una historia de lo rural en el cine español' traces how the favoured location of dictatorship-approved cinema gradually shifted from the countryside to towns as a reflection of the changing economic policies of the regime (1988: 19–24).
2. *El pacto de olvido* obliged the transitional government after Franco's death to follow a policy of '*la desmemoria*' (disremembering) which ensured there would be no accountability for the many crimes committed in the name of the dictatorship. In 2007, this law was overturned with the creation of the *Ley de Memoria Histórica* (Historical Memory Law), which formally recognised all victims of political, religious and ideological violence during both the Civil War and Franco's regime.
3. The term 'post-heritage' was coined by Claire Monk (1995/2001) to reflect the greater emphasis on sex and violence that these films contain compared to conventional heritage cinema. A recent example is the critically acclaimed, Catalan-language film, *Pa negre* (*Black Bread*, Agustí Villaronga, 2010), which exposes the bitter rivalries and prejudices in Spanish society after the

Civil War. For more about Spanish post-heritage films, see Faulkner (2013: 264–78, 2015: 214–24).
4. The 'tourist gaze' is coined by Urry to characterise the complex dynamics of how tourist sites are seen and experienced by both visitors and those responsible for their production and maintenance. His suggestion that 'Gazing is a performance that orders, shapes and classifies, rather than reflects the world' (Urry and Larsen 2011: 2) echoes Lefebvre's conceptualisation of *espacio conçu*.
5. Despite been released before the founding of the dictatorship, *La aldea maldita* (*The Cursed Village*, Florián Rey, 1930) reveals a vision of rural Castile as the ideological heartland of benign Spanish patriarchy that chimes well with what would later become official Francoist rhetoric (D'Lugo 1997: 30), a notion reflected by Rey's sound remake of the film in 1942. Although Katherine Kovács argues that the film does not 'extol the values of rural life' (1991: 20), a series of static landscape shots are deployed to evoke the classical paintings that celebrated the nation's glorious past.

Works Cited

Aguilar, C., ed. 1988. *El campo en el cine español*. Valencia: Banco de Crédito Agrícola/Filmoteca Generalitat Valenciana.
Anderson, B. 1991. *Imagined communities*, 2 edn. London: Verso.
Blanco Rodríguez, J.A. 1998. Sociedad y régimen en Castilla y León bajo el primer Franquismo. *Historia Contemporánea* 17: 287–359.
D'Lugo, M. 1997. *Guide to the cinema of Spain*. Westford: Greenwood Press.
———. 2010. Landscape in Spanish cinema. In *Cinema and landscape*, eds. G. Harper and J. Rayner, 119–129. Bristol/Chicago: Intellect.
Davies, A. 2012. *Spanish spaces: Landscape, space and place in contemporary Spanish culture*. Liverpool: Liverpool University Press.
Delgado, M., and R. Fiddian, eds. 2013. *Spanish cinema 1973-2010: Politics, landscape and memory*. Manchester: Manchester University Press.
Derrida, J. 1994. *Specters of Marx: The State of the Debt, the Work of Mourning and the New International*. New York & London: Routledge.
———. 2008. Of Grammatology. *Baltimore & London: The John Hopkins* University Press.
Faulkner, S. 2006. Nostalgia and the middlebrow Spanish ruralist cinema and Mario Camus's *Los santos inocentes/The holy innocents*. In *Representing the rural: Space, place and identity in films about the land*, eds. C. Fowler and G. Helfield, 35–47. Detroit: Wayne State University Press.
———. 2013. *A history of Spanish film: Cinema and society 1910–2010*. New York/London: Bloomsbury.

———. 2015. Spanish heritage cinema. In *The Europeanness of European cinema: Identity, meaning, globalization*, eds. M. Harrod, M. Liz, and A. Timoshkina, 213–226. London: I.B. Tauris.
Fowler, C., and G. Helfield, eds. 2006. *Representing the rural: Space, place and identity in films about the land*. Detroit: Wayne State University Press.
Gellner, E. 1964. *Thought and change*. Chicago: University of Chicago Press.
González Requena, J. 1988. Apuntes para una historia de lo rural en el cine español. In *El campo en el cine español*, ed. C. Aguilar, 13–27. Valencia: Banco de Crédito Agrícola/Filmoteca Generalitat Valenciana
Harper, G., and J. Rayner, eds. 2010. *Cinema and landscape*. Bristol/Chicago: Intellect.
Harrod, M., M. Liz, and A. Timoshkina. 2014. *The Europeanness of European cinema: Identity, meaning, globalization*. London: I. B. Tauris.
Herrero, C. 2010. Edgy art cinema: Cinephilia and genre negotiation in recent Spanish rural thrillers. *Studies in European Cinema* 7(2): 123–134.
Higson, A. 1995. *Waving the flag: Constructing a national cinema in Britain*. Oxford: Oxford University Press.
Hjort, M., and S. Mackenzie, eds. 2000. *Cinema and nation*. London: Routledge.
Hopewell, J. 1986. *Out of the past: Spanish cinema after Franco*. London: British Film Institute.
Jordan, B., and M. Allinson. 2005. *Spanish cinema: A student's guide*. London: Hodder Arnold.
Kinder, M. 1993. *Blood cinema: The reconstruction of national identity in Spain*. Berkley: University of California Press.
Kovács, K.S. 1991. The plain in Spain: Geography and national identity in Spanish cinema. *Quarterly Review of Film and Video*. 13(4): 17–46.
Labanyi, J. 2000. History and hauntology; or, what does one do with the ghosts of the past? Reflections in Spanish film and fiction of the Post-Franco Period. In *Disremembering the dictatorship: The politics of memory in the Spanish transition to democracy*, ed. Ramón J. Resina, 65–82. Amsterdam/Atlanta: Rodopi.
———. 2001a. Engaging with ghosts; or, theorizing culture in modern Spain. In *Constructing identity in contemporary Spain: Theoretical debates and cultural practice*, ed. J. Labanyi, 1–14. Oxford: Oxford University Press.
———. ed. 2001b. *Constructing identity in contemporary Spain: Theoretical debates and cultural practice*. Oxford: Oxford University Press.
Lefebvre, H. 1991. *The production of space*. Oxford: Blackwell.
Marsh, S. 2014. Editor's introduction. Untimely materialities: Spanish film and spectrality. *Journal of Spanish Cultural Studies* 15(1): 1–6.
Monk, C. 1995/2001. Sexuality and heritage. *Sight and Sound* 5(10): 32–34. Republished in *Film/literature/heritage: A sight & sound reader*, ed. G. Vincendeau. London: British Film Institute.

———. 2011. *Heritage film audiences: Period films and contemporary audiences in the UK*. Edinburgh: Edinburgh University Press.
Pavlović, T. 2009. *100 years of Spanish cinema*. Chichester: Wylie-Blackwell.
Perriam, C. 2001a. Engaging with ghosts; or, theorizing culture in modern Spain. In *Constructing identity in contemporary Spain: Theoretical debates and cultural practice*, ed. J. Labanyi, 1–14. Oxford: Oxford University Press.
Perriam, C. 2003. *Stars and masculinities in Spanish cinema: From Banderas to Bardem*. Oxford: Oxford University Press.
Ramon Resina, J., ed. 2000. *Disremembering the dictatorship: The politics of memory in the Spanish transition to democracy*. Amsterdam: Rodopi.
Richardson, N. 2011. *Constructing Spain: The re-imagination of space and place in narrative and film 1953–2003*. Lewisburg: Bucknell University Press.
Triana-Toribio, N. 2003. *Spanish National Cinema*. Abingdon & New York: Routledge.
Tumarkin, M. 2005. *Traumascapes: The power and fate of places transformed by tragedy*. Melbourne: Melbourne University Press.
Urry, J., and J. Larsen. 2011. *The tourist gaze 3.0*. London: Sage.
Vidal, B. 2012. *Heritage film: Nation, genre and representation*. New York: Columbia University Press.
Whittaker, T. 2011. *The films of Elías Querejeta: A producer of landscapes*. Cardiff: University of Wales Press.
———. 2013. *La noche de los girasoles/The Night of the Sunflowers*: palimpsests of genre, palimpsests of violence. In *Spanish cinema 1973-2010: Politics, landscape and memory*, eds. M. Delgado and R. Fiddian, 158–168. Manchester/New York: Manchester University Press.
———. 2014. Ghostly resonance: Sound, memory and matter in *Las olas* and *Dies d'agost*. *Journal of Spanish Cultural Studies* 15(3): 323–336.

CHAPTER 8

Adapting Balzac in Jacques Rivette's *Ne Touchez pas la hache* (*Don't Touch the Axe*): Violence and the Post-Heritage Aesthetic

Andrew Watts

Violence is no stranger to heritage cinema. In France, some of the most well-known heritage films produced since the 1980s have featured violence ranging from the graphic and disturbing to more innocent slapstick. In 1986, Claude Berri framed his adaptation of the Marcel Pagnol novel *Jean de Florette* between two violent deaths, the murder of the farmer Pique-Bouffigue, and the tragic demise of the eponymous hunchback, who dies as a result of his attempts to blast a well in the Provençal rock. More controversially, Patrice Chéreau's 1994 film *La Reine Margot*, a reworking of the historical novel by Alexandre Dumas, sought deliberately to shock audiences with its extreme violence, including a gruesome recreation of the St Bartholomew's Day Massacre which prompted the *Guardian* newspaper to describe the film as 'heritage gore' (cited in Powrie 2006: 229). These eruptions of screen violence have helped to define the register of French heritage films, which are typically much darker in tone than their British counterparts. As Ginette Vincendeau observes, in arguing for a wider study of different national approaches to heritage filmmaking,

A. Watts (✉)
University of Birmingham, Birmingham, UK
e-mail: a.j.watts.2@bham.ac.uk

© The Editor(s) (if applicable) and The Author(s) 2016
P. Cooke, R. Stone (eds.), *Screening European Heritage*, Palgrave European Film and Media Studies,
DOI 10.1057/978-1-137-52280-1_8

French period productions 'tend not to present a rosy view of the past and thus differ significantly from the turn-of-the-century domesticity of British films' (2001: xix–xx). Such generalisations invite us to explore further the artistic specificities of French heritage films and the unique ways in which they have engaged with the pervasive theme of violence. Over the past 30 years, the violence that has so often fascinated the country's heritage directors has taken multiple forms, most obviously physical and emotional, but also social, economic and political. It has been expressed in a variety of different ways on screen, through cinematography and *mise-en-scène*, and in the recurrence of specific images and metaphors. Moreover, some of the violence depicted in heritage films has sparked vigorous critical debates, especially in the case of *La Reine Margot*, which at the time of the film's release Chéreau invited spectators to interpret as a commentary on twentieth-century conflicts including the Bosnian War. As well as being a prominent theme in French heritage cinema, violence underpins the ways in which key films in this style have been presented on screen, and the reactions they have provoked in spectators.

This chapter considers the representation of violence in *Don't Touch the Axe*, Jacques Rivette's 2007 adaptation of a Balzac novella, *La Duchesse de Langeais* (*The Duchess of Langeais*). Rivette's film appears as an intriguing case study through which to explore the relationship between violence and heritage cinema, not least because its plot revolves around the romantic battle of wills between a Bonapartist soldier, Armand de Montriveau, and a married noblewoman, Antoinette de Langeais. As a point of departure for my analysis, I begin by explaining why Rivette decided to adapt *La Duchesse de Langeais*, focusing especially on his desire to redress some of the omissions made by Jacques de Baroncelli's 1942 version of the story, which had elided key elements of Balzac's plot in adaptation. The second part of the chapter examines the ways in which Rivette evokes the violence of the source text, and the array of cinematic images he uses to translate the passionate struggle between the two protagonists into his own medium. In particular, I wish to probe the director's artistic fascination with images of cutting and brutal rupture, and the ways in which these prove highly reminiscent of Balzac's novella. Finally, and most importantly, this chapter reflects on what *Don't Touch the Axe* can tell us about the sometimes conflicted evolution of heritage cinema in France. More specifically, I argue that this film occupies a liminal space between different strands of heritage filmmaking, namely the nostalgic literary adaptations of the late 1980s and early 1990s and the 'post-heritage' films of more recent times, which have sought typically to rethink and redefine the boundaries of the genre. With its historically authentic decors, period costumes and obsessive pursuit of fidelity to the source material, *Don't Touch the Axe* cultivates the 'museum aesthetic' that Vincendeau identifies as a key feature of heritage cinema (2001: xviii). As this chapter demonstrates, however, Rivette also delights in cutting himself free from these conventions and pushing heritage in new artistic directions. *Don't Touch the Axe* reflects in particular his enthusiasm for redeploying the personalities associated with his own previous films, most notably Jeanne Balibar, whose performance as Antoinette de Langeais recalls her earlier role as an actress in Rivette's 2001 film *Va savoir* (*Who Knows?*). Far from merely perpetuating or subverting the conventions of heritage film, *Don't Touch the Axe* embraces openly its connections to other works of cinema, and in so doing illustrates the artistic flexibility of the genre.

LA DUCHESSE DE LANGEAIS ON SCREEN

First published in 1834, *La Duchesse de Langeais* has long captivated filmmakers. To date, there have been at least seven adaptations of the story for film and television. Between 1909 and 1912, silent cinematographers in France recreated Balzac's novella on no fewer than three occasions. In 1942, during the German Occupation of the country, Jacques de Baroncelli added his own version to this corpus of films, working from a screenplay by the celebrated playwright Jean Giraudoux. Outside of France, filmmakers have also adapted *La Duchesse de Langeais* for their own national audiences. In the United States, the text inspired Frank Lloyd's 1922 film *The Eternal Flame*. In Germany, Paul Czinner also reworked the story under the title *Liebe* (*Love*) in 1927. That filmmakers have returned time and again to *La Duchesse de Langeais* is by no means surprising given that the source text combines a portrait of love and frustrated passion with moments of intense drama. Balzac's narrative begins in 1823, on an unnamed island off the coast of Spain. As the fictional Montriveau sits in the chapel of a Carmelite convent, he recognises a melody being played on the organ. Unable to see who is playing the music behind the altar curtains, the General concludes—correctly, it transpires later—that he has found his beloved Antoinette, for whom he has been searching for five years. Montriveau succeeds in obtaining a meeting with the Duchess, who is now living as a nun under the name Sœur Thérèse. This encounter comes to a sudden end, however, when

Antoinette/Sœur Thérèse admits to the Mother Superior that Montriveau is in fact her lover. Following this opening sequence, Balzac transports the reader to Paris five years earlier, and Antoinette's first meeting with the famous General de Montriveau. Under the pretext of hearing the story of how he once survived in the Egyptian desert, the Duchess invites the soldier to visit her apartment every evening, where over several months she teases him with her coquetry without ever giving herself to him entirely. The balance of power in their relationship shifts only when Montriveau kidnaps Antoinette and threatens to brand her with a hot iron—a threat of violence that ignites her passion, to which the General is now indifferent. When finally he surrenders to the Duchess's increasingly desperate attempts to win his love, Montriveau arrives too late to prevent her from leaving Paris. In a final, tragic development, his plan to kidnap her from the convent with the aid of a secret society also ends in failure, when he enters her cell only to discover that she is already dead.

While it is perhaps tempting to speculate that Rivette recognised immediately the adaptive potential of Balzac's novella, the origins of *Don't Touch the Axe* are actually to be found in the more prosaic realities of the film industry. Before alighting on this text, the director had intended to make a science fiction film with Balibar and Guillaume Depardieu entitled *L'Année prochaine à Paris* (*Next Year in Paris*). However, when he was unable to secure studio funding for this production, Rivette took the unusual step of retaining the two actors and embarking on a search for a script that would suit them, rather than starting afresh with a new project. As he explained subsequently in the press pack that accompanied the release of *Don't Touch the Axe*, he and his production team scoured 'the whole of western literature' (Rivette 2007: online)[1] before settling on *La Duchesse de Langeais* and casting Balibar and Depardieu as Antoinette and Montriveau. Given his longstanding fascination with *La Comédie humaine* (*The Human Comedy*), Balzac's multi-volume magnum opus, which includes this novella, Rivette's choice was a natural one. The director had first been introduced to Balzac's work in the early 1950s by fellow New Wave filmmaker Eric Rohmer, who told him that the two novelists that all cinematographers should read were Balzac and Dostoevsky. 'I read Dostoevsky belatedly,' Rivette admitted in 2007. 'As for Balzac, I "discovered" him one night during a bout of insomnia by stumbling across *Une ténébreuse affaire* (*A Murky Business*). This novel converted me and provided the key to read the whole of his collected works' (Rivette 2007: online). Since awakening to the artistic possibilities presented by

Balzac's work, Rivette has continued to adapt material from *La Comédie humaine* in a variety of innovative ways. His earliest attempt at reimagining Balzac was the 1971 film *Out 1: noli me tangere* (*Out 1*), a sprawling twelve-and-a-half-hour film inspired by the prologue to Balzac's *Histoire des Treize* (*The Thirteen*), which recounts the search for a secret society in post-1968 Paris, and in which Rivette playfully cast his friend Rohmer as a Balzac specialist. Twenty years later, in 1991, Rivette returned to Balzac in *La Belle Noiseuse*, a loose reworking of *Le Chef-d'œuvre inconnu* (*The Unknown Masterpiece*), which updated the story of the tormented artist Frenhofer to contemporary Provence. The film, which in its original version ran to almost four hours, was well received by critics, winning the Grand Prix at the 1991 Cannes Film Festival. For Rivette himself, however, the challenge of representing the process of painting on screen, in real time, proved arduous, and appeared to signal the end of his interest in reinventing works from *La Comédie humaine*. Balzac, he declared following the completion of *La Belle Noiseuse*, was 'utterly unadaptable' (cited in Trémois 2007: 376).

After waiting another 15 years before returning to Balzac, Rivette settled on a different approach to the novelist's work in *Don't Touch the Axe*. Rather than modernise his source material, as he had done in *Out 1* and *La Belle Noiseuse*, he would recreate *La Duchesse de Langeais* as a period piece, adopting as his guiding principle scrupulous fidelity to the original work. Accordingly, Rivette follows Balzac's plot closely, seeking not only to capture the content but also the pace and rhythm of the source narrative. As Anne-Marie Baron has noted, *Don't Touch the Axe* invents only two scenes that do not feature in the novella (2007: 524). In the first of these sequences, the Duchess's servants frolic in the kitchen, their laughter striking a contrast with the grave intensity of the conversation between their employer and Montriveau in the salon. In the second additional scene, the General is held up by two friends just as Antoinette waits to see if he will respond to her anguished declaration of love. The delay—exacerbated by Montriveau's slow clock—sets in motion the tragic *dénouement*, as the soldier emerges from his apartment moments after the Duchess has departed the city. These sequences aside, Rivette's awareness of the shortcomings of earlier versions of *La Duchesse de Langeais* motivated him to attempt a uniquely faithful recreation of the story. One of his key cinematic reference points in this respect was Baroncelli's 1942 adaptation, which in order to evade German censorship had softened the violence of the original story by omitting the scene in which Montriveau threatens to brand the Duchess, as well as the soldier's subsequent attempt to kidnap her from the convent.[2] In preparing the script for *Don't Touch the Axe*, the director and his team identified the replacement of this material as crucial to achieving an authentic reworking of the text. As screenwriter Pascal Bonitzer explained, the fundamental aim of the production was to 'remain as faithful as possible to the letter of Balzac's work, contrary to what Giraudoux had done for Jacques de Baroncelli's film, which at the end of the day told a completely different story to the one written by Balzac' (Rivette 2007: online). For Rivette, Bonitzer and the film's second screenwriter Christine Laurent, fidelity to Balzac did not mean simply transposing the novelist's words to the screen, but replacing some of the brutality that Baroncelli's earlier adaptation had removed.

Violence and the Post-Heritage Aesthetic

Rivette's determination to adapt the most violent passages in Balzac's novella was by no means surprising given the profound aesthetic and ideological developments that heritage cinema had undergone by the time *Don't Touch the Axe* went into production in 2006. In their attempts to appeal to a broad and increasingly international audience, heritage filmmakers in the late 1980s had tended to prioritise conservatism and comforting nostalgia over the depiction of savagery and bloodshed. As Claire Monk has argued, however, in the early 1990s period films began to challenge cultural taboos and broach questions of gender, sexuality and violence more overtly, a shift that prompted Monk to classify such films under the now familiar identifier 'post-heritage'. 'The strand', she writes, 'can be dated to early 1993 and the international success of Sally Potter's *Orlando* […]; by 1994, the trend had been consolidated not only in Britain […] but also globally, with the appropriation and renewal of the costume/literary film by Jane Campion (*The Piano*) and Martin Scorsese (*The Age of Innocence*)' (cited in Vincendeau 2001: 7). In France, 1993 and 1994 saw the release of a number of films which, though still grounded in the heritage tradition of faithful adaptation, also reflected the emergence of a 'post-heritage' aesthetic. In 1993, Berri's *Germinal*, based on Émile Zola's 1885 novel about miners in northern France, engaged forcefully with the themes of violence and sexual exploitation. Refusing to gloss over the harsh social realities described by Zola, the film featured a particularly graphic scene in which the fictional grocer Maigrat is publicly castrated by the miners' wives in punishment for his demanding sexual favours in return for desperately needed food supplies. In 1994, Yves Angelo's reworking of another Balzac text, *Le Colonel Chabert*, also foregrounded violence by opening with a bloody depiction of the aftermath of the Battle of Eylau (1807) in which the bodies of dead soldiers are shown being stripped of their clothes and valuables before being tipped into a mass grave. Coupled with the release earlier in 1994 of *La Reine Margot*, with its portrayal of incest, orgies and brutal slaughter, these films saw 'post-heritage' establish itself at the heart of French period cinema, just as it had done internationally.

While *Don't Touch the Axe* does not seek to shock audiences with blood and gore, like these earlier literary adaptations the film engages closely with the notion of violence, both at the level of plot and in its cinematography. The opening sequence of the film establishes the key importance of violence to the story by incorporating a series of menacing images. The film begins with a shot of the Carmelite convent seen from the ocean. Focusing in on the chapel at the top of the cliff, the director employs a zoom which, as Antoine Thirion points out, is divided roughly into three shots, thus evoking the chopping motion of the axe featured in the film's title (2007: 10). The camera then pans slowly across the chapel floor, alighting first on a mosaic depicting a griffin with a missing head, and then rising to show the altar behind an imposing set of bars. An intertitle separates these images from the introduction of Montriveau, who sits in the congregation listening to the organ. The sequence reflects the emotional turmoil that engulfs the General as he recognises the melody Antoinette used to play at home in Paris. First, he drops his cane, which falls noisily onto the stone floor. As he rushes outside into the blistering heat, he then stumbles on the chapel steps—an accidental slip which resulted from actor Guillaume Depardieu's wearing a prosthetic leg—before making his way across the courtyard. Once he reaches the parapet wall overlooking the ocean, he stares out to sea, the squawking of the seagulls continuing to echo his troubled state of mind. This sound, together with the fragmented images of the chapel and the movements performed by Depardieu, prepare the spectator for the passionate struggle between Antoinette and Montriveau. Moreover, the violence evoked by this combination of elements reflects the opening of the source text. In the novella, Balzac infuses his description of the convent with threatening imagery. Despite its apparent tranquillity, the building, he declares, sits atop an imposing rock 'sheered off on the seaward side' (Balzac 1976–81, 5: 906) and surrounded by dangerous currents. Having underlined the harshness of the physical environment, Balzac invites the reader to imagine the surge of emotions that Montriveau experiences upon finding his beloved Antoinette, a discovery the narrator compares to a volcanic eruption. As this opening section of the novella illustrates, Balzac delights in generating images of violence which foreshadow the story still to unfold, a technique readily appropriated by Rivette in his adaptation.

As the opening sequence of *Don't Touch the Axe* underscores the violence of Balzac's plot, so Rivette's subsequent depiction of the affair between Antoinette and Montriveau proves equally reminiscent of the source text. As James Mileham has observed in his analysis of *La Duchesse de Langeais*, Montriveau treats love as a war of attrition. In evoking the General's first visit to Antoinette's apartment, Balzac describes how this veteran of the Napoleonic Wars plans to declare his love 'as if it were the first cannon shot on a battlefield' (Balzac 1976–81, 5: 951). As one might expect of a military man, Montriveau looks upon the Duchess as territory to be conquered. 'Her body is a battlefield that Armand overruns place by place,' writes Mileham. 'First, he wins the right to kiss her hands, then her forehead; later, we see him kiss the hem of her dress, her feet, her knees, and it is implied that he goes farther' (2003: 211). The Duchess, for her part, seeks to impede Montriveau's relentless physical campaign. Delighting in the admiration of her suitor but not wanting to surrender to him completely, she erects a series of barriers, refusing first to betray her husband, then citing her duties both to religion and her social class. By allowing Montriveau to disarm these objections, Antoinette encourages him to believe that he is winning his campaign, only then to block his progress with fresh obstacles. Rivette's cinematography emphasises this tension between conquest and resistance, and the emotional stalemate in which it results for the two protagonists. In a scene that shows Montriveau's passion at boiling point, the soldier arrives at Antoinette's home determined to make her his mistress. After tracking his enraged stride through the apartment, the camera cuts to inside the Duchess's bedroom as Montriveau bursts through the door. Warning him of the impropriety of his actions, Antoinette orders her uninvited guest to leave, only for the General to grab her, the camera echoing his tightening grip by means of a subtle zoom. Startled by Montriveau's anger, she then flees to a corner of the room, prompting the soldier to advance towards her from out of frame. After he reveals his intention to cement their relationship by embracing her in public, she then moves towards the window, causing Montriveau to follow her again. In this series of movements, the officer advances repeatedly towards his target, only for her to move away. In a final assault, he vows through gritted teeth that he will take what he wants, a threat heavy with the implication of rape. The encounter ends without a clear victory for either party, as Montriveau retreats angrily through the apartment before the screen fades to black, signalling a temporary cessation in the couple's hostilities.

The fierce intensity of the struggle between Antoinette and Montriveau is closely linked in Rivette's film with images of bladed weapons and cutting.[3] As Francesca Dosi observes, the title of the film evokes the violence associated with the act of cutting at the very outset. Rivette shifts the emphasis of his film away from the social connotations of the title *La Duchesse de Langeais*, preferring instead the original title of the novella, which Balzac discarded in order to focus the reader's attention squarely on the character of Antoinette. Dosi postulates that in choosing this menacing imperative, the director may have wished to highlight the symbolic castration of Montriveau at the hands of the Duchess. The title also recalls the blade of the guillotine to which thousands of French aristocrats had lost their heads during the Revolution (2014: 396).[4] The factor that Dosi omits from her discussion, however, is that images of blades and cutting underpin Balzac's portrayal of violence in the novella itself. At the level of plot, such images feature prominently in his descriptions of the Duchess. In summarising her capacity to inflict emotional wounds on Montriveau, the narrator compares her to an executioner who toys with the soldier as one might an insect. Subsequently, Balzac labels her a 'woman as cold and cutting as steel' (Balzac 1976–81, 5: 985) who stings Montriveau with her short, arrow-like sentences. Rivette picks up on these references to cutting and incorporates them into the film's plot and cinematography to reflect the conflicted relationship between the protagonists. The director's artistic fascination with cutting is neatly illustrated by the sequence in which Montriveau prepares to implement his plan to kidnap the Duchess from a society ball. As he arrives at the home of the Comtesse de Sérizy, the General declares his intention to do battle with Antoinette in terms which recall the crossing of swords in a duel: 'Steel against steel. We shall see whose heart is sharpest.' An intertitle then abbreviates his vow in a manner that echoes the importance of the theme of cutting in this sequence, trimming Montriveau's words to read simply 'steel against steel'. After the camera moves inside the ballroom, the first dance shows couples waltzing with their arms raised and bent at the elbow, forming a shape reminiscent of a dagger. Finally, when Antoinette comes to rest at the edge of the ballroom, Montriveau is recounting to the Comtesse de Sérizy the story of his visit to London, where he claims to have heard a guard at the Palace of Westminster warn a visitor not to touch the axe that had been used to behead Charles I. In Montriveau's retelling, the anecdote becomes a sinister warning to Antoinette of the revenge he intends to exact for her coquettish behaviour, prompting her to ask whether he would like to see her own head roll. In both its plot development and cinematic features, this sequence rearticulates the images of cutting so integral to the representation of violence in the source text (Fig. 8.1).

If *Don't Touch the Axe* throws into relief Balzac's thematic interest in cutting, the film also reflects the ways in which Rivette uses cutting and editing to engage with the different forms of violence present in the source text. Despite aspiring to produce a highly faithful version of *La Duchesse de Langeais*, the director necessarily cuts material from the novella in order to accommodate the story within his own medium, and to make it accessible to a contemporary audience. As a result, the film elides Balzac's lengthy political attack on the aristocracy of the Faubourg Saint-Germain, which he accused of failing to live up to its responsibility to lead the nation. Similarly, Rivette provides no equivalent of the passage in which the Marquis de Ronquerolles suggests to Montriveau that women such as

Fig. 8.1 Montriveau warns Antoinette of the punishment that awaits her

Antoinette respond only to beatings—advice that the filmmaker perhaps considered too misogynistic for the sensibilities of twenty-first-century spectators. In an interview to mark the release of *Don't Touch the Axe*, Rivette explained the process of adapting Balzac by comparing his work to that of the sculptor César Baldaccini (1921–98), who pioneered the technique of using a hydraulic press to crush cars and scrap metal into new works of art. In recreating *La Duchesse de Langeais* for his own medium, Rivette sought to condense the source text while simultaneously retaining what he perceived to be the jagged, sometimes jarring rhythms of Balzac's writing. 'From the beginning,' the director revealed in the same interview, 'what interested us [...] was transposing Balzac's writing into cinematic terms. This writing plays on contradictory forces which generate power like a combustion engine: the long sentences interrupted by parentheses, the surprising changes of pace' (Rivette 2007: online). Rivette's adaptation of the sequence in which Montriveau kidnaps and threatens to brand Antoinette illustrates the way in which the film employs cutting and editing to foreground a sudden eruption of violence in the plot. As critics have often noted, the kidnapping represents one of the most incongruous episodes in the novella, since it disrupts a largely subtle, private drama with a passage reminiscent of Gothic horror. Rivette captures this change of registers by using editing to isolate the kidnapping sequence within the main narrative. As Antoinette leaves the ball, her carriage advances towards the camera before a masked man steps out of the shadows to bring the vehicle—and metaphorically the first part of the story—to a halt. The roughly edited series of shots that follows reflects the fear and disorientation of the Duchess as she is tied and blindfolded in the semi-darkness of the carriage before being taken down the stairs to Montriveau's apartment. After the General has outlined and ultimately renounced his plan, the camera cuts back to inside the Comtesse de Sérizy's apartment, where a secret door opens to allow Antoinette to return to the ball and then closes softly behind her, metaphorising the end of this Gothic interlude in the narrative. As Rivette suppresses the political vitriol and overt misogyny of the source text, so cutting and editing enable him to call attention to the pivotal moment of violence in the plot, in a manner befitting of Balzac's own narrative technique.[5]

In addition to foregrounding the violence depicted in *La Duchesse de Langeais*, cutting forms part of Rivette's wider interest in the themes of separation and rupture. Images of violent separation abound in *Don't Touch the Axe*, emphasising the way in which the two protagonists are slowly pulled apart by society, religion and their own stubbornness. The prologue to the film underscores such images at the outset. After returning to the chapel to confirm his suspicions that Antoinette was responsible for the music being played on the organ, Montriveau finds the altar curtains closed, prompting him to utter and then shout her name furiously at the fabric partition. The subsequent meeting between the General and Antoinette/Sœur Thérèse continues these allusions to the barriers that separate the couple. Having gained access to the convent, Montriveau finds that he must converse with Antoinette through a set of iron bars. A further barrier cuts short this exchange, however, when the Mother Superior, upon learning that Montriveau is in fact Antoinette's lover, pulls the curtain angrily. As Rivette demonstrates, the emotional violence inherent in such moments of rupture is often exacerbated by the protracted nature of the separation. In a later sequence set in Antoinette's home, the director's staging emphasises the turmoil that Montriveau experiences as the Duchess attempts to break off their relationship. After the soldier orders her not to attend confession again, Antoinette bids him a permanent farewell, and then retreats to her bedroom. Montriveau, however, remains in the salon, where he pokes the fire vigorously, a reflection, argues James Romney, of the character's 'barely contained sexual frustration' (2008: 67). An intertitle informs the audience that an hour has elapsed before Montriveau lets himself into Antoinette's bedroom, where she admits to never having loved him. Even this revelation, however, does not bring a definitive end to their relationship. Instead, Antoinette draws the General back into the salon by playing *Tage River*—an 1819 ballad about the pain of separation—on the piano, before claiming that she does love him after all. The closing scene in the film echoes this idea that separation is a torturous process that often remains incomplete. After the members of the Thirteen attempt to kidnap Antoinette from the convent, Ronquerolles suggests—in a final act of violence—that her body be thrown into the ocean, before advising Montriveau to consign the memory of her to the past 'like a poem read during our childhood'. However, the final shot of the film, in which Montriveau stares out across the vast expanse of water, reflects that, while this particular chapter of his life is over, he will continue to bear the scars of the emotional violence it engendered (Fig. 8.2).

La Duchesse de Langeais foreshadows Rivette's film by structuring its own plot around instances of violent separation.[6] Such moments of rupture are exemplified by the relationship between Antoinette and her husband. Though the couple live apart, the threat of violence looms over

Fig. 8.2 Montriveau stares out to sea in the closing shot of the film

their marriage. Thus, when Antoinette attempts to declare her love for Montriveau publicly by sending her carriage to wait outside his home, her aristocratic family is immediately fearful of the consequences. 'You have compromised your husband and your social position,' the Duchess's aunt warns her. By continuing to humiliate her husband, Antoinette is told, in terms which recall her earlier kidnapping, 'you will be bound, gagged by the laws' (Balzac 1976–81, 5: 1017). As well as helping to shape the plot of *La Duchesse de Langeais*, notions of violent separation underpin the narrative on a textual level. In the preface to the *Histoire des Treize*, the trilogy of fictions to which *La Duchesse de Langeais* belongs, Balzac declared his intention to reject the overblown violence associated with the Gothic novel in favour of the more understated dramas of private life. 'Plays dripping with blood, dramas filled with terrors, novels with secret beheadings, have been confided to his ears,' he wrote of himself as author. 'But he has preferred to recount the sweetest adventures' (Balzac 1976–81, 5: 788). However, despite condemning the triteness of Gothic fiction, Balzac refused to cut himself free of the genre entirely. An enthusiastic reader of the works of Matthew Lewis, Ann Radcliffe, and E.T.A. Hoffmann, he adapted the literary conventions they had popularised in order to add layers of depth and meaning to his own work. While the episode in which Montriveau threatens to brand Antoinette represents the author's most obvious debt to the Gothic novel, Balzac draws on the genre at other key junctures in the text. When Montriveau ceases to visit her apartment in the days prior to her kidnapping, the Duchess becomes increasingly tormented by thoughts of the extreme violence he might perpetrate against her. 'Would she be murdered?' she asks herself. 'Would this bull-necked man disembowel her and toss her over his head? Would he trample her underfoot?' (Balzac 1976–81, 5: 987). Moreover, when the General persists in sending only his card rather than visit in person, Antoinette begins to hallucinate, and imagines that the card is covered in blood. In evoking the terror experienced by his fictional heroine, Balzac clearly revels in the violent clichés of Gothic horror while simultaneously claiming to separate himself from them.

Rivette and the Redefining of Heritage

If violence is central to Balzac's exploitation of his literary predecessors, so, too, does it inform Rivette's engagement with the conventions of heritage cinema. *Don't Touch the Axe* displays many of the formal features typically associated with heritage productions. In seeking to achieve a faithful adaptation of its canonical source, the film places special emphasis on authenticity. The actors wear period costume, while the Château de Baville, near Arpajon, provided a historic location in which to recreate the home of Antoinette de Langeais. Echoing Balzac's disavowal of the well-worn imagery of Gothic fiction, Rivette nevertheless eschews some of the key techniques of heritage filmmaking. 'Not for Rivette the self-congratulatory shots over expensive exterior locations or tracks through stately homes,' write Morrey and Smith. 'For most sets, only a single, sparsely-furnished room will be used, the rest of the property glimpsed through an open doorway' (2009: 243). The casting of Guillaume Depardieu as Montriveau reflects this tension between the continuation and rejection of the heritage mode in *Don't Touch the Axe*. On the one hand, the actor's involvement in the project links this film inextricably to the figure of Gérard Depardieu and, by extension, to the tradition of nostalgic period films that Depardieu senior helped popularise in the late 1980s and early 1990s. On the other hand, the casting of Depardieu's son, Guillaume, illustrates Rivette's desire to move away from the familiar conventions and personalities of heritage cinema without abandoning them completely. Violence appears as a key locus of this tension in *Don't Touch the Axe*, not least because Guillaume Depardieu's own troubled past forms an integral part of his screen persona.[7] As well as having a difficult relationship with his father, the actor (who died in 2008 at the age of 37) had previously been imprisoned, fought drug addiction, and suffered a motorbike accident that resulted in 17 operations and the eventual amputation of his leg in 2003. Rivette's reworking of the source text plays very clearly on Depardieu's personal history of violence. In the scene in which Montriveau is introduced to Antoinette for the first time, the camera tracks the soldier's rigid movement across the salon, while the soundtrack records the dull thud of his prosthetic leg, recalling the injuries sustained both by the actor and the fictional war veteran he plays. As he mobilises Depardieu's screen persona, Rivette can thus be seen to reflect openly and self-consciously on the way in which violence shapes his own creative process. In so doing, he distances himself from the conservatism commonly associated with heritage adaptations of the late 1980s and early 1990s while at the same time acknowledging his artistic debt to this earlier corpus of films.

The casting of Jeanne Balibar as Antoinette proves similarly—if more subtly—important to Rivette's interest in the relationship between violence and heritage cinema. Prior to securing her role in *Don't Touch the Axe*, Balibar had established her professional reputation working mainly in the theatre, most notably for the prestigious Comédie-Française in Paris. Her screen persona thus loaned itself readily to the portrayal of the fictional Antoinette, who uses her own dramatic abilities to spark a violent passion in Montriveau. As she waits for the soldier to pay his first visit to her home, the Duchess sits in front of her dressing table mirror as if preparing for a stage performance. Having decided against wearing a long necklace—an object which anticipates her subsequent ensnarement of Montriveau—she moves to the salon, where she experiments with adopting different postures on the sofa before asking her valet to remove some of the candles from the room, thereby creating a more intimate atmosphere. When Montriveau enters the salon moments later, the Duchess continues to play the part of a coquettish woman, claiming first that she is too unwell to receive any visitor other than him, and then kicking away a cushion so that the General will notice her delicate feet. This carefully stage-managed display has a profound effect on Montriveau, whose desire for Antoinette eventually erupts in a declaration of his love for her. However, Rivette does not restrict himself to exploiting Balibar's theatrical persona in this sequence. Antoinette's manipulation of Montriveau also recalls Balibar's earlier role in another Rivette film, *Who Knows?* (2001), a romantic comedy in which she played a stage actress, Camille Renard.[8] In a scene which bears striking similarities to Antoinette's seductive display in *Don't Touch the Axe*, Camille visits the gambler and lothario Artur in order to retrieve a stolen ring. Wearing a tight-fitting dress, Camille arrives at the apartment and leans provocatively against the doorframe as she initiates her plan to entice the thief into bed. Like Antoinette with Montriveau, the actress proceeds to awaken Artur's desire, asking him first where the stairs lead in his apartment, and then embracing him passionately. Finally, she asks him to reflect on her offer to spend only one night with him while she goes to the bathroom. Such is the intensity of Artur's desire, however, that Camille has not even left the room before he blurts out his acceptance of her proposal, just as Montriveau is suddenly overwhelmed by his own passion in Antoinette's salon. Our ability to understand *Don't Touch the Axe* by no means depends on our recognising the parallels between these sequences. However, by exposing this connection to his earlier romantic comedy, Rivette playfully tempers the emotional violence of Balzac's story and, more importantly, demonstrates the capacity of contemporary heritage films to redeploy the artistic resources of other cinematic works, not least his own.

Rivette's ability to combine literary adaptation with romantic comedy provides compelling evidence of his determination to rethink and re-energise heritage cinema in unexpected ways. In choosing to rework *La Duchesse de Langeais*, the director added himself to a list of international filmmakers who have each been drawn to the dramatic potency of Balzac's novella. Among the seven film and television adaptations of the story to have appeared to date, *Don't Touch the Axe* stands out for the way in which it places violence at the heart of its artistic concerns. At the level of plot, the film evokes the rich network of allusions to blades, cutting and brutal separation which underpin the source text. Moreover, violence proves a key driver of Rivette's cinematography. As Owen Heathcote argues in relation to Balzac, in terms which can be applied equally to Rivette, 'violence is not just a material force but a means to reflect on that force and possibly re-channel it in different, more positive ways' (2009: 19). From the subtle zoom which echoes Montriveau's tightening grip around Antoinette's waist, to the rough editing of the pivotal kidnap sequence, *Don't Touch the Axe* illustrates that violence can act as a powerful stimulant to the cinematic imagination. Most importantly, however, the representation of violence in this film yields precious insights into the evolution of heritage cinema in France since the late 1980s. Just as Balzac both condemned and embraced the stereotypical imagery of Gothic horror, Rivette spurns some of the established techniques of heritage filmmaking without discarding them entirely. Through his casting of Jeanne Balibar and Guillaume Depardieu, he negotiates his own position between the nostalgic period films of the late 1980s and early 1990s and the more self-conscious engagement with violence that would later characterise post-heritage cinema. In *Don't Touch the Axe*, he asserts the flexibility of heritage films to engage both with the history of the genre and with a much wider corpus of cinematic material. Ultimately, therefore, the film captures contemporary French heritage cinema at a liminal, and highly productive, stage in its development. Far from seeking to destroy this type of historical drama in a manner befitting of the violence it portrays, *Don't Touch the Axe* shows heritage stretching its own boundaries in the pursuit of new and original cinema.

Notes

1. Unless otherwise stated, all translations of French quotations in this chapter are my own.
2. For an overview of the omissions made by Baroncelli's adaptation, see for example Lioure (1991: 312–13).
3. For a further discussion of this theme in relation to Rivette's portrayal of the relationship between Montriveau and Antoinette specifically, see Baron (2008: 50–1).
4. On the possible parallels between the character of Antoinette de Langeais, Queen Marie-Antoinette and the Revolutionary Terror, see Buchet (2001).
5. Chollet (1965) notes that the episode in which Montriveau threatens to brand the Duchess has its origins in another Balzac short story, 'Dezesperance d'Amour' ('The Despair of Love'), in which the jealous protagonist disfigures his lover with a sword.
6. For a broader discussion of Balzac's treatment of the theme of separation in *La Duchesse de Langeais*, see Roy-Reverzy (1995).
7. For further brief analysis of the screen personas of Guillaume Depardieu and Jeanne Balibar, see Dosi (2014: 461 n.683).
8. On Balibar's performance in *Who Knows?*, see for example Morrey and Smith (2009: 209–12) and Wiles (2012: 91–8).

Works Cited

Balzac, H. de. 1976–81. In *La Comédie humaine*, ed. P.-G. Castex 12 vols. Paris: Gallimard/Bibliothèque de la Pléiade.
Baron, A.-M. 2007. *Balzac au cinéma: La Duchesse de Langeais de Balzac à Rivette*. *L'Année balzacienne*: 523–527.

---. 2008. *Romans français du dix-neuvième siècle à l'écran. Problèmes de l'adaptation*. Clermont-Ferrand: Presses Universitaires Blaise Pascal.

Buchet Rogers, N. 2001. De 93 à l'*Histoire des Treize*: la terreur de (Marie-) Antoinette de Langeais. *Revue d'histoire littéraire de la France* 101(1): 71–80.

Chollet, R. 1965. De *Dezesperance d'Amour* à *La Duchesse de Langeais*: un exemple de l'unité de la création balzacienne. *L'Année balzacienne*: 93–120.

Dosi, F. 2014. *Trajectoires balzaciennes dans le cinéma de Jacques Rivette*. La Madeleine: LettMotif.

Heathcote, O. 2009. *Balzac and violence: Representing history, space, sexuality and death in 'La Comédie humaine'*. Bern: Peter Lang.

Lioure, M. 1991. Roman, théâtre, cinéma: *Le Film de la Duchesse de Langeais*. *Cahiers Jean Giraudoux* 20: 311–324.

Mileham, J.W. 2003. Desert, Desire, Dezesperance: Space and Play in Balzac's *La Duchesse de Langeais*. *Nineteenth-Century French Studies* 31(3–4): 210–225.

Morrey, D., and A. Smith. 2009. *Jacques Rivette*. Manchester: Manchester University Press.

Powrie, P. 2006. *The cinema of France*. London: Wallflower.

Rivette, J. 2007. *Ne Touchez pas la hache*. Press pack. [Online]. Available at: www.filmsdulosange.fr/uploads/presskits/df47d20aff01c7ab942b70bef-8f25750823c4d46.pdf. Accessed 14 July 2015.

Romney, J. 2008. Don't Touch the Axe. *Sight & Sound* 18(1): 67–68.

Roy-Reverzy, E. 1995. *La Duchesse de Langeais*: un romanesque de la séparation? *L'Année balzacienne*: 63–81.

Thirion, A. 2007. Etourdissant. *Cahiers du cinéma* 621: 10–11.

Trémois, C.-M. 2007. *Ne Touchez pas la hache*, de Jacques Rivette. *Esprit* 3: 375–378.

Vincendeau, G., ed. 2001. *Film/literature/heritage*. London: BFI.

Wiles, M.M. 2012. *Jacques Rivette*. Urbana/Chicago/Springfield: University of Illinois Press.

CHAPTER 9

The Ironic Gaze: Roots Tourism and Irish Heritage Cinema

Ruth Barton

Writing in 2004 on Irish cinema, I identified a trend that had emerged in the previous decade of films defined by nostalgia for a pre-modern Ireland. Such films—*Hear My Song* (Peter Chelsom, 1991), *Into the West* (Mike Newell, 1992), *War of the Buttons* (John Roberts, 1993), *Broken Harvest* (Maurice O'Callaghan, 1994), *The Run of the Country* (Peter Yates, 1995) and others—were distinctive for being structurally and thematically conservative, particularly in terms of their gender representations. They were also all rural-based and many centred their narratives on children, whose state of innocence became a palimpsest for Ireland of old, and by extension the innocent Irish people of bygone times. The impetus behind this wave of heritage films was, I concluded, a desire to make a break with the pervasive legacy of The Troubles and the image of a country defined by lawlessness and violence. In this, the films had much in common with Irish Tourist Board (Fáilte Ireland) campaigns designed to persuade tourists that a visit to Ireland was a visit to a country of timeless and ancient beauty, populated by welcoming natives who had no axe to grind with foreigners (particularly the lucrative UK tourist market). Drawing on theories of the

R. Barton (✉)
Trinity College, Dublin, Ireland
e-mail: ruth.barton@tcd.ie

tourist gaze, it appeared that many of the films replicated such a gaze as part of their aesthetic (Barton 2004: 148–56).

It is remarkable how that situation has changed. Irish cinema of today is overwhelmingly urban-based in terms of its settings, and almost without exception prefers contemporary narratives. Although a number of Irish historical films have been made in recent years (*The Magdalene Sisters* [Peter Mullan, 2002], *The Wind That Shakes the Barley* [Ken Loach, 2006], *Philomena* [Stephen Frears, 2013], *Jimmy's Hall* [Ken Loach, 2014]), these are not strictly indigenous productions. Such a statement needs to recognise the difficulty of establishing a country of origin for many contemporary films; however, all of the above originate outside of Ireland, are directed by British directors, and speak as much to a global audience as to an indigenous Irish one. Nor is there any convincing argument to be made that they conform to heritage filmmaking practices. Instead, they rehearse traumatic narratives of institutional abuse and wartime tragedy.

I have elsewhere considered the reasons for this shift from heritage productions (Barton 2014). Briefly, they arise from the ending of The Troubles and the abeyance of the National Question, the introduction of new digital technologies that favour more contemporary, edgy filmmaking, a generational desire to move away from the older paradigms of the cinema of the 1980s and early 1990s, and the elevation of the city over the countryside as the locus of identity formation.

One category of heritage cinema has, however, survived the transformation and it is to these films that I turn in this chapter. The productions in question foreground, in one way or another, tourist visits to Ireland; all are global productions, and several are rom-coms. They include: *The Matchmaker* (Mark Joffe, 1997), *P.S. I Love You* (Richard LaGravenese, 2007), *Leap Year* (Anand Tucker, 2010) and *Ek Tha Tiger* (*Once There Was a Tiger*, Kabir Khan, 2012). Although what unites all of them is their intersection with heritage, what distinguishes certain of them is a playful and ironic attitude towards the activity of tourism. In this, they are not uniquely Irish but form part of a wider cycle of films of which the best example is another Irish-themed production, Martin McDonagh's *In Bruges* (2008). This opens the door to a reappraisal of heritage cinema as postmodern in the sense of 'knowing and playful', rather than as defined by nostalgia and pastiche. Such films, it will be argued, recognise the inauthenticity of the tourist experience, while knowingly and playfully enacting that tourist encounter. Before discussing these works in more detail, it is useful to detour into a brief overview of related academic work on tourism and cinema.

Rethinking the Tourist Gaze

As I have already mentioned, the branch of tourism theory that overlaps most productively with film studies is that of the tourist gaze. Following John Urry's pioneering *The Tourist Gaze* (1990/2009), some considerable attention has been paid to how his model can be developed and applied to heritage cinema. As Sarah Gibson (2006: 60) notes, for example, in relation to Merchant-Ivory's E.M. Forster adaptations, these were films made primarily for consumption by a global audience who viewed them with the immobility of armchair tourists. While, she argues, the English have misrecognised these films as representing a particular national identification, American audiences have enjoyed the films as a form of cultural tourism. Gibson further discusses how a film such as *A Room With a View* (James Ivory, 1985) comments on the activity of tourism through positioning one of its central characters, Lucy Honeychurch (Helena Bonham-Carter), as a tourist in Italy (what I term 'the tourist-within-the-text'). When the film relocates to England, however, this diegetic engagement with tourism is dropped in favour of an unmediated view of middle-class English rural life. This view is just as informed by the tourist impulse but in a disguised manner. Although Gibson does not quite phrase it thus, the armchair tourist can now immerse herself in the pleasure of gazing at English heritage without being reminded of the act of looking. This distinction between the tourist-within-the-text versus the unmediated tourist gaze, as I will discuss below, can help us reconsider the relationship between tourism and heritage in the cinematic context.

In their article '*The Beach*, the gaze and film tourism', Lisa Law et al. (2007) identify an alternative positioning of the tourist-within-the-text. In Danny Boyle's 2000 version of Alex Garland's best-selling novel, American backpacker Richard (Leonardo DiCaprio) finds his way to the remote beach of the title as a consequence of his rejection of the inauthenticity of 'staged' Thai tourism. Of course, in doing so, he simply expands the frontiers of the tourist industry and comes no closer to engagement with the 'real' Thailand than if he had taken a package holiday. Law et al. distinguish four gazes at play within tourist films: the first gaze—of the camera; the second/third gaze—the conventional tourist gaze/the alternative tourist gaze; the fourth gaze—beyond the frame, of local activists who deliberately resist the first/second/third gazes and, if successful, disrupt the look of the spectator/tourist by drawing attention to the consequences for the environment of their practices of looking (which one could extend generally to the response of the film viewer). They even posit a fifth gaze, that of the academic/researcher at the film site.

Equally interesting is the concept of the host gaze. Currently, most of the research conducted in this area is sociological, drawing on interviews with workers within the tourist industry. As Omar Moufakkir and Yvette Reisinger note in their introduction to their edited collection, *The Host Gaze in Global Tourism*:

> Just as the tourist gaze is dynamic [...], the host gaze is also changing, depending on who is the tourist and who is the host [...]. Just as there is no single tourist gaze, the host gaze must also vary by society, social group and historical period. Host gazes are constructed through cultural similarities and dissimilarities [...]. Surely, there must be different gazes from the same gazer upon different gazees. (2013: xi)

Incorporating theories of the host gaze into analyses of tourist narratives restores some element of mutual agency to the encounter. Just as in the field, in cinema all gazes are not equal, nor do they carry the same ontological weight within any one film, or from film to film. In cinematic narratives, the host may well gaze back at the tourist and in doing so fundamentally destabilise the relationship between the two.

Another useful concept is that of post-tourism, or ironic tourism. Maxine Feifer (1985) suggests that the post-tourist recognises that tourism is always performative, and part of the pleasure of post-tourism is evaluating the quality of that staging. Thus, for instance, shopping for kitschy gifts is a knowing rather than an innocent act of pleasurable consumption. Urry follows Feifer by arguing that post-tourists 'almost delight in the inauthenticity of the normal tourist experience. "Post-tourists" find pleasure in the multiplicity of tourist games. They know that there is no authentic tourist experience, that there are merely a series of games or texts that can be played' (Urry 2009: 12).

Evidently, not all tourists are knowing tourists, and cinema likes to treat as humorous those who genuinely engage in tourist activities, to wit, the sequence in *2 Days in Paris* (Julie Delpy, 2007) where Jack (Adam Goldberg) wilfully misleads a group following in the steps of *The Da Vinci Code*. What Jack fails to understand, however, is that he is not an insider in the city, but as much an outsider as the Americans. In *In Bruges*, by contrast, the tourists-within-the-text are consciously acting parts. The older of the two gunmen on the run, Ken (Brendan Gleeson), patiently, and with some sincerity, instructs his resistant sidekick, Ray (Colin Farrell), how to sightsee. Given that Ken and Ray are Irish, one of the potential viewing pleasures on offer is the positioning of the Irish as subjects rather than objects of the tourist gaze.

The impact on specific locations of serving as a film setting is another commonly discussed aspect of film tourism. Sue Beeton's *Film-induced Tourism* (2005) serves as a useful introduction to the discipline, drawing on case studies from productions as diverse as the *Lord of the Rings* trilogy (Peter Jackson, 2001–3), the *Harry Potter* films (Chris Columbus, Alfonso Cuarón, Mike Newell, David Yates, 2001–11) and television shows such as the Australian *SeaChange* (1998–2000). As she demonstrates, the impact is not always beneficial, even if at the planning stage it promises to be. She and others also refer to the short-term impact of much film/television-induced tourism; in other words, as the film or television programme's impact dwindles, so does tourism to the site. In a more recent overview article, Joanne Connell adds that:

> Essentially, film tourism is tourist activity induced by the viewing of a moving image, and is accepted as encompassing film, television, pre-recorded products (e.g. video/DVD/Blu-Ray) [...] and now extends to digital media. Some distinction should be made between the form (i.e. a film or television programme) and the medium through which the image is transmitted, in that there are numerous ways of viewing film and filmic images and viewing can take place in an increasing multitude of environments. (Connell 2012: 1009)

Elsewhere, Connell has discussed the impact on the Isle of Mull, Scotland where the children's TV programme *Balamory* is set (Connell, 2005). Other case studies include failed sites, such as Cephalonia, the setting for *Captain Corelli's Mandolin* (John Madden, 2001), which, as Simon Hudson and J.R. Brent Ritchie (2006) discuss, did not manage to capitalise on the opportunities offered by the release of the film (and book before it).

Drawing on this model, David Martin-Jones (2014) has explored the significance of the film version of *The Da Vinci Code*'s (Ron Howard, 2006) use of Rosslyn Chapel as a setting. As he illustrates, in this case, VisitScotland actively worked with Sony Pictures to create tie-in promotions to the production. He further demonstrates how the original novel had already created considerable tourist interest in the chapel, and that Scotland in general carries pre-existing semiotic weight as a heritage site, due not least to its ties with its own diaspora (Martin-Jones 2004). He describes a cycle of processes, with the location influencing the film (evidenced by alterations in the adaptation from Dan Brown's novel), and the film influencing the tourist impact on the location.

Martin-Jones' case study illustrates the benefits to the tourist economy of a successful (and strategic) heritage release. To return to the case of Irish cinema, it is surprising, given the importance of tourism to the Irish economy, how little empirical scholarship has been specifically dedicated to the intersection of tourism and filmmaking. Noelle O'Connor and Sangkyun Kim's article 'Pictures and prose: exploring the impact of literary and film tourism' (O'Connor and Kim 2014) provides exploratory comments but the argument remains underdeveloped. According to the Irish Film Board, in 2010, 20 per cent of all tourists cited film as an influencing factor on why they visited Ireland (Irish Film Board 2015). This is, however, a somewhat optimistic reading of the Fáilte Ireland Report on Visitor Attitudes of that year, which actually states, 'Contemporary culture, incorporating performing and visual arts, film, literature, architecture, etc. appeared to have the least appeal with two in five interested to some extent, but one in four uninterested' (Fáilte Ireland 2010: 15). In advance of the publication of the 2013 *Visitor Attitude Survey*, Fáilte Ireland evidently asked the question, and only three per cent of tourists mentioned 'Films/Movies' as the motivation for their visit to Ireland (Fáilte Ireland 2013). Anecdotal evidence suggests that John Ford's *The Quiet Man* (1952) inspires visitors to make the journey to Cong, where the film was made. The 'Atlantic Film Trail' brings the visitor to Ireland from Youghal where *Moby Dick* (John Huston, 1956) was partially shot, and around the coast to Donegal where *Dancing at Lughnasa* (Pat O'Connor, 1998) is set (but not filmed). On the way it takes in the settings for *Poitín* (Bob Quinn, 1979) and *The Ballroom of Romance* (Pat O'Connor, 1982). As anyone who has seen the latter two films will testify, these are rigorously anti-romantic visions of Irish rural life that deliberately set out to undermine the image of the country so embedded in tourist-inflected representations, and it is hard to imagine that anyone seeing either film would have the least inclination to visit its setting. The film trail is accompanied by a booklet (Fáilte Ireland 2015a). A look at the publication suggests that the same idea occurred to the authors, which would explain the omission of any description of the films' plots or aesthetic.

Regrettably, the 2013 *Visitor Attitude Survey* did not elucidate which films had motivated the tourists in question to travel to Ireland. However, we can speculate that the low numbers involved are a consequence of several factors. The first is the absence of any recent high-profile international productions (such as *The Da Vinci Code*) that would obviously motivate travel. Beeton discusses how the economic decision to shoot certain sequences of *Braveheart* (Mel Gibson, 1995) in Ireland did not deter visitors from visiting Stirling where the actual battle was fought. In fact, although none of the filming took place in Stirling, the location has benefitted from a massive increase in visitors as a consequence of Gibson's film (Beeton 2005: 58–60). Ireland, it seems, has not.

Most empirical research on film tourism suggests that the viewer's emotional bond with the diegetic narrative, and the effect created by its mise-en-scène, are important in motivating a visit. Thus, a 'feel-good' film is more likely to create knock-on tourism than one that portrays poor or violent interpersonal relations and/or is set in a disadvantaged area with few recognisable tourist sights. The shift in Irish filmmaking from heritage productions to films with contemporary urban settings and focusing on traumatic narratives must thus be taken into consideration as deterring film-induced tourism to the country. An exception is *Once* (2007), a film that taps into Irish musical heritage through its casting of Glen Hansard of *The Frames* (whose other notable screen appearance was as Outspan in *The Commitments* [Alan Parker, 1991]) and its celebratory depiction of Dublin as a music capital. As Pat Brereton has noted in a paper that campaigns for some form of 'environmental tourism' to be replicated in Irish film:

> More recently, however, most home-grown narratives have appeared less interested in valorising a touristic landscape and have been more focused on emulating Hollywood generic product to achieve commercial success. Contemporary filmmakers […] emulate a universal and materially wealthy post-colonial urban environment, which frequently ignores the past and re-purposes landscape for younger audiences rather than nostalgic, diasporic ones. (Brereton 2006: 407)

Indeed, few Irish films, excepting those mentioned above as global products, have enjoyed much visibility overseas in the last decade or so and thus the opportunities to develop film tourism are limited. The most successful export currently comes from Northern Ireland, and the region is actively promoting *Game of Thrones*-related tourism (Game of Thrones Tours 2015).

New Tourists and the Ironic Gaze

In the absence, therefore, of any compelling empirical research, I want to focus for the remainder of this chapter on a discussion of the tourist-within-the-text, and in particular on the concept of the ironic gaze. As I will argue, this ironic gaze is both elicited by the knowing tourist-within-the-text, and by the host within the text, who gazes back and reframes the tourist. Or it may simply frame the narrative through storylines and aesthetic turns that mark the film as engaging ironically with heritage tropes.

Inevitably, such an enquiry returns us to the *ur*-Irish film, *The Quiet Man*. In *The Irish-American in Popular Culture*, Stephanie Rains has discussed how, as diasporic subjects increasingly become removed from their originating home, so they relate to that imagined space through narrative (Rains 2007: 68–70). Ford's film was to become a key component in the play of images through which Irish-Americans reconstructed a vision of Ireland. At the same time, the film was released when a vacation to the home country was becoming a viable option for the diaspora, and Rains further demonstrates how *Quiet Man*-type imagery was crucial to presenting Ireland as a tourist space. In this manner, the home country commodified the dreams of the diaspora and sold them back to them (Rains 2007: 99–143).

Critical responses to *The Quiet Man* have been divided between those who deride it for its artifice and others who celebrate precisely that artifice, pinpointing within it strategies of ironic disavowal (Barton 2004: 71–6). The opening sequences of the film stage an exchange between the returning emigrant, Sean Thornton (John Wayne), and the locals at Castletown, where his train stops, which provides a commentary on just the kind of tourist discourse that the promotional films were to reproduce (without the accompanying irony). Understanding it as ironic disavowal enables a reading of the positioning of both diasporic subject and indigenous Irish less as dupes of the system than as willing participants in a relay of looks and exchanges (Fig. 9.1).

As the train pulls in, a voiceover introduces the scene: 'Well then now, I'll begin at the beginning. A fine soft day in the Spring it was when the train pulled in to Castletown three hours late as usual and himself got off. He didn't have the look of an American tourist at all about him. Not a camera on him. What was worse, not even a fishing rod.' Thornton alights from the train while a woman in a shawl who has been moving towards the train left of frame comes towards him as do the train driver, the station manager and two porters. Thornton asks, 'Is this the way to Innisfree?' The gathered locals all offer directions, each one less helpful than the last. 'Now tell me

THE IRONIC GAZE: ROOTS TOURISM AND IRISH HERITAGE CINEMA

Fig. 9.1 'Now tell me this, Yank, what is it you're after? Is it trout or salmon?' *The Quiet Man* (John Ford, 1952)

this, Yank,' the driver asks. 'What is it you're after? Is it trout or salmon?' After furher exchanges, the jarvey, Michaeleen Óg Flynn (Barry Fitzgerald) steps forward, picks up Thornton's bags and carries them out to his waiting horse and trap. 'Innisfree, this way,' he announces. Thornton, who all the time has been surrounded by the locals in a series of mid-shots, looks through the window at Flynn, smiling. At the end of the sequence, the camera cuts to the men and the shawled woman now all looking out of the frame, one assumes at the departing Thornton. 'I wonder now why a man would go to Innisfree,' the train driver muses. The camera then pans across the wall to reveal the rest of the group, including the shawled woman. All shake their heads in disbelief at the notion (Fig. 9.2).

The sequence cues a number of perspectives. There is the tourist gaze of the camera, picking out the details of the idyllic country station and the emerald green of the train. The use of Technicolor heightens the almost painterly effect. The scene comes to life with the movement and dialogue of the locals who perform according to longtime expectations of Irish locals. They exhibit no sense of time or of the importance of reaching a destination, they offer kind but useless advice, and they speak the language

Fig. 9.2 'I wonder now why a man would go to Innisfree.' *The Quiet Man* (John Ford, 1952)

of the clan: 'My sister's third young one is living in Innisfree and she'd be only too happy for to show you the road,' the shawled woman offers Thornton, curtsying. 'Oh, ho, well, fine,' Thornton responds, bending to pick up his luggage. 'No, no,' the woman quickly adds, 'if she was here.' In a key argument, Dean MacCannell borrows from sociologist Ervin Goffman to conceptualise tourist space as divided between a 'front', where tourist encounters are played out, and a 'back', the private space of the hosts that tourists seldom see but dream of entering (MacCannell 1976: 101–2). Once they have played their part, the Irish locals move, as MacCannell proposes, from the foreground space of the tourist encounter, to the background of their own space, and train their own/host gaze back on the 'Yank'. As the (roots) tourist-in-the-text, Thornton will struggle throughout the film to assert the dominance of his own gaze and access the 'back' space. The entire sequence is presented to the gaze of the viewer who is expected to understand the ironies at play. That is, if they read it in this manner. Read straight, all that the viewer sees is a romanticised and kitschy film, and that is indeed how many viewers have responded to *The Quiet Man* since its release.

The heritage cinema of the 1980s and early 1990s that I previously identified displays none of this ironic and self-aware understanding of the interplay between gazer and gazee. More recent iterations of the tourist encounter, however, play it out to rich comic effect. Thus, turning to television, when the Simpsons travel to Ireland so that Grandpa Simpson can visit the old country (2009), their arrival sees Lisa quickly having to explain to the family that Ireland is at the forefront of Europe's tech boom. They drive into the village of Dunkilderry past hoardings advertising multinational consumer operations. Strolling leprechauns discuss plasma televisions and holidays in Tuscany. The episode ends with Homer being deported back to America for operating an illicit pub.

Here it is less the case that the characters, with the possible exception of the ever-informed Lisa, are post-tourists so much as the film assumes its audience to be. Its play with the indices of Irish heritage is reliant on an assumption of viewer familiarity with Irish tourist themes and imagery, much of it likely encountered through the media. In this manner, the armchair heritage tourist evolves into the heritage post-tourist.

One needs, however, to be careful not to rush to embrace all recent iterations of the cinematic heritage tourist encounter as informed by postmodern irony. Neither *P.S. I Love You* nor *Leap Year* displays any overwhelming desire to question its own parameters. The former is an adaptation of Cecilia Aherne's best-selling novel of the same name; the latter concerns the decision by its central character, Anna Brady (Amy Adams), to travel to Ireland where she believes it is a custom to propose to your boyfriend on 29 February. Both films' narratives are driven by the quest of a single, female roots tourist. Both also undermine and reframe her gaze by allocating equal, sometimes superior, weight to the gaze of the local back at the tourist. Thus, in *Leap Year*, Anna meets Declan (Matthew Goode), whom she hires to take her to Dublin where she plans to propose to Jeremy (Adam Scott). Declan is quick to dismiss Anna's materialism, epitomised by her Louis Vuitton luggage and her occupation (she decorates apartments before their sale to make them more attractive to purchasers). In the course of their road trip, she is literally divested of her materialism (the luggage goes astray) and Declan educates her gaze away from the contemporary world of consumer capitalism to the mystical world of Irish romance as he guides her around a ruined castle narrating the old myth of the lovers Diarmuid and Gráinne (Fig. 9.3).

Fig. 9.3 *Leap Year* (Anand Tucker, 2010): Anna (Amy Adams) learns to abandon materialism and embrace Irish romanticism

Internet noticeboards suggest that *Leap Year*'s viewers responded as Fáilte Ireland might have hoped to a viewing of the film:

> After watching this movie, I just want to go to Ireland, get lost, and find this guy. Didn't find him that attractive at the beginning of the film, totally loved him by the end! Personality and character really do make a man cuter or less attractive. Most attractive men I've known are guys I didn't pay much attention to at first glance but whose character changed my perception of their physical appearance greatly. Anyhoo, I just want to go to Ireland now!) (Green Lantern Girl 2011)

However, local Irish viewers aligned themselves promptly with the fourth gaze of tourist exchanges:

> Ireland is nothing like it is in this film!!! this film gives a horrible backwards impression of us!!!! people aren't stupid and there are big cities, irish people arent like people in this film!!! AND NO ONE SAYS "top of the morning to yee"!!! (stench_blossom 2011)

The Matchmaker, on the other hand, is constructed so as to simultaneously offer the conventional indices of tourist consumption and to treat tourism, specifically roots tourism, as inauthentic. The story opens in Boston, where Marcy Tizard (Janeane Garofalo) acts as advisor to Senator John McGlory (Jay O. Sanders). When it becomes evident that his faltering election campaign might be rescued by the Irish-American vote, his advisor Nick (Denis Leary) dispatches Marcy to Ireland to trace McGlory's ancestors. After a predictable series of cultural misunderstandings, she and the local village bartender, Sean (David O'Hara), fall in love but their affair is shattered when Sean's estranged wife, Moira (Saffron Burrows), shows up. McGlory travels to Ireland and discovers that Moira's middle name is Kennedy. They become engaged in time for him to take the election in Boston and free up Sean and Marcy to continue their relationship. The film's final revelation is that McGlory is in fact of Hungarian descent and his name was changed when the family arrived at Ellis Island.

Throughout *The Matchmaker* the perspective oscillates from the look of the outsider, Marcy, at the Irish locals, to the locals back at Marcy. As with the other romantic comedies, this exchange of looks is complicated by its gendering. While Marcy may indeed construct the host with her gaze, her authority to look is constantly undermined. In common with her rom-com cousins, Holly (Hilary Swank) in *P.S. I Love You* and Anna in *Leap Year*, she is defined by her lack (here of a suitable male partner) (Lapsley and Westlake 1992). Condemned, as rom-com heroines inevitably are, to behave in a ditzy manner because of their incomplete status as individuals, all three women have to be rescued by their 'better'/'other' halves, all of whom turn out to be handsome Irish males. Upon arrival in Ballingra (the literal translation from the Irish being 'town of love'), a series of mistaken gazes adds to the general joke that Marcy has arrived at a matchmaking festival. When she looks at one of the local men, he looks back at her, wrongly interpreting her gaze as desiring, only to bang his head against the wall when he realises his mistake. Throughout the film, Marcy is coded as 'uptight', where the Irish are relaxed and fun-loving (Fig. 9.4).

In common with the other rom-coms, *The Matchmaker* trades in the signifiers of Irish heritage tourism. The soundtrack features Shane MacGowan, Sinéad O'Connor, Van Morrison and The Chieftains. Much of the filming took place in the picturesque costal village of Roundstone, and the narrative includes a sea journey to the Aran Islands. The locals are delightfully feckless, and spend much of their day frequenting pubs. None of the action is set in Ireland's cities. Yet, as the film's concluding revelation establishes, its entire premise is based on a fiction. Scratch the surface and Marcy might as well have been in Brigadoon.

If *The Matchmaker* nods to the cynical post-tourist in its self-positioning as a performance and its repeated scenes of performance, while simultaneously offering itself to be read straight, then my final example, *Ek Tha Tiger*, takes this premise far beyond Mark Joffe's production. Kabir Khan's

Fig. 9.4 *The Matchmaker* (Mark Joffe, 1997): reversal of the gaze as the locals look back at the tourist, Marcy (Janeane Garofalo)

massive Bollywood hit concerns Indian government agent, Tiger (Salman Khan), whose pursuit of subversives takes him across several continents and into the arms of Zoya (Katrina Kaif), who is revealed to be spying for Pakistan. Part of *Ek Tha Tiger*'s appeal is its incorporation of armchair tourism into a global spy caper. Tiger travels to Dublin, Istanbul and Cuba on his mission, and later, when he absconds with Zoya, is sighted in Venice, Cape Town, Zurich and London. Dublin in Khan's version becomes a modern, exciting city, where old (Trinity College Dublin) and new (the Luas tram) spiritedly co-exist. In Dublin, Zoya is taking a dance class and, in a key set piece, she and Tiger stage a Riverdance-style number that opens on Trinity College's iconic Dining Hall steps and Front Square, and segues into the junction with Grafton Street, Dublin's upmarket shopping area. Filmed at the close of the Celtic Tiger economic boom, the sequence incorporates a panoply of Irish tourist imagery, much of it familiar from Dublin's Mardi Gras-influenced, restyled St Patrick's Day festivities. Dancers wear leprechaun hats and cheerleader costumes and perform against a background of exotic floats. In one segment, a group is dressed in the colours of the successful Kilkenny hurlers. Zoya appears as a bagpiper, a hurler and in a chic summer dress. The street scenes feature men cast to look like the Polish and Eastern European workers who migrated to Dublin in large numbers during the boom. As the desiring and desirable male, Tiger's central positioning within the frame of the film and of the narrative is unproblematic. He sits down beside one of the city's living statues who turns round and nudges him; he poses between two Dublin guards (police), performs with a group of buskers, and in one startling sequence a nun hands him a bouquet of flowers which he carries down the street as fans lean forward to kiss him. The entire sequence is set to a remix of one of its own tracks, 'Banjaara', now integrating Irish traditional music sounds and performed by Sukhwinder Singh (Fig. 9.5).

The sequence is constructed around a vision of Ireland that is made available for the pleasure of the tourist gaze and performed as a knowing post-tourist display. In a sense, the performative aspect is simply a consequence of its mode of production as a Bollywood film, yet it remains interesting from a local perspective because of the heritage tropes it deploys. Gone is the 'real Ireland' of tourism campaigns after *The Quiet Man*. In its place comes a celebration of the city-break as a contemporary vacation opportunity. This aligns it much more with films such as *2 Days in Paris*, and the Richard Linklater trilogy of *Before Sunrise* (1995), *Before Sunset* (2004) and *Before Midnight* (2013). Yet, unlike these films, and more like *In Bruges*, it foregrounds its own tourist aesthetic and invites the audience to share in the pleasures of tourism as performance. From an indigenous perspective, too, the positioning of local participants in the dance number endows them with an agency that allows them to participate in the forward-drive of the film, rather than operating in a separate time/space (outside of modernity) as the Irish so often have in more conventional heritage/roots tourist productions.

As the above examples suggest, the intersection of tourism and cinema remains an important aspect of Irish-set films, even following the demise of the indigenous Irish heritage film. These newer films could easily be

Fig. 9.5 In *Ek Tha Tiger* (Kabir Khan, 2012), Salman Khan dances with Katrina Kaif, here dressed as a Kilkenny hurler

dismissed as global entertainment with little to say about Irish identity formations. In a sense, this is true. In another sense, they demonstrate the global's ability to incorporate the local (only an Irish audience is likely to recognise the colours of the Kilkenny hurlers), and the globalisation of Irish heritage, in particular music and dance. Yet, at the same time, it is reductive to dismiss them as inauthentic without recognising that it is exactly their inauthenticity that complicates their representation of Irish identities and spaces. Their premise, that Ireland functions semiotically as nothing else but a tourist attraction, in whose 'front' space locals engage in pre-rehearsed identity performances, may be as accurate a construction of Ireland on film as any other. It is not, however, one that we may anticipate will form the basis of Fáilte Ireland campaigns to come.

Works Cited

Barton, R. 2004. *Irish national cinema*. London and New York: Routledge.

———. 2014. Between modernity and marginality: Celtic Tiger cinema. In *From prosperity to austerity. A socio-cultural critique of the Celtic Tiger and its aftermath*, eds. E. Maher. and E. O'Brien, 183–194. Manchester and New York: Manchester University Press.

Beeton, S. 2005. *Film-induced tourism*. Clevedon/Buffalo: Channel View Publications.

Brereton, P. 2006. Nature tourism and Irish film. *Irish Studies Review* 14(4): 407–420.

Connell, J. 2005. 'What's the story in Balamory?': The impacts of a children's TV programme on small tourism enterprises on the Isle of Mull, Scotland. *Journal of Sustainable Tourism* 13(3): 228–255.

———. 2012. Film tourism—Evolution, progress and prospects. *Tourism management* 33(5): 1007–1029.

Fáilte Ireland 2010. Visitor attitudes survey 2010 [Online]. Available at: http://www.failteireland.ie/FailteIreland/mdia/WebsiteStructure/Documents/3_Research_Insights/4_Visitor_Insights/Visitor-Attitudes-Survey-Exec-Summary.pdf?ext=.pdf. Accessed 22 Feb 2015.

———. 2013. *Visitor attitudes survey 2013* [Online]. Available at: http://www.failteireland.ie/FailteIreland/media/WebsiteStructure/Documents/3_Research_Insights/4_Visitor_Insights/The_Visitor_Attitudes_%28Port%29_Survey_Report_2013.pdf?ext=.pdf. Accessed 22 Feb 2015.

———. 2015. The Atlantic film trail [Online]. Available at: http://www.discoverireland.ie/getmedia/62055fe3-79d7-45de-a3b5-db3af0a6d2c9/Atlantic-Film-Trail-Brochure-FINAL.aspx. Accessed 22 Feb 2015.

Feifer, M. 1985. *Going places*. London: Macmillan.

Game of Thrones Tours. 2015. [Online]. Available at: http://www.gameofthronestours.com/. Accessed 23 Feb 2015.

Gibson, S. 2006. A seat with a view: Tourism, (im)mobility and the cinematic-travel glance. *Tourist Studies* 6(2): 157–178.

Green Lantern Girl. 2011. IMDB posting [Online]. Available at: http://www.imdb.com/title/tt1216492/board/nest/178613021?ref_=tt_bd_2. Accessed 24 Feb 2015.

Hudson, S., and J.R.B. Ritchie. 2006. Film tourism and destination marketing: The case of Captain Corelli's Mandolin. *Journal of Vacation Marketing* 12(3): 256–268.

Irish Film Board. 2015. Facts and figures [Online]. Available at: http://www.irishfilmboard.ie/irish_film_industry/Facts_amp_Figures/35. Accessed 4 Dec 2015.

Lapsley, R., and M. Westlake. 1992. From Casablanca to pretty woman: The politics of romance. *Screen* 33(1): 27–49.

Law, L., T. Bunnell, and C.-E. Ong. 2007. The beach, the gaze and film tourism. *Tourist Studies* 7(2): 141–164.

MacCannell, D. 1976. *The tourist: A new theory of the leisure class.* Berkeley/Los Angeles/London: University of California Press.

Martin-Jones, D. 2014. Film tourism as heritage tourism: Scotland, diaspora and The Da Vinci Code (2006). *New Review of Film and Television Studies* 12(2): 156–177.

Moufakkir, O., and Y. Reisinger, eds. 2013. *The host gaze in global tourism.* Wallingford, Oxfordshire, Boston, M.A.: CABI.

O'Connor, N., and S. Kim. 2014. Pictures and prose: Exploring the impact of literary and film tourism. *Journal of Tourism and Cultural Change* 12(1): 1–17.

Rains, S. 2007. *The Irish-American in popular culture, 1945–2000.* Dublin and Portland: Irish Academic Press.

Stench-Blossom. 2011. IMDB posting [Online]. Available at: http://www.imdb.com/title/tt1216492/board/nest/178613021?ref_=tt_bd_2. Accessed 24 Feb 2015.

Urry, J. 2009 [1990]. *The tourist gaze.* London: Sage.

PART III

Modes of Consumption

CHAPTER 10

Historical Films in Europe: The Transnational Production, Circulation and Reception of 'National' Heritage Drama

Andrew Higson

To live in Europe in the 2010s is to live through challenging times. On the one hand, the idea of Europe as a collective entity is at the time of writing as robust as it has ever been, and the coordinating function of the supranational European Union remains strong and far-reaching. On the other hand, the European project is threatened by financial crises, concerns about immigration, insular nationalist politics and Eurosceptic lack of interest at best and downright hostility at worst. As the great Norwegian actress and film director Liv Ullmann argued in 2014, European film and European cultural institutions 'are more important than ever' in this context: through cross-European collaboration and cooperation, it is possible to 'develop understanding and knowledge of each other's countries, art, culture and human dignity' and protect 'our common democratic culture' (2014: 11).

As Ullmann implies, cinema can be one of the most potent means of enabling citizens to encounter other cultures sympathetically; by extension, historical drama can be one of the most potent ways of enabling those same

A. Higson (✉)
University of York, York, UK
e-mail: andrew.higson@york.ac.uk

citizens to come to terms with the history of their own nation, histories of other nations, and indeed the shared but often internecine history of Europe. If there is such a thing as a common European culture, then it is a culture with a long, complex and multifaceted history, a past that European filmmakers have in various ways sought to present on screen.

The idea of a common European culture is not an easy one to sustain, however. Europe is an ever-changing network of nations, cultures, languages, identities and spaces. The production and circulation of films about the past is one way in which that network is exploited, reproduced, challenged, renewed and reinforced. Identities and cultures are rarely if ever pure or non-complex, caught up as they are in transnational, intercultural flows and negotiations. Historical films narrativise those identities and cultures, and the values and beliefs they embody. The circulation of and engagement with films about other European pasts than those with which one is most familiar has the capacity, therefore, to enhance understanding and communication within and between nations and cultures.

Intercultural, transnational and translingual encounters do not take place outside prevailing power relations, however. If Europe is an ever-changing network, it is clear that some connections are much stronger than others, that some parts of the network seem peripheral, and that the degree and experience of integration and connectedness is very uneven, whether at the level of culture, language, markets or industry infrastructure. The distribution of political and economic power across Europe cannot be ignored, given the impact it has on the nature and extent of cultural production, cultural flow and cultural reception. Within the European film business, there are some relatively powerful production centres and others that can only be described as marginal from the perspective of Europe as a whole.

The patterns of cultural flow are then decidedly asymmetrical. In this context, some films are so disconnected from the core business networks that they prove inexportable, and remain confined to their sometimes tiny domestic markets, while others work only within regional networks such as the Scandinavian or Nordic blocs, the Baltic nations, Eastern Europe, the Balkans, and so on. Language is vital in this respect, given the historical role of national languages in establishing modern European nations as distinct, culturally unique entities. While such ties remain strong, other cultural proximities enable some films to travel across borders.

The Relative Visibility of European Historical Drama

As the introduction to this volume notes, some commentators place historical films at the centre of contemporary European film culture. This seems a reasonable argument: even in the period since 2005, European-made historical dramas include *Das Leben der Anderen* (*The Lives of Others*, Florian Henckel von Donnersmarck, 2006), *El laberinto del fauno* (*Pan's Labyrinth*, Guillermo del Toro, 2006), *Perfume: The Story of a Murderer* (Tom Tykwer, 2006), *Coco avant Chanel* (*Coco Before Chanel*, Anne Fontaine, 2009), *Das Weisse Band* (*The White Ribbon*, Michael Haneke, 2009), *The King's Speech* (Tom Hooper, 2010), *The Artist* (Michel Hazanavicius, 2011), *En kongelig affære* (*A Royal Affair*, Nikolaj Arcel, 2012), *Ida* (Pawel Pawlikowski, 2013), *Mr Turner* (Mike Leigh, 2014) and the various *Astérix* films made in this period. Such a rich array of films suggests that historical drama might be a mainstay of European film production, one of the film genres most able to travel across internal European borders. If audiences are prepared to engage with such films, we might conclude that there is a potent fascination with the otherness of other nations' heritages, but also the otherness of much of what passes as one's own national heritage. Unfortunately, as this chapter demonstrates, the facts of distribution, exhibition and reception do not really support such arguments.

What follows draws on extensive statistical analysis of the European film market undertaken by Huw Jones and others through the HERA-funded project, Mediating Cultural Encounters Through European Screen (MeCETES 2015). In terms of the assumed prominence of European historical films within the European market, five broad conclusions can be drawn from this research. First, European films generally don't circulate very effectively, even within Europe—and historical films are no different. Cultural flow and intercultural encounters are in this sense quite limited. Second, while most European countries produce one or two nationally specific historical dramas each year, and these often fare well with domestic audiences, few of them travel far beyond their home territory. Rather than national differences appealing as exotic heritage cultures, the histories of many European nations or regions thus remain unfamiliar to the citizens of other countries.

Third, while some films that might be viewed as representations of 'national' heritage have proved highly exportable, this phenomenon is really limited to English-language historical films with a strong UK connection at the level of production, story or setting, and such films dominate the lists of European films that travel well. Fourth, historical dramas, whether imports, co-productions or national productions, are not actually much favoured by European audiences. Fifth, even in terms of the numbers of films made, historical drama is not particularly prominent in Europe. The following sections explore these issues in more detail, focusing on the period since 2005, and providing case studies of various types of historical films from different production contexts and with varying degrees of European visibility.

European Historical Dramas that Travel Well

In the period 2005–14, according to the LUMIERE database produced by the European Audiovisual Observatory (2015), some 10,000 films were made in Europe (unless otherwise indicated, all admissions figures are taken from this source). If we focus only on feature-length fiction films that actually made it into distribution, the number already drops off sharply. By identifying films that might be described as well travelled within Europe, we have whittled the number down to just 109. These are the only films that were distributed in at least 20 European territories, recorded more than one million admissions outside their country of origin but within Europe, and achieved a penetration rate of at least 0.5 per cent of the population in at least three of those non-domestic territories. Of these 109 films, some 46 are in some sense historical dramas, defined as films with settings before 2000—though it would be completely inappropriate to describe them all as national heritage dramas. Even so, we can conclude that around half of the well-travelled European films of the period since 2005 were historical dramas—while at the same time noting that this is less than 0.5 per cent of the European films made in that period.

Those 46 European historical dramas that did actually travel reasonably well within Europe can be classified by subgenre and mode of production, a process that reveals a marked relationship between budget, period, narrative type and production values. Thus action-adventure movies tend to be set in the distant past and have high budgets and high production values, while films set in the more recent past tend to have more modest budgets, and include several films that, by the standards of the international film business, are decidedly low-budget, specialised, 'quality' films, with production values to match.

The big-budget action-adventure films set in the past were designed to appeal to mainstream audiences and in many ways mimic Hollywood blockbuster production values—not least because they often depend on Hollywood investment. This small group of films has budgets of more than $70 million and makes extensive use of special effects and star casts (information about budgets, here and below, is taken from *Box Office Mojo* 2015 and *The Numbers* 2015). Such films tend to focus on legendary historical characters from the distant past, often a version of ancient or medieval history. Some of them are national legends, like *Robin Hood* (Ridley Scott, 2010), but others, such as *Kingdom of Heaven* (Ridley Scott, 2005), are less nationally specific. The two live-action, French-led *Astérix* films (*Astérix aux jeux olympiques* [*Astérix at the Olympic Games*, Frédéric Forestier and Thomas Langmann, 2008]; *Astérix & Obélix: Au service de sa Majesty* [*Astérix and Obélix: God Save Britannia*, Laurent Tirard, 2012]) might also be included in this category, given their budgets and setting, although their family-oriented blend of historical action, drama and comedy marks them out as slightly different. Again, they clearly speak to a certain sense of national history, but they also succeed because they are based on very well-known source texts.

There is also a group of more modestly budgeted films with more varied historical settings, stretching from the Viking period to the late twentieth century, which are again addressed to family audiences. Several are animated films, but there are also the two live-action Nanny McPhee films (*Nanny McPhee* [Kirk Jones, 2005]; *Nanny McPhee Returns* [Susanna White, 2010]). The budgets for these films were between $25 million and $35 million, with the exception of the $55 million UK/US inward investment production *The Pirates! Band of Misfits* (Peter Lord and Jeff Newitt, 2012).

A fourth production trend is medium-budget historical dramas set in the relatively distant past, from the sixteenth to nineteenth centuries, including *Perfume, Oliver Twist* (Roman Polanski, 2005), *Elizabeth: The Golden Age* (Shekhar Kapur, 2007) and *Les Misérables* (Tom Hooper, 2012). Once again, the pre-sold property is a vital ingredient, with several of these films being adapted from canonical and/or highly successful works of literature. This production trend depends upon well-known actors, high production values and budgets somewhere between $25 million and $65 million, and is designed to appeal to both mainstream audiences and those crossover audiences who feel more at home in independent or art-house cinemas.

The final three production trends involve more modestly budgeted historical dramas set in the more recent, twentieth-century past. A good number of these films are biopics about the (private) lives of internationally famous people, including *Coco Before Chanel*, *La Mome* (*La Vie En Rose*, Olivier Dahan, 2007), *The King's Speech*, *The Queen* (Stephen Frears, 2006) and *Rush* (Ron Howard, 2013). While the latter film cost $38 million, most of these biopics were made for between $12 million and $30 million. In this same budget range, there is another batch of adaptations set in the twentieth century, such as *Tinker, Tailor, Soldier, Spy* (Tomas Alfredson, 2011), *Potiche* (François Ozon, 2010) and *Philomena* (Stephen Frears, 2013). Such films again endeavour to attract mainstream and crossover audiences by playing on well-known casts and relatively high production values.

Finally, a small group of films with much smaller budgets of $8 million or less focuses on historically significant, but not necessarily well-known, people or events of the twentieth century, and features much less familiar casts and non-spectacular aesthetics designed to appeal to film aficionados, the sorts of audiences that are more likely to visit an art-house cinema than a multiplex. Such films include *The Wind That Shakes the Barley* (Ken Loach, 2006), *Des hommes et des dieux* (*Of Gods and Men*, Xavier Beauvois, 2010), *The Lives of Others* and *Ida*. To this list, we might add three more crossover films with budgets in the mid-teens: *The Artist*, *Pan's Labyrinth* and *The White Ribbon*.

Of the 46 European-led historical dramas that proved popular outside their domestic markets, 31 were shot in the English language (although most will have been dubbed into other languages for distribution in Europe). The majority of these films were in some way (European) co-productions. As will be evident from the titles, more than half were majority UK productions; 14 were French-led productions, five were German-led, with the rest led by Spain, Poland, Belgium and Ireland. Around half of the films also received MEDIA or Eurimages funding from the EU.

While one of the defining features of these 46 films is that they are historical dramas with strong European connections, it is difficult to escape the American connection, which inevitably has an impact on budget. Twelve of the films received US backing, while seven of the UK-led films are inward investment co-productions with American companies. Even so, there is no absolute correlation between budget size and the ability to travel well within Europe. Thus, the most popular of these 46 historical dramas in non-domestic European territories was *The King's Speech*, with a $15 million budget (and American support, admittedly). The next four most popular films in non-domestic European territories all had budgets of between $60 million and $200 million, but the eighth most successful traveller on the list was *The Lives of Others*, with a tiny $2 million budget, while three others budgeted in the mid-teens, including *The Artist*, were not far behind. Even so, most of the best-travelled historical dramas had budgets of $30 million or above, and most European films have far smaller budgets than that. According to the European Commission, 'The average EU production budget ranges from nearly €11 million the UK, €5 million in Germany and France to €300,000 in Hungary and Estonia' (European Commission 2014a). With the exception of *The King's Speech*, the relative success of these films in Europe was also out of kilter with their global performance. The numbers of tickets sold in non-domestic European territories was limited, too: only three of the 46 historical dramas sold more than ten million tickets, while 12 sold fewer than three million.

Acclaimed European Historical Dramas

Such statistical analysis deals only with theatrical box-office success, and not with critical success or user ratings, or with the viewing of films online or on television. How does the picture change if we focus instead on the 20 European-produced historical dramas released between 2005 and 2014 that best caught the public imagination regardless of where or how the films were screened, that were most admired by critics, and that were part of the official selection for the annual European Film Awards (European Film Academy 2015)? All but one of these 20 films was either nominated for or won at least one European Film Award. All of the films have a 'metascore' of at least 81 per cent ('universal acclaim') on Metacritic.com (2015), which is based on published reviews by film critics. In addition, these are the top 20 such films in terms of MOVIEmeter website traffic on the Internet Movie Database (2015), which records how many users view a film's profile page on IMDb.com, thus indicating a high level of public awareness and/or interest.

Just over half of these 20 films also appear in the list of 46 historical dramas that travelled well theatrically within Europe, including *The White Ribbon*, *Of Gods and Men*, *The Artist*, *The King's Speech* and *The Wind That Shakes the Barley*. These are films at the lower end of the budget range, but which aim for the respectability and appeal of the 'high-quality' specialised or art-house film. The more expensive films—the three Working

Title productions, *Pride and Prejudice* (Joe Wright, 2005), *Atonement* (Joe Wright, 2007) and *Tinker, Tailor, Soldier, Spy*—had budgets between $28 million and $32 million, and were clearly designed to cross over into the mainstream; but all the rest had budgets of $18 million or less.

Two of the nine films that appear in this list but not on the list of well-travelled films had budgets of $13 million (two more UK-led, English-language dramas, *Mr Turner* and *'71* [Yann Demange, 2014]), but all the rest had budgets of $7 million or less—much less in some cases, with *El secreto de sus ojos* (*The Secret in Their Eyes*, Juan José Campanella, 2009), *Hunger* (Steve McQueen, 2008), *4 luni, 3 săptămâni și 2 zile* (*4 Months, 3 Weeks and 2 Days*, Cristian Mungiu, 2007) and *This Is England* (Shane Meadows, 2006) all costing $2 million or less. It is therefore not surprising that these films did not travel as well as some of the higher-budgeted historical dramas: they simply did not have the same appeal for non-specialist audiences; nor did they have the marketing budgets or distribution deals that those other films had. Again, however, it should be noted that two films with budgets of $2 million do appear in the lists of both the best-travelled and most acclaimed films: *Ida* and *The Lives of Others*. They are thus exceptional, in both senses of the term.

This list of historical dramas that were acclaimed by critics, film professionals and users is thus dominated by small-scale films that tended to circulate as specialised or art-house films. Six were set in the first half of the twentieth century, and 12 were set between 1960 and the turn of the millennium. Compare this to the fact that, of the previous list of 46 historical dramas that travelled well theatrically within Europe, the three production trends involving more modestly budgeted films were made up entirely of dramas set in the twentieth century, with a good proportion set in the period since 1960. Historical drama productions inevitably attract additional costs due to the need to recreate a particular historical period. It is therefore significant that the more modestly budgeted films were set in the relatively recent past, thus requiring less in the way of historical reconstruction.

Only two of the acclaimed historical dramas were set prior to the twentieth century, and both of those were British-led productions, *Mr Turner* and *Pride and Prejudice*, with the latter benefitting from the involvement of Working Title and therefore Universal. Working Title's involvement was also crucial for European films set prior to the twentieth century and which travelled well theatrically within Europe, accounting for *Anna*

Karenina (Joe Wright, 2012), *Elizabeth: The Golden Age*, *Les Misérables*, *Pride and Prejudice* and the *Nanny McPhee* films (they also produced the twentieth-century-set *Atonement*). By contrast, it was unusual for high-profile, live-action historical dramas set before the twentieth century to be led by a production company based outside the UK. Of the films on either of the two lists above, only six meet that criterion: *Perfume* and *The Three Musketeers* (Paul W.S. Anderson, 2011), both led by German companies, and *Oliver Twist*, *Bandidas* (Joachim Running and Espen Sandberg, 2006) and two of the *Astérix* films, all led by French companies. With the exception of the *Astérix* films, they were shot primarily in the English language, and featured English-speaking and/or Hollywood-attuned stars. If we also take into account the fact that half of the 20 most acclaimed European historical dramas were UK-led, English-language productions generally dealing with aspects of British history, it is once more evident that we Europeans encounter a fairly limited range of European pasts and a fairly restricted approach to historical representation in recent successful European films.

The prominence of Working Title owes much to the fact that the company is a wholly-owned subsidiary of the major American studio, Universal, and their investment in the films noted above can be seen as a means of securing a strong foothold in the European market (Townsend 2014). While the British connection is important, *Anna Karenina* has a Russian setting and *Les Misérables* a French setting, while *Elizabeth: The Golden Age* deals with England's relations with other leading European states in the sixteenth century. Subject matter and setting aside, one of the reasons why these films were able to find a foothold in European markets was because they were distributed primarily by Universal, UIP or a local subsidiary, sometimes in conjunction with another local distributor. In other words, they were able to benefit from well-resourced global distribution operations. But even Universal's distribution agencies have to negotiate sales with a whole series of small local companies in order to cover Europe—at least 7–10 per film within the territories monitored by the LUMIERE database.

In order to minimise risk, each of these films was based on a pre-sold property—three classic European novels, a more recent critically acclaimed novel, a children's book series, and a prior film and very famous historical figure in Queen Elizabeth I. In various ways, then, Working Title's strategy was much more about pitching to the market than about making a self-consciously national heritage drama—but pitching to a European market, as much as an American market, which was presumably what appealed to Universal about these productions. As far as Working Title's executive producer, Eric Fellner, was concerned, 'The whole nationality issue is a red herring... I work in a global business' (2014). On the other hand, these films were important for Universal's global business precisely because they tapped into nationally specific English, French and Russian heritages that have proved to be attractive globally.

Audience Preferences

None of this should lead us to assume that European historical drama is necessarily popular across Europe. Indeed, according to a recent European Commission report (2014b), historical drama is not high on the list of genre preferences for European film audiences. Europeans particularly like to watch comedies (44 per cent say they watch these 'often'), followed by action (40 per cent) and adventure films (34 per cent). Of course, some of those action and adventure films may also be set in the past. But only 16 per cent of Europeans say they watch history films 'often', only 15 per cent say they watch war films 'often', and only nine per cent say they watch biographies 'often'. Despite these low numbers, there does appear to be strong demand for these genres: when asked about the types of stories they 'do not see enough of in films', European film viewers above all mention 'historical films' and 'biographies'.

The EC survey also suggests a geopolitical skew in audience preferences, with history films, war films and biographies consistently more popular in Eastern European countries than in Western European countries. Leaving aside national biases, the report also suggests that 'Europhiles'—those 14 per cent of European film viewers who regularly watch European films, and who tend to live in towns and cities within easy reach of cinemas—are also fans of historical films. If we combine this information with the evidence above about the relative exportability of small-scale, auteur-led, art-house films—even if it is often only through the festival circuit—and the critical prominence of such films, we might conclude that, among European audiences, those that are most likely to engage with unfamiliar histories are university-educated, Europhile, middle-class film aficionados.

The Performance of Historical Dramas in Their Domestic Markets

This sense that historical drama is not high on the agenda of most European film audiences also has an impact on which domestically produced films are most favoured by the audiences in that particular nation. If the most popular domestic films across Europe tend to be comedies, followed by romance, family films and contemporary dramas, the LUMIERE database demonstrates that most European countries also produce one or two popular domestic historical dramas each year.

In 2012, for instance, some 14 European countries saw at least one home-made historical film of some sort in the top five most successful films showing in domestic cinemas that year. There are some trends worth noting here. First, few of these domestically popular historical dramas travelled to the rest of Europe. Most appear to be made specifically for their own territory, and either do not travel beyond that territory or are distributed only in one or two neighbouring countries. Second, even these small-scale, domestically popular, historical dramas tend to be European co-productions rather than purely national productions, although this probably has more to do with issues of financing than the nature of the story or the presumed exportability of these films. Third, most of these domestically popular historical dramas deal with periods of great domestic social and political upheaval, such as revolutions, wars and foreign occupations. Indeed, many are set during the Second World War.

Aniko Imre (2012: 8–9) notes a fascination with national historical dramas in Eastern European countries in recent years. Take, for instance, three recent Latvian historical dramas that were successful in the Latvian market: *Rigas sargi* (*Defenders of Riga*, Aigars Grauba, 2007), *Rudolfa mantojums* (*Rudolf's Gold*, Janis Streics, 2010) and *Sapnu komanda* 1935 (*Dream Team 1935*, Aigars Grauba, 2012). Like other Eastern European historical dramas, these films self-consciously work over and reclaim key moments in the national history as a means of asserting a new sense of self-identity in a post-communist world. Such films are generally made only for the home market. They may be relatively costly as national productions, and highly successful with national audiences, but they are often highly localised epics, with strongly patriotic and/or nationalistic storylines, and impoverished production values by international standards—and they rarely travel. None of the three Latvian historical dramas was distributed further than Lithuania, for instance.

The performance of such films constitutes a fourth trend worthy of note among nationally popular historical dramas. The domestic success of such films is tiny compared with the box office of those films that do travel. But they are also generally quite different to equally low-budget art-house films that may be critically acclaimed, and that often actually travel abroad much better, even if only on the festival circuit. The flipside of this is that few historical dramas that are critically acclaimed outside the national context achieve genuine popular success with their domestic audience. Nonetheless, these films do travel relatively well within art-house and festival circuits. In other words, while domestically popular historical dramas do not travel well within Europe, critically acclaimed historical dramas often do, as the above lists demonstrate.

The three Latvian historical dramas, for instance, were among only four Latvian-produced feature films to gain more than 40,000 admissions in Latvian cinemas in the period from 2005 to 2013, and only one of those, *Defenders of Riga*, can be considered a significant success, with 205,000 admissions. Those four films were also the only Latvian productions to appear in the domestic-box-office top-ten lists in the period 2008–13 (European Audiovisual Observatory 2015; Baltic Films 2008–14). Indeed, *Defenders of Riga* was the most successful film, from Hollywood or elsewhere, to appear in Latvian cinemas in the period since 1991, a record previously held by *Titanic* (James Cameron, 1997) (Brūvere 2012). This is a unique success, however, by the most expensive Latvian production to date, and by far the largest market share of the Latvian box office in those years was taken by Hollywood films. So all but eight of the other films in the Latvian top ten for 2008–13 were American productions, or European films that benefitted from American investment; the only film without a Hollywood connection was a Russian film, *Ironiya sud'by. Prodolzheniye* (*The Irony of Fate. Sequel*, Timur Bekmambetov, 2007). Indeed, between 2005 and 2013, around 80 per cent of cinema tickets sold in Latvia were for Hollywood films, with Latvian films accounting for between 2.5 per cent and 6.9 per cent each year, and films from other European countries 14 per cent (European Audiovisual Observatory 2015; Baltic Films 2008–14).

The production company Platforma Films was responsible for all three of the Latvian films noted above, and their aim was to produce films that would please regular Latvian film viewers—'local examples of mainstream cinema' (Balcus 2012)—and they were prepared to invest in those productions on a scale few other Latvian filmmakers have been able to do since the fall of communism. All three films focused on key moments in Latvian national history, combining a sense of 'spectacle' with a 'patriotic look at our past' (Balcus 2012). *Defenders of Riga* is about the battle for Riga against Russian and German forces in Latvia's 1919 War of Independence. In the words of one Latvian commentator, 'by Latvian standards this is an epic film with a budget of $4 million', a domestic crowd pleaser that aims for neither 'subtlety' nor 'historical accuracy', and which 'plays on some of their most firmly held mythology and themes' (Makwitz 2008).

SMALL NATIONAL CINEMAS AND THE EXPORT MARKET

Latvia is a prime example of a small-nation cinema rebuilding itself in the post-communist era. Denmark is another small European nation, but with a much stronger, better developed and modern production base. Even so, few of its historical dramas have travelled well. The Second World War drama, *Hvidsten gruppen* (*This Life*, Anne-Grethe Bjarup Riis, 2012), for instance, was one of the most successful Danish-led productions in the Danish market in 2012 and won prizes at two international festivals, but it did not travel theatrically outside Denmark. In the same year, *A Royal Affair*, a romantic costume drama set during the Danish Enlightenment, was a domestic box-office success that also secured distribution in 26 other European territories. Its success outside Denmark and France was very modest indeed, however, with almost three quarters of its box-office gross takings garnered in the domestic market. While it was a mainstream success in Denmark, it was a very low-profile art-house release in the UK, although it did win the Silver Bear at the Berlin Festival in 2012, and was nominated for the Best Foreign Language Film Oscar in 2013.

These, then, are further examples of films about a particular national heritage that have very little access or appeal to non-national audiences—even though *A Royal Affair* was at the level of funding a transnational European project: a Danish-Swedish-Czech co-production, it also received funds from Eurimages and the MEDIA programme as well as various national and regional Scandinavian sources. But even in national markets, locally specific historical dramas will occasionally fail to make any impact with audiences. The UK production of *Wuthering Heights* (Andrea Arnold, 2011), for instance, set in the nineteenth century, was made for a budget not much smaller than *A Royal Affair* ($5 million, compared to the latter's $7 million budget), but where the Danish film received a mainstream release in its home market and recorded over 500,000 admissions, the British film was distributed as an art-house film even in the UK—and even taking into account its similar release in some 16 other European territories, it achieved only 250,000 admissions in total. It did, however, win prizes at three European film festivals.

Seeking exposure at international film festivals has been an important strategy for film industries in both small nations and larger nations rebuilding their industries after the fall of communism. Occasionally, those industries will work collaboratively, as with the 'Off The Wall' project in Eastern Europe, an initiative supported by the MEDIA strand of the EU's Creative Europe programme. 'Off The Wall' has collected documentary, animated and historical fiction films from Central and Eastern Europe for exhibition at major film festivals. The programme is designed to 'share the human experience of living in Eastern Europe with the audiences in the West':

> Over the last five years [2009–14], various filmmakers in Eastern Europe have made artistically significant works shaped by a common past and shared experiences. This generation of directors, born from the 1970s onwards, spent their childhoods in the last throes of the communist system. (Off The Wall 2014)

Films about living in a communist state, or about the fall of communism, constitute an important strand of the recent output in Central and Eastern European countries, and include such productions as *Ida*, *The Lives of Others* and *4 Months, 3 Weeks and 2 Days*, set in communist Poland, East Berlin and Romania respectively. All three of these films travelled widely to, and were acclaimed at, festivals around the world; all three also won the Best Film Award at the European Film Awards, while the first two won Best Foreign Language Movie at the Oscars, and the Romanian film won the Palme d'Or at the Cannes Film Festival. The domestic box-office success of these three films varied considerably. *The Lives of Others* sold 7.3 million tickets in its home territory, Germany, which would have made it the twelfth most successful film in Germany in 2007 had all its tickets been sold in a single year (the film was first released in 2006), and the third most popular German production. *4 Months, 3 Weeks and 2 Days* sold only 89,000 tickets in Romania in 2007, but this was enough to make it the seventh most popular film at the Romanian box office that year, and the most popular Romanian film. But while *Ida* sold more tickets (149,000) in its home market, Poland, than *4 Months* sold in Romania, this was only enough to make it the 119th most successful film in Poland that year; nor did it get into the top ten most successful productions of 2013.

To look at the reception of some of these films in the UK is to recognise just how small the UK market for foreign-language films is, and how resistant UK audiences are generally to European cultural products and unfamiliar histories (Jones 2014). Focusing solely on Amazon UK customer reviews, it is clear that those who are already familiar with low-budget European drama with 'quality' production values are relatively receptive to foreign-language films set in unfamiliar places and times, while others feel alienated. Thus several customer reviews of *Ida* reported that the film was something of a history lesson, with words such as 'insight', 'revelation' and 'truth' and ideas of authenticity and sincerity often being used in a positive sense.

By contrast, many Amazon UK customers expressed disappointment having purchased *A Royal Affair*—or rather, what they encountered as *A Royal Affair*—thinking it was an English-language historical drama; this error prompted heated discussion with voices both for and against foreign-language film on the reviews page. Clearly, several felt misled by the marketing for the film and did not watch it once they realised it wasn't in English (see, for example, Rawlings 2013). Others were more sympathetic to these transnational cultural encounters: 'I love these obscure stories from around Europe. We in Britain are so isolated, insecure and prejudicial... [and] movies like this are a great joy!' (Hermit 2014).

NATIONAL HERITAGE AND HISTORICAL FILMS: *THE KING'S SPEECH*

While such comments are revealing in terms of how different audiences relate to diverse European films, stories, characters and languages, as Bangert et al. (2013) point out, historical films 'often generate major national debates on the role of the past in contemporary national identity construction'. *Ida*, *The Lives of Others* and *4 Months, 3 Weeks and 2 Days* are cases in point, with all three generating controversy about their subject matter, the way this was handled and the wider national heritages and cultural identities into which they tapped (see, for example, Pulver 2015; Godeanu-Kenworthy and Popescu-Sandu 2014; Cooke 2013). In the case of *Ida*, for instance, a nationalist organisation, the Polish Anti-Defamation League (Reduta Dobrego Imienia), launched a petition against the film, accusing it of 'being "anti-Polish" and possessing 'serious flaws' of historical fact' (Pulver 2015).

The debate about heritage cinema has been closely bound to debates about national cinema and national identity. Central to the way in which we have, over the years, theorised heritage cinema has been a sense that it is primarily a national project. Such films present a national past, imagining the nation historically and contributing to the maintenance of particular constructions of national identity and national community (Higson 2003, 2011).

Yet as the nationalist case against *Ida* reminds us, ideas of heritage, identity and belonging are rarely uncontested. At the same time, *Ida*'s success abroad, at festivals, award ceremonies and art houses in Europe and the USA, invested Poland as a nation with considerable cultural capital and drew international attention to the idea of contemporary Polish cinema. There is, then, an interesting tension around such films, between the national and the transnational—not least since *Ida* was actually a Polish-Danish co-production. There is, of course, nothing unusual about this: a great deal of what passes as (national) heritage cinema is actually the product of transnational circumstances and pitched at transnational, even global markets, even if these are sometimes global art-house and festival markets. That is to say, such films are very often transnational productions, hybrid bundles of attractions that can be enjoyed by a range of audiences at the level of the text, and relatively exportable commodities at the point of exhibition (Higson 2003, 2011).

The King's Speech certainly fits this model, since it is both a highly acclaimed European historical drama and the one that has travelled most widely within Europe since 2005, selling more tickets (13.5 million) than any other outside its own domestic market (and another 7.5 million in the UK). This is a film about the British past, which dwells on the monarchy, one of the key institutions of the national heritage. After the James Bond and Harry Potter films, it was also the most successful British film of any genre in other European markets, as well as one of the most successful European productions of the last ten years: with a budget of only $15 million, its global box-office takings of $411 million were huge.

Of this, $135 million was taken in the USA; another $74 million was taken in territories outside North America and Europe, the relative modesty of the figure demonstrating just how important the North American and European markets are. The remaining $202 million came from Europe, which was thus significantly more lucrative than the North

American market. But it is important to note just how fragmented that European market is, with at least 22 separate distributors handling this film in 31 separate territories.

The EU attempts to mitigate this market fragmentation through its MEDIA programme, which is designed to encourage distribution of films outside the countries in which they are made, and *The King's Speech* received €562,000 in distribution support from this fund to promote distribution outside the UK (European Commission 2011). Even so, the distribution picture shows serious market inequalities across Europe. Within Europe, there are five big markets (the UK, France, Germany, Spain and Italy), in each of which the film enjoyed a mainstream release, showing on between 200 and 600 screens, and securing between $12 million and $75 million gross—with the total box-office takings for these five territories being greater than those for the USA. The takings in the UK were $75 million, roughly 37 per cent of the European market for *The King's Speech*. In the next tier of territories, mainly the smaller Western and Central European nations, the film showed in 40 to 100 cinemas, taking between $2 million and $6 million (Poland) in each territory, or between one and three per cent of the European gross. In another 14 countries, mainly in Eastern Europe, the Balkans, and former Soviet states, the film received a very modest release, sometimes showing in just a handful of cinemas, sometimes up to as many as 20, but never taking more than $2 million in any country, which is less than one per cent of the European box office. Sales agents and distributors thus had to work very hard to maximise their income, but in this particular case the work paid off.

For the film industry, *The King's Speech* is a beacon of cultural enterprise and a marketing triumph. From the perspective of what commentators variously call the heritage industry and the heritage sector, the success of the film as a cultural export has played a key role in maintaining England as a tourist destination and keeping Brand UK in the global consciousness. And for nationalist and/or patriotic British commentators and Anglophiles, it was applauded for its patriotic presentation of the royal family as a charming national institution.

From other perspectives, however, such nationalist visions are invariably highly contested. The values, beliefs and identities promoted by a conservative, patriotic and/or Anglophile reading of the film are challenged by others on the left of the political spectrum, for whom the idea of the British monarchy as being at the very heart of the national heritage may be highly troubling. Likewise, the idea that it makes perfect sense for the *English* royal family to act as figureheads of the *British* nation. Or the idea of the heterosexual, white, highly privileged nuclear family as an entirely normative role model, in the sense of the film offering no challenge to this assumption. Or the idea that the role of the UK's former colonies should be to provide discreet but also in some ways reformative support for the privileged old world.

From a leftist perspective, it is of course somewhat perturbing that diverse audiences within the UK, across Europe and indeed globally might be fascinated by this particular sense of national heritage and national identity. But such mediated encounters with other cultures are always complex and multidimensional, and audiences may also take away a more humanistic set of values from the film—for instance, that an empathetic understanding of disability is vital (given the focus on Bertie/King Edward's speech impediment), and that there is something to applaud in the 'ordinary' person, the flawed protagonist of the narrative, becoming heroic by rising above their bodily and psychological disabilities. It is the combination of all of these factors, these ways of engaging with the film, and more besides, that render this relatively modest independent production exportable and allow it to transcend a merely national experience.

For audiences beyond the British nation-space, which is ostensibly the film's domestic market and natural home, the past on offer is fascinating in part because of its otherness, its difference from their present experiences, but also from their own national pasts. But in part, the past on offer is utterly familiar, dealing as it does with universal humanistic values, character types and narrative trajectories. There are complex issues of identity and belonging at stake here: on the one hand, there may be a sense of one's self-identity encountering cultural difference; on the other hand, there may be an experience of recognition, of a relatively familiar other, perhaps even a sense of shared belonging to a larger complex, which we might call European culture.

Another key factor in the success of *The King's Speech* is that the film itself was a transnational production, with funding from the US and Australia, and was therefore never conceived as an entirely insular production. It can certainly help a film to cross borders if it is designed from the outset as a transnational production that might appeal to audiences beyond the domestic market. If some cultural products seem to travel better than others, this is in part because of a sense of cultural proximity between the domestic and export markets, in terms of shared values, beliefs, narratives, genres (narrative types) and cultural identities (character types).

The King's Speech might be understood as a business project in which cultural proximity was bundled into a co-production arrangement that embodies what Mette Hjort calls 'affinitive transnationalism' (2010).

As noted above, however, within the European context it is American investment in UK-led productions, not inter-European co-productions, that is more likely to ensure box-office success. To put it another way, it is often so-called UK heritage films that are the non-Hollywood films that travel best, speak most fluently to non-national audiences and attract non-national funding: *The King's Speech*; *Pride and Prejudice*; *Elizabeth: The Golden Age*; *Atonement*; *Mr Turner*, et cetera. But even the considerable box-office success of *The King's Speech* pales into insignificance alongside Hollywood's full-scale historical productions. Again, a major part of their appeal is that these foreign imports are actually highly familiar across Europe. Hollywood has so long played a central role in European film culture that its brand of cinema seems very familiar indeed in terms of cultural content, but also in terms of cultural form and all that substantial budgets can buy in terms of production values and star casting.

Perfume: A European Historical Drama with an American Accent

Perfume: The Story of a Murderer is a good example of a non-UK European historical drama that adopted a similar production strategy to that which had proved successful with Hollywood, UK-USA and UK films. Thus, it was a relatively big-budget film at $65 million, shot in English, with big English-speaking stars and high production values, and adapted from a pre-sold property, Patrick Suskind's immensely successful and widely translated novel of 1985. But it was also unusual, in that it was a German-led co-production, one of the very few well-travelled European historical dramas that was not led by either the UK or France. Thus, it was made by the German company Constantin, with a German producer, director and co-writer; Suskind's novel was originally written in German; and funding came from German banks and other investors, plus German public funds. But it was also a self-consciously *European* film, a German-Spanish-French co-production, with finance from all three countries, as well as Eurimages co-production funds. Set in France, the film was shot in Spain, with studio and post-production work carried out in Germany, using English and German leading actors, and with an English co-writer.

But if it was a self-consciously European film, it also had a strong American accent. Indeed, the biggest star in the film was Dustin Hoffman, whose presence underlines the extent to which the film was addressed to audiences familiar with Hollywood production strategies. This was no refined frock flick, but a crime thriller in costume, a hybrid genre product designed to maximise its audiences. The fact that it was a German-led production, but shot in English, is also clearly crucial—and ironic, since it had to be dubbed into German for the German market. The overall production strategy was successful to the extent that *Perfume* was the fifth best-travelled European historical drama in the period 2005–14, with six million European tickets sold outside Germany, another five and a half million in Germany and global box-office takings of $135 million.

If the film depended largely on German public and private finance, this was in order to exploit a highly attractive tax shelter scheme that provided 'no-strings-attached film funds', a 'complicated, opaque tax structure that allowed the financially savvy film fund managers to flourish'. This in turn encouraged companies such as Constantin to shoot relatively big-budget films like *Perfume* and the *Resident Evil* franchise (2002–12) entirely in English with a mainly non-German cast (Hollywood Reporter 2005; see also Cooke 2012: 45–9).

Like most of the big-budget European historical dramas, carefully pitched to international markets and working with Hollywood-style entertainment values, *Perfume* was not a film that generated debate about national heritage or historical representation. Indeed, as a historical crime thriller, adapted from a German novel, but set in France and shot in English, in many ways it worked with a self-consciously invented version of the past, and there is no evidence that the film was intended to raise issues about the relationship between history and the present or about cultural identity. Its relative success at the box office suggests, however, that audiences are quite prepared to engage with transnational cultural products and highly fictionalised representations of the imagined past. The film did generate public debate about the sorts of films that should be made in Germany—and by extension, in Europe more generally: small-scale, esoteric films that appeal only to art-house audiences, or more populist films like *Perfume* that might command more mainstream audiences (Rohrbach 2007).

Conclusion

There is, then, no easy relationship between national heritage and global entertainment, or between representations of the past and contemporary debates about nationhood, Europeanness and cultural difference. There clearly are still national melodramas that rework ideas of national heritage—but these are often very modestly budgeted local films that stay close to home: they may be popular with domestic audiences but they don't travel well to other European countries. Some historical dramas do travel much more successfully, however, either because they are equally low-budget films that appeal to the transnational festival and art-house crowd, or because they have much more substantial budgets (often thanks to American investment), are shot in the English language and adopt Hollywood-style production values. UK films about the English past and English historical figures are the exceptions that prove these 'rules', effectively straddling all three of these contrasting film types: they are often treated as melodramas of English heritage and national identity; they frequently adopt an aesthetics of quality that transnational art cinema audiences find engaging; and they are shot in the English language, often having larger budgets than can be commanded by historical dramas in other European countries—frequently because they are able to attract American funding in some guise or other. It is also clear that the more modest a film's budget, the more likely it is to be set in the relatively recent twentieth-century past.

Platforma's Latvian national epics may have pleased local audiences by dramatising key moments in national history. They may have commanded big budgets by Latvian standards, but they did not travel well because of their insistently patriotic nationalism at the level of content, and their poverty of production values by international standards. UK films with larger, but by Hollywood standards still modest, budgets like *The King's Speech*, *The Duchess* (Saul Dibb, 2008) or *The Queen*—all dealing with the English aristocracy or monarchy—aimed for a less pejorative type of character and story development. This was also true of European films with much lower budgets like *Ida* or *The Lives of Others*. Such films achieved a universality of emotional engagement that enabled them to travel more easily, even while dealing with insistently national histories and characters (and for the most part, twentieth-century histories). Bigger-budget transnational collaborations such as *Kingdom of Heaven*, *Perfume* or *Elizabeth: The Golden*

Age were carefully packaged to appeal to mainstream and culturally diverse audiences and to engage with a variety of tastes.

Much of the analysis above has depended on quantitative research about the nature of the industry and the distribution and consumption of films. Numbers on their own can only tell us so much, and we need to be asking the right questions to make sense of the statistical evidence. Why do so few European historical dramas reach mainstream audiences outside their national market, for instance? And why do audiences watch some films but not others? The answers are in part about industrial organisation, ownership and control, which has a major impact on which films get made, which circulate and which get seen. Crucial here is the role of distributors, and the decisions they make as gatekeepers about what they think will travel outside national markets. It is also important to understand the force of cultural and industrial policies, the official regulation of financial and legal frameworks, whether at local, national, regional or EU level, and the relationship between state power, nation-building and transnational collaboration. But we cannot set aside matters of cultural practice. Some films prove inexportable because they simply do not translate well to other cultural contexts and audiences, lacking as they do a sufficient sense of cultural affinity. Questions of language are clearly vital, and are negotiated in various ways, through dubbing and subtitling, or simply by distributors or audiences turning their backs on foreign-language films.

Overall, it does seem that we Europeans encounter a fairly limited range of European pasts and a fairly restricted approach to historical representation in recent successful European films. Historical dramas made in Europe rarely reach the cultural mainstream outside their own domestic markets. Those audiences that are prepared to engage with less familiar histories tend to be a small minority of cosmopolitan, university-educated, Europhile, middle-class film aficionados. Hollywood, by contrast, is much more successful at enabling mainstream European audiences to encounter relatively exotic and diverse European histories through films about classical cultures, the middle ages and the Second World War, and through investing in English historical dramas. Regrettably, there is little here to suggest that cinema is doing much to enable a more unified sense of Europe that celebrates cultural diversity at the level of the mainstream. Nor is there much evidence that European institutions and policies are proving particularly successful in enabling a dynamic, Europe-wide film industry and film culture.[1]

Note

1. My thanks to Huw Jones, Steven Roberts, Nathan Townsend and Roderik Smits for their admirable research assistance.

Works Cited

Balcus, Z. 2012. Narrative trends in recent Latvian fiction film. *KinoKultura* 13 [Online]. Available at: http://www.kinokultura.com/specials/13/balcus.shtml. Accessed 1 Dec 2014.

Baltic Films. 2008–2014. *Facts and figures*. Riga/Tallinn/Vilnius: Baltic Films.

Bangert, A., P. Cooke and R. Stone 2013. Screening European heritage. *Viewfinder* [Online]. Available at: http://bufvc.ac.uk/articles/screening-european-heritage.

Box Office Mojo. 2015. Available from: http://www.boxofficemojo.com/. Accessed 13 May 2015.

Brūvere, K. 2012. Aigars Grauba: *The defenders of Riga* (*Rīgas Sargi*, 2007). *KinoKultura* [Online]. Available at: http://www.kinokultura.com/specials/13/rigadefenders.shtml. Accessed 1 Dec 2014.

Cooke, P. 2012. *Contemporary German cinema*. Manchester: Manchester University Press.

———, ed. 2013. *'The Lives of Others' and contemporary German film: A companion*. Berlin: De Gruyter.

European Audiovisual Observatory. 2015. LUMIERE data base on admissions of films released in Europe [Online]. Available at: http://lumiere.obs.coe.int/. Accessed 4 Dec 2015.

European Commission. 2011. And the Oscar goes to... Major success for EU-backed film 'The King's Speech'. EC Press Release (ref IP/11/239), Brussels, 28.2.11 [Online]. Available at: http://europa.eu/rapid/press-release_IP-11-239_en.htm?locale=en. Accessed 21 Oct 2012.

———. 2014a. New European film strategy aims to boost cultural diversity and competitiveness in digital era. EC Press Release (ref IP/14/560), Brussels, 14.5.14 [Online]. Available at: http://europa.eu/rapid/press-release_IP-14-560_en.htm. Accessed 4 Mar 2016.

———. 2014b. *A profile of current and future audiovisual audience—Final report*. Luxembourg: Publications Office of the European Union.

European Film Academy. 2015. European Film Awards [Online]. Available at: https://www.europeanfilmacademy.org/Archive.39.0.html. Accessed 2 Nov 2015.

Fellner, E. 2014. Unpublished interview with Nathan Townsend. London, 14 March.

Godeanu-Kenworthy, O., and O. Popescu-Sandu. 2014. From minimalist representation to excessive interpretation: Contextualizing '4 Months, 3 Weeks and 2 Days' (2007)'. *Journal of European Studies* 44(3): 225–248.

Hermit, L. 2014. Good movie well presented [Online]. Available at: http://www.amazon.co.uk/gp/customer-reviews/R10XBISYS89ZU4/ref=cm_cr_pr_rvw_ttl?ie=UTF8&ASIN=8377783053. Accessed 2 Oct 2015.

Higson, A. 2003. *English heritage, English cinema: Costume Drama since 1980.* Oxford: Oxford University Press.

———. 2011. *Film England: Culturally English filmmaking since the 1990s.* London: I.B. Tauris.

Hjort, M. 2010. On the plurality of cinematic transnationalism. In *World cinemas, transnational perspectives,* eds. N. Durovicova and K. Newman. London: Routledge.

Hollywood Reporter. 2005. German film funding situation [Online]. Available at: http://www.nexis.com/results/docview/docview.do docLinkInd=true&risb=21_T21616989366&format=GNBFI&sort=DATE,A,H&startDocNo=76&resultsUrlKey=29_T21616866744&cisb=22_T21616989374&treeMax=true&treeWidth=0&csi=12015&docNo=78. Accessed 9 Dec 2015.

Imre, A. 2012. Introduction: Eastern European cinema from *No End* to The End (As We Know It). In *A companion to Eastern European cinemas,* ed. A. Imre. Chichester: Wiley Blackwell.

Internet Movie Database. 2015. What are STARmeter, MOVIEmeter & COMPANYmeter? [Online]. Available at: http://www.imdb.com/help/show_leaf?prowhatisstarmeter. Accessed 1 Nov 2015.

Jones, H.D. 2014. The circulation and reception of foreign-language European films in the UK. Working paper available on the MeCETES website [Online]. Available at: http://mecetes.co.uk/wp-content/uploads/2015/06/Jones-Circulation-and-Reception-of-NNE-films-in-UK.pdf. Accessed 4 Dec 2015.

Makwitz, A. 2008. A local blockbuster [Online]. Available at: http://www.imdb.com/title/tt0471359/. Accessed 30 Nov 2014.

MeCETES. 2015. Mediating cultural encounters through European screens project website [Online]. Available at: http://www.mecetes.co.uk. Accessed 4 Dec 2015.

Metacritic. 2015. How we create the metascore magic [Online]. Available at: http://www.metacritic.com/about-metascores. Accessed 2 Oct 2015.

Off The Wall. 2014. Off The Wall project website [Online]. Available at: http://www.offthewallproject.eu/concept. Accessed 2 Oct 2015.

Pulver, A. 2015. Polish nationalists launch petition against Oscar-nominated film Ida. *The Guardian* [Online]. Available at: http://www.theguardian.com/film/2015/jan/22/ida-oscars-2015-film-polish-nationalists-petition. Accessed 22 Jan 2015.

Rawlings, J. 2013. An expensive mistake (16.1.13) [Online]. Available at: http://www.amazon.co.uk/gp/customer-reviews/R1B9X8RWFUOPZ3/ref=cm_cr_pr_rvw_ttl?ie=UTF8&ASIN=B008RYLY06. Accessed 2 Oct 2015.
Rohrbach, G. 2007. Das Schmollen der Autisten. *Der Spiegel*, January 22.
The Numbers. 2015. The Numbers: Where data and the movie business meet [Online]. Available at: http://www.the-numbers.com/. Accessed 4 Dec 2015
Townsend, N. 2014. *Working title films and transatlantic British Cinema*. PhD thesis, University of York.
Ullmann, L. 2014. Foreword. In *Stork flying over pinewood: Nordic-Baltic film cooperation, 1989–2014*, ed. J.E. Holst. Oslo: Kom Forlag.

CHAPTER 11

From 'English' Heritage to Transnational Audiences: Fan Perspectives and Practices and Why They Matter

Claire Monk

The Introduction to this volume sets out a number of propositions about the 'key role[s]' played by historical and heritage-film dramas—in reality, a convenient shorthand for a generically, thematically and aesthetically diverse field of 'period screen fictions' set in the past or addressing historical subjects close to the present (see Monk 2002: 176)—across Europe. At the national-cultural and nation-state level, these films (and their television drama equivalents) are said to contribute to national (or regional and sub-national) film cultures; are tasked with generating wider economic as well as cultural value across diverse sectors—the 'national' film, heritage and tourism industries—by 'acting as an international "shop window"'; and are also said to generate 'major' domestic debates 'on the role of the past in contemporary national identity construction' (Bangert, Cooke and Stone 2016: xvii). Historical and heritage films are also argued to contribute to the (more abstract, less tangible) pan-European project of articulating and promoting a notionally European heritage, not least via the mesh of formal and informal interactions between the films themselves

C. Monk (✉)
De Montfort University, Leicester, UK
e-mail: cmonk@dmu.ac.uk

© The Editor(s) (if applicable) and The Author(s) 2016
P. Cooke, R. Stone (eds.), *Screening European Heritage*,
Palgrave European Film and Media Studies,
DOI 10.1057/978-1-137-52280-1_11

and 'tourist sites, the digital sphere and the heritage industries' (Bangert et al. 2016: xvii).

Importantly, the *Screening European Heritage* project has also highlighted questions of the circulation, distribution and consumption of historical or heritage films and television dramas: of how (and whether) they reach audiences; which audiences they reach; and via what platforms and modes of consumption. In the twenty-first century, however, this circulation and these modes are no longer (or not wholly) boundaried and determined by pre-digital terrestrial and territorial geographies, whether national, European or beyond. Rather, they occur across deterritorialised digital sites of audience access, circulation and consumption—not merely across large and small screens, but across a wider diversity of platforms and access points and within a proliferation of reception contexts.

Despite the transnational character of the twenty-first-century film and entertainment industries, and the transformation of modes of consumption by the interlinked impacts of globalisation, digitisation, media convergence and 'Web 2.0' social media and participatory internet culture, academic discourse around 'heritage cinema' has nonetheless persisted in framing it as a national 'project'. The *Screening European Heritage* study's own research questions hinge upon the presumed, even 'key', importance of heritage films within *national* and *European* film culture(s) and in supporting film industries and the heritage and tourism sector alike at nation-state level. Indeed, the very notion of 'European heritage' tacitly presumes a relatively direct, self-evident relationship between putative heritage representations, formations of national and European identity, and a relatively coherent, knowable 'European audience'. The inevitable disjunctures between the unity-in-diversity aspirations of 'the European project' and the highly plural subjectivities and (self-)perceptions of actual Europeans on the ground make both notional concepts elusive at best. Overlaying this is the further—and, I would argue, more fundamental—problem of whether audiences or fans living in Europe even perceive themselves centrally as 'Europeans' or in terms of the 'national'.

As Andrew Higson correctly observes, however, 'a great deal of what passes as (national) heritage cinema is actually the product of transnational, even global, markets' (2016: xxxi). In this chapter, I expand upon this notion by venturing beyond the transnational production, finance and commercial logics that shape much post-2000 'culturally English' heritage (and post-heritage: Monk 1995/2001) film production (as explored in

Higson 2010) to focus on transnational audience, and especially fan, perspectives on 'English' heritage films.

Methodologically, my approach proposes that the transnationalism of much 'English' heritage cinema is located—and merits consideration—across at least three sites. First, in the films' institutional and production origins and commercial logics (as explored in Higson 2010, and the later chapters of Higson 2003), to which I would add creative agency. As this chapter's core case study (the transnational and trans-temporal fan reception of the 1980s–90s 'English' heritage films of Merchant Ivory Productions) makes abundantly clear, the transnational production and creative origins of many exemplary 'culturally English' heritage films are far from new. Nor, of course, is the broader history of transnational production collaborations, initiatives and exchanges in British and European cinema (indicatively, see the instances explored in Higson and Maltby eds 1999; Bergfelder and Cargnelli eds 2008; and—on Merchant Ivory themselves—Pym 1983). Second, in the (to date, little-studied and only fragmentarily known) specifics of the films' transcultural circulation, (re-)framing and reception once they reach—diverse, non-homogeneous—global markets, which will differ significantly within different cultures, and potentially within the same culture. Examples include the distinctions between US Anglophilic engagements with 'English' heritage films and TV dramas (and further, generational, and old versus new media, subdivisions within these) and the different and distinctive local cultural and institutional specifics of the same films' place, reception and significance in Japanese film and fan culture since the 1980s.

Last—overlapping with questions of transcultural reception, but also extending beyond them into a field of potentially 'infinite' (Monk, 2011b: 450–1) transtextuality and creative play—this transnationalism is acutely manifested in the continuing presence and circulation of iconic 'English' heritage films produced in the 1980s and 1990s (and their source novels) in twenty-first-century, internet-based, global fan culture and practices, where these 'heritage' texts are received, consumed, appropriated, creatively reworked and mashed with other texts (film, media, music, popular-cultural, literary…) in plural, knowing and unexpected ways. It is in this third—virtual, deterritorialised—arena, where fans whose passions include (but are rarely confined to) 'English' heritage films and their actors enthuse (or, in fan vocabulary, 'flail' and 'squee'), interact and create that the transnationalism of so-called heritage cinema is thrown into sharpest relief. While heritage films themselves have always transcended national, continental and transatlantic boundaries, global internet fan culture (across its various manifestations) affirms, amplifies and transforms this established (institutional and textual) transnationalism.

My chapter draws on my recent empirical study of heritage-film audiences (Monk 2011a) and my ongoing research on the complex, fascinating—and unpredictably evolving—place of 'English' heritage films in twenty-first-century participatory internet fan culture and social media ('Web 2.0') (Monk 2011b). In line with this earlier work, I will focus centrally on twenty-first-century, transnational and transcultural, fan engagements, discourses and practices around some of the most iconic, popular—but, in many academic and critical circles, reviled—'English' heritage films of the 1980s and 1990s, the adaptations from the novels of E.M. Forster (all written and set—or, in the case of Forster's posthumous gay novel *Maurice*, first drafted—during the Edwardian period 1905–14, followed by *A Passage to India* in 1924) made by Merchant Ivory Productions: *A Room with a View* (James Ivory, 1985), *Maurice* (Ivory, 1987) and *Howards End* (Ivory, 1992). The 1980s–90s cycle of Forster film adaptations also included *A Passage to India* (David Lean, 1984) and *Where Angels Fear to Tread* (Charles Sturridge, 1991).

Of course, twenty-first-century fans also embrace, and form fandoms around, numerous contemporary heritage or historical TV-drama, film (and literary) texts—from the global TV-industry phenomenon *Downton Abbey* (ITV/PBS Masterpiece, 2010–16) to such diverse recent examples as *The White Queen* (BBC/Starz, 2013, financially a French co-production shot largely in Flanders), the rebooted *Poldark* (BBC/PSB Masterpiece, 2015–), or *Jonathan Strange & Mr Norrell* (BBC/BBC America, 2015). However, the surprising persistence (or new visibility) of time-shifted fan enthusiasm around some of the most exemplary late-twentieth-century 'English' heritage films is especially fascinating, in part because of its trans-temporal, trans-generational character—fans ranging from teenage to middle age can be witnessed responding to films made a quarter-century earlier, often *as though* they were contemporary—and because this activity focuses most intensely on the least commercially successful of the three 'Merchant-Forster-Ivory' films, Ivory's 1987 film of Forster's self-suppressed gay novel *Maurice*. (As I expand upon in Monk 2011b: 435, 451, internet engagements around *Maurice* since the mid-2000s repeatedly display more pronouncedly 'fannish' qualities—intensity, warmth, the building of *Maurice* fan communities, and a small but coherent body of fan fiction—than those around the other Forster films or novels.)

The transnational appreciation of *Maurice* (a century after Forster dedicated his first draft to 'a happier year' in which same-sex love might be legal)—among strikingly young, sexually diverse new generations as well as enduring older fans—gains a special poignancy from *Maurice*'s resonance with twenty-first-century same-sex marriage-equality campaigns; the fierce anti-LGBT (lesbian, gay, bisexual and transgender) clampdown in Putin's Russia; the wider resurgence of virulent homophobia in parts of post-Communist Europe; and continuing struggles for tolerance and LGBT rights in many other parts of the world. Attention to the broader (and less 'serious') forms of twenty-first-century fan engagement around the 1980s–90s 'Merchant-Forster-Ivory' films similarly reveals that these films are today consumed, appreciated and (re-)appropriated within generic, media, fannish and transtextual contexts that depart markedly from notions of heritage cinema or narrowly national interpretative frameworks—from vast transnational media fandoms such as the BBC's *Sherlock* (2010–) or the *Harry Potter* franchise (2001–11), via contemporary young-adult fiction, to LGBT activism.

Rather than replicating the detailed account of the specifics of fan responses and creative outputs (such as fan fiction) presented in Monk 2011b), this chapter takes a more selective approach, delineating key aspects and examples relevant to a consideration, and enhanced understanding, of how 'English' and European heritage films are actually consumed, understood, enjoyed and used by global fans. My overarching purpose is to illustrate why serious, empirically grounded attention to fan perspectives and practices is essential to a full account of the 'screening', consumption, reception and afterlives of 'English' or European heritage cinema.

Forms and Sites of Online Fan Activity

In the pre-'Web 2.0' reception context, and mindful of the audience segments and demographics most prominently and stereotypically associated with heritage films (both as projected by the films' detractors, and as verified in the responses of the two contrasting audience segments studied in Monk 2011a), we might rationally have *expected* heritage films to attract forms of audience/fan appreciation that were relatively 'unfannish'. By this, I mean more *reactive* than *participatory*; characterised by a *differentiated* focus on specific texts, genres, cycles or performers, as opposed to blurring into and feeding off the vast mesh, or continuum, of '*infinite fandom*' (Monk 2011b: 450) around mainstream media texts and franchises; and typically both *respectful* and *respectable*: characterised by notions of respect for canon, source authors, directors, 'their creations', characters and performers, rather than the implied antitheses (overtly libidinous or transgressive forms of engagement, or an embrace of canon-busting genres and practices). As I explored in detail in 'Heritage Film Audiences 2.0' (Monk 2011b: 445–68), however, contemporary fan behaviour around (what used to be defined as) 'heritage films' is a complicated field, where *more or less* participatory, differentiated and dis/respectful forms of fandom coexist, and *cut across* the various forms and forums of online audience/fan activity.

How can we account for this entry of 1980s–90s heritage films into the mainstream of convergence-era media fandom (albeit still as marginal, 'rare' fandoms in comparison with giants such as the *Star Trek*, *Harry Potter* or *Lord of the Rings* franchises)? The answers lie in intertextualities of casting between Ivory's 1980s–90s 'English' heritage films and the most familiar of contemporary media fandom texts; coupled with certain thematic affinities between Forsterian and twenty-first-century young-adult concerns; and the appeal of the films' queer and homoerotic elements within a contemporary fan culture preoccupied with both sexual identity politics and the pleasures of slash appropriation. Helena Bonham Carter, the young star of Ivory's *A Room with a View* (as Lucy Honeychurch) and *Howards End* (as Helen Schlegel), is well known to young audiences now as Bellatrix Lestrange in the *Harry Potter* films, and for her film roles for her former husband Tim Burton. Other new young (and not-so-young) fans have discovered Ivory's *Maurice*, and *A Room with a View*, thanks to the cross-casting of Rupert Graves (*A Room with a View*'s Freddy Honeychurch, *Maurice*'s Alec Scudder), a quarter century later, as D.I. Lestrade in the BBC's *Sherlock*: one of the biggest, most instantaneous and most strategically promoted transmedia-fandom phenomena of the past decade (Monk 2011b: 449–50). *Maurice* was almost immediately appropriated within the *Sherlock* fandom as a source of off-the-peg slash (homoerotic) content for use in crossover mash-ups. But it has also found a new appreciation in its own right—sometimes, fascinatingly, expressed by fans themselves in terms which assert *Maurice*'s longer-standing place in fan culture: as an ur-text of slash literature, or even (because of Forster's Utopian insistence on writing a gay happy ending) as a work of proto-fan fiction itself.

One way to map this field of online fan activity is in terms of the types of websites or web platforms where it can be observed, including blogs and (more pictorial) microblogs (currently epitomised by Tumblr); fanfiction archives, both commercial (fanfiction.net) and non-profit/fan-led (AO3/Archive of Our Own); video-sharing and photo-sharing sites (such as YouTube and Vimeo or Flickr and Photobucket, respectively); and

User Comments (YouTube) and discussion or review boards (the Internet Movie Database/IMDb). In these last categories, participants may comment and interact on sites—such as the IMDb—where the bulk of content is professionally generated and managed, or those—such as YouTube—which, in practice, combine user-*generated* content with professionally produced content (feature films, DVD extras, promotional videos, media interviews, etc.) *uploaded* and shared by users (often in extracted or edited form). As this list is starting to imply, however, for the purposes of this chapter, this field is most usefully mapped in terms of the forms of audience/fan *activity* and/or user-generated *content* themselves. Taking this approach, the forms of such online activity currently observable around 'heritage films'—including Ivory's *Maurice*—can be mapped as follows:

1. **Posting of films, film extracts and DVD extras or other professionally generated ancillary material** on YouTube.
2. **Fan talk**. Appreciation, discussion and criticism of the above—typically at its most detailed in the interactive spaces of YouTube Comments threads and IMDb Message Boards—as well as posting (non-interactive) user reviews (IMDb). (For a discussion of representative examples, see Monk 2011b: 456–8, 454–60.)
3. Making and posting **fan videos** (YouTube): transformative works which remix, mash up and/or re-purpose film or television (and sometimes ancillary) footage.
4. **Posting and re-posting static screen-caps** (captured still images) **or GIFs** (simple animated files) from the films. These are characteristically posted on Tumblr (and, prior to that, LiveJournal) fan-blogs, commonly as an act of actor or character appreciation, but also for cinephilic, aesthetic, humorous or satirical purposes, and as commentary. High-quality screen-caps (of favourite/significant screen moments or sequences) are sometimes also posted on photo-sharing sites such as Flickr, or occasionally on specialised sites devoted to recording (virtually) a whole film, or an actor's entire performance, in screen-caps.
5. **Fan art (both digital and analogue), including icon-making, 'manips' and 'edits'**. Examples—often derived from favourite characters, actors and/or screen moments—are commonly posted and shared within fan-blogs on Tumblr, or on the older, dedicated art-sharing website DeviantArt. Icons or avatars—stamp-sized artworks—are used by fans (as self-identifiers and expressions of their fandom) across a range of platforms and contexts within online cultures of fan interaction and productivity. Many icons consist of digital 'manips' (manipulations) of existing

still images or screen-caps—whether of characters, pairings, highly precise narrative situations and references or other 'iconic' images. 'Edits' aesthetically rework existing still images or raw screen-caps. The overall field of online fan art spans both digital and analogue forms of drawing and painting, alongside digital manips and edits.
6. **Fan fiction**. Encompasses both stories inspired by a specific text, and hybrid or crossover fictions meshing together characters, narrative events and/or settings drawn from more than one source text or franchise—in both cases, spanning a range of genres. (For an overview of trends, and case studies, in *Maurice* fan fiction—canonic, crossover and crack—see Monk 2011b: 446, 464–8.)
7. **Individual blogs or virtual fan communities** devoted to the appreciation and discussion of specific films, TV shows, their actors, characters or pairings, or in other cases with reference to the 'source' novel(s), other related literary texts, authors and lives. (For a brief history of *Maurice*-specific internet fan communities and blogs since 2004, see Monk 2011b: 461–2.)
8. Last, there are **fan-run blogs or websites dedicated to period films and costume dramas in general**. In contrast with the other forms of fan activity mapped above, and the norms of fan culture, sites of this kind are more likely to focus on the conventional pleasures that heritage films are presumed, stereotypically to offer their audiences (such as historical costume, period styling, or the 'elegance' of the past), and to exhibit a 'respectable' orientation towards the films (Monk 2011b: 453). It is relatively rare for such sites to focus directly on queer-heritage-film texts such as *Maurice*.

'Heritage' Fanworks: Some Notes on Genre and the Slash Sensibility

The (potentially intersecting) varieties of heritage-film fan video (discussed with reference to detailed examples in Monk 2011b: 448–9, 462–4) draw heavily upon genres and practices already well established within large-scale media fan culture. Forms of fan video drawing on a single film text (or TV show, or ancillary material) include videos that comment upon, parody or condense a specific film; videos paying tribute to a specific actor (whether via a montage of favourite roles and performance moments, or by condensing their full performance in one film into one short video);

numerous videos celebrating or commenting upon a specific character pairing/relationship, typically edited to emphasise highly affective screen moments; and an equally great variety of pop and other music videos (which, similarly, are frequently dedicated to the fan's preferred relationship pairing or 'OTP', the 'one true pairing'). This emphasis on emotions and love relationships is epitomised in the slash genre—widespread across fan fiction and fan art as well as video—which may celebrate same-sex pairings, but more commonly *creates* them by 'slashing' together (usually) same-sex characters into a relationship or 'ship' (see below). Fan videos also frequently mash together footage from multiple films/texts for a variety of purposes: to create crossover or AU (alternative universe) narratives, 'crack' (absurdist, humorous mixing of anachronistic sources and references) and, again, slash. Last, it must be noted that the music-video form crosses virtually all of these genres.

The widespread popularity of slash—simultaneously a fan genre and practice, spanning fan video, fan art and fan fiction—is fundamental to fully understanding the positioning of *Maurice* (both novel and film) within twenty-first-century fan culture. As the fan-scholars Kristina Busse and Karen Hellekson explain, 'slash stories [and, equally, fan-produced slash narratives and representations in visual media] posit a same-sex relationship, usually one imposed by the author and based on a perceived homoerotic subtext' (2006: 10). Slash (videos, stories, art, all originating in fan discussions or imaginings: 'head-canon') is widely understood as a practice of queering existing 'straight' popular-cultural material or texts—with the complication that the term centrally denotes male/male romantic and/or homoerotic scenarios, stories and images imagined and created by, and for, predominantly female fans (of all sexual orientations, by no means solely heterosexual). It is important to note that fans practise, create and consume slash first and foremost for pleasure, rather than invariably with conscious pro-LGBT activist or representationally progressive agendas. Indeed (as the case studies explored by Hunting 2012 and Stasi 2013 both illustrate) female fan culture's libidinous and appropriative investments in male/male sex and romance are not invariably progressive or anti-heteronormative. Nonetheless, debates within the fan community and fan scholarship predominantly argue for slash as a feminist as well as queer(ing) practice (see, for instance, Driscoll 2006).

As noted earlier, one school of thought among fans themselves regards *Maurice* (novel and film) as a *prototype or inspiration* for slash tastes and practices, rather than merely a text adopted or appropriated *by* female slashers (including for crossover uses in, or fusions with, other fandoms). Similar ambiguities resurface when attempting to account for the more locally specific factors driving the success of Ivory's *Maurice* in Japan—where *Maurice* opened in January 1988, as an exclusive run at Tokyo's new Cine Switch mini-theatre—and its widely acknowledged and enduring impact on a generation of young Japanese women. *Maurice* became one of the first and most significant box-office successes of Japan's late-1980s mini-theatre boom (Tazuka 2011: 85–6): during its 15-week run, it was seen by an audience of 95,000, and grossed 122 million yen (almost $94,000 at 1988 exchange rates); a decade later, it remained Cine Switch's third-highest-grossing film of all time (Morimoto 2015a, citing Otaka 1998: 217). This success was underpinned by the novelty, specific features (luxurious design and comfort) and programming strategies of the mini-theatres themselves, which consciously targeted young female audiences (Tazuka 2011: 82–4). However, the main draw for the so-called Office Ladies (OLs) and 'Japanese schoolgirls' who flocked to see *Maurice* (as recalled by the film's lead actors, James Wilby and Rupert Graves, in the *Story of Maurice* documentary, Merchant Ivory Collection, double-DVD edition, 2004: see Monk 2011b: 458–60) was undoubtedly the male homoerotic, refracted via the (occidentalist) cultural othering evident in the 'hedonism of [Japanese] women's pleasure in [...] the beauty of white men' (to quote Japanese critic Hirō Otaka 1998: 44).

From *Maurice* onwards, the mini-theatres' biggest box-office hits were invariably imports with (from a Japanese perspective) *abunasa* (subversive or 'edgy') appeal (Otaka and Inaba 1989: 38–9)—a category which included Jim Jarmusch's 1980s New York indie films *Stranger Than Paradise* (1984) and *Down by Law* (1986) (both, incidentally, made with West German co-finance). However, it was 'the sexual subversiveness of gay [male] films that became emblematic of mini-theatre' (Tezuka 2011: 84) and provided its greatest hits—centrally, via a diverse mix of 1980s British films that included *My Beautiful Laundrette* (Stephen Frears, 1985) and *The Angelic Conversation* (Derek Jarman, 1985) as well as the gay heritage films *Maurice* and *Another Country* (Marek Kanievska, 1984) (Otaka and Inaba 1989: 49). And, I would argue, from a female audience and fan perspective, this should come as no surprise. Where transnational fan culture has slash, Japan has its own popular-cultural traditions and forms of homoeroticism *expressly aimed at* teenage girls and young women—which have, today, permeated or fused with global fan culture: the longstanding *bishōnen* (beautiful boy) aesthetic (Morimoto 2015b), widespread across *shōjo* manga, the *shōnen-ai* (boy-love) genre in manga and anime, and *shōnen-ai*'s sexually explicit cousin, *yaoi*.

While *bishōnen* and *yaoi* tastes shed light on *Maurice*'s popularity in Japan, their potential influence on gendered and cross-cultural reception of gay representations is not unproblematic, including in relation to the specific representational ethos of Ivory's film (at once anti-camp and homonormative) and Forster's novel. In particular, *yaoi*'s fetishisation of fixed *seme* (top/active) and *uke* (bottom/receptive) sexual roles runs counter to the ideal of mutuality and reciprocity (both cross-class and erotic) that Forster was striving towards in his writing of the Maurice Hall/Alec Scudder pairing, both informed by and reworking Platonic philosophies of male/male love (see Martin 1983; Endres 2007).

Fan Perspectives and the Problem of 'The National'

It will already be apparent that the terms in which convergence-era fans worldwide engage with *Maurice*—variously emotional, erotic, intensely character-invested, and as an activist queer text—are at odds with its established critical framing as a 'heritage film'. However, there are further reasons why fan perspectives are especially challenging and disruptive to notions of 'the national', 'Englishness' or a coherent 'Europeanness' as the guiding contexts within which heritage films are enjoyed by, or meaningful for, their audiences—and not only because of the deterritorialised nature of the internet and digital consumption. Rather, the culture of fandom itself shifts the consumption and interpretation of 'English' 'heritage' films further away from 'the national'. Committed fans, given easeful global access to other fans in the age of social and user-generated media, perceive *fandom itself* as a self-evidently transnational and deterritorialised 'community' or 'family'—but one in which pseudonymous online identities and interactions are the norm. In this context, the spaces of fandom may strongly reveal *or* conceal nationality, region or other salient facets of 'real-life' identity.

Although the 'community' of twenty-first-century internet fandom is self-evidently transnational, it remains delimited by the distinction between (global) English speakers able to participate (to a greater or lesser extent) in English-language platforms and communities, and the (separate but overlapping) fans and fan communities based on non-English-language platforms. Examples include Europe's largest social-networking site, VK—comparable to Facebook—which is available in several languages but most heavily used by Russian speakers, the Russian online journal community diary.ru, comparators in Japan and China, and the German-language fan-fiction archive fanfiktion.de, comparable to the US-owned and predominantly English-language fanfiction.net. Although the main English-language platforms are US-owned and (statistically and, in the larger media fandoms, culturally) dominated by North American users, the full spectrum of fans who participate in them is almost comprehensively international, drawn from every continent and region. However, while some fans identify and make reference to their national location and cultural or ethnic identities—or reveal fascinating local specifics of fandom, consumption and context—many do not. Thus the place of national/regional identities (or European versus American versus wider Anglophone versus rest-of-world distinctions) in relation to fannish investments and textual understandings often remains unstated—and, it is important to allow, may in some cases be irrelevant.

Above all, fan perspectives on these films demonstrate the immense pitfalls, problems and limitations of 'the national' or 'the European' as primary explanatory frameworks for understanding so-called heritage films and their appeals, meanings and pleasures for their audiences. Indeed, the terms in which twenty-first-century fans respond to these films in many cases render the classification 'heritage film', or even 'Merchant Ivory film', as redundant as 'the national'.

Even in the late 1990s, one (male, 39-year-old) participant in my *Heritage Film Audiences* study (Monk 2011a) asserted this redundancy on textual grounds, arguing that 'the complexities' of the heritage films' (characteristically Forsterian) themes'—'issues of class and sexuality which have remained central to our literary tradition and to the structures of our social, economic and psychological experiences'—'makes [sic] the term "heritage films" especially redundant/inadequate' (Monk 2011b: 443). Audience and fan engagements with these films *since* the 1990s—both stimulated and made newly visible by the rise of the participatory internet, related new technologies (digital media, broadband), the consequent proliferation of web platforms, communities and (fan-fiction and fanworks) archives pertinent to fan activity (see Monk 2011b: 461–2), and hence the new, public, visibility of fandom, fan communities and fanworks—underscore this redundancy. As I concluded in 2011, if we revisit what Merchant Ivory's 1987 'heritage' adaptation of Forster's posthumous gay novel *Maurice* means, *not* as framed by the critics of heritage cinema, but *as understood through audience and fan cultures* (witnessed in the passions and preoccupations expressed on YouTube or IMDb [Internet Movie Database] discussion boards and fan activity on [the virtual community] LiveJournal and [microblogging platform] Tumblr), the validity of ['heritage'] classifications today is far from clear. A fandom-led, 2.0-era reformulation might more accurately classify *Maurice* as *all at once* a classic romance, a paradigm-shifting and life-changing queer cultural object, and a slash[-fiction] text; for some fans, as porn (in terms of the responses the film *permits*, particularly with the assistance of DVD and screencapping technologies, as distinct from its advertised intentions); and as a cult film. (Monk 2011b: 451; my italics)

Far from constituting freakish, marginal or 'illegitimate' responses, such fan investments (*Maurice* as a groundbreaking gay film, ignored as such by many critics, but intensely important to queer—*not* solely gay male—audiences) and appropriations (adopted for its homoerotic and homoromantic pleasures by the overwhelmingly female—but *not* solely straight—community of slash fan-fiction writers and readers) in fact provide a valuable prism through which we can usefully return to, and reappraise, the films themselves. Such fan perspectives encourage us, I would argue, to refocus on precisely those aspects of the films—including production impetus and creative agency as well as audience appeal—that their persistent critical and scholarly framing in 'national' and 'heritage' terms serves to suppress or occlude perhaps even strategically and knowingly.

Merchant Ivory: Transcultural Filmmakers and 'English' Heritage

In the case of Merchant Ivory Productions' 'English' heritage films, these suppressions (by detractors and the wider British media) have extended to the long-established, deep-rooted, transcultural character of the Merchant Ivory partnership itself. The self-styled 'wandering company' (Pym 1983), and their story sources and settings, actors, crew and sources of finance, have always been more transnational than the post-1990 debates framing their films as exemplars of conservative English heritage were willing to concede. In certain cases, their films were also distinctly European: for example, their adaptation of *Quartet* (James Ivory, 1981), Jean Rhys's semi-autobiographical account of her unhappy relationship with the older novelist Ford Madox Ford, set in 1927 Paris and starring Isabelle Adjani.

Quartet also marked Ivory's first collaboration with the French cinematographer Pierre Lhomme. Lhomme—the cinematographer of two key French heritage films of the 1980s–90s, the artist biopic *Camille Claudel* (Bruno Nuytten, 1988), again starring Adjani, and *Cyrano de Bergerac* (Jean-Paul Rappeneau, 1990)—returned as Ivory's director of photography on the—visually stunning and iconographically exact—'English' Forster adaptation *Maurice* (1987); the uneasy, controversial, historically based US/French co-production *Jefferson in Paris* (Ivory, 1995), which broached the subject of future US president Thomas Jefferson's sexual relationship with his 15-year-old slave Sally Hemings against the backdrop of the French Revolution; and the (wholly US-funded) French–American culture-clash romcom *Le Divorce* (Ivory, 2003).

Moreover, the hostile critical (re-)framing of Merchant Ivory's films as the epitome—or nadir—of 'English' 'heritage' filmmaking reversed the terms in which the—transcultural, nomadic and postcolonial—producer-director-screenwriter trio of (Indian Muslim) Ismail Merchant, (white American) James Ivory and (German-born Jewish émigré) Ruth Prawer Jhabvala had always articulated their own identity. A page heading on the 1990s version of Merchant Ivory's official website proclaimed: 'We are proud of our roots.' Until the breakout international success of *A Room with a View* in 1986, and the subsequent emergence of the anti-heritage-film critique (and mood) in the UK, the trio's self-framing of the Merchant Ivory project—as nomadically cross-cultural—was mirrored in the media reception of their films, and in celebratory publications such as John Pym's 1983 book *The Wandering Company*:

> In 1961 Indian film producer Ismail Merchant and American director James Ivory paid a visit to German-born writer Ruth Prawer Jhabvala, then living in Delhi, with a proposal to make a film of her novel *The Householder*. Thus was born one of the most productive partnerships in the history of cinema. [...] Many of their films, appropriately, have been concerned with the meeting of cultures; all of them are marvelously evocative of time and place. (Pym 1983: cover copy)

In the face of such facts, however, the dominant lines of criticism that emerged around 'English' heritage films and their makers, especially in the early 1990s, repressed or ignored these transnational-collaborative creative origins and inputs in favour of generalised national-cultural and national-ideological readings. At its most perverse—yet persistently influential—this critique specifically targeted Merchant Ivory's Forster adaptations, condemning them as vessels of a pernicious 'ideology of Englishness', and their—patently non-British and transnational—makers as 'enthralled by a repressed Englishness, and blind to the particularities of other cultures' (Dodd 1991).

MAURICE, TRANSCULTURAL FAN RECEPTION AND FAN TOURISM

Interestingly, this same line of critique simultaneously condemned the 'Merchant-Forster-Ivory' films for their *presumed* (consumerist, 'theme-park') appeals and address to *international* audiences, transatlantic and beyond. As the Scottish literary scholar Cairns Craig memorably complained (in a polemical feature commissioned by Dodd for the same issue of the relaunched *Sight & Sound*): 'It is film as conspicuous consumption: the country houses, the panelled interiors, the clothes which have provided a good business for New York fashion houses selling country style to rich Americans [...] for an international audience, the England these films validate and advertise is a theme park of the past' (1991: 10).

It is both fascinating and instructive to contrast these (characteristically puritanical, anti-pleasure and genre-blind) assertions and anxieties about the *presumed* appeals of Ivory's 'English' Forster films to international audiences with the actual instances—and issues—of transcultural fan engagement, interpretation and comprehension which can be observed within the arena of twenty-first-century internet fan culture. Of course, US Anglophilic engagements with 'English' heritage films and TV dramas do form one subsection of these transnational responses—but, as already touched upon in the opening section of this chapter, 'Anglophilia' itself takes differentiated forms (among different generations, demographics and social fractions, and across 'old' and 'new' modes of consumption) that will also evolve across time. The form of 'Anglofil[m]ia' theorised by Martin A. Hipsky—who explained the US success of Merchant Ivory's films in terms of their appeal to economically redundant forms of (liberal-arts) cultural capital, providing reassurance to a beleaguered 'college-educated elite' (1994: 102–3)—differs from that of the 'ladies who went shopping at Bergdorf's and then dropped into a matinee of *A Room with a View*' whom the *New York Times* feared would be shocked by *Maurice*'s 'defiant [...] salute to homosexual passion' in the midst of the

AIDS crisis (Nightingale 1987). The self-proclaimed Anglophilia of convergence-era US female fans differs again, focusing heavily on shows with ultra-contemporary settings (such as the BBC's *Sherlock*) as much as films or TV dramas set in the past—but structured above all around an intense cross-cultural adulation of British actors (invariably male), coupled with a highly selective construction of the UK as a liberal Utopia in perceived contrast with the conservatism(s) of the USA.

The cultural, linguistic, tonal, idiomatic—and, not least, societal and historical—content of 'English' heritage films can, of course, present a range of challenges for their transnational audiences that differ from those presented by mainstream Hollywood cinema. On the one hand, *Maurice* (novel and film) traces the journey of its young, upper-middle-class, Edwardian gay male protagonist to self-discovery and sexual and emotional fulfilment in 'deceptively simple' narrative terms—'boy meets boy, loses boy, and meets another,' to quote gay US critic Thomas Waugh (1987/2000: 188)—combined (in Ivory's film) with the universal visceral appeal of a 'swoony [...] intoxicating tuxedo-ripper' (Kempley 1987). (Waugh's precise words are echoed by Maurice's own co-screenwriter Kit Hesketh-Harvey in *The Story of Maurice* documentary: one of many extras on the Merchant Ivory Collection 2004 double-DVD release, which was a key stimulus to the emergence of visible fannish activity around Maurice online: Monk, 2011b: 461–462.). On the other hand, to gain a deeper understanding of *Maurice*'s Edwardian British historical and cultural contexts and themes, transnational fans—who engage passionately with the detail and nuances of texts in online discussions—must navigate specialised areas such as Edwardian English society and its class system, contemporary laws (as well as social attitudes) on homosexuality, and Forster's broader themes of social hypocrisy and cross-class connections.

Examples of such discussions can be seen (indicatively) in the archives of the English-language www.mr-edna-may.livejournal.com—the first known online *Maurice* community (founded in 2004, the same year as the Merchant Ivory Collection DVD release); the (members-only) Russian *Maurice* community at www.maurice1987.diary.ru (founded in late 2010, a few months after the debut of the BBC's first *Sherlock* series); and more than one Japanese *Maurice* fan site, as well as many other platforms such as YouTube Comments. (For a timeline and a brief overview of the emergence of *Maurice*-specific fan websites, see Monk 2011b: 461–2.) The class positioning of the three main protagonists—suburban stockbroker Maurice Hall (played by James Wilby in Ivory's film), representative of the fading landed gentry Clive Durham (Hugh Grant in his first starring role), and sexually enterprising under-gamekeeper Alec Scudder (Rupert Graves), with whom Maurice eventually finds happiness—and the narrative implications of these differences, are easily misread by Anglophone US film critics, let alone non-Anglophone fans. Conversely, however, some transnational fans respond to *Maurice* with a refreshing directness that cuts straight through such minutiae to the core of the protagonists' dilemmas, while others bring historical insights most British viewers would lack. One German fan described literally shaking her fist and shouting at the screen when Maurice initially refuses Alec's plea to 'sleep the night with me' at a shabby hotel because he is due to attend a business dinner: '*Nein*! What *does* your engagement matter?' A new, passionate *Maurice* fan from Argentina wrote: 'Imagine my surprise when I realised they were talking about my country'—mentioned in the film when Maurice recommends an investment in 'Argentine Northern Land' to Clive's future wife, Anne, prefiguring the stealthy introduction of Alec, who (in both novel and film) is due to emigrate to 'the Argentine', but will instead miss his boat to remain with Maurice in an England which 'belonged to them' (Forster 1971: 239). This fan (not alone in spotting, and speculating upon, these references) was able to immediately explain this detail with reference to specifics of the history of British neo-colonial interests in Argentina.

One topic that remains especially hotly debated, and anguished over, by fans is the sexuality and psychology of Clive—who, painfully for Maurice, insists upon chastity throughout their three-year relationship, then abandons him for a sterile (and seemingly hypocritical) heterosexual marriage. Ivory's film motivates this turning point differently from Forster's novel, foregrounding the societal and legal perils—and fear—Maurice and Clive both face (even, in Edwardian England, in a chaste relationship) by introducing the entrapment, arrest, trial and (following the fate which destroyed Oscar Wilde) imprisonment with hard labour of Risley (Mark Tandy), a Cambridge friend of Clive's, on a (gay, sexual) 'immorality charge'. As the fandom-history wiki Fanlore notes in its entry on *Maurice*, discussion topics in the mr-edna-may LiveJournal community included 'Clive's sexuality, the novel's timeline, revisions made to the novel over Forster's lifetime, differences between the novel and the film, and the application of "slash" to a canonically gay source' (Fanlore, undated).

This last focus—alongside fans' wider framings of both Forster's and Ivory's *Maurice* in relation to fan fiction and slash noted earlier, and indeed the existence of sites such as Fanlore—illustrates the importance within fan culture of 'meta': meta-analysis *by* fans of both canon texts and aspects of fandom itself. Fan fiction, too, is written within a distinct culture with its own set of established practices, including writing challenges, fic prompts and commissions, and beta-ing (fannish proof-reading and supportive feedback on drafts). Indeed, one specialised form of beta-ing, 'Brit-pick', refers specifically to checking fan fictions set in the UK but written by (predominantly) US fans to ensure that the details of story, settings, dialogue, spelling and slang are all convincingly British. In addition, (high-quality) English-language fan fictions are written by authors for whom English is not their native language, including several *Maurice* fan fics, and at least one in the smaller field of *A Room with A View* fics, by writers from Italy, France and beyond. Two of the most compellingly realised *Maurice* fics are the work of writers from Denmark. In *Somebody With Whom to Dance* (Ea [eacalendula], 2010), a post-canon story set in the late 1920s, Clive Durham, holidaying in Cornwall with his wife Anne but haunted by memories of Maurice, forms a connection (emotional, then physical) with a lonely, bereaved gay man, Oliver, who is working as a professional dancing partner. The seven-chapter *Happy Ending* (devo79 2007/2012; discussed in Monk 2011b: 465), superbly researched, follows the fate of Maurice and Alec during World War I.

Alongside the writers who strive (often with considerable skill) to achieve a tone, style and historical verisimilitude close to the narrative universe of the film and Forster's novel, the field of *Maurice* fan fiction also includes crossovers and crack fics. But, on the whole, it is visual fanworks which are most likely to mash together 'English' heritage-film source material with hybrid trans/cultural specifics and popular-cultural elements—for example, in heritage-film pop videos, or in fan art which translates *Maurice* and wider 'Merchant-Forster-Ivory' content (most often, favourite actors and/or characters) into genres and styles owing more to wider fan culture. This is evident, for example, in the widespread (international) adoption of fan-art styles which draw their aesthetics and genres from the Japanese (and Korean or other East Asian) manga and anime traditions—including *chibi* ('small person' or 'small child' representations) (Fig. 11.1, left) and *bishōnen* styles (Fig. 11.1, right)—alongside many other styles ranging across the spectrum of Western art history and popular culture.

The soundtrack choices of *Maurice* music-video makers invoke a variety of cross-cultural and contemporising contexts. In relation to the film's gay themes, these range from the pairing of *Maurice* with songs and

Fig. 11.1 Manga- and anime-influenced styles of fan art. *Left: Chibi* ('small person') representations of British actor James Wilby in his two main roles in Merchant Ivory Productions' E.M. Forster adaptations: as Maurice Hall in *Maurice* (1987) and Charles Wilcox in *Howards End* (2012). By ma10-mato (Japan), Tumblr, 2015, who works in a range of styles. *Right:* Maurice Hall and Clive Durham's first tentative embrace at Cambridge, *Maurice* (1987), drawn in a *bishōnen* style by endymiasyzygy (UK), 2008, DeviantArt

artistes closely associated with the New York gay club scene of the 1970s onwards, from Blondie to the Scissor Sisters (see Monk 2011b: 448–9) to a more explicit curation of such videos with reference to gay experience, closetry and rights. While, as we have seen, the place of *Maurice* (and wider examples) in twenty-first-century fan culture owes much to the pleasures of young (and not so young) women, it is essential to note that *Maurice*'s circulation in participatory internet culture *simultaneously* serves vitally important functions for the promotion of LGBT equalities and rights worldwide—including as a (sometimes below-the-radar) source of LGBT hope, comfort and consciousness-raising for individuals in oppressive family circumstances or homophobic and oppressive regions (from post-Communist Central and Eastern Europe to the US Bible Belt states). One positive value of fan culture, in this context, is that it provides an ambiguous, anonymised arena in which LGBT issues can be discussed while identities and nationalities remain vague. *Maurice* remains a banned film in some countries (including Thailand and Singapore) and (on the evidence cited below) was so heavily cut in Russian territories that, on its delayed release, Ivory's 140-minute film ran to less than 90 minutes.

Maurice's LGBT-rights importance in such circumstances can be gleaned from small details. A Polish-subtitled copy of the film on YouTube (now taken down) was shared by a user named 'antihomofob'. An early thread on the Russian-language *Maurice* community at www.maurice1987.diary.ru/ asked its members: 'In the beginning was the word… or a movie? As well as a poll, anyone can share memories of your first meeting with *Maurice*. How, how did you hear about it in the censored country?' (18 March 2011). The very first reply was 'We thank God the internet is not yet censored', with the same member adding later that, among 200 films they had watched on 'the theme' (presumably homosexuality), *Maurice* was 'for me one of the best'. A later contributor reports: 'I first saw the film at all in the castrated version released [here] in the 1990s [1997]—just 90 minutes, there was no Alex [Alec Scudder] at all(!), it all ended with the wedding of Clive. A couple of years later I got the book and was shocked that the product was not at all about that, and with a happy ending. [Another] couple of years—finally the complete film (of course, all that time it had been available on VHS under the counter. :)))))' The original poster responds: 'Alex was not in it at all… HORROR!!!!!! After watching such a movie, the unaware person might easily shoot or hang himself.'

The same thread also diversifies into non-censorship topics of common interest to *Maurice* fans around the world, including comparisons between *Maurice* and *Brokeback Mountain* (Ang Lee, 2005) (also a mainstay since 2006 of the *Maurice* IMDb Message Boards) and members' shifting structures of (loss of) sympathy in relation to Clive Durham. Although the site's wider content abundantly displays the usual fannish and slash pleasures, the background context of LGBT equality struggles is evident in the community's choice of wallpaper (website background theme), which reproduces (in English, and in an appropriately romantic cursive script) the text of the UK marriage vow ('To have and to hold…')—resonating with Maurice's

Fig. 11.2 Resonant sites and queer heritage in *Maurice* (1987). *Left*: A pair of Assyrian lamassu at the British Museum, London, watch over and fascinate cross-class lovers Alec Scudder (Rupert Graves) and Maurice Hall (James Wilby) at the pivotal turning point in their relationship. Screen captures from *Maurice*, Merchant Ivory Productions. *Right*: A British Museum visitor touches one of the same lamassu, 2013. Photograph by Claire Monk

(and Forster's) dream of 'someone to last your whole life', but also, of course, with worldwide twenty-first-century campaigns for marriage equality.

In conclusion, it should be noted that this grassroots character of convergence-era *Maurice* fandom as it stands in the period 2004–16—in stark contrast with commercialised, industry-promoted Big Fandoms— also typifies the forms of fan/heritage tourism the film inspires. As I have discussed elsewhere (Monk 2013), contrary to the assumptions shaping 1990s British anti-heritage-film criticism, the presumed relationship between Merchant Ivory's 'English' heritage films and the UK heritage industry has never been a very direct or official one—in particular because many of the 'heritage properties' used as locations in their films have been privately owned homes not accessible to the pub-

Fig. 11.3 Maurice and Alec at the British Museum as visualized by one of *Maurice* (1987)'s twenty-first-century fan artists. Alec exclaims in astonishment at the size of the lamassu, while Maurice gazes adoringly at Alec. Part of a larger set by zzigae (South Korea), drawn in 2012, posted in 2014, Tumblr.

lic. Wilbury Park in Wiltshire—used as the Durham family's crumbling Penge (novel) or Pendersleigh Park (film) country estate in *Maurice*—was, at the date of filming, the home via marriage of the late, Russian-born, actress Maria Britneva/Maria St Just, one-time muse of the gay American playwright Tennessee Williams, and the executor of his literary estate. Britneva (who had already appeared briefly as Cecil Vyse's mother in Ivory's *A Room with a View*) allowed Ivory to film *Maurice* at Wilbury Park on condition that he gave her a cameo role. *Maurice*'s Wilbury Park location is thus steeped in personal connections and queer cultural heritage—but neither exploited nor exploitable as a commodified heritage visitor attraction.

In fact, the location from *Maurice* that resonates most powerfully with fans, and that fans from around the world—as well as the UK—love to visit, has nothing to do with upper-class, 'country-house' conceptions of the heritage industry, nor 'English' heritage, and everything to do with the emotional resonances of both the film and queer ancient history. At the British Museum in London, the crisis between cross-class lovers Maurice and Alec is transformed into mutually acknowledged—and permanent—love in front of a pair of giant matching statues of five-legged Assyrian bull-men (lamassu: protective spirits or deities) (Fig. 11.2). The scene, first written by Forster with no expectation of publication, even alludes to the possibility of same-sex marriage. *Maurice* fans (of all genders and sexual orientations) love to visit the bull-men, to see, photograph and perhaps touch them at a site that holds deep emotional resonance (and also inspires fan artists: Fig. 11.3). Perhaps most remarkably, however, this site illustrates how 'unofficial' heritage and fan tourism, and activist and fannish passions alike, may sometimes converge to remake—and become—official heritage. Since 2013, the British Museum's gift book *A Little Gay History* (Parkinson 2013: 28, 90), alongside a related Desire and Diversity trail (British Museum 2013), expressly highlights the importance of this scene in *Maurice*, and celebrates both the queer historical significance and plot function of its museum setting.

In closing, however, the example of *Maurice* and its fans also draws attention tellingly to the divergent fates of 'English' heritage cinema's two 'market leaders' of the 1980s–90s, 'Merchant–Forster–Ivory' and Jane Austen (Monk 2011b: 110–15), in the post-2000 global image market. The free labour/gift economy of *Maurice* fandom (around a film yet to be released on Blu-ray)—and even the relative austerity of the novel's centenary conference (St Andrews, 2012), where, in a bitterly cold November, the heating broke down and one speaker quipped, 'We know how Maurice and Alec kept warm'—stand in stark contrast to the unstoppable, continuing, twenty-first-century ascendancy of the Hollywood-backed Jane Austen media/heritage franchise (Higson 2010: 161–90) with its proliferating cross-media merchandising, spin-offs, and lavish circuit of events. Against this backdrop, the twenty-first-century afterlives of the 1980s–90s 'Merchant–Forster–Ivory' films emerge as a counter-narrative—but an unexpected, fascinating and even moving one, important in ways their 1980s–90s detractors might never have anticipated.

WORKS CITED

Bangert, A., P. Cooke, and R. Stone. 2016. Introduction. In *Screening European heritage*, eds. P. Cooke, and R. Stone, xvii–xxxiv. Basingstoke: Palgrave Macmillan.

Bergfelder, T., and C. Cargnelli, eds. 2008. *Destination London: German-speaking emigrés and British cinema, 1925–1950*. Oxford and New York: Berghahn.

British Museum. 2013. Desire and diversity. [Online]. Available from: www.britishmuseum.org/visiting/planning_your_visit/object_trails/desire_and_diversity.aspx#16. Accessed 24 Nov 2015.

Busse, K., and K. Hellekson. 2006. Introduction: Work in progress. In *Fan fiction and fan communities in the age of the internet*, eds. K. Hellekson and K. Busse, 5–32. Jefferson, NC: McFarland.

Craig, C. 1991. Rooms without a view. *Sight & Sound* 1(2), 10–13. In 2001. *Film/literature/heritage: A sight & sound reader*, ed. G. Vincendeau, 3–6. London: British Film Institute.

devo79. 2007/2012. *Happy ending*. [*Maurice* fan fiction in seven chapters.] *LiveJournal*, 23 June–21 September 2007. [Online]. Available from: http://devo79.livejournal.com/11956.html. Accessed on 20 Aug 2011.

Dodd, P. 1991. An English inheritance. *Sight & Sound* 1(2): 3.

Archive of Our Own [AO3]. 16 April. [Online]. Available from: http://archiveofourown.org/works/384649/chapters/629756. Accessed 21 Nov 2015.

Driscoll, C. 2006. One true pairing: The romance of pornography and the pornography of romance. In *Fan fiction and fan communities in the age of the internet*, eds. K. Hellekson and K. Busse, 79–96. Jefferson, NC: McFarland.

Ea (eacalendula). 2010. *Somebody with whom to dance*. [*Maurice* fan fiction.] Archive of Our Own [AO3] [Online]. Available from: http://archiveofourown.org/works/64775. Accessed 21 Nov 2015.

Endres, N. 2007. Plato, Platotude and blatancy in E. M. Forster's *Maurice*. In *Alma parens originalis?: The receptions of classical literature and thought in Africa, Europe, the United States, and Cuba*, eds. J.L. Hilton and A. Gosling, 177–200. Bern: Peter Lang.

endymiasyzygy. 2008. *Maurice*. [Fan art.] DeviantArt, 21 January. [Online]. Available from: http://endymiasyzygy.deviantart.com/art/Maurice-75255275. Accessed 22 Nov 2015.

Fanlore. No date. *Maurice*. [Wiki entry.] *Fanlore*. [Multi-authored fandom-history wiki encyclopaedia.] [Online]. Available from: http://fanlore.org/wiki/Maurice. Accessed 28 June 2015.

Finch, M., and R. Kwietniowski. 1988. Melodrama and *Maurice*: Homo is where the het is. *Screen* 29(3): 72–80.

Forster, E.M. 1971. *Maurice*. New York: W. W. Norton.

Higson, A., and R. Maltby, eds. 1999. *Film Europe and Film America: Cinema, commerce and cultural exchange, 1920–39*. Exeter: University of Exeter Press.

Higson, A. 2003. *English heritage, English cinema: Costume drama since 1980*. Oxford: Oxford University Press.

———. 2010. *Film England: Culturally English filmmaking since the 1990s*. London: I.B. Tauris.

———. 2016. Historical Films in Europe: The Transnational Production, Circulation and Reception of 'National' Heritage Drama. In *Screening European heritage*, eds. P. Cooke, and R. Stone, 183–207. Basingstoke: Palgrave Macmillan.

Hipsky, M.A. 1994. Anglophil(m)ia: Why does America watch Merchant–Ivory movies? *Journal of Popular Film and Television* 22(3): 98–107.

Hunting, K. 2012. *Queer as Folk* and the trouble with slash. *Transformative Works and Cultures* 11. [Open-access e-journal, no pagination.] [Online]. At: http://journal.transformativeworks.org/index.php/twc/article/view/415. Accessed 4 Dec 2015.

Ingersoll, E. G. 2012. *Filming Forster: The Challenges of Adapting E. M. Forster's Novels for the Screen*. Lanham MD: Lexington Books.

Jenkins, H. 1992. *Textual Poachers: Television Fans and Participatory Culture*. London and New York: Routledge.

Kempley, R. 1987. *Maurice*. [Film review.] *Washington Post*, 2 October. www.washingtonpost.com/wp-srv/style/longterm/movies/videos/mauricerkempley_a0ca53.htm. Accessed 4 June 2013.

Martin, R. K. 1983. Edward Carpenter and the double structure of *Maurice*. In: Kellogg, S., ed. *Essays on Gay Literature*. New York: Harrington Park Press, pp. 35–46.

ma10-mato. 2015. *Maurice* (1987), Maurice Hall. [Chibi fan art.] Tumblr, 14 October. http://ma10-mato.tumblr.com/post/131099775692. [Accessed 22 ovember 2015.]

ma10-mato. 2015. *Howards End* (1992), Charles Wilcox. [Chibi fan art.] Tumblr, 16 October. http://ma10-mato.tumblr.com/post/131272953582. [Accessed 22 November 2015.]

Monk, C. 1995/2001. Sexuality and heritage. *Sight and Sound* , 5(10): 32–34. Republished in *Film/literature/heritage: A sight & sound reader*, ed. G. Vincendeau, 6–11. London: British Film Institute.

Monk, C. 2002. The British heritage-film debate revisited. In: Monk, C. and Sargeant, A. eds. *British Historical Cinema: The History, Heritage and Costume Film*. London: Routledge, pp. 176–198.

Monk, C. 2011a. *Heritage Film Audiences: Period Film and Contemporary Audiences in the UK*. Edinburgh: Edinburgh University Press.

Monk, C. 2011b. Heritage Film Audiences 2.0: period film audiences and online fan cultures. *Participations: Journal of Audience & Reception Studies*. 8(2), pp. 431–477. www.participations.org/Volume%208/Issue%202/3h%20Monk.pdf.

Monk, C. 2013. From political critique to online fandom: Claire Monk on British heritage film, its origins and afterlife. Interviewed by Bangert, A. *Screening European Heritage* project website, 25 July. http://arts.leeds.ac.uk/screeningeuropeanheritage/956/.

Morimoto, L. H. 2015a. The first 'beautiful British boy boom' (1988–1989). [Blog post.] lorimorimoto.org, 22 January. http://lorimorimoto.org/2015/01/22/the-first-beautiful-british-boy-boom-1988-1989/ [Accessed 6 July 2015.]

Morimoto, L. H. 2015b. Setting the stage: the origins of modern foreign 'boy booms' in Japan. Fan Studies Network Third Annual Conference, University of East Anglia, UK, 28 June.

Nightingale, B. 1987. A gay 'love story'. *New York Times*, 13 September. www.nytimes.com/1987/09/13/movies/a-gay-love-story.html. [Accessed 30 May 2015.]

Otaka, H. and Inaba, M. 1989. *Mini-Theatre o Yoroshiku (All the Best to Mini-Theatre)*. Tokyo: JiccShuppankyoku.

Otaka, H. 1998. *Mini ShiatāTeki: EigaGa Motto MottoSuki Ni Naru Hon (Mini-Theatre Style: A Book to Make You Love Movies More)*. Tokyo: WēbuShuppan.

Parkinson, R. B. 2013. *A Little Gay History: Desire and Diversity Across the World*. London: British Museum Press.

Pym, J. 1984. *The Wandering Company: Twenty-One Years of Merchant Ivory Films*. London and New York: British Film Institute and Museum of Modern Art.

St Andrews. 2012. E. M. Forster's *Maurice*: A conference marking the centenary of Forster's writing of the novel. University of St Andrews, UK, 24–25 November.

Stasi, M. 2013. 'You? Omega. Me? Alpha. ... I can't help it. That's basic biology for you': New forms of gender essentialism in fan fiction. Conference paper, *Console-ing Passions*, De Montfort University, Leicester, UK.

svebara. 2015. 'It isn't,' he said to Mr Ducie, 'and I've a serious charge to bring against this gentleman.' [*Maurice* fan art.] Tumblr, 21 November. http://svebaraart.tumblr.com/post/133651153304. [Accessed 27 November 2015.]

Tezuka, Y. 2011. *Japanese Cinema Goes Global: Filmworkers' Journeys*. Hong Kong: Hong Kong University Press.

Waugh, T. 2000. *The Fruit Machine: Twenty Years of Writings on Gay Cinema*, Durham, NC: Duke University Press.

zzigae. 2014. Some of *Maurice* (written by E. M. Forster), doodle drawn in 2012. [*Maurice* fan art.] Tumblr, 21 November. http://zzigae.tumblr.com/post/73564937341. [Accessed 22 November 2015.]

CHAPTER 12

From 'Auschwitz-land' to *Banglatown*: Heritage Conflicts, Film and the Politics of Place

Paul Cooke

'Auschwitz-land' is the provocative term coined by Tim Cole to describe what he sees as the reductive way in which the complex of over 43 concentration and extermination camps located on the outskirts of the Polish town of Oświęcim is now presented to tourists. 'The tourist's experience of "Auschwitz-land" starts at the gate proclaiming *Arbeit macht frei*, and ends at the reconstructed Crematorium. It is a manipulated tour which makes claims to the authentic, and yet owes much more to the constructed symbol "Auschwitz"', which, Cole argues, has come to stand 'as *the* symbol of the Holocaust' (emphasis in original), the presentation of Auschwitz as a physical place, where specific groups of people with specific histories were abused and murdered, having been subsumed within a globally recognised 'brand name' (Cole 2000: 105–11).

The status of Auschwitz as the symbolic 'brand name' for the Holocaust has long been particularly visible in cinema. That said, film has also had an uneasy relationship with Auschwitz as 'brand'. Steven Spielberg, for example, was famously refused permission to film scenes of *Schindler's*

P. Cooke (✉)
University of Leeds, Leeds, UK
e-mail: p.cooke@leeds.ac.uk

List (1993) in the camp itself. Yet, the international success of the film has been hugely influential in raising awareness of, and generating visitors to, the camp and other sites connected to the Holocaust, to the extent that it was, for a time at least, one of the only cultural phenomena to have the potential to challenge the symbolic power of even the Auschwitz 'brand', Omer Bartov going so far as to suggest in the mid 1990s that the movie had become 'for the present generation the most important source of historical information affecting popular perceptions of the Holocaust' (Bartov 1996: 169). Or, as Cole puts it, 'for some, *Schindler's List* has almost the status of a primary source. It is not seen as simply representation, but as the "real thing"', a development that is evidenced, he argues, in *Schindler's List* tours of locations represented in the film. Here tourists 'do not so much see sites of "Holocaust" history, as sites of *Schindler's List* history', this blurring of 'image and reality' ultimately feeding into the creation of the Holocaust as a 'myth' with the potential to overwhelm and usurp the place of the 'Holocaust as history' (Cole 2000: 75). For many commentators, Spielberg's film was, for this reason, deeply problematic, and this is not to mention its presentation of a finally uplifting image of the period focused on the narrative of a few survivors which, it is argued, creates a fundamentally skewed impression of the Holocaust as history.[1] In the process, although the custodians of the Auschwitz memorial reject the representation of history in Spielberg's film, for Cole, both the film and the memorial are part of the same global trend towards a mythologisation of the Holocaust. Indeed, the similarly problematic nature of the visitor's experience at Auschwitz and the spectator's experience of watching a Hollywood version of the Holocaust such as *Schindler's List* is, Griselda Pollock suggests, fundamentally 'structural'. Radicalising the foundational work of John Urry on the 'tourist gaze' (Urry 1990) by drawing parallels between the physical 'tourism' (if it can be described as such) of visiting the camp and what she defines as the virtual tourism of consuming film, Pollock argues that both involve 'the spectacularization of the work or experience of the other', which fails to make enough of a distinction 'between the place that can be visited and left, and the problematic burned into Western European culture' (Pollock 2003: 181–8). If, as Urry suggests, the tourist's gaze is intent upon domesticating and controlling the 'other' through spectacle, the challenge with the Holocaust as heritage is both to acknowledge this structural relationship and also, in the process, problematise it. While the tourist can visit and leave this history, so many of the historical actors involved could not.

The relationship between Cole's notion of 'Auschwitz-land' and the cinematic representation of the Holocaust in film is made more complex still if it is considered in conjunction with Michael Rothberg's concept of 'multidirectional memory' and the various ways in which analogies with, and references to, the Holocaust have become 'unavoidable building blocks or *morphemes* of public memory' (Rothberg 2011: 524). Rothberg traces the variety of ways the Holocaust has become a key orientation point in discussions of a whole host of histories, particularly, he suggests, in contemporary debates around post-colonialism, multiculturalism and transnational, diasporic experience. In his discussion of the use of Holocaust memory in a wide variety of contexts, Rothberg rejects the common 'misrecognition of collective memory as a zero-sum game', namely that to compare traumatic histories is to elide differences between them (Rothberg 2009: 11). 'Proximate pasts,' he argues, 'are neither "separate and unique" nor "equal"; rather, a form of modified "double consciousness" arises capable of conjoining them in an open-ended assemblage' (Rothberg 2011: 527–8). But how is one to achieve this kind of balance? How can one acknowledge—indeed, instrumentalise—the *fact* that the Holocaust provides a representational grammar for exploring a whole range of traumatic histories, while also recognising the concerns of commentators such as Cole and Pollock, and the need to respect the particularity of the experience of those engaging with, or who have been engaged by, the history in question?

In this chapter, I wish to examine the tension between the call for a recognition of the specific and competing subject positions of all those connected to Auschwitz as a heritage site and the potential of Rothberg's multidimensional memory in a number of case studies where we similarly find critical encounters between traumatic moments of history, heritage sites and film—all of which also invoke Rothberg's discursive framework—before returning to the symbolic place of Auschwitz as heritage site. In so doing, I suggest that while reference to the Holocaust as a '*morphem*[*e*] of public memory' in the debates often sparked by films that engage with physical heritage sites frequently do seem to run roughshod over the kind of nuanced approach to the specificity of individual historical contexts that both Rothberg and Pollock, in their different ways, ultimately call for, in the films discussed here, one finds an attempt to strike a balance between Pollock's demand for specificity, on the one hand, and the potential of Rothberg's conceptualisation of memory as 'open-ended assemblage' on the other. However, before turning to my specific case studies, it is useful to reflect further on the relationship between film, heritage and tourism more generally. In the process, I hope to show how tensions in the assumed relationship between the consumer of a given heritage site and their actual experience can also provide us with tools to find this balance.

Tourism, Film and Questions of Embodiment

Although engaging a fundamentally different set of ethical issues than those explored in the 'consumption' of the Holocaust by visiting tourists to Auschwitz, the same *structural* equivalence identified by Pollock is to be found in a whole range of encounters between physical heritage sites and their real, or imagined, consumption via visual culture. David Martin-Jones, for example, identifies a similar structural correspondence between film and heritage tourism in his discussion of VisitScotland's location marketing strategy. However, what is seen as deeply problematic for Pollock is, for VisitScotland, presented as helpful. Focusing on the way that the tourist board worked in partnership with Sony Pictures to market the Scottish locations featured in the blockbuster hit *The Da Vinci Code* (Ron Howard 2006), Martin-Jones highlights the manner in which the film constructs a specific sense of national identity that VisitScotland sought to use to attract visitors from the Scottish overseas diaspora. The film's conspiracy-theory version of European history culminates in a visit to Rosslyn Chapel near Edinburgh by the film's transnational group of protagonists. This visit creates a very attractive 'association of Scotland with a past steeped in myth and romance' (Martin-Jones 2014: 161). At the same time, it provides the resolution to the film's quest to find the Holy Grail along with a strong sense of homecoming for the film's female lead (Audrey Tautou). Working in a long tradition of 'roots-tourism' filmmaking, most famously exemplified by John Ford's *The Quiet Man* (1952), which spoke to diasporic Irish-American identity, Martin-Jones points to what VisitScotland and Sony see as a symbiotic relationship between film and heritage tourism, the ostensibly straightforward and, crucially, singular reading of history presented in this and similar films providing a mythical sense of belonging for the implied target spectator. While the correspondence between heritage tourism and film is at the heart of the ethical problem raised in the encounter between the visitor and Holocaust history, as Martin-Jones and other commentators point out, it is the ability of films such as *The Da Vinci Code* or *The Quiet Man* to work in concert with the heritage/tourist industry that makes them so valuable to this sector, allowing the relevant tourist board to present Scotland or Ireland as a readily consumable 'heritage landscape' that, in turn, potentially enhances the experience of watching the films (Martin-Jones 2014: 172; Rains 2003).

That said, the kind of one-to-one mapping of film onto heritage site and then onto the visitor experience is fundamentally troubled by the question of what Rodanthi Tzanelli defines in her work on cinematic tourism as 'embodiment', a question which ultimately returns us to the tension between the positions of Pollock and Rothberg outlined above. Tzanelli questions readings of film and heritage tourism predicated on the implied spectator/visitor, ostensibly constructed by the film/curatorial strategy of the site in question. Discussing the nature of 'virtual tourism' through film, as well as other media, Tzanelli notes that 'the embodied viewer is both a spectator and an actor who can challenge the objectivity of the camera', defining the consumers of such products as 'virtual flâneurs [...], hermeneutic agents because they often precede any interpretation of the film's marketing value by local and global tourist providers' (Tzanelli 2007: 17). Conceptualising the consumer of such cultural products as an 'embodied viewer' allows for a far more 'dynamic relationship of interaction [between film and tourism/heritage] which often has unpredictable outcomes' (Tzanelli 2007: 5). At the same time, and returning to Pollock's discussion, it is also necessary to be mindful of the embodied nature of the historical subject and *their* status as (frequently silenced) actors whose position in the historical narrative must equally be acknowledged and, Pollock insists, problematised within the process of consumption. It is the challenge of acknowledging the place of the embodied spectator and the embodied historical subject, while also exploring the potential for emotional yet critical and, at the same time, 'open-ended' engagement with heritage culture—to cite Rothberg once more—that I wish to examine in the rest of this chapter.

I look now at three very different cultural encounters, all of which point to the possibility of a dynamic engagement between film and heritage that can open up new ways of exploring the past and its multiple meanings for the present.

Brick Lane and Banglatown

Sarah Gavron's 2007 production of Monica Ali's best-selling novel *Brick Lane* (2003) highlights many of the tensions outlined above, most obviously the need to address questions of embodiment, and in particular 'the *embodied* nature of creating and claiming space' when dealing with difficult histories and contested heritage, as Claire Alexander puts it in her discussion of the setting of Ali/Gavron's texts (2011: 204, emphasis in original). *Brick Lane* focuses on the changing nature of life for the London Bengali community in the run-up to and aftermath of the events of 11 September 2001, telling the story of Nazneen (Tannishtha Chatterjee) who was brought from rural Bangladesh to the borough of Tower Hamlets (where Brick Lane is found) in the 1980s as a very quiet 17-year-old, and given in marriage to the much older and somewhat self-deluded Chanu (Satish Kaushik). During its production the film provoked a vicious controversy, much reported in the media. Members of the Bengali community were unhappy about the proposed film and refused permission for the production company, Ruby Films, to use locations on the street, insisting that Ali's book was a patronising and insidious misrepresentation of their community, which they did not want turned into a film. The protestors cited, among other examples, a scene that was apparently to be included in which a leech was to fall from the hair of a Bengali woman into a pot of curry in a Brick Lane restaurant (a scene, it should be noted, that does not appear in the film and which the production company insists was never intended to). Ali had not lived on Brick Lane, they pointed out. She was not from the Sylhet region of Bangladesh, from where the majority of the local inhabitants came. Consequently she had no right to speak for them. Book burnings were even planned and violence hinted at, if the film crew did not leave the area (Lea and Lewis 2006). Publicity for this protest grew when the writers and public intellectuals Germaine Greer and Salmon Rushdie entered the debate, Greer siding with the protestors, claiming that Ali was irresponsible. 'Brick Lane is a real place,' she insisted. 'Bengali Muslims smart under an Islamic prejudice that they are irreligious and disorderly, the impure among the pure, and here was a proto-Bengali writer with a Muslim name, portraying them as all of that and more'(Greer 2006). Rushdie, on the other hand, insisted upon Ali's right to freedom of speech, attacking Greer's position as 'philistine, sanctimonious, and disgraceful', the venom of which was rooted in a much older argument between the two writers, sparked when Greer refused to support Rushdie's right to publish *The Satanic Verses* (1988) (Lea and Lewis 2006).

Oblique echoes of Rothberg's thesis could be found throughout the debate the film sparked. The *Independent*'s Johann Hari, for example, described the protest as 'The Battle of Brick Lane', recalling the violent clashes between Oswald Mosley's Fascists and the Jewish community, as well as other minorities in the 1930s in the East End of London, referred to as 'The Battle of Cable Street' (Hari 2006), a connection further underlined in

Hazuan Hashim and Phil Maxwell's recent documentary *From Cable Street to Brick Lane* (2012). Hari even compared Ali's book to the work of the Jewish intellectual and Holocaust survivor Elie Wiesel, suggesting that *Brick Lane* similarly gave voice to problematic subject positions in order to challenge them (Hari 2006).[2] Like the other debates mentioned in this chapter, central to the discussion about the film was the status of Brick Lane itself as a heritage site, and who had the right to define its meaning. The driving force behind the protest was the Brick Lane Traders' Association, a group that had a keen interest in protecting the recent economic regeneration of the area as a London heritage tourist attraction that offered visitors the opportunity to 'experience' Bangladeshi culture, part of Brick Lane having being rebranded as 'Banglatown' (Oakley and Pratt 2010). On one level, the reason for the protest appeared clear, particularly in light of the discussion of Auschwitz as a heritage site, as well as the work of VisitScotland. The central community actors considered the book to present an image of Brick Lane that ran counter to their core message, seeming to suggest that their community was simply a group of unenlightened extremists. If the film were to be made, this image would surely be significantly amplified. This was not, it appeared, a case of a film and heritage attraction working in harmony. However, the relationship between the protestors, the film and 'Banglatown' is, in fact, far more complex than this analysis would suggest.

As Alexander argues, 'Banglatown has become a highly contested site within the local Bengali community around issues of religion, region, gender, generation, commercialization and so on' (Alexander 2011: 214). That said, the press debate actually allowed the protestors to transcend these issues and present a very particular and, crucially, unified image of 'Banglatown' to the outside world. Deliberately played out predominantly in the pages of centre-left newspaper the *Guardian*, the discussion provided a platform for the protestors to portray Banglatown as an 'authentically edgy' space in a way that was likely to be attractive to the readership of this newspaper (Brouillette 2009: 441). At the same time, given that in the world of entertainment there generally is no such thing as bad publicity, the protest also helped keep the book on the bestseller lists and advertise the forthcoming film. Thus it would seem that this was, contrary to first impressions, a further example of heritage and film working in a mutually supportive manner in order to construct and communicate a singular reading of Brick Lane as a cultural symbol.

However, what was not discussed in the original debate the film sparked was that the Brick Lane protests also raised questions that challenged the status of this singular reading, asking us to re-examine the nature of Brick Lane as heritage site, and who has the right to represent it. This area has acted as an arrival point for migrant communities since at least the sixteenth century, beginning with the French Huguenots. Bangladeshis are the largest community to inhabit the area at the moment. However, there is a fear that this community is now under threat, at this point from encroaching gentrification as the affluence of the City of London moves ever eastwards. Banglatown was an attempt to protect, as Sarah Brouillette puts it, 'an essentialized image of Bangladeshi identity', aimed at ensuring the economic viability of this community by drawing in new visitors (Brouillette 2009: 435). For some commentators, the apparently essentialising impulse behind the Banglatown project is problematic for a number of competing reasons. On the one hand, it presents Brick Lane today as a 'mono-cultural enclave' (Jacobs 1996: 100). Yet as the film *Our Brick Lane* (2007)—produced by the local volunteer group Eastside Community Heritage in the wake of the *Brick Lane* controversy—makes clear, over 10,000 Somalis also live in the area. Furthermore, as the echoes of Rothberg's 'multidirectional memory' in the debate mentioned above highlight, although they had largely left by the 1960s, there are still traces of the Jewish community to be found in the area, traces which also have a claim to be part of any celebration of Brick Lane as heritage site. On the other hand, the creation of Banglatown can in fact also be seen as part of the *same* process of gentrification that is challenging the future of Brick Lane as a Bangladeshi space and in response to which it was created in order to protect this very community. The regeneration of the area is bringing in new, more affluent, inhabitants who are ultimately changing the area's fundamental nature. In so doing, it would seem to be ushering in a moment of community transition in an area that has a long tradition of such transitions. As a result, the apparently essentialising impulse behind Banglatown instead highlights the constructed, transitory and non-essentialist nature of Brick Lane as a community space, while at the same time presenting it as a space in which meaning is, somewhat ironically, embodied in the performance of an essentialist notion of community identity.

This tension is also central to Gavron's film itself. The narrative of both the book and the film is told from the point of view of Nazneen, who we meet in the film at a point when she has been living in London with Chanu for 16 years and has two daughters. On one level, the film can be viewed as an attempt to deconstruct the 'root tourism' tradition of filmmaking to be found in John Ford. Rather than telling the story of what happens when the migrant returns 'home'—the central conceit of *The Quiet Man* and its depiction of the return of Sean Thornton (John Wayne) to rural Ireland—in *Brick Lane* returning home is held out as an aspiration for Nazneen and Chanu, much to the chagrin of their eldest daughter, who is fully integrated into London life with no understanding of, or wish to learn about, life in rural Bangladesh. Nonetheless, 'home' is presented in a chocolate-box, nostalgic aesthetic reminiscent of Ford's film. Nazneen's life in her Tower Hamlets' flat is punctuated by a series of flashbacks, in which we watch her as a child playing with her sister, the rich red and gold colour palette of these sequences contrasting starkly with the pallid shots of her drab and isolated life in the East End. Nazneen and Chanu's status as rootless outsiders in the UK is continually underlined by the way they are positioned either as subjects or objects of tourist culture. On the one hand, Chanu forces his family to take on the role of tourist, 'to see the sites' of London. He even has their picture taken in front of Buckingham Palace in a ridiculous performance that insists upon their 'otherness' to mainstream British heritage, as if they had not been living in London for years. On the other, we see Nazneen flinch as she is snapped by a visitor to Banglatown, here the uncomfortable object of the tourist's gaze, unwilling to be 'domesticated'—to invoke Urry once more—by UK tourist culture (Fig. 12.1).

Fig. 12.1 Chanu orchestrating his family's performance of the role of tourist

Over time, Nazneen grows in confidence, to the point that she decides to have an affair with a young man she meets when she begins to take in sewing to help support the family. Karim (Christopher Simpson) falls in love with Nazneen, believing her to be 'the real thing', a 'village girl' from a homeland he himself has never visited. And, as their love blossoms, the colour palette of the Bangladeshi sequences begins to spread to Tower Hamlets, the shots of the couple in bed having a similar red-golden hue, suggesting that Nazneen has now found a new sense of belonging within the Bangladeshi diaspora. However, as Karim begins to radicalise in the face of increased racist attacks before and after the events of 11 September 2001—presented as a moment of profound traumatic rupture for this community—Nazneen rejects him and his politics. Simultaneously, she begins to find a new respect for her husband. Although still a buffoon, Chanu refuses the kind of essentialist, and ultimately mythical, version of Bangladeshi identity propagated by Karim, in favour of a more pragmatic understanding of identity construction based on their present circumstances. Finally the couple split up, amicably. Chanu returns to Bangladesh, well aware that it will not be the same place he left decades before. Nazneen and her daughters remain in London, having decided that this is their home, now fully embracing the grainy, cool tones of Tower Hamlets, the final shot of her making snow angels with her daughters outside their flat acting as a 'realist' counterweight to the colourful, nostalgic shots of her playing with her sister in Bangladesh. While the novel ultimately seemed to play into the essentialising message the Brick Lane traders wished to project for Banglatown, *Brick Lane* the film explicitly rejects the notion of identity or community as essentialist categories. Nazneen and Chanu finally realise that both identity and community can only exist through a process of individual embodied performance, rather than being externally constructed. This suggests a process of embodiment with the potential for a far more 'open-ended' understanding of community identity than was suggested in the initial debate the film's production sparked (Rothberg 2011: 528).

CHALLENGING *STASILAND* THROUGH EMBODIMENT: *DAS LEBEN DER ANDEREN* (*THE LIVES OF OTHERS*, 2006)

Although engaging another, very different, historical context to that of either *Schindler's List* or *Brick Lane*, the debate sparked by Florian Henckel von Donnersmarck's hugely successful *The Lives of Others* picked up many of the issues that were at the heart of both these other debates. Beyond the explicit reference to Spielberg's film in the press discussion of von Donnersmark's film, and thus to Rothberg's thesis, it also, more significantly, once again raised questions about the nature of embodiment, the right to historical representation and the ownership of heritage space. *The Lives of Others* tells the story of Stasi officer Gerd Wiesler (Ulrich Mühe), who is ordered to organise a surveillance operation on the GDR playwright Georg Dreyman (Sebastian Koch). Over the course of the narrative, Wiesler becomes increasingly attracted to the artistic world of his target, to the point that he falsifies reports in order to protect the writer from further punishment by the State. Internationally, the film was widely praised, receiving numerous prizes, not least the Oscar for best foreign language production. In Germany, however, its reception was more mixed, the film sparking a huge debate.[3] On the one hand, there were those who saw the film as an important corrective to earlier cinematic representations of the GDR, most notably so-called *Ostalgie* (East German nostalgia) comedies such as *Good Bye, Lenin!* (Wolfgang Becker, 2003) and *Sonnenallee* (*Sun Alley*, Leander Haußmann, 1999), which, their critics suggested, played to contemporary impulses to fetishise the material culture of the GDR and play down the oppressive reality of life under its communist regime. Supporters cited the film's ostensible quest for authenticity and its painstaking attention to detail, down to its use of genuine bugging devices from the period in its recreation of a Stasi surveillance operation (Handke 2007). For Germany's Federal Agency for Political Education (bpb), the film's attention to authentic detail made it an ideal text for teaching schoolchildren about life in the East (Falck 2006), and the positive reviews from the various film screenings specifically for children seemed to support this view, the organisers of such events precisely seeing the film as a way for the younger generation to gain a non-*Ostalgie*-tainted picture of the GDR (Harmsen 2006).

On the other hand, there were those who condemned the film precisely for its *lack* of authenticity. As Anna Funder, the author of the best-selling English-language account of the Stasi's activities *Stasiland* (2003), notes in one of the few critical foreign reviews the film received, the Stasi would never have let a single individual run an operation like this. Consequently, a lone officer betraying the Stasi could never have had such a large impact on an operation, and this is not to mention the fact that there is little or no evidence that such conversions among members of the organisation ever took place (Funder 2007: 18). Others went far beyond pointing out specific historical inaccuracies to challenge the film's underlying ideological position, and, as we see in the *Brick Lane* debate, the right of this particular director (in this case a West German) to tell this story, which is about life in the East. It is here, moreover, that we once again find points of correspondence with Rothberg's discursive framework. Günter Jeschonnek, for example, provocatively suggested that von Donnersmarck's ultimate aim was to turn Wiesler into 'a State Security Schindler', making a 'straight-edged perpetrator into a sensitive good person, then into a hero and finally into a pitiable victim' (Jeschonnek 2006). If this is the case, it would seem unsurprising, then, that the film should receive official endorsement by organisations such as the bpb, since it would seem to play into a dominant trend in the official reading of the GDR, which Bill Niven identifies as positing the former East German State as a 'continuation of National Socialism', by continually stressing in official discourse 'equational thinking' between the two German dictatorships. In the process, however, rather than allowing for a more nuanced understanding of the GDR via a comparison with this earlier German dictatorship, such comparisons tend to elide important differences between these two moments in German history and, most importantly, the relative culpability of the general population for crimes carried out by the Nazis on the one hand and the East German Communist Party on the other (Niven 2001: 58–9).

Of particular interest to the wider discussion of this chapter is the response to the film by Hubertus Knabe, director of the Berlin-Hohenschönhausen Memorial, which is housed on the site of the Stasi's main remand prison. Knabe publicly refused permission for von Donnersmarck to film at the memorial, much to the annoyance, and expense, of the filmmaker, who was consequently forced to rebuild parts of the former prison for his opening sequences. For Knabe, the conversion of Wiesler was the major stumbling block. In his view, allowing the film to shoot on the site would have been a betrayal of the former victims of the organisation, some of whom now actually carry out tours at the museum: 'One cannot abuse a location in which people have suffered, and which they might then recognise in the cinema as the set for a film which treats history so casually' (Knabe 2007). Knabe tried to convince the director to change this aspect of his story, but to no avail, and so permission to shoot there was refused. In Knabe's account of his engagement with von Donnersmarck, *Schindler's List* is once again invoked, the filmmaker ostensibly citing Spielberg in his justification of the conversion plotline, thus seeming to underline the validity of Jeschonnek's criticism mentioned above. However, as Knabe insists, the criticisms of Spielberg's film already discussed above notwithstanding, 'Schindler was a real person, Wiesler wasn't'. Knabe's demand for authenticity has all the urgency of commentators such as Cole and Bartov, who call for a similar level of authenticity in representations of the Holocaust as heritage in the face of those who would deny the fact of its historicity. He cites the increasingly well-organised interventions by former members of the Stasi who attempt to challenge his museum's presentation of history, suggesting that, even today after so many revelations have surfaced about the Stasi's activities, the majority of its members refuse to accept any guilt for their participation in past human rights violations (Knabe 2007). Knabe's position on the film is understandable given the museum's particular approach to presenting this aspect of history, which is based, as André Kockisch, the museum's press officer, notes, upon the primacy of the witness's experience, a perspective that provides the museum's visitors with a 'unique emotional entrance point' to the past (Ward 2014). The museum sets great store in its approach. History is embodied for the visitor in the experience of the tour guides, an encounter that can, moreover, have a therapeutic function for the guides themselves, empowering former inmates who now literally hold the key to their one-time prison. The Hohenschönhausen memorial provides a powerful emotional bridge to the past via the testimony of the witnesses who work there. In so doing, as Knabe notes, it is also the museum's duty to respect the primacy of their memory.

While the museum did not endorse what it saw as a problematic representation of history in the film, like *Schindler's List*, the film clearly has had an impact on the site, not least in terms of visitor numbers. Karsten Harfst, a member of the educational team at the museum, for example, states that the number of younger visitors noticeably increased in the wake of the film's success. Tour guides also have to engage with the film in the questions posed by visitors (Harfst 2007). For Kockisch, at least, despite the museum's critical position on the film, the fact that the museum now has to discuss the film's representation of the past is not problematic. Indeed, discussion of the film allows the museum staff to distance themselves from what they see as the inauthenticity of the film's presentation of history, giving them the opportunity to restate the museum's ethical position—and legal mandate—to teach visitors about the GDR's system of political repression, and to give its former victims a voice (Ward 2014).

The debate between the film and Hohenschönhausen has much in common with the other encounters already mentioned. However, what was missed in the debate the film sparked, and which offers a new dimension to this present discussion, is the way the film actively interrogates the 'dynamic relationship of interaction' between the past as heritage and its representation through film; to return for a moment to Tzanelli's formulation, a direction of enquiry that allows the spectator to move beyond the kind of 'equational thinking' between the two German dictatorships identified by Niven in public debates on the legacy of the GDR for Germany and which, once again, calls for a more 'open-ended' approach to working through, in this case, Germany's problematic history, an approach that also takes into account the specific experience of both those who were there and those who have come afterwards.

Wiesler's surveillance operation is focused on listening to conversations in the flat below him. The central conceit of the narrative is the way in which Wiesler uses what he *hears* to create, via his imagination, a visual, and ultimately embodied, understanding of Dreyman's life. He longs to inhabit Dreyman's world *physically*. We see, for example, his posture echoing that of Dreyman, embracing the cord of his headphones as he listens in to the apartment below in a similar fashion to the way we see Dreyman embracing his partner. However, the film ultimately makes clear that Wiesler cannot live Dreyman's life. The experiences he imagines are not his own, and cannot be embodied by him. This, in turn, leads to a more complex understanding of the relationship between authenticity and historical representation than that to be found in the original debate the film generated. In so doing, the film also begins to ask broader questions about the nature of embodiment and the ownership of the historical record.

Of central importance to the wider significance of the film's understanding of what Tzanelli sees as the dynamic relationship between history and heritage is the film's encounter with the Stasi files as archive, and the dominant place of this archive as holder of the historical record of GDR authoritarianism. Immediately after the fall of the Wall, numerous figures were outed as 'unofficial' Stasi collaborators, from Lothar de Maizière, the GDR's only democratically elected president, to some of the country's most prominent cultural figures such as Christa Wolf and Heiner Müller, fuelling the impression that the GDR was fundamentally a 'this Stasi State influence' where, as Jürgen Habermas famously described it, this giant octopus-like organisation stretched its tentacles through the whole of society, leaving no aspect of life free from its influence (Bathrick 1995: 221), a view that is also reinforced in Funder's *Stasiland*, based on eyewitness accounts of life in the East and what she sees as the continued aftershocks of the organisation in unified Germany. The importance of the Stasi archive for our contemporary understanding of the GDR should not be underestimated. However, through Dreyman's engagement with the files as an historical record, their status as the repository of absolute truth, as the final word on the 'reality' of life in the GDR as they have been construed either implicitly or explicitly in countless popular readings of the period, is called into question. Towards the end of the film, Dreyman goes to the Stasi archive to read his file, in order to find out 'the truth' about his treatment at the hands of the state. Reading his file, he discovers that the unknown Stasi officer in charge of his case fabricated reports in order to protect him. Crucially, the Stasi file is only helpful to Dreyman because it does *not* hold the truth. Like the rest of the archive, Dreyman's file is a written text constructed within a specific socio-political context by people with their own agendas, abilities and competing desires. Dreyman can only establish 'the truth' by reading between the lines of his file, by engaging with this textual representation in conjunction with his own, embodied, experience of the past.

The film ultimately suggests the complexity of the relationship between the material remains of the past, heritage and memory, and the need to engage with this past without resorting to comparisons with the crimes of other times in German history, comparisons that would frequently seem to elide the kind of nuanced approach to the engagement with historical trauma called for by Rothberg. This would, ironically, also seem to underline the position of the *Ostalgie* comedies, to which *The Lives of Others* was ostensibly a corrective. As the publicity information for *Sonnenallee*, for example, suggests: 'It's time that people talked about what else the GDR was apart from the Wall, the Stasi and the Ruling Central Committee' (Cafferty 2001: 253). Through its exploration of GDR material culture, *Sonnenallee* was an attempt to give a voice to the experience of ordinary people who lived in the GDR. In so doing, the film seeks to de-exoticise the lives of East Germans for those in the West and to challenge official discourses that seemed to present the former East German State exclusively as a conquered evil 'Other', a continuation of National Socialism in a different guise, which stood in opposition to the enlightened Federal Republic. For Knabe, of course, this is a worrying trend, an impulse that supports contemporary protests by former members of the organisation who refuse to accept culpability for the past. However, while protesting Stasi officers would clearly appear to be apologists for the past, *The Lives of Others* insists upon the need for continued engagement with the problematic, material legacy of this period of history. This is not to forgive those who would tell lies about history. Rather, it is to insist upon the active engagement with competing memories of the past that respect the importance, and yet fallibility, of its material remains while also insisting upon an engagement with the competing embodied subject positions of those who were there. Dreyman must engage with the physical archive to understand his history. However, this understanding cannot be achieved through the archive alone.

AM ENDE KOMMEN TOURISTEN (*AND ALONG COME TOURISTS*, 2007)

In the discussion generated by *The Lives of Others* and *Brick Lane*, one finds the limits of Rothberg's 'multidirectional memory' in practice. The invocation of the Holocaust and the crimes of National Socialism often elides the kind of open-ended, dynamic approach to history Rothberg seeks, and which can also respond to Pollock's call for the need to respect the subject position of all those involved in the historical narrative, both as historical 'actors' and contemporary 'consumers'. The films themselves, however, point to the need for precisely this kind of nuanced, open-ended engagement with the past, along with an understanding of the complex, present-day, cultural ramifications of the heritage in question. To conclude this chapter, I wish to return to the representation of Auschwitz in film in the light of this discussion, looking at Robert Thalheim's *And Along Come Tourists*, a film that seems to invert the dynamic one finds in many cultural encounters that engage with Rothberg's paradigm. Here we find a film that refuses even to allow the grammar of the Holocaust as a '*morphem[e]* of public history' (Rothberg 2011: 524) to be used straightforwardly to explore the role of the Holocaust itself as heritage.

And Along Come Tourists explores the place of Auschwitz as a contemporary heritage site, telling the story of 19-year-old Sven (Alexander Fehling) as he embarks on a year's work placement at the concentration camp memorial. Through Sven's eyes we are given multiple and competing views of Oświęcim, which, for its German visitors, is synonymous with the crimes of the Holocaust, in which Sven has no real interest, and for its Polish inhabitants is a place where they simply live and work. The camp itself, more often than not, appears as a notable absence in the film, not least because Thalheim, like Spielberg before him, was not given permission to film at the memorial. However, this constraint becomes an important dynamic within the film, helping

Thalheim to challenge the spectator's visual expectations of a narrative set in this particular town. In the opening sequence, for example, we are presented with a shot of Oświęcim's railway station, its tracks in the centre of the frame. This is an image that immediately calls to mind that archetypal Holocaust image of the Auschwitz railway tracks that brought millions to their death in the camps but which here bring a bemused Sven to his placement. Elsewhere, similarly iconic images are recontextualised, such as a shot of the camp's barbed-wired fence, which is used to frame an image of Sven and his young landlady, Ania (Barbara Wysocka), with whom he is falling in love, as they take a bicycle ride in the sunshine. A stock image of the Holocaust is consequently juxtaposed with a romantic image of young love (Fig 12.2).

Oświęcim is presented as a real place, in which real people live, rather than an 'authentic' image of the past. It is a place where the young form bands, go to discos and have fun, just like anywhere else, but where the overwhelming attitude to the population from the outside world is one of condescension and pity. The film asks the spectator to reflect upon well-worn images of the Holocaust anew, exploring how such images circulate in contemporary culture and how they relate to specific embodied experience. This is noticeable, for example, in the variety

Fig. 12.2 A train arriving in Oświęcim

of ways the film utilises as a motif the suitcases that were taken from prisoners on their arrival at the camp. We first encounter the suitcases during a tour of the memorial, led by Ania, where she is explaining their significance to a group of Germans, including Sven. The group all affect suitable facial expressions of horror and shame. For Sven, however, the significance of this encounter with the suitcases is not that it offers him a powerful material connection to the past but that it introduces him to the woman with whom he will fall in love. Sven's main duty on his placement is to look after Stanislaw Krzeminski (Ryszard Ronczewski), a survivor of the camp now in his eighties, who has continued to live there since its liberation by the Soviets. Stanislaw helped build the camp museum and now earns a living giving talks about his experience and repairing the suitcases that are exhibited in the memorial. The museum curators, however, no longer want Stanislaw's help with the suitcases, which for them are important historical artefacts that need to be authentically 'preserved' rather than 'repaired'. For Stanislaw, on the other hand, the suitcases form a crucial psychic link with the past. It was his job to collect them from the prisoners as they arrived, promising that he would look after their property until he could give it back. Unable to fulfil his promise, he spends his final days looking after the suitcases he took in order to assuage his guilt both for the lies he told his fellow prisoners and for surviving the ordeal himself.

The multilayered significance of the suitcases in the film becomes a microcosm of the multilayered transnational circulation of Holocaust memory, particularly as it impacts upon contemporary German-Polish relations. If, as Peter Bender argues, during the Cold War 'the Polish thought historically, the West Germans ideologically' when it came to their relationship (Bender 2005: 3), this has now become more complicated. History clearly defines Sven's encounters with the older generation in the town. 'Ask him if his Grandpa also worked here,' one of Stanislaw's friends quips when he realises that the man has a German carer. The young, on the other hand, are focused almost entirely on the opportunities of Western capitalism. While Sven can condemn the takeover of the local chemical plant by a German company as neo-colonial exploitation, made all the worse by Germany's historical crimes, for Ania, who is desperate to leave the town to become a translator for the EU in Brussels, it is a sign of economic hope. On the face of it at least, all German activity in the area is rooted in the quest to deal with the past, from the school teachers who bring their classes to the camp, to the German director of a newly constructed chemical works who engages Stanislaw to speak to her German workers about his experience. That said, the real focus of this specific engagement with the past is clearly economic, the success of the chemical works being contingent on eliciting good PR for a German chemical company that must be extraordinarily careful about its public perception in a town where memories of the exploitation of Jewish and Polish slave workers by the German IG Farben are never far from the surface.

Thalheim's film ultimately leaves open the key question it asks: where does German society go today in the process of coming to terms with the past, if it is going to mean anything beyond the kind of bland collective reflection on history seemingly propagated within the 'European Project', or in the unthinking declarations of 'nie wieder' (never again) that began in 1945 and that continue to be invoked every time the world fails to prevent another genocide. This is encapsulated, for example, in the well-meaning comments by one of the teachers Sven meets towards the end of the film, a man who already knows how he will respond to the material he will encounter at the camp before he even arrives there. What are the specific national constraints on the transnational circulation of Holocaust memory, and how do they relate to a European population faced with very different and competing social and economic challenges? These are the questions that the film asks in response to Sven's encounter with Auschwitz as a physical heritage space. As we have seen throughout this chapter, the term heritage, like that of identity and community, is both contingent and yet particular. Consequently, if the representational codes used to examine the Holocaust can be useful in the exploration of a range of historical and contemporary social contexts, as Rothberg suggests, great care must be taken to ensure that one continually reflects upon the competing demands of the call for historical specificity on the one hand and the potential of multidirectional memory on the other. Thalheim's film refuses to allow the spectator to have a clichéd response to Oświęcim as a place, and thus to Auschwitz as heritage. In so doing, it speaks to the key concern raised in all our case studies, be it the multilayered heritage of Brick Lane or the legacy of the Stasi within Germany. How can film help us understand the tension between the consumption of heritage as spectacle, *and* as physical encounter with history? How do heritage sites, and the films that present them, acknowledge, and shape, the experience of visitors, while also accepting our moral responsibility to protect, and yet to allow continued dynamic engagement with, the memory of those whose lives and communities have been defined by these sites?

Notes

1. For an overview of critical debates generated by the film see Loshitzky (1997).
2. The protest against the film soon petered out; there were no book burnings. However, the controversy was subsequently reignited when plans for the film to be premiered at the annual Royal Film Performance were cancelled at short notice, commentators presuming that Prince Charles wanted to avoid further protests from the Bengali community, a decision that gave fresh impetus to the discussion of artistic freedom versus the duty of the artist to represent 'real life' responsibly (Bakewell 2007).
3. For an overview of the debate and critical responses to the film see Cooke (2013).

Works Cited

Alexander, C. 2011. Making Bengali Brick Lane: Claiming and contesting space in East London. *British Journal of Sociology* 62(2): 201–220.

Bakewell , J. 2007. A dangerous message from Prince Charles. *The Independent*. 27 September.

Bartov, O. 1996. *Murder in our Midst: The Holocaust, industrial killing, and representation*. Oxford: Oxford University Press.

Bathrick, D. 1995. *The powers of speech. The politics of culture in the GDR*. Lincoln: University of Nebraska.

Bender, P. 2005. Normalisierung wäre schon viel. *Deutschland und Polen: Aus Politik und Zeitgeschichte* 5–6: 3–9.

Brouillette, S. 2009. Literature and gentrification on Brick Lane. *Criticism* 51(3): 425–449.

Cafferty, H. 2001. *Sonnenallee*: Taking comedy seriously in unified Germany. In *Textual responses to German unification*, eds. C. Costabile-Heming, R.J. Halverson, and K.A. Foell, 253–272. Berlin: de Gruyter.

Cooke, P. ed. 2013. *'The Lives of Others' and contemporary German film: A companion*. Berlin: De Gruyter.

Cole, T. 2000. *Selling the Holocaust: From Auschwitz to Schindler; how history is bought, packaged and sold*. New York: Routledge.

Falck, M. 2006. *Filmheft. Das Leben der Anderen*. Bonn: Bundeszentrale für politische Bildung.

Funder, A. 2007. Eyes without a face. *Sight and Sound* 17(5): 16–20.

Greer, G . 2006. Reality bites. *The Guardian*. 24. July.

Handke, S. 2007. Die Wanzen sind echt: Kinodebatte über *Das Leben der Anderen*. *Tagesspiegel*, 8 April.

Harfst, K. 2007. *Das Leben der Anderen*. Film und Wirklichkeit. *Nachrichteninfo* 8: 8–12. [Online]. Available from: http://www.foerderverein-hsh.de/documents/Nachrichteninfo_08_2007.pdf. Accessed 20 July 2014.

Hari, J. 2006. What's at stake in the Battle of Brick Lane. *The Independent*. [Online]. Available from: http://www.independent.co.uk/voices/commentators/johann-hari/johann-hari-whats-at-stake-in-the-battle-of-brick-lane-409992.html. Accessed 31 July 2015.

Harmsen, T. 2006. Irgendwie geht's um Stasi: 700 Schüler sehen auf Einladung Klaus Bögers. *Berliner Zeitung*, 4 April.

Jacobs, J.M. 1996. *Edge of empire: Postcolonialism and the city*. London: Routledge.

Jeschonnek, G. 2006. Die Sehnsucht nach dem unpolitischen Märchen: Ein kritischer Kommentar zum Stasi-Film *Das Leben der Anderen*. *Deutschland Archiv* 39(3): 424–442.

Knabe, H. 2007. Schindler gab es, Wiesler nicht. Bundesverband Deutscher Landwirte e.V. [Online]. Available from: http://www.deutsche-landwirte.de/060207b.htm. Accessed 17 July 2014.

Lea, R. and P. Lewis 2006. Local protests over Brick Lane film. *The Guardian* [Online]. Available from: http://www.theguardian.com/books/2006/jul/17/film.uk. Accessed 17 July 2015.

Loshitzky, Y. 1997. *Spielberg's Holocaust: Critical Perspectives on Schindler's List*. Bloomington: Indiana University Press.

Martin-Jones, D. 2014. Film tourism as heritage tourism: Scotland, diaspora and *The Da Vinci Code*. *New Review of Film and Television Studies* 12(2): 156–177.

Niven, W. 2001. *Facing the Nazi past: United Germany and the legacy of the Third Reich*. London: Routledge.

Oakley, K. and A.C. Pratt 2010. Brick Lane: Community-driven innovation. In *Local knowledge: Case studies of four innovative places*, 28–39. London: NESTA [Online]. Available from: www.nesta.org.uk/sites/default/files/local_knowledge.pdf. Accessed 27 Jan 2014.

Pollock, G. 2003. Holocaust tourism: Being there, looking back and the ethics of spatial memory. In *Visual culture and tourism*, eds. D. Crouch and N. Lübbren, 175–190. Oxford: Berg.

Rains, S. 2003. Home from home: Diasporic images of Ireland in film and tourism. In *Tourism in Ireland: A critical study*, eds. B. O'Connor and M. Cronin, 194–214. Channel View: Clevedon.

Rothberg, M. 2009. *Multidirectional memory: Remembering the Holocaust in the age of decolonization*. Stanford: Stanford University Press.

Rothberg, M. 2011. From Gaza to Warsaw: Mapping Multidirectional Memory. *Criticism*. 53(4): 523–548.

Tzanelli, R. 2007. *The cinematic tourist: explorations in globalization, culture and resistance*. New York: Routledge.

Urry, J. 1990. *The tourist gaze*. London: Sage.

Ward, E. 2014. Unpublished interview with André Kockisch.

CHAPTER 13

Cinematic Pilgrimages: Postmodern Heritage Cinema

Rob Stone

The heritage that inspires 'heritage cinema' is pre-existing. It may be contested as a version of history but nobody argues that King George VI, Solomon Northup or Abraham Lincoln never existed. Likewise, no one protests that Elizabeth Bennet, Charles Darnay and the second wife of Maxim de Winter are fictional, set as they are upon the pedestal of classic literature. Nevertheless, while the tourists who visit stately homes and regal residences are compelled to respect the factual evidence of historical figures while consuming evidence of their everyday existence, the tourism that seeks out the locations of films and television series tends to blur fact and fiction, searching for fictional characters in surroundings that exploit the confusion. The desire to visit the locations of events imagined for films and television series is a consequence of this tendency that has recently surged in popularity. Thus, in addition to visiting the house where Jane Austen lived in Chawton near Alton in Hampshire, fans of the films and television series derived from her novels seek out the stately homes that have formed the backdrops to various versions of *Pride and Prejudice*. Such day trips, like those to the settings of *Downton Abbey* (2010–) and the *Harry Potter* films, can significantly boost the takings of previously

R. Stone (✉)
University of Birmingham, Birmingham, UK
e-mail: R.Stone@bham.ac.uk

unremarkable or unheralded national and regional monuments, heritage sites and stately homes. There are several degrees or stages of film tourism, however, that range from simply sightseeing at filming locations to elaborate quests seeking to replicate the experience of the protagonists of the films. This gradation can suggest and even evoke a quasi-religious element in such cinematic pilgrimages, which extends from the merely observational day trip to the most intense peregrination of the hardcore and die-hard fanatic. As I shall both literally and theoretically explore, tracking this gradation via comparison with the arcane but relevant four stages of prayer invoked by Saint Teresa of Avila, the Spanish mystic and Roman Catholic saint of the sixteenth century, reveals a process for expressing similar passion, wherein four successive stages of pilgrimage can culminate in the ecstasy of communion with the cinematic object of desire in a way that bears comparison with the rapture enjoyed by the most religiously devout.

This analysis of the cinematic pilgrimage goes beyond recent analyses of film tourism that count footfall or tourist traffic in order to influence and impact upon commercial strategies and policies. Seeing 'film-induced tourism' (Beeton 2005) or 'set-jetting' as a two-way street paved with tourist gold, those who attract tourists to the cinema and filmgoers to holiday destinations have tended to indulge in the mutually beneficial foregrounding of images and imaginaries via movies and marketing that impact upon the imagination of the tourist/filmgoer. Ellen Strain (2003) claims such strategies exploit the viewers' lack of empirical experience by constructing a tourist gaze that is the product of an image's recycling. This display, in which certain films and some tourist destinations, such as the picturesque portraits of the beaches and small towns of a Greek island provided by *Captain Corelli's Mandolin* (John Madden, 2001) and the General Tourism Services of Kefalonia (Anon. 2016), collude, mediates a globalised sense of being in the world but delivers only second-hand experiences. This, too, is therefore distinct from cinematic pilgrimages, which are not just about affect in relation to an encounter with a film of a place, but about the impact on the tourist of actually being in a place that is meaningful *only* because it was filmed. Stefan Roesch examines the on-site encounters of such tourists with the landscapes that feature in such films as *The Lord of the Rings: The Fellowship of the Ring* (Peter Jackson, 2001) in *The Experiences of Film Location Tourists* (2009) but aims his findings at those who manage marketing and visitor expectations in the tourist industry. From the sociological standpoint, Rodanthi Tzanelli (2004, 2007) has explored the intersections of media and tourism in similar contexts, seeing the response of the New Zealand tourist industry to an influx of tourist-fans of the *Lord of the Rings* trilogy (2001–3) as tantamount to the simulation of a fantasy that appropriates local heritage for tourist consumption and thus has consequences for the authenticity of that heritage in matters of cultural self-recognition and national identity. Tzanelli argues that the way in which 'the New Zealand landscape is "consumed" by viewers is different from that we encounter in ecotourism, because it is governed by virtuality and simulation' (Tzanelli 2004: 24). She sees film tourism as 'a game of endless hermeneutics: by filmmakers (of novels), by audiences (of films) and by holiday providers (of audiences' film readings)' and she suggests that it is 'a type of capitalist exploitation that even Adorno and Horkheimer would not have anticipated' (Tzanelli 2004: 25). Tzanelli admits that her vision of film tourism is 'dystopian and rather deterministic' (Tzanelli 2004: 25) but she posits the resistance of individual tourists to the prefabricated tour as a possible response while regretting that her article 'does not include an analysis of actual *Lord of the Rings* tourists to New Zealand' (Tzanelli 2004: 25). In effect, this chapter takes up the empirical challenge of being embedded within, resisting and even breaking away from such tours, resulting in a greater understanding of those film tourists whose imaginative endeavour brings them closest to the cinema by means of pilgrimage to its postmodern heritage.

The range of cinematic pilgrimages explored in this chapter reveals the existence of postmodern heritage cinema as one in which precepts of fact, truth and history carry the same status as invention, fable and myth, and any rigidity or distinction in relation to these terms collapses. At the same time, the postmodern cinematic pilgrimage must be understood as being at least partly tongue-in-cheek because, as Peter and Will Brooker maintain, 'one of the most consistent signs of the postmodern has been its ironic self-referentiality. [It is] playful and allusive' (1997: 1). Instead of referring to the history of the actual building, monument or landscape that is visited, the cinematic pilgrimage to the filming location relocates its meaning in an intra-history of viewing experiences, while the touristic activity is above all recreational, moving beyond negative connotations of postmodernism as meaningless or nihilistic towards an appreciation of the value of such immersive entertainment. Fredric Jameson might well argue that the cinematic pilgrimage subjects the conventions of traditional heritage sites to 'the necessary failure of art and the aesthetic' (1983: 169) because of the apparent trivialisation of the sites, whose historical, geographical, political or religious importance is overridden by the affective response of tourists inspired by the alternative histories of fictions. The pleasure of the cinematic pilgrimage suggests, indeed, a parody of the conventions of heritage tourism and religious pilgrimage. The cinematic pilgrimage is less a parody than a pastiche, however, which is a 'parody that has lost its sense of humour' (Jameson 1983: 167), an act of absurdity that takes itself seriously and is unapologetic about its hyperbole. The cinematic pilgrimage adopts the aesthetics of the religious pilgrimage to places like Fatima, Lourdes or the Cathedral at Santiago de Compostela, which all impose opening hours, entrance fees, queues and gift shops on their visitors. It then transposes them onto something meaningful to the film tourist, who reproduces the mode of pilgrimage and appropriates its sacral status while also reinstating the conventions of quest, contact, communion, reflection and, as the comparison with the four-part strategy of Saint Teresa makes clear, even the possibility of transcendence, in a way that may be decoded to realise similar formulae for fulfilment.

Excluded from this study are theme parks such as Disneyland Paris and the Warner Brothers Harry Potter Experience in London, where everything is artificial, practised, limited and laid on. Here the cinematic artefacts are clearly displayed as such and the tourist is paying to peek behind an invisible curtain, as it were. The entertainment on offer can still engage the imagination of the tourists, but these ticket-holders, who strap themselves into fairground rides and dress up in a limited array of costumes for official photographs, mainly confirm the transaction of tourist currency for spectacle. When Donald Horne (1984) described the contemporary tourist as a modern pilgrim, carrying guidebooks as devotional texts, he was scorning their collective subservience and willingness to be educated in a specific and signposted manner. Horne argued that such tourism maintains the 'gap between "art" and the tourist's own environment' (1984: 16) but this is anathema to the immersion, union and transcendence sought by the cinematic pilgrim, who arguably reflects the anti-elitism of postmodernism. John Urry notes that 'even the sets of TV soap operas' (2002: 119) can be preserved in museums, but he sees their appeal purely in terms of their functionality, noting how exhibits like these tend to turn themselves inside out by revealing how they were made and, indeed, how they were made to appear authentic. Urry fails to recognise, however, that visitors to the mock-up of the Rovers Return public house that features prominently in the long-running soap opera *Coronation Street* (1960–) and is recreated in Manchester's *Coronation Street: The Tour*, for example, actively seek what might be called the authenticity of this inauthenticity and that enjoyment of the reality of its unreality is crucial to an understanding of, and engagement with, film tourism in general and cinematic pilgrimages in particular. Instead of dismissing cinematic pilgrimages as a lowbrow, trivial activity, this investigation seeks to participate in, and thereby appreciate, such activities in relation to film heritage as a series of imaginative and intuitive, participatory and postmodern ventures whose four stages resemble that which Saint Teresa of Avila described as a sequential search 'in which true wisdom is acquired, and to the soul a fulfilment most full of delight' (Saint Teresa of Avila 1957: 112).

Saint Teresa demarcated four successive stages of metaphysical engagement with God in her autobiography. In the first stage, the devout must withdraw from the outside world and focus on the task of prayer. In the second, they use routine and tools, which make the effort less, the distractions fewer and the rewards greater, such as the increased awareness of the ongoing transformation. The third stage is one of open understanding that approximates joy but is distinct from stage four because of the consciousness that anchors the rapture. This disappears in the final stage, wherein objective analysis of the experience is no longer possible and time, memory and imagination melt away leaving only the ecstatic union with the object of desire. This strategic framework is devoted to faith and therefore dismisses its critics for 'not advancing in freedom of spirit but hanging back through weakness' (Saint Teresa of Avila 1957: 81). It promises that on completion the soul 'conceives itself to be near God, and that it is left with such a conviction that it cannot possibly help believing' (Saint Teresa of Avila 1957: 127). The theory that inspires this study is that there are four types of cinematic pilgrimage, correlating to Saint Teresa's four stages of prayer. First, there are the loose and anecdotic guided tours around film studios such as Cinecittà outside Rome. Then there are the more independent explorations of still-standing film sets such as that of Western Leone in Almeria, southern Spain, where many spaghetti westerns were made and where a shift from observation to touristic participation is apparent. Then there are the tours offered to specific areas and landscapes such as those near Belfast in Northern Ireland, for example, where imagination and memory of previous viewing experiences of *Game of Thrones* (2011–) are required in order to make sense of the vistas that appear heavily disguised by computer-generated imagery in the television series. One such excursion—the Stones and Thrones tour—provides the third case study (Anon 2015). Finally, there are the uniquely personal, potentially metaphysical and occasionally transcendental experiences of wholly independent film *flânerie*, which consist of seeking out and happening upon the locations of favourite films in cities, such as the towers, canals and alcoves in Bruges of *In Bruges* (Martin McDonagh, 2008) or the places where *Vertigo* (Alfred Hitchcock, 1958) was shot in San Francisco, *Breaking Bad* (2008–13) was made in Albuquerque, *The Sopranos* (1999–2007) was set in New Jersey, and *Before Sunrise* (Richard Linklater, 1995) (which provides our final case study) was filmed in Vienna. Taken in stages, these cinematic pilgrimages extend the relation of cinema to heritage into a postmodern arena as well as a metaphysical realm in which the heritage sought is deliberately unreal and the experience of it increasingly uncanny, only visible via an imaginative leap that seeks a transcendental relocation of the tourist in a similar vein to Saint Teresa's exaltation of 'what the soul seeks' (Saint Teresa of Avila 1957: 119). The heritage sought and found via a cinematic pilgrimage also reveals how important are the structural myths of the cinema, while this need for communion with the object of desire casts a light back onto the complex interaction of foundational structures and affect that underpins the genre of heritage cinema.

Among the tourist destinations revealed and created by this fixation on filming locations, there emerges a wide range of what might be understood via self-referential address as a postmodern interpretation of heritage. From the spectacle of the pastiche of history, its cinematic representation and the history of filmmaking itself found in visits to film studios, to a tour of fictional settings that skirts self-parody, the cinematic pilgrimage offers a knowing, self-conscious assemblage of absurdity and serious intent. This results in an experience that resembles the rapture of Saint Teresa, which she describes as 'a time of vows, of heroic resolutions, and of strenuous desires, when the soul begins to loathe the world, and develops a very clear realisation of its own vanity' (Saint Teresa of Avila 1957: 128). Pulling a pint in the Rovers Return is a ritualistic act enacted for the camera that provides evidence—a photograph such as Fig. 13.1 that can be disseminated via social media—of communion with the 'faith' of fandom and contact with its hallowed 'relics'. The desire to visit these destinations may thus be compared to the psychological need for pilgrimage, which Jean Dalby Clift and Wallace B. Clift (1996) describe as an archetypical outer action with a unique inner meaning. Their Jungian analysis of pilgrimage supposes that the physical act of travel actualises an inner process that responds to 'the basic human need to make a connection with something outside themselves, some holiness or value which helps ground the pilgrim in a new being, in a new lease on life, in something which gives meaning and direction and which is frequently experienced as healing[, taking] the

Fig. 13.1 Visitors to the Rovers Return public house set of *Coronation Street* pretending to pull pints. Photograph courtesy of Megan Caine

pilgrim beyond the limitations of the worldview which had become static or empty' (Clift and Clift 1996: 152). Even setting aside the commercial exploitation of elements of any pilgrimage and the potential misrepresentation of local, national and even international history, however, the cinematic pilgrimage is arguably distinct from the religious kind because it pursues the heritage of a blatant fiction, thereby giving rise to a new kind of heritage that is focused on unreality and inauthenticity rather than what is real or verified by a secular authority or merely believed to be real by the pilgrims whose consensus grounds their actions in tradition, ritual and even (eventually) history.

Hardcore fans of *Before Sunrise*, *In Bruges* and *La grande bellezza* (*The Great Beauty*, Paolo Sorrentino, 2013) do not set out to explore the history and architecture of cities such as Vienna, Bruges and Rome, respectively, but the worlds of their beloved films instead. Thus, a cinematic pilgrim is more likely to be thrilled by finding out that a 'place' is *not* where it should be than if it is where he or she expected. For example, discovering that the cemetery visited by the wandering couple in *Before Sunrise* is actually a long way from Vienna's city centre and only reachable by taxi or two buses allows the pilgrim to feel 'in on' the magic trick of the filmmaking. This sense of discovery, which enhances the sense of pilgrimage, is even heightened in places like Northern Ireland, where *Game of Thrones* is filmed against landscapes later embellished with extravagant computer-generated imagery. Here the pilgrim is not disappointed by the lack of castles and dragons but exhilarated by both the demand on his or her memory and imagination and the immersive sense of being behind the curtain. Travelling to 'unreal' places, where cemeteries and dragons *cannot* be found, does not respond to traditional ideas of heritage cinema, which tend towards a basis in historical representation. Nevertheless, the blatant metaphysical gambit of moving from reality to unreality and back to reality again in the cinematic pilgrimage does tally with the aforementioned prayer system of Saint Teresa and suggests that a transposition of this strategy to four kinds of cinematic pilgrimage will permit understanding of a similarly progressive kind of union with the cinematic object of desire. Moving from the first stage of the loosely guided tour (Cinecittà in Rome) to the second stage of the more independent investigation of a single location (the spaghetti western town of Western Leone in Almeria), followed by the third stage of visiting various locations in an area (those of *Game of Thrones* in Northern Ireland) and the final exploration of a space via *flânerie* (the Vienna of *Before Sunrise*), my objective is to examine how the 'soul' that is inspired by postmodern heritage cinema to embark upon a cinematic pilgrimage rises 'from its wretched state, and receives some little intimation of the joys of heaven' (Saint Teresa of Avila 1957: 99).

First Stage

Cinecittà is a dusty relic residing on the outskirts of Rome, reached via metro to its eponymous station. Built during the Fascist era and famous for hosting Hollywood productions such as *Ben Hur* (William Wyler, 1959) as well as the extravagant film-parties of Federico Fellini, the studios suffered bankruptcy in 1997 and serious fires in 2007 and 2012. Today one can purchase an entrance ticket and wander inwards to be faced with pathways flanked with statuary left over from various epics and nondescript buildings housing a café, a small museum offering a potted history of the place and a more modern installation designed to represent various filmmaking skills. The real attraction, however, is the informal tour of the sets that remain from *Gangs of New York* (Martin Scorsese, 2002) and the HBO-BBC series *Rome* (2005–7). What remains of *Gangs of New York* is faded and in disrepair, while the little left standing from *Rome* is occasionally used as the backdrop for television commercials. The mock-up of New York's Bowery, the façade of ancient Egyptian monuments and the remnants of a Roman town are all held up by scaffolding. The tour guide is needlessly apologetic and the group of tourist-pilgrims is respectful and a little righteous. Their passion overflows at moments when they vie for greater recall, arguing which scenes took place in one alleyway or another, or grilling the bemused guide with the aim of displaying their own superior knowledge. When told to refrain from taking photographs of the central square from *Rome* because it is currently being used as the set for a commercial, the majority take snaps anyway (Fig. 13.2). Overriding the command to refrain from doing so counters the declared sacrality of the commercial production because it is *this* that trespasses upon the hallowed ground, not them.

Fig. 13.2 Tourists to the set of *Rome* in Cinecittà find themselves cordoned off because of a commercial shoot. Photograph by Rob Stone

The cultural dynamics bound up in the ability of film and television series to create heritage sites, whether they are exploitative, welcoming or indifferent, tend to focus the efforts of audiences to construct identities that incorporate an affective response to their entertainment. Financial gain from entrance fees, a minuscule amount of branded merchandise and the café is minimal at Cinecittà, whose threadbare heritage is so estranged from past glories as to seem bereft of value. Nevertheless, the distracted informality of the few employees who serve and guide suggests that it is easier to tolerate pilgrims than it might be to rebuff them. Empty sound-stages look like vacant warehouses, but this does not diminish the zeal of the visitors. Some are serious students of film history and all are fans, far more thrilled to see this mock-up of the Forum on the outskirts of Rome than they would be to enter the real one in the middle of the city. Indeed, these visitors have determinedly bypassed the real ancient ruins for a day and travelled to see their run-down simulacra instead. Thus, they are delighted by the dilapidated sets, expressing a reverence for their surroundings that the real Colosseum might not inspire. This is because, as Saint Teresa advises, these devoted few have purposefully withdrawn from the outside world (the city of Rome) and focused on the task of prayer instead (contemplation of the artificial city of *Rome*). Unlike the crowded and exploited tourist areas of the nearby metropolis, Cinecittà remains a sacred site whose inaccessibility and relative obscurity only adds to its appeal. It is not nostalgia that powers the quest but a kind of faith in film because, as Urry suggests, it is in such places that 'the fame of the object becomes its meaning' (2002: 118). That is to say, the locations where something was filmed and the extant evidence of that happening many years later are treated as sacred by the pilgrims to Cinecittà, who experience what David Martin-Jones calls 'a sense of return and belonging' (Martin-Jones 2014: 156), albeit to a place they have never been before, in his consideration of the effect on Scottish tourism of *The Da Vinci Code* (Ron Howard, 2006). Martin-Jones also writes of 'the *Braveheart* effect' in response to the 1995 film directed by Mel Gibson, which served to advertise the beauty of the highlands and functioned as a tourist draw (Martin-Jones 2014: 163), but these tourists mostly came to see Scotland and were not interested in or knowledgeable about the film's production history, or they would have gone to Ireland where much of it was filmed instead. Martin-Jones observes that 'even though seemingly ephemeral, with an impact likely to last only a few years after a successful film, film tourism actually belongs to a robust tradition with greater longevity, heritage tourism' (2014: 164). He connects this tourism with an interest in genealogy, particularly from the Scottish diaspora, and he notes that 'roots tourism is depicted as a grail quest' in *The Da Vinci Code*, too (2014: 170). But he does not pursue the notion of a cinematic pilgrimage, which differs from tourism because, whereas tourists seek the 'real' Scotland, neither the visitors to Cinecittà nor the film studio itself attribute what Horne describes as 'reverence to objects simply because of their aura of authenticity' (Horne 1984: 249), precisely because everything on show is deliberately inauthentic.

Second Stage

The cinematic pilgrim does not expect authenticity and therefore dismisses the kind of 'ceremonial agenda' that establishes 'what we should see and sometimes even the order in which they should be seen' in most museums and theme parks (Urry 2002: 118). Instead, the pilgrim appears to follow Saint Teresa's advice in the second stage of prayer in which 'the intellect now works very gently' (Saint Teresa of Avila 1957: 99). To this end, objective, intellectual observation gives way to participation and a greater reliance on intuition in a cinematic pilgrimage to the likes of Western Leone in Almeria. Found at the end of a long, uneven dirt road, the ruins of a western town complete with gallows, saloon, livery store, sheriff's office, stables, a Mexican homestead and a few wigwam tee-pees attract a steady trickle of visitors. Its stockade is solid but its gallows are rickety, which does not deter visitors from climbing up to put their heads through the noose for photographs. The dilapidation of Western Leone is part of its charm. The handful of employee-occupants doubles and trebles up as barkeeps, guides and desperados and the banter that blooms between them whenever tourists are near is hierarchical, with the Henry Fonda lookalike clearly the star (albeit dressed more like Clint Eastwood's 'Man With No Name') and the more swarthy Andalusian happy to be the butt of jokes and be dragged by a galloping horse in the showdown that occurs whenever tourist numbers prompt it. The main appeal for cinematic pilgrims is the well-kept saloon, which played the homestead in *Once Upon a Time in the West* (Sergio Leone, 1968). Its walls are decorated with framed photographs and faded posters that point out the heritage to be savoured in the surroundings. When the heat drives enough visitors inside, the resident gunfighters perform a gunfight skit to the music of Ennio Morricone emanating from a CD player beneath the counter. The playlet is witty, delivered in pantomime style but respectful of the iconography of the western in general, that of Leone in particular, and Fonda above all, whose stand-in uses his well-practised thousand-yard stare to scare children. Following the shoot-out, the audience is advised to relocate to the stoop of the sheriff's office to obtain the best views of the second act in which a convoluted tale of a bank robbery gone wrong results in horseplay, tumbles and the aforementioned stunt enjoyed by the supporting player and the small but appreciative crowd. Finding the tiny township 'just as Leone left it' relocates the pilgrim in the mind-map of *Once Upon a Time in the West* and shores up the sacred enterprise.

Western Leone is haunted by the ghosts of spaghetti westerns baked into the rough wood, cracked paint and peeling hoardings that inspire reverence and a great deal of amateur filming. The sense of 'return and belonging' is ripe here because the gaze invited by Western Leone is in no way 'socially organised and systematic', as Urry describes guided tourism (2002: 1). Instead, the direction of the tourist gaze is redirected by the agency of the visitor, who is free to wander the fabricated township. Western Leone thus rejects the assertion by Urry, following MacCannell, that 'all tourists [...] embody a quest for authenticity' (Urry 2002: 9), even as it supports his assertion that 'this quest is a modern version of the universal human concern with the sacred' (Urry 2002: 9), precisely because it is the *inauthenticity* of Western Leone that is sacrosanct. Thus, the postmodern gambit of such tourism depends upon the paradox that Western Leone is both *authentic* in being the actual place where *Once Upon a Time in the West* was filmed and *inauthentic* in being a mock-up of a western township. Crucially, the cinematic pilgrim delights in both sides of the paradox, finding logic and absurdity perfectly balanced. Urry claims 'the tourist is a kind of contemporary pilgrim, seeking authenticity in other "times" and other "places" away from that person's everyday life' (2002: 90). The particular fascination of the cinematic pilgrim, however, is not only with 'the "real lives" of others that somehow possess a reality hard to discover in their own experiences' (Urry 2002: 9), but with the pretence of Henry Fonda and Sergio Leone in the making of *Once Upon a Time in the West*, as well as with that of the welcoming gunfighter-guides and their maintenance of Western Leone. At the same time, therefore, enjoyment of Western Leone does not require the suspension of disbelief but the settling of faith, because the cinematic pilgrim is drawn to a location whose authenticity is inauthentic (because the realistic township is a mock-up) and whose inauthenticity is authentic because this *is* actually where *Once Upon a Time in the West* was filmed. Although it may be argued that all cultures are to some degree staged, invented, reorganised and self-reflexive, Western Leone disarms such criticism by being upfront about its performativity. The metaphysical element that allows for correlation between this second type of cinematic pilgrimage and the second stage of prayer invoked by Saint Teresa is thus apparent because Western Leone is a location wherein, as Urry supposes, 'like the pilgrim the tourist moves from a familiar place to a far place and then returns to a familiar place. At the far place both the pilgrim and the tourist engage in "worship" of shrines which are sacred, albeit in different ways, and as a result gain some uplifting experience' (2002: 11). This metaphysical element informs that which Urry describes as 'post-tourism' in which visitors 'delight in the inauthenticity of the normal tourist experience [finding] pleasure in the multiplicity of tourist games. They know that there is no authentic tourist experience, that there are merely a series of games and texts that can be played' (2002: 12). Western Leone upends this judgement with the authenticity of its inauthenticity, however, and vice versa. Instead of the complete fabrication of the tourist experience offered elsewhere, it effects a paradox that calls attention to the reality of film history as well as the fantasy of the films that were made there.

Third Stage

In Northern Ireland, meanwhile, the tour of locations featured in the *Game of Thrones* series deposits its enraptured pilgrims in a bare field, whereupon they race without prompting to a small mound and kneel to take photographs of their own beheading in a pose that commemorates some meaningful moment in the fiction. Taking paying pilgrims around the countryside in a jostling minibus on the promise of seeing nondescript fields and roads, the tour also takes in the Giant's Causeway, but this does not appear in the series and several day-trippers therefore sit this site out. Instead, the highlight of the Stones and Thrones tour is rapturously identified by all in the minibus on first sight as 'The King's Road'. Flanked by trees and busy with tractors, this lane featured in the final episode of the fourth series as two characters (Brienne [Gwendoline Christie] and Podrick [Daniel Portman]) came down it on horseback in a sequence that took six days to film. The guide, who also offers anecdotes about the cast members on furlough in Belfast, provides black-velvet capes and plastic swords and the pilgrims take turns posing in fighting or chivalrous mode.

The photograph is once more the holy relic that provides evidence of contact with the sacred. This is where the absurdity of the day trip is qualified by physical evidence of touching the world of *Game of Thrones*, where the bewilderment is focused and made demonstrable in the photograph that attests to actually being there, where 'there' is not just the country lane that it is to everyone else but 'The King's Road' to those in the know. The memories of those who pose for photographs populate the setting with fictional characters and their imaginations adorn it with CGI. Dressing up and standing in the landscape that is itself dressed up to play the fictional kingdom of Westeros clearly provokes a kind of rapture equivalent to Saint Teresa's third stage of prayer and its achievement of a 'glorious bewilderment, a heavenly madness' (Saint Teresa of Avila 1957: 112) (Fig. 13.3).

Indeed, any distinctions between reality and fantasy are inevitably muddled in these film and television heritage sites, which are subject to selection and a participatory imagination. There is therefore perhaps something

Fig. 13.3 Tourists on the Stones and Thrones tour of Northern Ireland pose as knights on 'The King's Road'. Photograph by Rob Stone

therapeutic in a *Game of Thrones* tour that so deliberately exploits a need for escapism and metaphysical contact with the object of desire. But there is also the possibility that the cinematic pilgrims and the postmodern heritage they encounter posit an equivalence between the fictional wars of Westeros and 'the troubles' of Northern Ireland, which inspire another tour available from the same local company, one which takes in Shankhill, Falls Road and the murals in an effort to explain the religious and political conflicts that have shaped the area and its people. The juxtaposition is not jarring, however. It is even possible to combine both the fictional and actual scenes of great conflict in one tour that spends the day moving between the reality of Northern Ireland and the unreality of Westeros and concludes with the view that *Game of Thrones*, with its triumphant impact upon prosperity, employment and tourism in the region, is the happy ending that 'the troubles' could never have foreseen. In other words, *Game of Thrones* offers a metaphysical resolution to the religious and political conflict in Northern Ireland that the pilgrimage tacitly acknowledges. Participation in such pilgrimages to these postmodern heritage sites of fictional worlds and histories arguably carries ethical implications for considering how such imagined heritage feels as real or even more real than actual historical artefacts. The suspension of disbelief in 'light' heritage sites such as 'The King's Road' should be at the opposite extreme of the encounter with the grimmest reality in 'dark' heritage sites such as the nearby Falls Road. However, the fact that tourists and locations of postmodern heritage clearly collaborate on making the experience, to a greater or lesser extent, pleasurable, educational and/or vital to an underpinning of individual and collective, or even national, identity calls into question the very notion of a reflective society, one that is able to distinguish between fantasy and reality and between 'light' and 'dark' heritage.

Further along the Stones and Thrones tour, there is evidence that the real inhabitants of the locations have collaborated in the treasure hunt, allowing their heritage to be purloined and even conspiring to celebrate the pretence. The locals of Ballintoy, for example, have exploited the alternate history of their harbour. What was once merely quaint has been rechristened Pyke Harbour and commemorated in a plaque that superimposes a poster-sized image of the return of the character Theon Greyjoy (Alfie Allen) to his childhood home of Pyke over the actual harbour (Fig. 13.4). The sense is that no one comes to Ballintoy any longer unless it is to visit Pyke. This redressing of natural landmarks such as Ballintoy, the Cushendun Caves and Carncastle as the locations of *Game of Thrones* further demonstrates that the unrestricted and unexamined proliferation of such postmodern heritage sites blurs the distinctions between an actual history involving terrorism and an unreal one involving dragons. Yet the fact that the inhabitants of the locations themselves participate in and encourage the metaphysical exercise by the cinematic pilgrims, and then use this to emphasise the metaphysical history of the place that rises up to meet them, reveals how the responsive cultural practices of the places that receive the pilgrims have their say in deciding what is heritage. In this case, cinematic pilgrimages to places like Ballintoy, which are keen to cast off their historical identities and assume new, postmodern ones, bring challenges to any rigid ideas of historical resilience. They also call into question responsible tourism and citizenship in relation to the transnational circulation of tourists, whose search for both authenticity and inauthenticity is served by heritage sites that corroborate both fact and fiction and even deliberately blend them.

Fig. 13.4 Ballintoy Harbour, renamed Pyke Harbour for the *Game of Thrones* tour of Northern Ireland. Photograph by Rob Stone

Business opportunities are inevitable (see McVeigh 2015). Research carried out by Creative England to measure the impact of so-called 'set-jetting' (tourism generated by famous locations) revealed that the *Harry Potter* series had massively boosted admissions at Alnwick Castle in Northumberland, which had stood in for a section of Hogwarts, Wollaton Hall in Nottingham, which had appeared in *The Dark Knight Rises* (Christopher Nolan, 2012) and Puzzlewood in the Forest of Dean in Gloucestershire, which features in *Doctor Who*, *Merlin* and *Star Wars VII: The Force Awakens* (J.J. Abrams, 2015). This is more than mere advertising of the kind that the animated film *Brave* (Mark Andrews and Brenda Chapman, 2012) is said to have managed for Scotland, generating £120 million for the Scottish economy after a tie-in collaborative marketing campaign by Visit Scotland and Disney. Yet the pilgrims, as opposed to the tourists, claim for themselves a quest and see queuing in a museum to do what everyone else does as banal. They are therefore likely to reject the campaign by Tourism Ireland that leads with the slogan 'Welcome to Westeros: Jump into Northern Ireland, *Game of Thrones* Territory' (Fig. 13.5) and promises signage and stunts because it

Fig. 13.5 Tourism Ireland campaign to lure fans of the *Game of Thrones* series to Northern Ireland

is too populist. Instead, the pilgrims expend effort and expense to achieve something that rejects the organisation or circumscription of travel in favour of their metaphysical progress to transcendence, of actually touching the settings and skies of their favourite television series and therefore knowing in a religious sense the object of faith and desire.

Fourth Stage

Filmed in the summer of 1994 as a hybrid of American indie and European art-house fare, *Before Sunrise* describes the *flânerie* of a young couple as they wander the streets of Vienna discussing love, life and death until dawn. Most of the filming locations in the Austrian capital that appear in the film are identifiable and joining the dots on a map of the city is a task enjoyed by numerous fans of the film, who attempt to retrace the steps of the couple. Organised tours are available, too, but these are for unambitious pilgrims without the time, energy or dedication necessary to spend plotting the key locations, a process which reveals several secrets and lies about the film. First, no logical or practical path exists between the locations if pilgrims are to follow the chronology of the film. Second, a few of the locations are inaccessible except by metro, such as the Weiner Prater fairground with its iconic Ferris wheel, and the aforementioned Friedhof der Namenlosen (cemetery of the nameless), which can only be reached by two buses or a taxi. Regardless, most of the key sites can be visited in a circular route and are still as they were when Linklater filmed them. Spotting fellow pilgrims is also easy as they mostly travel in romantic-minded couples, particularly on the 16 June, which is the anniversary of the events of the film. At such times there is a bottleneck of pilgrims in key locations or 'shrines' such as the booth in Café Sperl where the characters have a particularly intense conversation and the Schallplattenhandlung Teuchtler Alt & Neu record store, where the scene of the couple snatching glances at each other in a listening booth takes place. The pilgrimage also reveals the cheats of the filmmakers: the record store contains no listening booth, just a door that opens onto an interior patio, while the inside of the church they visit does not correspond to the one they are seen entering in the film. Nevertheless, discovery of such artifice only adds to the appeal of the pilgrimage for its followers are not ignorant but knowing, fully aware of the postmodern nature of their quest and delighted to incorporate artifice alongside what is revealed to be true. The trail is marked with subtle clues, including a poster of the film on the wall of Café Sperl and a framed record sleeve of the song—'Come Here' by Kath Bloom—that accompanies the scene in the listening booth, which the store owner will allow pilgrims to handle with the due care and reverence befitting a holy relic.

Crucial to this independent-minded pilgrimage is the fact that film tourism in this fashion actively replicates the action of the film itself. That is to say, those engaged in this film-flavoured *flânerie* around the streets of Vienna are both enjoying a unique exploration and discovery of the city for themselves *and* actively imitating the film's protagonists. This activity does not require dress-up or any pretence to resembling the characters, but it does demand dedication to the pilgrimage. At the same time, although the pilgrimage allows for a sense of personal discovery that may be similar to that experienced by the characters in the film, it can never be identical. Differences and digressions in the pilgrimage, which takes around ten hours to complete, allow the devout to approximate the experience of the events of the film, but in a way that is not wholly predetermined or circumscribed but open to chance, distractions and redirection. To the extent that this particular example of film tourism not only *resembles* a pilgrimage but actively *becomes* one, and thereby replicates the journey of self-discovery of the *flâneurs* that informs the film itself, it may be understood via comparison with the fourth stage of prayer described by Saint Teresa. Finding no valid objective stance from which to understand her experience of rapture in any purely intellectual manner, Saint Teresa wrote of a condition of ecstasy in which she supposed that her subjectivity was fused with that of God. Beside and beyond herself, the saint discovered that it was in this ecstatic state that 'the will must be fully occupied in loving, but does not understand how it loves. If it understands, it does not understand how it understands' (Saint Teresa of Avila 1957: 127). The act and its meaning are thus fused as the intellect gives way to pure feeling and the pilgrim achieves the desired state of transcendence that is equivalent to oneness with the object of desire. The heritage that is sought and traversed in the *Before Sunrise* pilgrimage is not that of Vienna, despite its monuments, architecture and museum culture, but that of a film in which such grandeur is only briefly glimpsed via a few cutaways to statuary and a discussion about an art exhibition that has not yet opened. The postmodern element that rejects a traditional, collective, predetermined touristic response to Vienna and elevates subjectivism instead is also self-reflexive, requiring the pilgrims to recognise the myriad influences that make up their selves as subjects in which a favourite film is as valid as any political or religious teaching. Cinematic pilgrims tend to understand that traditional heritage is crafted and deceptive and that its single-point perspective is limiting. Their actions therefore subvert the Althusserian principle that the idea of oneself as subject is an illusion fabricated by ideology because they select and subscribe to their own alternative ideology in their devotion to a particular film. Accusations of triviality do not diminish the meaning of the cinematic pilgrimage; rather they point to the idiosyncrasy of the venture in comparison with the multitudes who queue to pay to enter monuments and museums. In other words, faith is reclaimed as a personal choice in which a 20-year-old film becomes as sacred a text as any 2,000-year-old tale.

Conclusion

Despite the apparent playfulness of these four types of cinematic pilgrimage, it would be wrong to dismiss the activities without considering the needs that they fulfil. At first sight, the four stages of cinematic pilgrimage seem to move from the collective tourist gaze, which involves conviviality and 'a sense of carnival', to what Urry calls the romantic gaze in which 'solitude, privacy and a personal, semi-spiritual relationship with the object of the gaze are emphasised' (Urry 2002: 150). To an extent, the cinematic pilgrimage responds to that which Urry describes as 'the mediatised gaze', which is one that is 'a collective gaze where particular sites famous for their "mediated" nature are viewed' (Urry 2002: 151), and he offers as examples the aforementioned Rovers Return pub from *Coronation Street* and the Taj Mahal, because it is also the setting for many Indian films. Urry does not problematise the implied equivalence, however, which reflects the interplay of consumerism and globalisation that makes everything in the world subject to the tourist gaze. Indeed, the metaphysical tour that results from one's devotion to a particular film or television series subscribes to a lucid postmodern understanding of reality because the cinematic pilgrim knows all along that 'reality' is fake. Moreover, if 'reality' is recognised as fabricated to represent hegemonic values that the pilgrim finds it difficult to accept or share, then the cinematic pilgrimage offers a purposefully absurd way in which to subvert the expectation of compliance with a rigid version of history. That is to say, instead of accepting a limited or limiting view of a war or offering unquestioning respect for a religious relic, the cinematic pilgrim enjoys a relationship with a place or object that is transformative. The boundaries that separate the highbrow good taste of traditional heritage from lowbrow films and television series are dissolved by the postmodernist project, which dismantles the denomination of artefacts as carriers of historical importance and of places and things as 'to be seen'. The cinematic pilgrimage rejects nostalgia for what has been certified as authentic and embraces irony as a conduit to a new romanticism that is validated by emotional connections to popular culture. Finally, this culture is then authenticated by the ontology of the belief system that is reinforced by the cinematic pilgrimage, much like a politically minded visit to a particular war memorial or a faith-based visit to a certain shrine.

Postmodern heritage cinema and television is not about pre-existing history or religion, which postmodernism understands as made-up, biased and reductive anyway. The heritage of the film studio is that of the films that are inherited by successive generations of viewers, while the myths of the spaghetti western and television series such as *Game of Thrones* turn places like Western Leone and Northern Ireland into tourist destinations that advertise the paradox of being both authentic and inauthentic at the same time. The film *flâneur* in Vienna, meanwhile, is engaged in a digressive search for unreal times as well as real places, not simply visiting the locations but embodying the sensibility of what their favourite film is all about. All these cinematic pilgrimages reinforce emotional connections with films and television series and add a personal sense of nostalgia to repeat viewings. The pilgrim moves on from seeing Western Leone as the place where *Once Upon a Time in the West* was filmed to seeing *Once Upon a Time in the West* as the film that reminds them of their pilgrimage. It could be argued that this solipsistic and centripetal exercise creates a more hermetic sensibility for the pilgrim, whose questionable ability to see all things as equally real or equally unreal counters the essentially hierarchical belief systems that tend to dominate political, religious or economic dogma, while also resulting in an upturned belief system that prioritises irrelevancy. Turning away from so-called reality to so-called unreality and back again may even resemble a parody of metaphysical endeavor, if it were not for the fact that the true objective of the cinematic pilgrimage is not the increasingly privatised artefact or place but the unfettered and eccentric self who is engaged in the pilgrimage. Such activities might also be derided as escapism, for they provide a metaphysical journey from the real to the unreal, which may be prolonged by the most hardcore fanatical pilgrim in order to avoid what Saint Teresa called 'the distress of having to return to life' (Saint Teresa of Avila 1957: 144). Despite finding inspiration in commercial, populist entertainment, however, the cinematic pilgrimage also counters the commodifying of the past and the presumption of truthfulness that usually characterises traditional heritage sites by deflecting reverence and nostalgia towards blatantly fictional sources instead. The ruse is ironic, sceptical and evasive, but it is also significant to postmodern pilgrims, who experience rapture in visiting the locations where nothing real actually happened but everything meaningful to them was filmed.

Works Cited

Anon. 2015. The stones and thrones tour. [Online]. Available from: http://www.stonesandthrones.com. Accessed 4 Dec 2015.

———. 2016. General tourism services of Kefalonia. [Online]. Available from: http://www.kefaloniatravel.com/kefalonia_cephalonia_captain_corellis_mandolin.html. Accessed 4 Mar 2016.

Beeton, Sue. 2005. *Film-induced tourism*. Clevedon: Channel View Publications.

Clift, Jean Dalby, and Wallace B. Clift. 1996. *The archetype of pilgrimage: Outer action with inner meaning*. New York: Paulist Press.

Horne, Donald. 1984. *The great museum: The re-presentation of history*. London: Pluto Press.

Jameson, Fredric. 1983. Postmodernism and consumer society. In *Modernism/Postmodernism*, ed. Peter Brooker. Essex: Longman.

Martin-Jones, David. 2014. Film tourism as heritage tourism: Scotland, diaspora and The Da Vinci Code (2006). *New Review of Film and Television Studies* 12(2): 156–177.

McVeigh, Tracy. 2015. The stunning locations cashing in on Britain's film and TV. *The Guardian*. [Online]. Available from: www.theguardian.com/tv-and-radio/2015/mar/08/locations-cashing-in-britain-film-tv-fame?CMP=share_btn_fb. Accessed 8 Mar 2015.

Roesch, Stefan. 2009. *The experiences of film location tourists*. Bristol: Channel View Publications.

Saint Teresa of Avila. 1957. *The life of Saint Teresa of Ávila by herself*. St.Ives: Penguin Classics.

Strain, Ellen. 2003. *Public places, private journeys*. New Brunswick: Rutgers University Press.

Tzanelli, Rodanthi. 2004. Constructing the 'cinematic tourist'; The 'sign industry' of "The Lord of the Rings". *Tourist Studies* 4(1): 21–42.

———. 2007. *The cinematic tourist*. London: Routledge.

Urry, John. 2002. *The tourist gaze*. London: Sage.

INDEX

A
abolitionist movement, 100
aesthetic
    aesthetics of heritage cinema, xxii, xxviii
    aesthetics of representing Nazi perpetrators, xxix, 108
    fascist aesthetics, 72
    hybrid heritage aesthetic, 28
    museum aesthetics, 85
    sanitised aesthetics, 74
Age of Innocence, The, 150
Aimée & Jaguar, 94
Akelarre, xxiv
Akomfrah, John, 99, 103
Algerian War, 88–94. *See also* Franco-Algerian war
Ali, Monica, xv, 239
Almanya–Welcome to Germany, xxiv, 88, 94–8
Almanya-Willkommen in Deutschland (*see Almanya–Welcome to Germany*)
Am Ende Kommen Touristen (*see And Along Come Tourists*)

And Along Come Tourists, xxxii, 250–3
Anderson, Benedict, 42, 127, 133, 191
Angelic Conversation, The, 218
Anna Karenina, 191
Annaud, Jean-Jacques, xx
Another Country, 218
Antonioni, Michelangelo, 120–1
Arcel, Nikolaj, xix, 185
Argento, Dario, 50
Arliss, Leslie, xxii, 98
Armendáriz, Montxo, xix
Arnold, Andrea, xxiii, 195
Artist, The, 185, 188–9
Asante, Amma, 89, 98–101
Astérix (films), 185, 187, 191
Atonement, 190–1, 201
audience
    around the world, xxviii
    cinephilic audience, xviii
    conservative audience, xviii
    Danish audience, 12–15
    domestic audiences, xxv, 186, 203
    European audiences, xxxi, 11–13, 186, 192, 204, 223

280 INDEX

heritage-film audiences, xviii, 212
international audiences, xviii, xxii, 39, 46, 88, 150
modern audiences, 11
non-specialist audiences, 190
as spectators, xxx
transnational audience, xxvi, xxxi, 3, 209–32
in UK, 3, 14, 197, 200
young female audiences, 218
Au hazard Bresson (see *Zum Beispiel Bresson*)
Auschwitz, xxxii, 108, 117, 122, 235, 237–8, 250
Auschwitz as heritage site, 237–241, 250–1, 253. See also heritage and tourism
Auschwitz-land, 235–6, 235–53
Aus einem deutschen Leben (see *Death Is My Trade*)

B
Badehotellet (see *Seaside Hotel, The*)
Balamory, 167
Ballroom of Romance, The, 168
Balzac, Honoré de, xxx, 146–61
Bandidas, 191
Banglatown, 239–44
Barbara, xxii
Baroncelli, Jacques de, 146–7, 149–50
Basque cinema, xxiv
battaglia di Algeri, La (see *Battle of Algiers, The*)
Battle of Algiers, The, 127
BBC, 27, 31, 36–7, 212–14, 224, 265
BBC2, 31
Before Midnight, 177
Before Sunrise, xxxii, 177, 262–4, 274–5 (see also *flânerie* and Vienna)
Before Sunset, 177

Before the Fall (see *Napola*)
Belle, 89, 98–9, 101–4
Belle Noiseuse, La, 149
Ben Hur, 264
Benjamin, Walter, 79
Bernadeau, Miguel Ángel, xxiv
Bertolucci, Bernardo, 70–1, 74, 81n6
Better Times, 13, 17–18, 21
Big Shot's Funeral, 74–5
Bjarup Riis, Anne-Grethe, xxiv, 195
black identity, 99
Black Venus (see *Vénus noire*)
Bloch, Ernst, xxi
Bollywood, 76, 176–7
Bornedal, Ole, 19–20
Born in '45, xxi
Böttcher, Jürgen, xxi
Bouchareb, Rachid, 88–91, 93–4, 103
Brave, 273
Braveheart, 169, 266
Bresson, Robert, 118–21
Brick Lane, xxv, xxxii, 239–45, 250, 254
Bridge, The (see *Brücke, Die*)
British film industry, xix, 28–30
British heritage culture, xvii, xxiii
Britishness, xii, 25–6, 30, 40–1, 63
Broken Harvest, 163
Brücke, Die, 118
Buñuel, Luis, 119, 135

C
Cabiria, 46
Cahiers du Cinéma, 69
Call The Midwife, xxiv
Cambridge, xxii
Camille Claudel, 222
capitalist democracy, xxi
Captain Corelli's Mandolin, 167, 258
Capture of Rome, The (see *presa di Roma, La*)

Cartouches gauloises, 126
caza, La, 129
Chariots of Fire, xviii, 26
Chéreau, Patrice, 145–6
Chinese heritage, 70–1, 75
Christabel, 14
Chronicle of the Years of Fire (*see Chroniques des années de braise*)
Chroniques des années de braise, 91
Cinecittà, xxxii, 261, 264–7
Cinema Paradiso, 66–8
cinque giornate, Le, 85
Coco avant Chanel (*see Coco Before Chanel*)
Coco Before Chanel, 185, 188
cognitive individualism, 8
cognitive sociology, 8–9
cognitive universalism, 9
Comédie humaine, La, 148–9
Commitments, The, 169
communism, 195–6
community
   imagined community, 5, 14, 127, 133
   international community, 75
   national community, 4, 86, 198
   transnational community, 86
   (*see also* Europe)
Coronation Street, 260, 263, 276
Corti, Axel, 107–9, 112–14, 116–17, 123–4
Cows (*see Vacas*)
Cricket, xxii
Crouching Tiger, Hidden Dragon, 73
Cry, The (*see Grido, Il*)
Cuéntame, xxiv
Curse of the Golden Flower, 71
Cut, The, 88
Cyrano de Bergerac, 222

D

Dancing at Lughnasa, 168
dark heritage, xx, xxvii, xxix, 107–125, 271. *See also* heritage
Dark Knight Rises, The, 273
Darkness Fell on Gotenhafen (*see Nacht fiel über Gotenhafen*)
Davies, Andrew, 27
Da Vinci Code, The, 166–7, 169, 238, 266–7
Days of Glory, 88–9
Death Is My Trade, 108–11, 117–24
De Cataldo, Giancarlo, 51–2, 56
Defenders of Riga, 193–5
Denmark, xxvi, 13, 18–21, 195, 226
Derrida, Jacques, 130–3
diegetic narrative, 169
Dil Chahta Hai, 78
Divorce, Le, 222
Doctor Who, 273
dolce vita, La, 69
docudrama, 107, 113–14, 123
Don't Touch The Axe, xxx, 145–55, 158–61
Down by Law, 218
Downfall, 110–12, 117, 123–4
Downton Abbey, 3, 11–12, 18, 212, 257
dramas
   British historical drama, xix
   British television drama, xxvii
   costume drama, xviii, 40, 78, 89, 98, 103, 195, 216
   European historical dramas, xx, 186–190, 193, 201–2, 204
   historical dramas, xvii, xviii, xx, xxiii, xxvi, xxxi, xxxii, 3, 16, 185–95, 201–4
   period drama, xxii

Stasi Drama, xxv (*see also* Stasi and national heritage)
Dream Team 1935 (*see Sapnu komanda 1935*)
Duchess, The, 241
Duchesse de Langeais, La, 146–50, 152–60
Duchess of Langeais, The (*see Duchesse de Langeais, La*)

E
East is East, 88
1864, 37
1860: I mille di Garibaldi, 85
Ek Tha Tiger, 164, 175–7
Elsaesser, Thomas, xvii, xxxiii, 110
Elizabeth I, 11
Elizabeth: The Golden Age, 187, 191, 201, 203
Emperor and the Assassin, The, 71–2, 80–81n5
Enemy at the Gates, xx
English Civil War, xxx
Englishness, xviii, xxiv, 27, 63–4, 85, 119, 223
espíritu de la colmena, El, 135
ETA, xxv
Eternal Flame, The, 147
EU, xx, xxiv, xxv, xxvi, xxvii, 4–10, 27, 30, 35, 86, 183, 188–9, 196, 199, 204
Eurimages, xxv, 7, 54, 188, 195, 201
Eurocentrism, 79–80
Europe
  European conflict, xx
  European art-house, 119, 274
  European heritage dramas, xxxi
  Europeanness, 9–10, 203, 219
  as an imagined community, 5, 14, 127, 133
  post-Communist Europe, 213
European identity, 7–9, 13, 210

European Union. *See* EU
Europudding, xx, xxv
Euskal Telebista, xxv
EU treaty
  Maastricht Treaty, 5, 7
  Treaty of Rome, 5–7, 9

F
Fáilte Ireland, 163, 168, 174, 178. *See also* Ireland
Fascism, 47, 67, 89
  anti-fascist resistance, 92
  Fascist era, 264
female beauty, xxxviii, 66
Film Tax Credit (FTC), xxx
Five Days in Milan (*see cinque giornate, Le*)
Flanders, xxvii, 25–41
  Flanders Audiovisual Fund (VAF), 26, 34–8
  Flemishness, 41
  Location Flanders, 34–6
  Screen Flanders, 34–5, 38
flânerie, xxxii, 261–2, 264, 274–5, 277
  virtual *flâneurs*, 239 (*see also* Vienna)
Forbidden City, 70–1, 75
Forster, E.M., 165, 212–14, 219–20, 222–7, 229–32
4 luni, 3 săptămâni și 2 zile (*see 4 Months, 3 Weeks and 2 Days*)
4 Months, 3 Weeks and 2 Days, 190, 196–8
Frames, The, 169
Franco-Algerian war, 90, 94
Franco, Francisco, 127–8, 138, 140n2
  Francoism, 127–30, 136, 140n2
  Francoist nationalism, 128
  Francoist rhetoric, 141n5
  post-Franco, 131
  under Franco, 137

French heritage cinema, xxx, 146, 161
From Cable Street to Brick Lane, 240–1
Furrows (*see Surcos*)
Furtivos, 129

G

Game of Thrones, xxii, 169, 261, 264, 269–73, 277
Gangs of New York, 265
gangster film, 91–2, 103
gattopardo, Il (*see Leopard, The*)
Gavron, Sarah, xxv, 239, 242
GDR, xxi, 111, 245–9
Gernika bajo las bombas, xxv
Gesuzza the Garibaldian Wife (*see 1860: I mille di Garibaldi*)
Girl with a Pearl Earring, The, xix
Gli ultimi giorni di Pompei (*see Last Days of Pompeii, The*)
Godfather, The (trilogy), 91
Good Bye, Lenin!, 245
Gothic horror, 155, 158, 160
Gramsci, Antonio, 47–8, 50–2
grande bellezza, La, 68–9, 75, 263
Grido, Il, 120
Guernica under the Bombs (*see Gernika bajo las bombas*)

H

Harry Potter (films), 167, 199, 213–14, 257, 260, 273
hauntology, 127–40
  Derridean hauntology, 131
HBO, 36, 265
Heat, 91–2
Hear My Song, 163
Heat and Dust, 87
Henri 4, xx, xxiii
heritage

British heritage, xviii, xix, xxii, xxiii, 11, 25–7, 38–9, 40–1, 57, 75, 86, 243 (*see also* (drama))
diasporic heritage, xxviii, 87
English Heritage, 64, 66, 75, 98–9, 102–3, 165, 203, 209–32
European heritage, xxvii, xviii, xix, xx, xxv, xxvi, xxvii, xxix, xxxi, xxxiii, 4, 6, 9, 25, 41, 46, 79, 86, 110, 209–10, 213
Flemish heritage, xxvii
heritage aesthetic, xxiv, xxviii, xxx, 27–8; and Post-Heritage Aesthetic, 150–8
heritage culture, xviii, xx, xxviii, xxviii, 65, 185, 239
heritage fanworks, 216–19
heritage as a genre, xxx
heritage gore, 145
heritage iconography, xxii
heritage industry, xxxii, xxxiii, 25, 199, 229
heritage properties, 26, 229
heritage of the slave trade, 64
heritage space, 26–7, 76, 101, 245, 253
heritage television dramas, 26
heritage of trauma, xx, 65
heritage tourism, xxv, 138, 140, 175, 229, 238–9, 260
Holocaust as heritage, 236, 247
individual heritage sites, xxvi
Irish heritage, xxx
Italian heritage, 57, 67, 70
Muslim heritage, 77
national heritage, xx, xxvi, xxvii, xxix, xxxi, 6, 11, 15, 21, 25–6, 29, 45–7, 57, 79, 86–7, 94, 183, 185–6, 192, 195, 197–203
regional heritage, xxiii, 26, 39

Spanish heritage, xxix, 127–40
spectral heritage, xxix, 131, 135, 140
urban heritage, xxviii
working class heritage, xxiii
heritage cinema/film
   anti-heritage-film, xxiii, 229
   British anti-heritage-film criticism, 229
   counter-heritage film, 88, 103
   diasporic filmmakers, 86–7, 98, 102
   English heritage films, 210–14, 221–4, 229
   European heritage films, xix, xxv, xxix, 46, 86, 213
   film and television heritage, 270
   French heritage films, 145–6, 222
   German heritage films, xxix, 94
   German-language film heritage, 124
   hegemonic heritage cinema, 88
   heritage cinema criticism, 77
   Irish heritage cinema, 163–78
   post-heritage cinema/film, xxiii, xxxiv, 26, 130, 132, 140, 146, 161
   postmodern heritage cinema, 257–78
   prehistory of the heritage film, xxix
   as a public history, xxxi
   spectral heritage films, xxix
   world heritage cinema, 63–80
Hero, 71–5, 81nn7,9
Hindi films, 77
Hirschbiegel, Oliver, 110, 124
historical melodrama, 25
history
   community, xxxii
   intra-history, 259
   public, xxxi, 250
   traumatic histories, xxxiii, 237
Hitler, a Career, 124
Hitler, Adolf, xxix, 72, 107–15, 117, 120, 123–4

Hitler–eine Karriere (*see Hitler, a Career*)
Hitler: The Last Ten Days, 109
Hitler-Welle (Hitler wave), xxix, 108–9, 114
Hohenschönhausen, xxv, xxvii, 246–7
Holocaust, 110, 160, 235–8, 241, 247, 250–3
hommes et des dieux, Des (*see Of Gods and Men*)
homoeroticism, 218
homosexuality, 223–4, 228
Hooper, Tom, xvii, 11, 185, 187
Hors-la-loi (*see Outside the Law*)
Höß, Rudolf, 108–9, 111, 117–23
House of Flying Daggers, 71, 73
Howards End, 212, 214, 227
How They Became What They Were: A Young Man from the Inn Quarter–Adolf Hitler, 107–17, 121, 123–4
Hudson, Hugh, xviii, 26
Hum Aapke Hain Koun...!, 78
Hunger, 190
Hunt, The (*see caza, La*)
Hvidsten gruppen, xxiv, 195

I
Ida, 185
identity
   Bangladeshi identity, 242, 244
   black identity, 99
   contemporary national identity, xvii, xxviii, xxxii, 197, 209
   European identity, 7–10, 13, 210
   Indian identity, 77
   Irish-American identity, 238
   Irish identity, xvii, 178
   Italian national identity, xxviii, 57
   national identity, xxix, 9, 14, 21, 46, 49, 56–7, 110, 127, 198, 200, 203, 238, 259

real-life identity, 219
sexual identity, 214
Spanish identity, 128–9
transnational identity, 10
I for India, 93
Il gattopardo (*see Leopard, The*)
Immigrant Memories (*see Mémoires d'immigrés-l' héritage maghrébin*)
imperialism, 87
 imperial China, 70, 72
 imperial past, 25
 post-imperialist, 26
In Bruges, 164, 166, 177, 262–3
Inch'Allah dimanche, 88
Indian heritage, 79
Indigènes (*see Days of Glory*)
In nome del popolo sovrano, 50
In the Name of the Sovereign People (*see In nome del popolo sovrano*)
Intimate Enemies (*see L' ennemi intime*)
Into the West, 163
Ireland, xxx, 37, 163–4, 173–5, 177–8, 188, 239, 242, 266, 273
 Northern Ireland, xxxii, 28, 36, 169–70, 261, 264, 269–73, 277
Irish heritage cinema, xxx, 163–78
Ironiya sud'by. Prodolzheniye, 194
Irony of Fate. Sequel, The (*see Ironiya sud' by. Prodolzheniye*)
isla mínima, La, 130
Italian cinema/films, 45–6
Italianism, 68–9
ITV, 3, 31, 212
Ivory, James, xviii, xix, 87, 165, 212, 214–15, 218–19, 221–5, 228–9

J
Jahrgang 45 (*see Born in '45*)

Jameson, Fredric, 102, 259–60
Jane Eyre, 11–12
Jefferson in Paris, 222
JFK, 57
Jimmy's Hall, 164
Jodhaa Akbar, 63, 76–9, 81nn14,15
Jonathan Strange & Mr Norrell, 212
Joyeux Noël, xix, xx
Jyske Vestkysten (newspaper), 52

K
Kent, James, 26
Khan, Kabir, 164, 175–7
Kingdom of Heaven, 187, 203
King's Speech, The, xvii, 185, 188–9, 197–201, 203
kongelig affære, En (*see Royal Affair, A*)
Kotulla, Theodor, 108–109, 111, 117–24
Kracauer, Siegfried, 118
Krøniken (*see Better Times*)

L
laberinto del fauno, El, 185
Land Without Bread (*see Tierra sin pan (aka Las Hurdes)*)
L'Année prochaine à Paris, 148
Last Days of Pompeii, The, 46
Last Emperor, The, 70–1, 74–5, 79, 81n.6
Leap Year, 164, 173–5
Leben der Anderen, Das (*see Lives of Others, The*)
Lefebvre, Henri, 131–2, 135–7, 140, 141n.4
L'ennemi intime, 90
Leopard, The, 48, 52
LGBT, 64, 213, 217, 227–8

Liebe, 147
Linklater, Richard, xxxii, 177, 262, 274
Lives of Others, The, xvii, xxi, xxv, xxvii, 111, 185, 188–90, 196–7, 203, 244–50 (*see also Stasi*)
Living in Paradise (*see Vivre au paradis*)
Lord of the Rings, The (trilogy), 167, 214, 258–9
Lore, xxiii
Love (*see Liebe*)
LUMIERE (database), 186, 191, 193

M

Magdalene Sisters, The, 164
Man in Grey, The, 98
Marías, Luis, xxv
Marshland (*see isla mínima, La*)
Martone, Mario, xxvii, 45, 48, 50–7, 58n8, 59n11
Massingham, Richard, xxii
Matador, 13, 18–19, 21
Matchmaker, The, 164, 174–6
Maurice, xix, 212–22, 223–32
MEDIA programme, 4, 7, 195, 199
Mediterraneo, 66–7
Mein Vater, der Gastarbeiter, 93
Mémoires d'immigrés–l'héritage maghrébin, 93
memory
 collective memory, xxviii, 86, 93, 102, 237
 diasporic memory, xxviii, 85, 87, 103–4
 holocaust memory, 237, 252–3
Merchant, Ivory, 85, 165, 211–13, 218, 220–4, 226–7, 229–32
Merlin, 273
Merry Christmas (*see Joyeux Noël*)
Midsomer Murders, 18

mise-en-scène, 85, 121–2, 136, 146
Misérables, Les, 187, 191
Moby Dick, 168
Mollywood, 36–7
môme, La, 188
Mon colonel, 90
Mörder sind unter uns, Die, 119
movie-induced tourism, xxvii
Mr Turner, 185
Murderers Are Among Us, The (*see Mörder sind unter uns, Die*)
museum, xxv, 73, 104, 246–7, 252, 260, 264, 267, 273, 275–6
 British Museum, 229–31
 Migration Museum Project, 104
 museum aesthetic, xxx, 85, 101, 147 (*see also* memory)
My Beautiful Laundrette, 218
My Father, The Guestworker (*see Mein Vater, der Gastarbeiter*)
myths, xxxii, 277
 structural myths, 262

N

Nacht fiel über Gotenhafen, 118
Nanny McPhee (films), 187, 191
Napola, xix
national heritage, xx, xxvi, xxvii, xxix, xxxi, 6, 11, 15, 21, 25–6, 45–7, 57, 86–7, 94, 185–6, 192, 195, 197–203
 Department of National Heritage (DNH), 28 (*see also* heritage)
Nazism, xxix, 72, 92, 246
 Nazi perpetrators, xxix, 107–125
Ne Touchez pas la hache (*see Don't Touch The Axe*)
Next Year in Paris (*see L' Année prochaine à Paris*)
New Neapolitan Cinema, x, xvii, 54
Night of the Sunflowers, The, 127–40

Nine Muses, The, 99, 104
Nobleza baturra, 136
noche de los girasoles, La, xxix (*see Night of the Sunflowers, The*)
Noi credevamo (*see We Believed*)
nonsimultaneity, xxi
nostalgia, xix, xxx, 18, 27, 57, 86, 97, 127, 130, 132, 140, 150, 163–4, 266, 277
    cultural nostalgia, 131, 139
    East German nostalgia, 245
    for a pre-modern nation, xxx
    nostalgia drive, xxii

O

Obaba, xix
Of Gods and Men, 188–9 (*see also hommes et des dieux, Des*)
Olea, Pedro, xxiv
Oliver Twist, 187, 191
Once, 169
Once There Was a Tiger (*see Ek Tha Tiger*)
Once Upon a Time in America, 91
Once upon a Time in the West, 267–9, 277
Orientalism, 68–72
Orlando, xxiii, 150
Ostalgie, 245, 249
Oświęcim, xxxii, 235, 250–3
Other
    cultural heritage of others, 6
    evil Other, 249
    exotic Other, 133
    racially Other, 77
Otherness, xxi, 87, 185, 200, 243
Our Brick Lane, xxiv, 242
Out 1 (*see Out 1: noli me tangere*)
Out 1: noli me tangere, 149
Outside the Law, 88–94, 103

P

Pan's Labyrinth (*see laberinto del fauno, El*)
Parade's End, 12, 26, 28, 34–40
Pascual Duarte, 129
Passage to India, A, 83, 212
Pastrone, Giovanni, 46
Perfume: The Story of a Murderer, 185, 187, 191, 201–3
Philomena, 164, 188
Piano, The, 150
pilgrimages
    cinematic pilgrimages, xxxii, 257–78
    independent-minded pilgrimage, 275
    metaphysical journey, 277
    religious pilgrimage, 260, 298
    tourism as pilgrimage, xxxii (*see also* tourism)
Pillars of the Earth, 11–12
Poachers (*see Furtivos*)
Poitín, 168
Poldark, 212
Postino, Il, 66–7, 75
postmodernism, 259–60, 277
post-war film culture, xxix, 110
Potiche, 188
Potter, Sally, xxiii, 150
presa di Roma, La (*see Capture of Rome, The*)
Pride and Prejudice, 61, 190–1, 201, 257
P.S. I Love You, 164, 173, 175

Q

Quartet, 221–2
Queen, The, 188, 203
queer, xviii, 214, 217, 221, 229–30
    activist queer text, 219
    queer cultural heritage, 229, 230

queer-heritage-film, 216
Quiet Man, The, 168, 170–3, 177, 238, 242
Quo Vadis?, 46

R
Race (see *Raza*)
racism
   contemporary racism, 65
   racial equality, 99–100, 103
   racial ideology, 116
   racial oppression, 89
   racial selection, 115
   racially Other, 103
   racist attacks, 244
   scientific racism, 89
   subtle racism, 101
Raza, 128
Reine Margot, La, 145–6, 151
Revenge, The (see *Zemsta*)
Rigas sargi (see *Defenders of Riga*)
Risorgimento, xxviii
   films, 45–57
   of the post-war period, 47–8
   Risorgimento historiography, 57
   Risorgimento History, 49–50
Rivette, Jacques, xxx, 145–61
Robin Hood, 187
Rohmer, Eric, 148–9
Romanzo criminale, 86
Rome, xxxii, 47, 50, 57, 68–9, 75, 261, 263–6
   Treaty of Rome, 5–9
Rome, 265–6
Room With A View, A, xviii, 165, 212, 214, 222–3, 226, 229
Rosenstrasse, 130
Royal Affair, A, xix, xxiii, 185, 195, 197
Rudolfa mantojums, 193 (see also *Rudolf's Gold*)
Run of the Country, The, 163
Rush, 188
Rustic Chivalry (see *Nobleza baturra*)

S
Sailor's Return, The, 98
Saint Teresa of Avila, xxxii, 258, 261–2, 264, 267, 270, 275, 277
Samdereli, Yasemin, xxiv, 88, 96, 103
Sánchez-Cabezudo, Jorge, xxix, 129–30, 132–3, 135–40
Sapnu komanda 1935, 193
Schindler's List, 93, 236, 244, 246–7
SeaChange, 167
Seaside Hotel, The, 16–18
secreto de sus ojos, El, 190 (see also *Secret in their Eyes, The*)
Senso, 48
set-jetting, xxvii, 273
Sex, Drugs and Taxation (see *Spies & Glistrup*)
sexuality, xxiii, 26, 75, 150, 212, 219–20, 224–5
   sexual identity, 214
   sexual orientations, 217, 229
Sherlock, 213–14, 224
Shortland, Cate, xiii
slavery, 64–5, 99–100
Solino, 88
Song of Freedom, 98
Sonnenallee, 245, 249
Sontag, Susan, 72
Sopranos, The, 262
Sorrentino, Paolo, 68–9, 263
Sous les pieds des femmes, 90
spaghetti-western, xxxii, 26, 264, 268, 277
Spanish cinema, 128–9, 136
Spanish Civil War, xxv, 27–8, 127–8, 140nn2,3
Spanish heritage cinema, xxix, 127–40

Spanish post-heritage films, 140n3
Spielberg, Steven, 93, 235–6, 244, 246, 250
Spies & Glistrup, xxiii
Spirit of the Beehive, The (*see espíritu de la colmena, El*)
Stars Above (*see Tähtitaivas talon yllä*)
Star Trek, 214
Star Wars VII: The Force Awakens, 273
Stasi, xxv, xxxvii, 217, 245–9, 253
  Stasi archive, 248–9
  Stasi drama, xxv
  Stasi State, 248
Stasiland, 245, 248
Staudte, Wolfgang, 119
Stoppard, Tom, 36
Story of Maurice, 218, 224
Stranger Than Paradise, 218
subsidy disease, 34
Summer of '62 (*see Cartouches gauloises*)
Sun Alley (*see Sonnenallee*)
Sunday God Willing (*see Inch' Allah dimanche*)
Surcos, 128, 134

T
Tähtitaivas talon yllä, xix
Thalheim, Robert, xxxii, 250, 253
Thatcher, Margaret, xix, 29, 63
  Thatcherism, xviii, 26, 27
  Thatcherite Conservatism, 25
  Thatcherite ideology, 64
Third Reich, 108, 110–12, 117–19, 124
This is England, 190
This Life (*see Hvidsten gruppen*)
Three Musketeers, The, 191
Tierra sin pan (aka *Las Hurdes*), 135
Tinker, Tailor, Soldier, Spy, 188, 190
Titanic, 74, 194

Touch of Zen, A, 73
tourism
  cultural tourism, 165
  cynical post-tourist, 175
  English tourist sites, xxxi
  fan tourism, 223–32
  metaphysical tour, 276
  modern tourism, 132
  as a narrative, xxx
  tourist/filmgoer, 258
  tourist gaze, xxviii, 66, 69, 75, 80, 133, 134, 141n4, 164–78, 236, 258, 268, 276
  tourist traffic, xviii, 258
  touristic spectacle, 67
  pioneering tourist cinema, 71
  post-tourism, xxx, 166, 269
  roots-tourism, 238
  West German tourists, xxi (*see also* heritage; pilgrimages)
trauma
  trauma of the First World War, 40
  trauma of the Franco-Algerian war, 90
  traumas of the past, xxi
  traumascape, 136, 138, 140
  traumatic memories, 88
  traumatic narratives, 164, 169
  heritage of trauma, xx, 65
  historical trauma, 93
Triumph of the Will, 72
Troller, Georg Stefan, 107–9, 111, 113–17, 123–4
12 Years a Slave, 65, 89
2 Days in Paris, 166, 177
Tykwer, Tom, 185

U
UK Film Council (UKFC), 29
UNESCO, 66, 75, 79. *See also* World Heritage List

United Nations Educational, Scientific and Cultural Organization. *See* UNESCO
Untergang, Der (*see* Downfall)
Urry, John, 80, 133–4, 141n4, 165–6, 236, 243, 260, 266–8, 269, 276

V
Vacas, 133
Va savoir (*see Who Knows?*)
Venice Film Festival, 49, 176
Vénus noire, 89
Vertigo, 262
Vidal, Belén, xix, xx, 27, 64, 103, 112, 131
Vie en Rose, La (*see môme, La*)
Vienna, xxxii, 107, 112, 115–16, 262–4, 274–5, 277. *See also flânerie*
Vincendeau, Ginette, xix, 46, 80, 85, 145, 147, 150
Virgin Queen, The, 11
Visconti, Luchino, 48–9, 52
Vivre au paradis, 90
von Donnersmarck, Florian Henckel, xvii, 113, 185, 244, 246
VRT, 36–8

W
Wajda, Andrzej, xix
War of the Buttons, 163
Webber, Peter, xix
We Believed, xxvii, 45, 48–50, 52–5, 57
Weimar cinema, 118
Weisse Band, Das (*see White Ribbon, The*)

Western Leone, 261, 264, 267–9, 277
Where Angels Fear to Tread, 212
White Queen, The, 26, 28, 34–5, 37–40, 212
White Ribbon, The, 185, 188–9
White, Susanna, 60, 187
Who Knows?, 147, 159
Wicked Lady, The, xxii
Wie sie es wurden: Ein junger Mann aus dem Innviertel–Adolf Hitler (*see How They Became What They Were: A Young Man from The Inn Quarter–Adolf Hitler*)
Wind That Shakes the Barley, The, 164, 188–9
Witches' Sabbath (*see Akelarre*)
Wolf Hall, 11
World Heritage List, 75–6, 79. *See also* UNESCO
World War I/First World War, 26, 36, 40, 107, 115–16, 121, 226
World War II/ Second World War/ World War Two, xx, 47, 67, 88–9, 92, 110, 193, 195, 204
Wuthering Heights, xxiii, 195
Wuxia cinema 73

Y
Yorkshire, xxii, xxiii
 Screen Yorkshire, xxiii

Z
Zemsta, xix
Zerubavel, Eviatar, 8–9, 16
Zhang Yimou, 71–2, 75
Zum Beispiel Bresson, 118

The manufacturer's authorised representative in the EU is Springer Nature Customer Service Centre GmbH, Europaplatz 3, 69115 Heidelberg, Germany. If you have any concerns regarding our products, please contact ProductSafety@springernature.com

Printed and bound by CPI Group (UK) Ltd, Croydon, CR0 4YY
23/03/2026
02076673-0006